D0385635

BELL'S BRITISH THEATRE

1776-1781

BELL'S BRITISH THEATRE

General Editor, Byrne R.S. Fone
Introductions and Notes by Professor Fone

Byrne R.S. Fone is Associate Professor of English at The City College, The City University of New York. His work in theater history is known to scholars. Dr. Fone has published articles on eighteenth century theater, is editor of Cibber's *Love's Last Shift* and Cibber's *Apology,* and has published works on Boswell, Johnson and on various American writers.

BELL'S BRITISH THEATRE

1776-1781

In Twenty-One Volumes
of which this is
Volume Eleven

With a New Preface
by Byrne R.S. Fone and with
New Author and Play Indexes

AMS PRESS
NEW YORK

Library of Congress Cataloging in Publication Data

Bell, John, 1745-1831, ed.
    Bell's British theatre, 1776-1781.

    Reprint of the 1776-1781 ed. published by
J. Bell, London.

    Contains 100 plays, each with special t.p. and
separate pagination. Imprints vary.

    1. English drama.   I. Title.   II. Title:
British theatre.
PR1241.B4   1977   822'.08   76-44551
ISBN 0-404-00800-3

Reprinted from the edition of 1777, London
First AMS edition published in 1977
Manufactured in the United States of America

International Standard Book Number:
Complete Set: 0-404-00800-3
Volume Eleven: 0-404-00811-9

AMS PRESS INC.
NEW YORK, N.Y.

CONTENTS

PREFACE

Colley Cibber wrote so many plays that there is often some difficulty in distinguishing them, one from the other. *The Refusal* (1721) takes the furor over the South Sea Bubble as its topical occassion and weaves a comedy around that potentially farcical situation. But *The Refusal* is not a memorable play and makes use of Cibber's tricks and techniques, that is, a play designed for the enjoyment, the thoughtless enjoyment, of the town.

The Relapse (1697) was written as a counter-blast to Cibber's *Love's Last Shift*. It pretends to be a sequel to the play, and reverses the events of Cibber's sentimental comedy. It established the reputation of its author, Sir John Vanbrugh. It immediately delighted the audiences, who rightfully saw the elevation of Sir Novelty Fashion to the dignity of Lord Foppington as a masterstroke. Of its other characters, Hoyden and Sir Tunbelly Clumsy are masterful caricatures, and Vanbrugh does his best to stem the tide of sentimental comedy by having Loveless, who is reformed in Cibber's play, fall again to the lure of vice.

While *The Relapse* ought to be remembered as a genial milestone in English comedy, Joseph Addison's *The Drummer* should rightfully be forgotten. Its ineptness demonstrates that he was not a playwright, and the fact that he chose not to acknowledge the play demonstrates his agreement. Audiences too saw its failure as a play, and aided its demise by withholding their applause.

Dryden's *Amphitryon* (1690), which he had taken from Moliere who had taken it from Plautus, was a considerable success when it was performed. When John Hawkesworth (1715-1775) adapted it later its distinguished ancestry remained its primary merit. Hawkesworth's merit rests on his editorship of *The Adventurer*, a periodical, and further as Swift's editor. He was a gentleman writer who made contributions to the important periodicals, wrote at least one oriental tale called *Almoran and Hamet* and was a competent member of the minor literati of the day, and in that role he adapted the play which adaptation was equal to his talents.

Bell's

BRITISH THEATRE;

Comedies.

NATURE

Mortimer del.

Hall sc.

𝕷𝖔𝖓𝖉𝖔𝖓.

Printed for *John Bell* near *Exeter Exchange* in the
STRAND.

Robert del.   Publish'd for Bell's British Theatre April 5th 1777.   Thornthwaite Sculp.

M.ʳ MACKLIN, in the Character of S.ᴿ GILBERT WRANGLE.

Nay, I have them from all Nations, here's one now,
from an Irish Relation of my own.

BELL'S EDITION.

THE

REFUSAL;

OR, THE

LADIES PIHLOSOPHY.

A COMEDY,

As written by COLLEY CIBBER.

DISTINGUISHING ALSO THE

VARIATIONS OF THE THEATRE,

AS PERFORMED AT THE

𝕿𝖍𝖊𝖆𝖙𝖗𝖊-𝕽𝖔𝖞𝖆𝖑 𝖎𝖓 𝕮𝖔𝖛𝖊𝖓𝖙-𝕲𝖆𝖗𝖉𝖊𝖓.

Regulated from the Prompt-Book,

By PERMISSION *of the* MANAGERS,

By Mr. WILD, Prompter.

LONDON:

Printed for JOHN BELL, near *Exeter-Exchange*, in the *Strand.*

MDCCLXXVII.

P R O L O G U E.

Spoken by the Author.

GAllants! behold before your eyes the wight,
 Whose actions stand accountable to-night,
For all your dividends of profit or delight.
New plays resemble bubbles, we must own,
But their intrinsic value soon is known,
There's no imposing pleasure on a town.
And when they fail, count o'er his pains and trouble,
His doubts, his fears, the poet is a bubble.
As heroes by the tragic muse are sung;
So to the comic, knaves and fools belong:
Follies, to-night, of various kinds we paint,
One, in a female philosophic saint,
That wou'd by learning nature's laws repeal,
Warm all her sex's bosoms to rebel,
And only with Platonic raptures swell.
Long she resists the proper use of beauty,
But flesh and blood reduce the dame to duty.
A coxcomb too of modern stamp we show,
A wit——but impudent——a South-Sea beau.
Nay, more——our muses fire (but, pray, protect her)
Roasts, to your taste, a whole South-Sea director.
But let none think we bring him here in spite,
For all their actions, sure, will bear the light;
Besides, he's painted here in height of power,
Long ere we laid such ruin at his door:
When he was levee'd, like a statesman, by the town,
And thought his heap'd-up millions all his own.
No, no; stock's always at a thousand here,
He'll almost honest on the stage appear.
Such is our fare, to feed the mind our aim,
But poets stand, like warriors, in their fame;
One ill day's work brings all their past to shame.
Thus having tasted of your former favour,
The chance seems now for deeper stakes than ever.
As after runs of luck, we're most accurst,
To lose our winnings, than have lost at first;
A first stake lost has often sav'd from ruin,
But on one cast to lose the tout——is hard undoing.
But be it as it may——the dye is thrown,
Fear now were folly——Pass the Rubicon.

    DRA-

DRAMATIS PERSONÆ.

M E N.

Covent-Garden.

Sir *Gilbert Wrangle*,	—— ——	Mr. Macklin.
Frankly,	—— ——	Mr. Lewis.
Granger,	——	Mr. Mahon.
Wittling,	——	Mr. Lee Lewes.
Cook,	——	Mr. Dunftall.

W O M E N.

Lady *Wrangle*,	——	Mrs. Green.
Sophronia,	——	Mrs. Leffingham.
Maid,	——	Mifs Ambrofe.
Charlotte,	——	Mifs Macklin.

Servants, &c.

THE

' *Fran.* Was ever so desperate an indifference ?' I am impatient till I know her.

Gran. Even the sage and haughty prude, Sophronia.

Fran. Sophronia ! ' I hope you don't take her for a ' fool, Sir :' why, she thinks she has more sense than all her sex together.

Gran. ' You don't tell me that as a proof of her wit, ' I presume, Sir.

' *Fran.* No: but I think your humour's a little extra-
' ordinary, that can resolve to marry the woman you
' laugh at.

' *Gran.* It's at least, a sign I am in no great danger of
' her laughing at me, Tom ; the case of many a prettier
' fellow. But I take Sophronia to be only a fool of parts,
' that is however capable of thinking right; and a man
' must be nice indeed, that turns up his nose at a woman
' who has no worse imperfection, than setting too great
' value upon her understanding.' I grant it she is half mad with her learning and philosophy : what then ? so are most of our great men, when they get a little too much on't. Nay, she is so rapt in the pride of her imaginary knowledge, that she almost forgets she is a wo-
man, and thinks all offers of love to her person a dis-
honour to the dignity of her soul; but all this does not discourage me: she may fancy herself as wise as she pleases ; but unless I fail in my measures, I think I shall have hard luck, if I don't make that fine flesh and blood of I ...s, as troublesome as my own in a fortnight.

Fran. You must have better luck than I had then ; I was her fool for above five months together, and did not come ill-recommended to the family ; but could make no more impression than upon a vestal virgin ; and *yet*
' how a man of your cool reflexion, can think of at-
' tempting her, I have no notion.

' *Gran.* Psha ! I laugh at all her airs : a woman of
' a general insensibility, is only one that has never been
' rightly attacked.

' *Fran.* Are you then really resolved to pursue her ?

' *Gran.* Why not ? Is not she a fine creature ? Has
' not she the parts ? Would not half her knowledge, equally
' divided, make fifty coquettes all women of sense ? Is
' not

‘ not her beauty natural, her perfon lovely, her mien
‘ majeftic?——Then fuch a conftitution——

‘ *Fran.* Nay, fhe has a wholefome look, I grant you:
‘ but then her prudery, and Platonic principles, are in-
‘ fupportable.

‘ *Gran.* Now to me they are more diverting, than all
‘ the levity of a coquette: Oh, the noble conflicts be-
‘ tween nature and a proud underftanding, make our tri-
‘ umphs fo infinitely above thofe petty conquefts——
‘ Befides, are not you philofopher enough to know, my
‘ friend, that a body continent holds moft of the thing
‘ contained? ’Tis not your wafting current, but refer-
‘ voirs, that make the fountain play; not the prodigal’s,
‘ but the mifer’s cheft that holds the treafure. No, no,
‘ take my word, your prude has thrice the latent fire of
‘ a coquette. Your prude’s flafk hermetically fealed, all’s
‘ right within, depend upon’t; but your coquette’s a
‘ mere bottle of plague-water, that’s open to every
‘ body.

‘ *Fran.* Well, Sir, fince you feem fo heartily in earneft,
‘ and, I fee, are not to be difgufted at a little female
‘ frailty: I think I ought in honour to let you into a
‘ little more of her. You muft know then,’ this marble-
hearted lady, who could not bear my addreffes to herfelf,
has, notwithftanding, flefh and blood enough to be confoundedly uneafy, that I now pay them to her fifter.

Gran. I am glad to hear it. Pr’ythee, let me know
all; for ’tis upon thefe fort of weakneffes that I am to
ftrengthen my hopes.

‘ *Fran.* You know, I writ you word, that I thought the
‘ fafeft way to convey my real paffion for her fifter Char-
‘ lotte, wou’d be to drop my cold pretenfions to Sophro-
‘ nia infenfibly; upon which account I rather heightened
‘ my refpect to her: but as, you know, ’tis harder to
‘ difguife a real inclination, than to diffemble one we
‘ have not; Sophronia, it feems, has fo far fufpected the
‘ cheat, that, fince your abfence, fhe has broke into a
‘ thoufand little impatiences at my new happinefs with
‘ Charlotte.

‘ *Gran.* Good.’

Fran. But the jeft is, fhe can’t yet bring down her vanity to believe I am in earneft with Charlotte neither;
                                                    but

but really fancies my addreſſes there are all grimace ; the mere malice of a rejected lover, to give her ſcorn a jealouſy.

 Gran. Admirable ! ' but I hope you are ſure of this.

 ' *Fran.* 'Twas but yeſterday ſhe gave me a proof of it.

 ' *Gran.* Pray, let's hear.

 ' *Fran.* Why, as Charlotte and I were whiſpering at
' one end of a room, while we thought her wrapt up in
' one of Horace's odes at the other, of a ſudden I obſerved
' her come ſailing up to me, with an inſulting ſmile, as
' who ſhould ſay—I laugh at all theſe ſhallow arts——
' then turned ſhort, and looking over her ſhoulder, cried
' aloud,——*Ah, miſer !*

  ' *Quantâ laboras in Charybdi !*

 ' *Gran. Digne puer meliore flammâ*——Ah! methinks
' I ſee the imperious huſſy in profile, waving her ſnowy
' neck into a thouſand lovely attitudes of ſcorn and tri-
' umph! Oh, the dear vanity !' Well, when all's ſaid,
the coxcomb's vaſtly handſome.

 ' *Fran.* 'Egad, thou art the oddeſt fellow in the world,
' to be thus capable of diverting yourſelf with your miſ-
' treſs's jealouſy of another man.

 ' *Gran.* Pſha ! Thou'rt too refined a lover ; I am
' glad of any occaſion that proves her more a woman
' than ſhe imagines.

 ' *Fran.* But pray, Sir, upon what foot did you ſtand
' with her before you went to France ?

 ' *Gran.* Oh, I never pretended to more than a Platonic
' paſſion ; I ſaw, at firſt view, ſhe was inacceſſible by
' love.

 ' *Fran.* Yet, ſince you were reſolved to purſue her,
' how came you to think of rambling to Paris ?

 ' *Gran.* Why, the laſt time I ſaw her, ſhe grew ſo fan-
' taſtically jealous of my regarding her more as a woman,
' than an intellectual being, that my patience was half
' tired ; and having, at that time, an appointment with
' ſome idle company to make a trip to Paris, I ſlily took
' that occaſion, and told her, if I threw myſelf into a
' voluntary baniſhment from her perſon, I hoped ſhe
' would then be convinced, I had no other views of hap-
' pineſs, than what her letters might, even in abſence,
' as well gratify, from the charms of her underſtanding.
       ' *Fran.*

' *Fran.* Moſt ſolemnly impudent.

' *Gran.* In ſhort, her vanity was ſo blind to the ban-
' ter, that ſhe infiſted upon my going, and made me a con-
' ditional promiſe of anſwering all my letters ; in which
' I have flattered her romantic folly to that degree, that in
' her laſt, ſhe confeſſes an entire ſatisfaction in the Inno-
' cent Dignity of my inclinations (as ſhe ſtiles it) and
' therefore thinks herſelf bound in gratitude to recall me
' from exile : which gracious boon (being heartily tired
' at Paris) I am now arrived to accept of.

' *Fran.* The merrieſt amour that ever was ! Well,'
and, *Frank,* why don't you viſit her ?

Gran. Oh ! I do all things by rule—not till ſhe has dined ; for our great Engliſh philoſopher, my Lord Bacon,
tells you, that then the mind is generally moſt ductile.

Fran. Wiſely conſidered.

Gran. Beſides, I want to have a little talk firſt with the
old gentleman her father.

Fran. Sir Gilbert ! If I don't miſtake, yonder he comes.

Gran. Where, pr'ythee ?

Fran. There, by the bookſeller's ; don't you ſee him,
with an odd crowd after him ?

Gran. Oh ! now I have him——he's loaded with papers, like a ſoliçitor.

Fran. Sir, he is, at this time, a man of the firſt conſe-
quence, and receives more petitions every hour, than the
court of chancery in a whole term.

Gran. What ! is he lord treaſurer ?

Fran. A much more conſiderable perſon, I can aſſure
you ; he is a South Sea director, Sir.

Gran. Oh, I cry you mercy ! and thoſe about him, I
preſume, are bowing for ſubſcriptions.

Fran. That's their buſineſs, you may be ſure ; but ſee,
at laſt he has broke from them. *Let's*

' *Gran.* No : there's one has got him by the ſleeve
' again.'

Fran. ' What if we ſhould ' ſtand off, and obſerve a
little ?

Gran. With all my heart.

Sir Gilb. [*To a Man at the door.*] Pr'ythee, be quiet,
fellow ! I tell you I'll ſend the Duke an anſwer to-morrow morning.

[Within.]

[*Within.*] It's very well, Sir——

Sir Gilbert *speaks, entering with a great parcel of open letters in his hand, and others stuffing his pockets.*

Sir Gilb. Very well! aye, so it is, if he gets it then—Why! what! these people of quality, sure, think they do you a favour when they ask one—Huh, let him come for it himself! I am sure I was forced to do so at his house, when I came for my own, and could not get it neither—and he expects I should give him two thousand pounds only for sending a footman to me. Why! what! Does his Grace think I don't know which side my bread's buttered on? Let's see! 'who are these from? [*Reads 'to himself.*

' *Gran.* The old gentleman's no blind admirer of a 'man of quality, I see.

' *Fran.* Oh, Sir! he has lately taken up a mortal aver-'sion to any man that has a better title than himself.

' *Gran.* How so pray?

' *Fran.* As he grows rich, he grows proud; and among 'friends, had lately a mind to be made a lord himself; 'but applying to the wrong person, it seems he was dif-'appointed; and ever since piques himself upon despi-'sing any nobleman who is not as rich as himself.

' *Gran.* Hah! the right plebeian spirit of Old Eng-'land: but I think he's counted an honest man.

' *Fran.* Umph! Yes, well enough—a good sort of a 'mercantile conscience: he is punctual in bargains, and 'expects the same from others; he will neither steal nor 'cheat, unless he thinks he has the protection of the law: 'then indeed, as most thriving men do, he thinks ho-'nour and equity are chimerical notions.

'—*Gran.* That is, he bluntly professes what other peo-'ple practise with more breeding—But let's accost him.

' *Fran.* Stay a little.

' *Enter a Footman, with a Letter.*

' *Sir Gilb.* To me, friend!——What, will they never 'have done?

' *Footm.* Sir, my Lady Double-chin presents her ser-'vice, and says she'll call for your honour's answer to-'morrow morning.

' *Sir Gilb.* Very well ; tell my Lady, I'll take care—
' [*Exit Footman.*] to be exactly out of the way when she
' comes.

' *Gran.* Hah ! he'll keep that part of his word, I war-
' rant him.

' *Sir Gilb.* Let's fee : the old ſtory, I ſuppoſe—[*Reads.*]
' Um—um—yes, yes—only two thouſand—Hah ! does
' the woman take me for a fool ? Does ſhe think I don't
' know, that a two thouſand ſubſcription is worth two
' thouſand guineas ? And becauſe ſhe is not worth above
' fourſcore thouſand already, ſhe would have me give
' them to her for nothing. To a poor relation, ſhe pre-
' tends, indeed ; as if ſhe loved any body better than
' herſelf. A drum ! and a fiddle ! I'll greaſe none of
' your fat ſows, not I.'—No, no ; get you into the negative pocket—— Bleſs my eyes ! Mr. Granger !

Gran. Sir Gilbert, I am your moſt humble ſervant.

Sir Gilb. In troth, I am glad to fee you in England
again—Mr. Frankly, your humble ſervant,

Fran. Sir, your moſt obedient.

Sir Gilb. Well, how goes Miſſiſſippi, man ? What, do
they bring their money by waggon loads to market ſtill ?
Hay ! ha, ha, ha !

Gran. Oh, all gone ! Good for nothing, Sir ! Your
South Sea has brought it to waſte paper.

Sir Gilb. Why, ay, han't we done glorious things here,
ha ? We have found work for the coachmakers as well as
they, boy.

Gran. Ah, Sir, in a little time we ſhall reduce thoſe,
who kept them there, to their original of riding behind
them here.

Sir Gilb. Huh, huh ! you will have your joke ſtill, I
fee——Well, you have not ſold out, I hope.

Gran. Not I, faith, Sir ; the old five thouſand lies ſnug
as it was. I don't fee where one can move it and mend
it ; ſo e'en let it lie, and breed by itſelf.

Sir Gilb. You're right, you're right——hark you—
keep it—the thing will do more ſtill, boy.

Gran. Sir, I am ſure it's in hands that can make it do
any thing.

Sir Gilb. Have you got any new ſubſcriptions ?

Gran. You know, Sir, I have been abſent ; and it is
really

really now grown fo valuable a favour, I have not the confidence to afk it.

Sir Gilb. Pfha ! pr'ythee, never talk of that, man.

Gran. If I thought you were not full, Sir——

Sir Gilb. Why, if I were as full as a bumper, Sir, I'll put my friends in, let who will run over for it.

Fran. Sir Gilbert always doubles his favours by his manner of doing them.

Sir Gilb. Frankly, you are down for five thoufand pounds already, and you may depend upon every fhilling of it—Let me fee—what have I done with my lift ?—— Granger has a good eftate, and had an eye upon my eldeft daughter before he went to France. I muft have him in ; it may chance to bring the matter to bear. *[Afide.*

Gran. Where did you get all thefe letters, Sir Gilbert ?

Sir Gilb. Why, ay, this is the trade every morning ; all for fubfcriptions. Nay, they are fpecial ftuff—Here, pr'ythee, read that.

Fran. Who is it from, Sir ?

Sir Gilb. Oh, a North-Briton ! a bloody, fquabbling fellow, who owes me a thoufand pounds for difference, and that's his way of paying me. Read it.

Gran. [*Reading.*] " Wuns, Sir, de ye no tack me for a man of honour ! Ye need no fend to my ludging fo often for year pimping thoufand pound. An ye'll be but civil a bit, Ife order the bearer, my brocker, to mack up year balance ; an if ye wull but gee yourfel the trouble to put his name intull your own lift for a thoufand fubfcription, he'fe pay ye aw down upo' the nail : but an ye wunna do this fmaw jubb, the deel dom me an ye e'er fee a groat from me, as long as my name is

George Blunderbufs."

Fran. What can you do with fuch a fellow, Sir ?

Sir Gilb. Do with him ! why, I'll let him have it, and get my money. I had better do that, than be obliged to fight for it, or give it to the lawyers.

Fran. Nay, that's true too.

Sir Gilb. Here's another, now, from one of my wife's hopeful relations ; an extravagant puppy, that has rattled a gilt chariot to pieces before it was paid for. But he'll die in jail.

B

Fran. [*Reading.*]——" Dear knight."——I fee he is familiar.

Sir Gilb. Nay, it's all of a piece.

Fran. [*Reading.*] " Not to mince the matter ; yefter-day, at Marybone, they had me all bob as a Robin. In fhort, being out of my money, I was forced to come the cafter, and tumbled for five hundred, dead : befides which, I owe Crop, the lender, a brace ; and if I have a fingle Si-mon to pay him, rot me. But the queer coll promifes to advance me t'other three, and bring me home, provided you will let him fneak into your lift for a cool thoufand. You know it's a debt of honour in me, and will coft you nothing.　　　　　　　　　　　Yours in hafte,

　　　　　　　　　　　　　　　　Robert Rattle."

Fran. The ftile is extraordinary.

Gran. And his motives irrefiftible.

Sir Gilb. Nay, I have them from all nations ; here's one now from an Irifh relation of my own.

Fran. Oh ! pray, let's fee.

Sir Gilb. There.　　　　　　　　　　　[Frankly *reads.*

　　" Loving coufin, and my dear life.

　　" There is only my brother Patrick, and dat is two of us ; and becaufe we would have a great refpect for our relations, we are come poft from Tipperary, with a loving defign to put both our families upon one anoder. And though we have no acquaintance with your brave daugh-ters, we faw them yefterday at the cathedral church, and find they vil fharve us vel enough. And to fhew our fincere affections, we vil taak dem vidout never a penny of money ; only, as a fmall token of fhivility upon your fide, we defire the faavour of both of us each ten thou-fand in this fame new fubfcription. And becaufe, in our hafte, fome of our cloaths and bills of exchange were for-got, prydee be fo grateful as to fend us two fcore pounds, to put us into fome worfhip for the mean time. So dis was all from, my dear life,

　　　　　　　　　Your humble farvant,
　　　　　　　　　　And loving relation,
　　　　　　　　　　　　Owen Mac Ogle."

Fran. A very modeft epiftle, truly !

Sir Gilb. Oh, here's my lift—— Now, Mr. Granger, we'll fee what we can do for you. Hold, here are fome
　　　　　　　　　　　　　　　　　　people

people that have no bufinefs here, I am fure—ay, here is
Dr. Bullanbear, one thoufand—Why, ay, I was forced
to put him down to get rid of him. The man has no
confcience. Don't I know he's in every court-lift under
a fham name ? Indeed, Domine Doctor, you can't be
here. [*Scratches him out.*] Then here's another favourite
of my wife's too; Signor Caponi da Capo—two thoufand—What, becaufe he can get as much for a fong, does
he think to have it for whiftling too ?—Huh, huh, huh !
not I, troth ; I am not for fending our money into popifh
countries. [*Blots him out.*

Fran. Rightly confidered, Sir.

Sir Gilb. Let's fee who's next——' Sir James Baker,
' Knt. one thoufand.

' *Gran.* Who's he, Sir ?

' *Sir Gilb.* Oh, a very ingenious perfon ! he's well
' known at court ; he muft ftand ; befides, I believe we
' fhall employ him in our Spanifh trade——Oh ! here
' we can you fpare one, I believe—Sir Ifaac Bickerftaff,
' Knt. one thoufand.

' *Fran.* What, the fam'd cenfor of Great Britain ?

' *Sir Gilb.* No, no, he was a very honeft, pleafant fel-
' low ; this is only a relation, a mere whimfical, that
' will draw nobody's way but his own, and is always
' wifer than his betters. I don't underftand that fort of
' wifdom, that's for doing good to every body but him-
' felf. Let thofe lift him that like him ; he fhall ride in
' no troop of mine, odfheartlikins ! [*Blots him.*

' *Gran.* How he damns them with a dafh, like a pro-
' fcribing triumvir !

' *Sir Gilb.* Let's fee.'—I would fain have another for
you——Oh, here ! William Penkethman, one thoufand.
Ha, a very pretty fellow, truly ! What, give a thoufand
pounds to a player ! why, it's enough to turn his brain :
we fhall have him grow proud, and quit the ftage upon it.
No, no, keep him poor, and let him mind his bufinefs ;
if the puppy leaves off playing the fool, he's undone.
No, no, I won't hurt the ftage ; my wife loves plays, and
whenever fhe is there, I am fure of three hours quiet at
home—[*Blots, &c.*]—Let's fee ; one, three, four, five,
ay, juft Frankly's fum—Here's five thoufand for you,
Mr. Granger, with a wet finger.

Gran.

Gran. Sir, I shall ever be in your debt.

Sir Gilb. Pooh! you owe me nothing.

Fran. You have the happiness of this life, Sir Gilbert, the power of obliging all about you.

Sir Gilb. Oh, Mr. Frankly, money won't do every thing! I am uneasy at home for all this.

Fran. Is that possible, Sir, while you have so fine a lady?

Sir Gilb. Ay, ay, you are her favourite, and have learning enough to understand her; but she is too wise and too wilful for me.

Fran. Oh, Sir! learning's a fine accomplishment in a fine lady.

Sir Gilb. Ay, it's no matter for that, she's a great plague to me. Not but my lord bishop, her uncle, was a mighty good man; she lived all along with him; I took her upon his word; 'twas he made her a scholar; I thought her a miracle; before I had her, I used to go and hear her talk Latin with him an hour together; and there I—I—I played the fool——·I was wrong, I was wrong—I should not have married again—and yet, I was so fond of her parts, I begged him to give my eldest daughter the same fine education; and so he did—but, to tell you the truth, I believe both their heads are turned.

Gran. A good husband, Sir, would set your daughter right, I warrant you.

Sir G. He must come out of the clouds, then; for she thinks no mortal man can deserve her. What think you, Mr. Frankly, you had soon enough of her?

Fran. I think still, she may deserve any mortal man, Sir.

Gran. I can't boast of my merit, Sir Gilbert; but I wish you would give me leave to take my chance with her.

Sir Gilb. Will you dine with me?

Gran. Sir, you shall not ask me twice.

Sir Gilb. And you, Mr. Frankly?

Fran. Thank you, Sir; I have had the honour of my Lady's invitation before I came out.

Sir Gilb. Oh, then, pray don't fail; for when you are there, she is always in humour.

Gran. I hope, Sir, we shall have the happiness of the young lady's company too.

Sir

Sir Gilb. Ay, ay, after dinner I'll talk with you.

Fran. Not forgetting your favourite, Charlotte, Sir.

Sir Gilb. Look you, Mr. Frankly, I underſtand you; you have a mind to my daughter Charlotte, and I have often told you I have no exceptions to you; and therefore you may well wonder why I yet ſcruple my conſent.

Fran. You have a right to refuſe it, no doubt, Sir; but I hope you can't blame me for aſking it.

Sir Gilb. In troth, I don't; and I wiſh you had it, with all my heart. But ſo it is—there's no comfort, ſure, in this life; for, though, by this glorious ſtate of our flocks, I have raiſed my poor ſingle plumb to a pomgranate, yet if they had not riſen quite ſo high, you and I, Mr. Frankly, might poſſibly have been both happier men than we are.

Fran. How ſo, Sir?

Sir Gilb. Why, at the price it now is, I am under contract to give one of the greateſt coxcombs upon earth the refuſal of marrying which of my daughters he pleaſes.

Gran. Hey-day! What, is marriage a bubble too?

[*Aſide.*

Sir Gilb. Nay, and am bound in honour even to ſpeak a good word for him. You know young Witling.

Fran. I could have gueſs'd your coxcomb, Sir; but I hope he has not yet named the lady.

Sir Gilb. Not directly; but I gueſs his inclinations, and expect every hour to have him make his call upon my conſent according to form.

' *Fran.* Is this poſſible?

Gran. Sir, if he ſhould happen to name Sophronia, will you give me leave to drub him out of his contract?

Sir Gilb. By no means; credit's a nice point, and people won't ſuppoſe that would be done without my conni-
vance: ' beſide, I believe Sophronia's in no danger. But
' becauſe one can be ſure of nothing, gentlemen, I de-
' mand both your words of honour, that, for my ſake,
' you will neither of you uſe any acts of hoſtility.

' *Fran.* Sir, in this caſe, you have a right to com-
' mand us.

' *Sir Gilb.* Your hands upon't.

' *Both.* And our words of honour.

' *Sir Gilb.* I am ſatisfied'—If we can find a way to out-

wit

wit him, fo; if not—Odfo! here he comes—I beg your pardon, gentlemen; but I won't be in his way, till I cannot help it. Hum, hum!   [*Exit* Sir Gilb.

Gran. A very odd circumftance.

Fran. I am afraid there's fomething in it; and begin to think, now, my friend, Witling, (in his raillery yefterday with Charlotte) knew what he faid himfelf, tho' he did not care whether any body elfe did.

Gran. Sure it cannot be real! I always took Witling for a beggar.

Fran. So he was, or very near it, fome months ago; but fince fortune has been playing her tricks here, fhe has rewarded his merit, it feems, with about an hundred thoufand pounds out of Change-alley.

Gran. Nay, then he may be dangerous indeed.

Fran. I long to know the bottom of it.

Gran. That you can't fail of; for you know he is vain and familiar—and here he comes.

Enter Witling.

Wit. Ha, my little Granger! how doft thou do, child? Where the devil haft thou been this age? What's the reafon you never come among us? Frankly, give me thy little finger, my dear.

Gran. Thou art a very impudent fellow, Witling.

Wit. Ay, it's no matter for that; thou art a pleafant one, I am fure; for thou always makeft us laugh.

Fran. Us! What the devil doft thou mean by us, now?

Wit. Why, your pretty fellows, my dear; your *bons vivants*; your men of wit and tafte, child.

Gran. I know very few of thofe; but I come from a country, Sir, where half the nation are juft fuch pretty fellows as thou art.

Wit. Ha! that muft be a pleafant place indeed! What, doft thou come from Paradife, child? Ha, ha, ha!

' *Fran.* Don't you know he is juft come from France, ' Sir?

' *Wit.* You jeft!

' *Gran.* Why, ay—Now you fee, Witling, your vani' ty has brought you into a fool's Paradife.

' *Wit.* Oh, you pleafant cur! What, Paris, *quafi par* ' *diis*, or Paradife. Ha! I wifh I had been with you: I ' am fure you would have thought it Paradife then.

3   ' *Gran.*

'*Gran.* Nay, now he's fairly in.

'*Wit.* 'Tis impoffible to be out on't, Sir, in your company; wherever you are, it is always Paradife to me, depend upon't. Ha, ha!'

Fran. Faith, Granger, there I think he came up with you.

Gran. Nay, fince the rogue has money, we muft, of courfe, allow him wit: but I think he is one of your good-natur'd ones; he does not only find the jeft, but the laugh too.

Wit. Ay, and to hear thee talk, child, how is it poffible to want either? Ha, ha!

Fran. Good again! Well faid, Witling! Why, thou art as fharp to-day———

Wit. As a glover's needle, my dear; I always dart it into your leather heads with three edges, ha, ha!

Gran. Pr'ythee, Witling, does not thy affurance fometimes meet with a repartee that only lights upon the outfide of thy head?

Wit. Oh, your fervant, Sir! What, now your fre's gone, you would knock me down with the butt-end, would you? Ha! it's very well, Sir; I ha' done, Sir, I ha' done; I fee it's a folly to draw bills upon a man that has no affets.

Gran. And to do it upon a man that has no cafh o thine in his hands, is the impudence of a bankrupt.

Wit. Pfha! a mere flafh in the pan—'Well, well, it's all over'—Come, come, a truce, a truce; I have done; I beg pardon.

'*Gran.* Why, thou vain rogue, thy good-nature has more impudence than thy wit. Doft thou fuppofe I can ever take any thing ill of thee.

'*Wit.* Pfha! fie! what doft thou talk, man? Why, I know thou canft not live without me. Doft think I' don't know how to make allowances? Tho' if I have too much wit, and thou haft too little, how the devil can either of us help it, you know? Ha, ha!

'*Fran.* Ha, ha! honeft Witling is not to be put out of humour, I fee.

'*Gran.* No, faith, nor out of countenance——

'*Wit.* Not I, faith, my friend; and a man of turn may fay any thing to me—Not but I fee by his hu-

'mour,

' mour, fomething has gone wrong—I hold fix to four,
' now, thou haft been crabbed at Paris in the Miffiffippi.

' *Gran.* Not I, faith, Sir; I would no more put my
' money into the ftocks there, than my legs into the ftocks
' here.   There's no getting home again, when you have
' a mind to it.

' *Wit.* Ha! very good. But, pr'ythee, tell us; what,
' is the Quinquinpois as pleafant as our Change-alley
' here?

' *Gran.* Much the fame comedy, Sir, where poor wife
' men are only fpectators, and laugh to fee fools make
' their fortune.

' *Wit.* Ay, but there we differ, Sir; for there are men
' of wit too, that have made their fortunes among us, to
' my knowledge.

' *Gran.* Very likely, Sir; when fools are flufh of mo-
' ney, men of wit won't be long without it.   I hear you
' have been fortunate, Sir.

' *Wit.* Humh—'Egad I don't know whether he calls
' me a wit or a fool.

' *Gran.* Oh, fie! every body knows you have a great
' deal of money.

' *Fran.* And I don't know any man pretends to more
' wit.

' *Wit.* Nay, that's true too: but—'Egad, I believe he
' has me.'

Gran. But, pr'ythee, Witling, how came a man of thy
parts ever to think of raifing thy fortune in Change-alley? How didft thou make all this money thou art mafter of?

Wit. Why, as other men of wit and parts often do, by
having little or nothing to lofe.   I raifed my fortune,
Sir, as Milo lifted the bull, by fticking to it every day,
when 'twas but a calf.   I foufed them with premiums,
child, and laid them on thick when the ftock was low;
and did it all from a brafs nail, boy.   In fhort, by being
dirty once a day for a few months, taking a lodging at
my broker's, and rifing at the fame hour I ufed to go to
bed at this end of the town.   I have at laft made up my
accounts, and now wake every morning mafter of five-
and-twenty hundred a year, *terra firma*, and pelf in my
ocket; I have fun in my fob, befide, child.

Gran.

Gran. And all this out of Change-alley ?

Wit. Every ſhilling, Sir ; all out of ſtocks, puts, bulls, rams, bears, and bubbles.

' *Gran.* Theſe frolicks of Fortune do ſome juſtice at
' leaſt ; they ſufficiently mortify the proud and envious,
' that have not been the better for them.

' *Fran.* Oh, I know ſome are ready to burſt even at
' the good fortune of their own relations !

' *Wit.* 'Egad, and ſo do I ; there's that ſurly put, my
' uncle, the counſellor, won't pull off his hat to me now.
' A poor ſlaving cur, that is not worth above a thouſand
' a year, and minds nothing but his buſineſs——

' *Fran.* And ſo is out of humour with you, becauſe you
' have done that in a twelvemonth, that he has been
' drudging for theſe twenty years.

' *Wit.* But I intend to ſend him word, if he does not
' mend his manners now, I ſhall diſinherit him.'

Gran. What are we to think of this, Frankly ? Is Fortune really in her wits, or is the world out of them ?

Fran. Much as it uſed to be ; ſhe has only found a new channel for her tides of favour.

Wit. Pr'ythee, why doſt not come into the Alley, and ſee us ſcramble for them ? If you have a mind to philoſophize there, there's work for your ſpeculation ! 'Egad, I never go there, but it puts me in mind of the poetical regions of death, where all mankind are upon a level :
' there you'll ſee a duke dangling after a director ; here
' a peer and a 'prentice haggling for an eighth ; there a
' Jew and a parſon making up differences ; here a young
' woman of quality buying bears of a quaker ; and there
' an old one ſelling refuſals to a lieutenant of grenadiers.

' *Frank.* What a medley of mortals has he jumbled
' together !'

' *Wit.*' Oh, there's no ſuch fun in the univerſe !——
'Egad, there's no getting away. Periſh me, if I've had time to ſee my miſtreſs, but of a Sunday, theſe three months.

Gran. Thy miſtreſs ! What doſt thou mean ? Thou ſpeakeſt as if thou hadſt but one.

Wit. Why, no more I have not, that I care a farthing for : I may perhaps have a ſtable of ſcrubs, to mount my footmen

footmen, when I rattle into town, or fo ; but this is a choice pad, child, that I defign for my own riding.

Frank. Pr'ythee, who is fhe ?

Wit. I'll fhew you, my dear——I think I have her here in my pocket.

Gran. What doft thou mean ?

Wit. Look you, I know you are my friends ; and therefore fince I am fure it is in nobody's power to hurt me, I'll venture to truft you.—There ! that's whoo, child.

[*Shews a Paper.*

Fran. What's here ?   [*Reads.*

" To Sir GILBERT WRANGLE.

" Sir, according to your contract of the 11th of February laft, I now make my election of your younger daughter, Mrs. Charlotte Wrangle ; and do hereby demand your confent, to be forthwith join'd to the faid Charlotte in the fober ftate of matrimony. Witnefs my hand, &c.

WILLIAM WITLING."

Fran. What a merry world do we live in !

Gran. This indeed is extraordinary.

Wit. I think fo : I affure you, gentlemen, I take this to be a *coup de maître* of the whole Alley. This is a call now, that none of your thick-fculled calculators could ever have thought on.

Gran. Well, Sir, and does this contract fecure the lady's fortune to you too ?

Wit. Oh, pox ! I knew that was all rug before : he had fettled three thoufand a-piece upon them in the South Sea, when it was only about par, provided they married with his confent, which by this contract, you know, I have a right to. So there's another thirty thoufand dead, my dear.

Fran. But pray, Sir, has not the lady herfelf a right of refufal, as well as you, all this while ?

Wit. A right ! aye, who doubts it ? Every woman has a right to be a fool, if fhe has a mind to it, that's certain: but Charlotte happens to be a girl of tafte, my dear ; fhe is none of thofe fools that will ftand in her own light, I can tell you.

Fran. Well, but do you expect fhe fhould blindly confent to your bargain ?

Wit. Blindly, no, child : but doft thou imagine any
citizen's

citizen's daughter can refufe a man of my figure and fortune, with her eyes open ?

Gran. Impudent rogue ! 　　　　　　　　[*Afide.*

Fran. Nay, I grant, your fecurity's good, Sir : but I mean, you have ftill left her confent at large in the writing.

Wit. Her confent ! Didft thou think I minded that, man ? I knew, if the ftock did but whip up, I fhould make no more of her than a poached egg. But to let you into the fecret, my dear, I am fecure of that already ; for the flut's in love with me, and does not know it : ha, ha, ha !

Fran. How came you to know it then ?

Wit. By her ridiculous pretending to hate me, child : for we never meet, but 'tis a mortal war, and never part, till one of us is rallied to death : ha, ha, ha !

Fran. Nay then, it muft be a match ; for, I fee, you are refolved to take no anfwer.

Wit. Not I, faith ! I know her play too well for that : in fhort, I am this very evening to attack her in form ; and to fhew you I am a man of fkill, I intend to make my firft breach from a battery of Italian mufic, in which I defign to fing my own Io Pæan, and enter the town in triumph.

Fran. You are not going to her now ?

Wit. No, no, I muft firft go and give the governor my fummons here. I muft find out Sir Gilbert ; he's hereabouts : I long to make him growl a little ; for I know he'll fire when he reads it, as if it were a *fcire facias* againft the company's charter. Ha, ha, ha ! 　[*Exit* Wit.

' *Fran.* When all's faid, this fellow feems to feel his
' fortune more than moft of the fools that have been
' lately taken into her favour.'

Gran. ' Pox on him ! I had rather have his conftitu-
' tion than his money.' Pr'ythee let's follow, and fee how the old gentleman receives him.

Fran. No ; excufe me ; I can't reft till I fee Charlotte : you know, my affairs now require attendance.

Gran. That's true ; I beg you take no notice to Sophronia of my being in town ; I have my reafons for it.

Fran. Very well ; we fhall meet at dinner. Adieu.
　　　　　　　　　　　　　　　　[*Exeunt feverally.*

End of the First Act.

A C T

A C T II.

SCENE, *Sir* Gilbert's *Houfe.*

Sophronia *and* Charlotte.

CHARLOTTE.

HA, ha, ha !

Soph. Dear fifter, don't be fo boifterous in your mirth : you really over-power me ! So much vociferation is infupportable.

Char. Well, well, I beg your pardon—but, you know laughing is the wholfomeft thing in the world; and when one has a hearty occafion——

Soph. To be vulgar, you are refolved to appear fo.

Char. Oh, I cannot help it, I love you dearly ; and, pray, where's the harm of it ?

Soph. Look you, fifter, I grant you, that rifibility is only given to the *animal rationale* ; but you really indulge it, as if you could give no other proof of your fpecies.

Char. And if I were to come into your fentiments, dear fifter, I am afraid the world would think I were of no fpecies at all.

Soph. The world, fifter, is a generation of ignorants : and, for my part, I am refolved to do what in me lies, to put an end to pofterity.

Char. Why, you don't defpair of a man, I hope !

Soph. No ; but I will have all mankind defpair of me.

Char. You'll pofitively die a maid ?

Soph. You, perhaps, may think that dying a martyr ; but I fhall not die a brute, depend upon't.

Char. Nay, I don't think you'll die either, if you can help it.

Soph. What do you mean, Madam ?

Char. Only, Madam, that you are a woman, and may happen to change your mind ; that's all.

Soph. A woman ! That's fo like your ordinary way of thinking ; as if fouls had any fexes—No—when I die, Madam, I fhall endeavour to leave fuch fentiments behind me, that—*(non omnis moriar)* the world will be convinced my purer part had no fex at all.

‘ *Char.*

' *Char.* Why truly, it will be hard to imagine, that
' any one of our fex could make fuch a refolution;
' though, I hope, we are not bound to keep all we make
' neither.

' *Soph.* You'll find, Madam, that an elevated foul may
' be always mafter of its perifhable part.'

Char. But, dear Madam, do you fuppofe our fouls are
crammed into our bodies merely to fpoil fport, that a
virtuous woman is only fent hither of a fool's errand?
What's the ufe of our coming into the world, if we are to
go out of it, and leave nobody behind us?

Soph. ' If our fpecies can be only fupported by thofe
' grofs mixtures, of which cookmaids and footmen are
' capable, people of rank and erudition ought certainly
' to deteft them.' Oh, what a pity 'tis the divine fecret
fhould be loft! I have fomewhere read of an ancient na-
turalift, whofe laborious ftudies had difcovered a more
innocent way of propagation; but, it feems, his tables
unfortunately falling into his wife's hands, the grofs
creature threw them into the fire.

Char. Indeed, my dear fifter, if you talk thus in company, people will take you for a mad-woman.

' *Soph.* I fhall be even with them, and think thofe mad,
' that differ from my opinion.

' *Char.* But I rather hope the world will be fo chari-
' table, as to think this is not your real opinion.'

Soph. I fhall wonder at nothing that's faid or thought
by people of your fullied imagination.

Char. Sullied! I would have you to know, Madam, I
think of nothing but what's decent and natural.

Soph. Don't be too pofitive, nature has it indecencies.

Char. That may be; but I don't think of them.

Soph. No! Did not you own to me juft now, you were
determined to marry?

Char. Well; and where's the crime, pray?

Soph. What! you want to have me explain? But I
fhall not defile my imagination with fuch grofs ideas.

' *Char.* But, dear Madam, if marriage were fuch an
' abominable bufinefs, how comes it that all the world
' allows it to be honourable? And I hope you won't ex-
' pect me to be wifer than any of my anceftors, by think-
' ing the contrary.

C   ' *Soph.*

' *Soph.* No ; but if you will read hiftory, fifter, you
' will find that the fubjects of the greateft empire upon
' earth were only propagated from violated chaftity :
' the Sabine ladies were wives, 'tis true, but glorious
' ravifhed wives. Vanquifhed they were indeed, but
' they furrendered not : they fcreamed, and cried, and
' tore, and as far as their weak limbs would give them
' leave, refifted and abhorred the odious joy——

' *Char.* And yet, for all that nicenefs, they brought
' a chopping race of rakes, that bullied the whole world
' about them.

' *Soph.* The greater ftill their glory, that though they
' were naturally prolific, their refiftance proved they
' were not flaves to appetite.

' *Char.* Ah, fifter ! if the Romans had not been fo
' fharp fet, the glorious refiftance of thefe fine ladies
' might have been all turned into coquettry.

' *Soph.* There's the fecret, fifter : had our modern
' dames but the true Sabine fpirit of difdain, mankind
' might be again reduced to thofe old Roman extremi-
' ties ; and our fhamelefs brides would not then be led,
' but dragged to the altar ; their *fponfalia* not called a
' marriage, but a facrifice : and the conquered beauty,
' not the bridal virgin, but the victim.

' *Char.* Oh, ridiculous ! and fo you would have no
' woman married, that was not firft ravifhed, according
' to law ?

' *Soph.* I would have mankind owe their conqueft of
' us rather to the weaknefs of our limbs, than of our
' fouls. And if defencelefs women muft be mothers, the
' brutality, at leaft, fhould lie all at their door.'

Char. Have a care of this over-nicenefs, dear fifter,
left fome agreeable young fellow fhould feduce you to
the confufion of parting with it. You'd make a moft
rueful figure in love !

Soph. Sifter, you make me fhudder at your freedom !
I in love ! I admit a man ! What, become the voluntary, the lawful object of a corporeal fenfuality ! Like
you, to choofe myfelf a tyrant ! a defpoiler ! a hufband !
Ugh.

Char. I am afraid, by this diforder of your thoughts,
dear

dear fifter, you have got one in your head, that you don't know how to get rid of.

Soph. I have, indeed ; but it's only the male creature that you have a mind to.

Char. Why, that's poffible too ; for I have often obferved you uneafy at Mr. Frankly's being particular to me.

Soph. If I am, 'tis upon your account, becaufe I know he impofes upon you.

Char. You know it ?

' *Soph.* I know his heart, and that another is miftrefs ' of it.

' *Char.* Another !

' *Soph.* Another ; but one that to my knowledge will ' never hear of him ; fo don't be uneafy, dear filter, all ' in my power you may be affured of.

' *Char.* Surprifingly kind, indeed !

' *Soph.* And you know too I have a great deal in my ' inclination ———

' *Char.* For me or him, dear fifter ?

' *Soph.* Nay, now you won't fuffer me to oblige you ; ' I tell you, I hate the animal ; and for half a good word ' would give him away.

' *Char.* What ! before you have him ?

' *Soph.* This affected ignorance is fo vain, dear fifter, ' that I now think it high time to explain to you.

' *Char.* Then we fhall underftand one another.'

Soph. You don't know, perhaps, that Mr. Frankly is paffionately in love with me ?

Char. I know, upon his treating with my father, his lawyer once made you fome offers.

Soph. Why then you may know too, that upon my flighting thofe offers, he fell immediately into a violent defpair.

Char. I did not hear of its violence.

' *Soph.* So violent, that he has never fince dared to ' open his lips to me about it ; but to revenge the fecret ' pains I gave him, has made his public addreffes to you.

' *Char.* Indeed, fifter, you furprife me : and 'tis hard ' to fay, that men impofe more upon us, than we upon ' ourfelves.

' *Soph.*

'*Soph.* Therefore by what I have told you, you may
' now be convinced he is falfe to you.

'*Char.* But is there a neceffity, my dear Sophronia,
' that I muft rather believe you than him? Ha, ha,
' ha!'

Soph. How, Madam! Have you the confidence to
queftion my veracity, by fuppofing me capable of an endeavour to deceive you?

Char. No hard words, dear fifter: I only fuppofe you
as capable of deceiving yourfelf, as I am.

Soph. Oh, mighty probable, indeed! You are a perfon
of infinite penetration! Your ftudies have opened to you
the utmoft receffes of human nature; but let me tell
you, fifter, that vanity is the only fruit of toilette lucu-
brations. I deceive myfelf: ha, ha, ha!

Char. One of us certainly does! Ha, ha!

Soph. There I agree with you. Ha, ha!

Char. Till I am better convinced then on which fide
the vanity lies, give me leave to laugh in my turn, dear
fifter.

Soph. Oh, by all means, fweet Madam! Ha, ha!

Both. Ha, ha, ha!

Char. Oh, here's mamma; fhe perhaps may decide
the queftion. Ha, ha!

Enter Lady Wrangle.

L. Wrang. So, Mrs. Charlotte! what wonderful nothing, pray, may be the fubject of this mighty merri-
ment?

Soph. Nothing indeed, Madam; or, what's next to
nothing; a man, it feems. Ha, ha!

L. Wrang. Charlotte, wilt thou never have any thing
elfe in thy head?

Char. I was in hopes, nothing, that was in my fifter's
head, would be a crime in mine, Madam,

L. Wrang. Your fifter's! What? How? Who is it
you are laughing at?

Char. Only at one another, Madam; but, perhaps,
your ladyfhip may laugh at us both: for, it feems, my
fifter and I both infift, that Mr. Frankly is pofitively in
love but with one of us.

L. Wrang. Who, child?

Soph. Mr. Frankly, Madam.

L. Wrang.

L. Wrang. Mr. Frankly in love with one of you!

Soph. Ay, Madam; but it feems we both take him **to** ourfelves.

L. Wrang. Then Charlotte was in the right in one point.

Soph. In what, dear Madam?

L. Wrang. Why, that for the fame reafon you have been laughing at one another, I muft humbly beg leave to laugh at you both —— Ha, ha!

Char. So, this is rare fport.   [*Afide.*

L. Wrang. But pray, ladies, how long has the chimera of this gentleman's paffion for you been in either of your heads?

Soph. Nay, Madam, not that I value the conqueft; but your ladyfhip knows he once treated with my father upon my account.

L. Wrang. I know he made that his pretence to get acquainted in the family.

Soph. Perhaps, Madam, I have more coercive reafons, but am not concerned enough at prefent to infift upon their validity.

L. Wrang. Sophronia, you have prudence. [*Sophronia walks by and reads.*] But what have you to urge, fweet lady? How came this gentleman into your head, pray?

Char. Really, Madam, I can't well fay how he got in, but there he is, that's certain: what will be able to get him out again, heaven knows.

L. Wrang. Oh, I'll inform you then; think no more of him than he thinks of you, and I'll anfwer for your cure. Ha, ha, ha!

Char. I fhall follow your prefcription, Madam, when I am once fure how little he thinks on me.

L. Wrang. Then judge of that, when I affure you, that his heart is utterly and folely given up to me.

Soph. Well! I did not think my Lady had been capable of fo much weaknefs.   [*Afide.*

Char. How! to you, Madam? How is that poffible, unlefs he makes you difhonourable offers?

L. Wrang. There's no occafion to fuppofe that neither; there are paffions you have no notion of: he knows my

vir-

virtue is impregnable : but that——preferves him mine.

Char. Nay, this does puzzle me indeed, Madam.

Soph. If you had ever read Plato, fifter, you might have known, that paffions of the greateft dignity have not their fource from veins and arteries.

L. Wrang. Sophronia, give me leave to judge of that ; perhaps I don't infift that he is utterly Platonic neither : the manfion of the foul may have its attractions too ; he is as yet but *udum & molle lutum*——and may take what form I pleafe to give him.

Char. Well, Madam, fince I fee he is fo utterly at your ladyfhip's difpofal, and that 'tis impoffible your virtue can make any ufe of him in my vulgar way ; fhall I beg your good word to my father, only to make me miftrefs of his mortal part ?

L. Wrang. Heavens ! what will this world come to ? ' This creature has fcarce been two years from fchool, ' and yet is impatient for a hufband?' No, Madam, you are too young as yet ; but—— *Cruda marito.* Your education is not yet finifhed ; firft cultivate your mind, ' correct and mortify thefe fallies of your blood ;' learn of your fifter here, to live a bright example of your fex ; refine your foul ; give your happier hours up to fcience, arts, and letters ; enjoy the raptures of philofophy, fubdue your paffions, and renounce the fenfual commerce of mankind.

Char. Oh, dear Madam, I fhould make a piteous philofopher ; indeed your ladyfhip had much better put me out to the bufinefs I am fit for : here's my fifter has learning enough o'confcience for any one family ; and, of the two, I had much rather follow your ladyfhip's example, and ufe my humble endeavours to increafe it.

L. Wrang. My example ! Do you fuppofe then, if I had been capable of grofs defires, I would have chofen your father for the gratificator of them ?

Char. Why not, Madam ; my papa's a hale man, and though he has twice your ladyfhip's age, he walks as ftraight, and leads up a country-dance as brifk as a beau at a ball.

L. Wrang. Come, none of your fenfual inferences
from

from thence; I was governed by my parents, I had other views in marrying Mr. Wrangle.

Char. Yes, a fwinging jointure. [*Afide.*

L. Wrang. When you have gone through my ftudies, Madam, philofophy will tell you, 'tis poffible a well-natured mind, though fated to a hufband, may be at once a wife and virgin.

Char. Prodigious! [*Afide.*

L. Wrang. What is't you fmile at, Madam?

Char. Nothing, Madam, only I don't underftand thefe philofophical myfteries; but if your ladyfhip will indulge me, in marrying Mr. Frankly, as for dying a maid afterwards, I'll take my chance for it.

L. Wrang. What a giddy confidence! But thou art ftrangely vain, Charlotte, to be fo importunate for a man, that, as I have told thee, has the misfortune to be paffionately in love with me.

Char. Indeed, indeed, Madam, if your ladyfhip would but give him leave to open his mind freely, he would certainly tell you another ftory.

L. Wrang. I will fend for him this minute, and convince you of your error.

Enter a Servant.

Serv. Madam, Mr. Frankly.

L. Wrang. He never came more opportunely: defire him to walk in.

Enter Mr. Frankly.

L. Wrang. Oh, Mr. Frankly, the welcomeft man alive.

Fran. Then I am the happieft, I am fure, Madam.

L. Wrang. Oh, fy! is there any one of this company could make you fo?

Fran. There's one in the company, Madam, has a great deal more in her power, than I'm afraid fhe'll part with to me.

Soph. Are you this hard-hearted lady, fifter? Does this defcription reach you, pray? [*Afide.*

Char. The power does not defcribe you, I'll anfwer for it. [*Afide.*

L. Wrang. Nay, now you grow particular——You have fomething to fay to one of thefe ladies, I'm fure.
[*To* Frankly.

Fran.

Fran. I have fomething, Madam, to fay to both of them.

Soph. Shall we let him fpeak, fifter?

Char. Freely.

L. Wrang. Which of thefe two, now, if you were free to choofe, could you really give up your heart to?

Fran. Oh, Madam! as to that, I dare only fay, as Sir John Suckling did upon the fame occafion.

Soph. Pray, what was that?

Fran. He fure is happieft that has hopes of either;

Next him is he that fees you both together.

L. Wrang. Perfectly fine—Nor is there more wit in the verfes themfelves, than in your polite application of them—Mr. Frankly, I muft beg your pardon—I know it's rude to whifper; but you have good-nature; and, to oblige a woman——

Fran. Is the bufinefs of my life, Madam—What the devil can all this mean? I have been oddly catechized here—Sure they have not all agreed to bring me to a declaration for one of them—It looks a little like it—' But then, how comes Charlotte into fo vain a project? Nay, ' fo hazardous! She can't but know, my holding the ' other two in play, has been the only means of my get- ' ting admittance to her—Perhaps they may have piqued ' her into this experiment—not unlikely.' But I muft be cautious.   [*Afide.*

L. Wrang. Nay, ladies, you can't but fay I laid you fairly in his way. [*Apart to* Soph. *and* Char.] And yet you fee from how palpable a regard to me he has ingenioufly avoided a declaration, for either of you, at leaft.

Soph. Your ladyfhip won't be offended, if, for a moment, we fhould fufpend your conclufion.

L. Wrang. Not in the leaft; if fufpenfe can make you happy, live always in it.

Char. But, pray, Madam, let him go on a little.

L. Wrang. Oh, you fhall have enough of him. Well, you are a horrid tyrant, Mr. Frankly. Don't you plainly fee, here are two ladies in this company, that have a mind you fhould declare in favour of one of them?

Fran. Yes, Madam; but I plainly fee, there are three ladies in the company.

L. Wrang. What then?

Fran.

Fran. Why, then, Madam, I am more afraid of offending that third perfon, than either of the other two.

L. Wrang. [*To* Soph. *and* Char.] Obferve his diffidence, his awe; he knows I love refpect.

Soph. With fubmiffion, Madam, I never was familiar with him.

' *L. Wrang.* Come, now, do you both afk the quef-
' tion, as I have done, each exclufive of herfelf.

' *Char.* Your ladyfhip's in the right————[*Afide.*
' Sir, without any apology then, I am obliged to afk you,
' whether it be my Lady or my fifter, you are really in
' love with ?

' *Fran.* So, now it's plain. [*Afide.*] When either of
' them afk me, you'll be out of the queftion, I can affure
' you, Madam.

' *L. Wrang.* Ha, ha !

' *Soph.* Who's in the queftion now, fifter ?

' *Char.* If I had put myfelf in, you would not have
' been there, I'll anfwer for him.   [*Afide.*

' *Soph.* Then, I'll do you that favour, Madam.

' *Fran.* So, now the other——but I am ready for
' her too.

' *Soph.* You fee, Sir, the humour we are in : though
' don't fuppofe, if I afk you the fame queftion, 'tis from
' the fame motive ; but fince thefe ladies have obliged
' me to it——Which of them is it you fincerely are a
' flave to ?

' *Fran.* Since I find your motive is only complaifance
' to them, Madam, I hope you will not think it needs an
' anfwer.

' *Soph.* I am fatisfied—Your ladyfhip was pleafed to
' mention refpect—I think there's refpect and demonftra-
' tion too, Madam.   [*Afide to* L. Wrang.'

L. Wrang. I grant it ; ' but both to me, child.' But I will fpeak once more for all of us—Sir, that you may not be reduced to farther ambiguities, fuppofe we are all agreed, you fhould have leave to declare which of us, then, your heart is utterly in the difpofal of ?

Fran. Then I muft fuppofe, Madam, that one of you have a mind I fhould make the other two my enemies.

L. Wrang. All your friends, depend upon us.

Fran. So were all the three goddeffes to Paris, Madam, till

till he presumed to be particular, and rashly gave the apple to Venus—You know, Madam, Juno was his immortal enemy ever after.

—— ——Manet altâ mente repôstum
Judicium Paridis, spretæque injuria formæ.

L. Wrang. Sir, you are excus'd; the modesty and elegance of your reply has charmed me.

Soph. Now, sister, was this delicacy of his taste and learning shewn to recommend himself to me or you, think you?

Char. Oh, I don't dispute its recommending him to you.

Soph. He thinks it does, depend upon't.

Char. Though I can hardly think that of him, yet I can't say, indeed, he has taken much pains to recommend himself to me all this while. I see no reason, because they are to be respected, forsooth, that I may not be pleased in my turn too.   [*To herself.*

Fran. And now, ladies, give me leave to ask you a question.

L. Wrang. You may command us, Sir.

Fran. Then, whose cruel proposal was it to urge me to a declaration of my heart, when you all knew there was not one of you, from the disposition of whose mind or circumstances, I could hope the least favour or mercy.

L. Wrang. Explain yourself.

Fran. Why, first, Madam, as to your ladyship, you are honourably disposed of; from you my utmost vanity could no more form a hope, than could your virtue give it—And here, [*To Soph.*] if possible, my fate were harder still—here I must have to encounter rivals numberless and invincible.

Soph. Rivals!

Fran. Ay, Madam, is not every volume in your library a rival? Do you not pass whole days, nay, sometimes, happier nights, with them alone? ' The living and ' the dead promiscuous in your favour?' Old, venerable sages, even in their graves, can give you raptures, from whose divine enjoyment no mortal lover can persuade you.

Soph. [*To Char.*] Is this to please you, sister?

Char. Truly, I think not——he has mistaken the way, at least.

Fran. [*Turning to Char.*] And here, Madam——
                                                L. Wrang.

L. Wrang. Hold, Sir; a truce with your negatives, left they grow too vehement in their affirmation. You have hitherto my efteem, preferve it by your difcretion, and force me not to revoke the freedom I have this day given you. Sophronia, I have carried this matter to the very utmoft limits of difcretion. I hope you and your fifter are now delivered from your error; if not, I'll inftantly withdraw, and leave you to a full conviction. [*Exit.*

Fran. I am afraid my Lady takes fomething ill of me.

Soph. Sir, what you have done was from her own defire; and fince I partly am the occafion, it is but juft I ftand engaged for your reconciliation.

Fran. Then give me leave to hope, Madam——

Soph. From what pretenfion, Sir? From any weaknefs of my behaviour? Hope! Do you confider the licentious and extenfive confequences of that odious word? Hope! You make me tremble at the thought.

Fran. Madam, I only mean——

Soph. I know your meaning, Sir: and therefore muft not hear it.

Fran. This is new with a vengeance! [*Afide.*

Soph. Sifter, ' I am forry our argument has reduced ' me to ftand fo outrageous an inftance of your conviction; ' but you may profit from the infult:' you may now learn to moderate your vanity, and to know yourfelf. Oh, 'tis a heavenly leffon!——*E cælo defcendit gnothe feauton.* [*Exit.*

Fran. What a folid happinefs is now crept into her mind through the crack of her brain?—I hope you are not going too, Madam?

Char. I don't know any bufinefs I have here.

Fran. So——'Egad, I have difobliged them all, I believe. [*Afide.*] You are not out of humour?

Char. I don't know whether I am or no.

Fran. So cold, Charlotte, after I have had my wits upon the ftretch this half hour, to oblige you?

Char. What, in blowing up other people's vanity at my expence?

Fran. Would you have had me blown up their jealoufy, at the expence of my being well with you?

Char. You, that are fo dexterous in impofing upon others, may impofe upon me too, for ought I know.

' *Fran.*

'*Fran.* Come, come, don't impofe upon yourfelf,
' Charlotte, by this groundlefs, this childifh refentment.

'*Char.* She that has no refentment at all, may be un-
' der-treated as long as fhe lives, I find.'

Fran. Pray, think a little. Is my having made them
ridiculous by your own confent, expofing you to them,
or them to you?

Char. I don't know how the matter's contrived; but I
certainly find myfelf uneafy, and you can't perfuade me
I am not fo.

Fran. Well, well; fince you can't juftify your being
in an ill humour, it's a fair ftep, at leaft, to your coming
into a good one.

Char. Come, I will not be wheedled now.

Fran. Nay, but hear me.

Sophronia *enters unfeen, while* Frankly *feems to entertain*
Charlotte *apart.*

Soph. What can thefe creatures be doing alone together? ' I thought I left my fifter in too ill a humour to
' retire with him; but I fee thefe carnage lovers have
' fuch a meannefs in their fouls, they'll overlook the
' groffeft ufage to accommodate their fenfual concorpora-
' tion.' 'Tis fo—her eyes have loft all refentment already.
But I muft not be feen, left they miftake my innocent curiofity for jealoufy.

Char. Well, but you might have thrown in a civil thing
to me in my turn too.

Fran. Alas, poor lady! Pray, what one civil thing did
I mean to any body but yourfelf? Befides, was not you
one of the three goddeffes, Mifs Charlotte? Which of
the company do you fuppofe I meant by Venus, pray?

Char. How filly you make me?

Fran. Nay, I was going to fay a great deal more to you,
if my Lady had not ftopped my mouth.

Soph. Is it poffible?   [*Afide.*

Char. Why, then, I beg your pardon; for, in fhort, I
find I have only been fool enough to be uneafy, becaufe
they had not fenfe enough to be mortified.

Fran. A pretty innocent confeffion, truly!

Soph. Have I my fenfes?

Char. Well, but tell me, what was it you had a mind
fay to me?

Fran.

Fran. Nothing to what I now could say——Oh, Char-lotte, my heart grows full of you; the leaft look of kindnefs foftens me to folly !—Indeed I love you.

Soph. Soh——

Chor. And for what, after all ?   [*Smiling.*

Fran. For that, and for a thoufand charms befide. [*Preffing her hand.*] There's fomething in your looks fo foft, fo gentle, fo refign'd, and plaintive ; I loved before I knew it, and only thought I gave the pity that I wanted.

Char. What tranfport's in the paffion, when the ten-dernefs is mutual !

Soph. Oh, the enormous creature! but I'll begone, left her intoxication fhould know no bounds—No, on fecond thoughts, I'll ftay ; ' this odious objeĉt may be ufeful ;
' vipers, if rightly taken, are prefervatives : and as the
' Spartans taught their children to abhor intemperance,
' by fhewing them their flaves expofed, and fenfelefs in
' their wine ; fo I, in contemplation of this folly, may
' be fortified againft it.'   Oh, the abandoned wantons !—
' What a riotous diforder now muft run through every
' vein of her whole fyftem ? How can they thus deface
' the dignity of human being ?'—[*During this* Fr. *and* Char. *feem in an amorous difpute, till he kiffes her.*] —A kifs ! nay, then, 'tis infupportable. [*She goes to them.*] Sifter, I am amazed you can ftand trifling here, when my father is come home, and you know he wants you.

Char. She has certainly feen us. •   [*Afide to* Fran.

Fran. No matter; feem eafy, and take no notice.
                                   [*Apart to* Char.

Soph. Shall I tell him you will not come, Madam ?

Char. Well, do not be in a paffion, dear fifter.

Fran. Oh, fie ! why fhould you think fo ? But is Sir Gilbert come in, Madam ? I have a little bufinefs with him. If you pleafe, Madam, I'll wait upon you to him.

Char. With all my heart.

' *Fran. Amante fpofo,* &c.   [*finging.*
                          [*Exeunt* Fran. *and* Char.

Soph. What means this turbulence of thought ? ' Why ' am I thus difordered !' It cannot, nay, I will not have it jealoufy—No, if I were capable of folly, Granger might miflead me ; yet ftill I am difturbed—' Yes, 'tis
                D   ' plain,

' plain, I am incenfed, provoked at him ;' but can I not
affign the caufe ?—Oh, I have found it !—Having firft
offered up his heart to me, his giving it to another, without
my leave, is an infult on my merit, and worthy my refentment—that's all—How, then, fhall I punifh him ? By
fecuring her to his rival. Witling fhall have her; I'll
work it by my Lady ; fhe feems his friend— ' Yes, yes,
' that will entirely eafe my heart. How I rejoice to find
' 'tis only decent pride that has difturbed me. Yes, I'll
' certainly refent it, to their mutual difappointment.'

Thus both fhall fuffer, doom'd to different fates :

His be defpair ; be hers, the man fhe hates.

　　　　　　　　　　　　　　　　　　　　　　[*Exit.*

END of the SECOND ACT.

A C T　III.

Lady Wrangle, *and* Sophronia.

LADY WRANGLE.

IMPOSSIBLE ! You amaze me ! Kifs her, fay you ?
　What, as a lover, amoroufly, voluptuoufly ?

Soph. Infamoufly, with all the glowing fervour of a libertine.

L. Wrang. Then I am deceived indeed. ' I thought
' that virtue, letters, and philofophy, had only charms for
' him : I have known his foul all rapture in their praifes ;
' nay, and believed myfelf the fecret object of them all.
' But is he vulgar, brutal, then, at laft ? No Punic faith
' fo falfe. 'Tis well ; he has deceived me, and I hate
' him. Oh, that forward creature !

' *Soph.* She warms as I could wifh.　　　　　[*Afide.*

' *L. Wrang.*' But, tell me, dear Sophronia, how did
that naughty girl behave to him ? Was the fhame chiefly
his ? Did fhe refift, or——' how was this odious kifs ob-
' tained ? Were his perfuafions melting, or her allure-
' ments artful ? Was he enfnared, or did his wiles feduce
' her ?' Oh, tell me all his bafenefs ! I burn to know,
yet wifh to be deceived.

Soph. —*Speratque miferrima falli*—Directly jealous of
him ; but I'll make my ufes of it. [*Afide.*] Nay, Madam,
　　　　　　　　　　　　　　　　　　　　　　　　I muft

I muſt own the guilty part was chiefly hers. Had you but ſeen the warm advances that ſhe made him, ' the ' looks, the ſmiles, the toying glances; Oh, ſuch wanton ' blandiſhments to allure him!' you would think his crime, compared to hers, but frailty.

L. Wrang. Oh, the little forcereſs! But I ſhall ſtop her in her looſe career: I'll have her know, forward as ſhe is, her inclinations ſhall wait upon my choice; and ſince ſhe will run riot, I'll have her clogged immediately. I'll marry her, Sophronia; but where I think fit. No, Mr. Witling is her man, or ſhe's a maid for ever.

Soph. That, Madam, I doubt, ſhe will never be brought to; ſhe mortally hates him.

L. Wrang. So much the better; I do not deſign him, therefore, as her happineſs, but her puniſhment.

Soph. This is fortunate; ſhe even prevents my pur-poſe. [*Aſide.*

L. Wrang. Oh, that a man of his ſublime faculties could fall from ſuch a height! Was ever any thing ſo mean, Sophronia?

Soph. I am ſurprized indeed. My ſiſter, too, is ſo illi-terate, Madam.

L. Wrong. To contaminate his intellects with ſuch a chit of an animal; *O tempora!*

Soph. O mores! 'Tis a degenerate age, indeed, Madam.

' *L. Wrang.* Nothing but noiſe and ignorance; girls ' and vanity have their attractions now.

' *Soph.* Oh, there's no living, Madam, while coquettes ' are ſo openly tolerated among a civilized people!

' *L. Wrang.* I proteſt, they are ſo inſolently inſidious, ' they are become mere nuiſances to all innocent ſociety.

' *Soph.* I am amazed the government ſhould not ſet ' the idle creatures to work.

' *L. Wrang.* The wiſdom of our anceſtors reſtrained ' ſuch horrid licences; and, you ſee, the laws they made, ' deſcribed them all by the modeſt term of ſpinſters only. But I'll take care of her, ' at leaſt; and ſince ſhe is be-' come a public miſchief, to humble her will be a public ' good.' I'll ſend to Mr. Witling this moment, and in-vite him to dine here. I deſire you will be in the way, child, and aſſiſt me in bringing this matter to a ſpeedy concluſion. [*Exit.*

Soph.

Soph. Yes, I shall assist you, Madam; though not to gratify your resentments, but my own. Poor lady! is this then all the fruit of your philosophy? ' Is this her
' conduct of the passions, not to endure another should
' possess what she pretends to scorn? Are these her self-
' denials? Where, where was her self-examination all this
' while? The least inquiry there had shewn these passions
' as they are: then had she seen, that all this anger at
' my sister was but envy: those reproaches on her lo-
' ver, jealousy; even that jealousy, the child of vanity,
' and her avowed resentment, malice!' Good Heaven! Can she be this creature, and know it not?——And yet 'tis so—so partial's Nature to herself,
   ' That charity begins, where knowledge shou'd,
   ' And all our wisdom's counsell'd by the blood:'
   The faults of others we with ease discern,
   But our own frailties are the last we learn.

            [*Going off she meets* Frankly *and* Charlotte ? Ha! perpetually together!

Char. In contemplation, sister? I am afraid we dis-turb you: come, Mr. Frankly, we'll go into the next room.

Soph. No, Madam, if you have any secrets, I'll retire,

Char. Nay, we have none now, sister, but what I dare swear you are certainly let into: ha, ha, ha!

Fran. So she must have a gentle insult, I find; but it will be prudent in me to keep the peace.   [*Aside.*

Soph. These taunts are insupportable! but to confess the smart, were adding to her triumph.   [*Aside.*

Char. Why so grave, Sophronia?

Soph. Why that question, Madam? Do you often see me otherwise?

Char. No; but I thought, upon your supposing we had secrets, you drew up a little.

Soph. 'Tis possible, I might not be in a laughing hu-mour, without thinking any of your secrets important.

Fran. People, Madam, that think much, always wear a serious aspect.   [*To* Char.

Soph. As the contrary, sister, may be a reason for your continual mirth.

Char. Well, well; so I am but happy, sister, I am content you should be wise as long as you live.

                        Soph.

Soph. You have one fign of wifdom, I fee: a little thing contents you—There's no bearing her. [*Ex.* Soph.

Char. She's in a high miff.

Fran. I am afraid there is no good towards us : I obferved my lady, as fhe paffed too, had much the fame cloud upon her brow.

Char. Then fhe has certainly told her how fhe caught us fooling together.

Fran. No doubt on't; therefore we muft expect all the mifchief that either of them can do us.

Char. My fifter can't do us much, at leaft.

Fran. She can blow up my lady; and, you know, my lady governs your father.

Char. She does a little overbear him indeed ; not but he will make his party good with her upon occafion : I have known it come to a drawn battle between them, efpecially when he has any body to ftand by him. A fad life though, Mr. Frankly, when conjugal engagements are only battles; does not their example frighten you ?

Fran. I can fee no hazard, in taking my chance with you, Madam.

Sophronia *returns, and ftops fhort, feeing* Frankly *taking* Charlotte's *hand.*

Soph. So ! clofing again the minute they are alone; but I fhall make bold with them. [*Goes forward.* Pray, fifter, what did you do with that book of mine you took up this morning ?

Char. What book ?

Soph. The Confucius, you know, in my chamber.

Char. Oh, I did not mind it ; I left it upon the green table.

Soph. Very well—— that's all——I beg your pardon. What a melancholy fight fhe is !

[*Exit, and drops her handkerchief.*

Fran. This book was only a pretence to break in upon us.

Char. Plainly——fhe haunts us like the ghoft in Hamlet. But pray, what talk had you with my father juft now ?

Fran. A great deal; we are upon very good terms there, I can tell you : but his confcience, it feems, is under the moft ridiculous dilemma, fure, that ever was.

Char.

Char. What do you mean ?

Fran. If you will have patience to hear it, I'll tell you.

Char. I fhall have no patience till I do hear it.

Fran. You muft know then, fome time ago, ' Sir Gil-
' bert happened in a mixed company in Change-Alley,
' to join in a laugh at Mr.' Witling, ' for his folly (as it
' was then thought) in giving out premiums for the re-
' fufal of South-Sea ftock at an extravagant price : the
' beau being piqued to an intemperance, to fee his bar-
' gains a jeft, offered, in heat of blood, to back his judg-
' ment with more money, for a harder bargain, and ten
' times as·chimerical.

' *Char.* Ay, now let's hear.

' *Fran.* Thus it was : he' told an hundred guineas into your father's hand ; in confideration of which, (if
Witling could prove himfelf worth fifty thoufand pounds
within the year, and the South-Sea ftcck fhould in that
time mount to a thoufand per cent. why then, and on
:hofe conditions only) your father was to give him the
refufal of you, or your fifter, in marriage. ' This whim-
' fical offer turned the laugh of the company to the
' beau's fide, at which Sir Gilbert, impatient of his
' triumph, and not being in the leaft apprehenfive
' either of the ftocks rifing to that price, or that this
' rattle-headed fellow could poffibly make fuch a for-
' tune in that time, fairly took the money, and figned
' the contract.' Now the ftock, it feems, is come up to
his price, and the fpark has actually proved himfelf worth
near double the fum he conditioned for.

Char. For heaven's fake ! am I to take all this feri-
oufly ?

Fran. Upon my life 'tis true : but don't miftake the
matter ; Sir Gilbert has left his daughter's inclinations
free : there is no force to be put upon them in the bargain.

' *Char.* Oh, then I can take my breath again.

' *Fran.* No, no ; you are fafe as to that point : you
' may do as you pleafe ; he has only tied up his own
' confent. But Witling having this call upon it, Sir
' Gilbert is incapable, as he fays, of giving it, at pre-
' fent, to me.

' *Char.*

' *Char.* Well; but in the mean time, suppose he
' should give it to you; what's the penalty?

' *Fran.* That's true; I had like to have forgot it:
' the penalty is this; if Sir Gilbert refuses his consent,
' then he is to give Witling an alternative of the three
' thousand pounds stock only, at two hundred. So low
' it seems was the price when this bargain was made.

' *Char.* A pinching article: I am afraid my good fa-
' ther has not distaste enough for a coxcomb, to part
' with his stock, and not toss him a daughter in the
' bargain.

' *Fran.* Ay, but confider; Sir Gilbert is not to part
' with his stock neither, if you refuse to marry the gen-
' tleman.'

Char. Why then the fool has given his money for
nothing; at least I am sure he has, if he makes his call
upon me.

' *Fran.* Ay, but here's the misfortune; the fool has
' been wise enough to do that already: Sir Gilbert tells
' me, he has insisted upon you; and you may be sure
' my lady, and your sister, will do all in their power to
' hold your father to his bargain: so that, while the
' contract's valid, it will not be even in your power,
' Charlotte, to complete my happiness this half year.

' *Char.* It gives me at least occasion to shew you a new
' proof of my inclination; for I confess, I shall be as
' uneasy as you, 'till, one way or other, this ridiculous
' bargain is out of that coxcomb's hands again.'

Fran. Oh, Charlotte! lay your hand upon my heart,
and feel how sensibly it thanks you.

Char. Foolish!

Sophronia *enters, as looking for her handkerchief, and ob-
serves them.*

Soph. Monstrous! actually embracing him! What
have her transports made her blind too? Sure she might
see me.

Char. Be but ruled, and I'll engage to manage it.

' *Fran.* I have a lucky thought, that certainly——'

Char. Peace! break thee off! Lo! where it comes
again.

Fran. Speak to it, Horatio——   [*Seeing* Soph.

Char. Do you want any thing, sister?

Soph.

Soph. Ay! did not I drop an handkerchief here?

Char. I did not see any————Oh, here——I believe this is it.   [*Gives it her.*

[*They all stand gravely mute for some time, at last,*
          Charlotte, *as uneasy at her company, speaks.*

Char. Do you want any thing else, sister?

Soph. [*Turning short upon her.*]——Yes, Madam—— Patience——to support me under your injurious assurance.

Char. Keep your temper, sister, lest I should suspect your philosophy to be only an affectation of knowledge you never could arrive at.

Soph. There are some surprises, Madam, too strong for all the guards of human constancy.

Char. Yet I have heard you say, Madam, 'tis a narrowness of mind to be surprised at any thing.

Soph. To be amazed at the actions of the unjust, and the abandoned, is a weakness that often arises from innocence and virtue: you must therefore pardon me, if I am astonished at your behaviour.

' *Fran.* So! I suppose I shall have my share pre-
' fently.'   [*Aside.*

Char. My behaviour, Madam, is not to be asperfed by outrage; and if I am not astonished at yours, 'tis because the folly of it ought to move no passion but laughter.

Soph. This to me! to me, Mrs. Charlotte?

Char. Ay, ay! to you, Mrs. Sophronia.

Fran. I beg your pardon, ladies, I see you have private business.   [*Going.*

Soph. No, Sir,——hold——you are at least an accomplice, if not the principal, in the injury I complain of.

Fran. You do me a great deal of honour, Madam, in supposing any thing in my power could disturb you; but pray, Madam, wherein have I been so unhappy as to injure you?

' *Soph.* In the tenderest part; my fame, my sense,
' my merit, and (as the world esteems it) in my sex's
' glory.

' *Fran.* Accumulated wrongs, indeed! But really,
' Madam,

' Madam, I am yet in the dark; I muft beg you to ex-
' plain a little farther.'

Soph. Then plainly thus, Sir: you have robbed me
of my right; the vows of love you once preferred to
' me, are by the laws of honour, without my confent,
irrevocable: but, like a vile apoftate, you have fince
prefumed to throw your fcornful malice on my attractions, by bafely kneeling to another.

Char. Oh, the painful conflicts of prudery !   [*Afide.*

Fran. ' This is hard indeed, Madam, that the lofs of
' what you never thought worth your acceptance, fhould
' be worth your refentment.' If a beggar fhould afk you
charity, would you call it an injury, if, upon refufing
it, the wretch fhould beg of the next paffenger ?

Char. Well ; is not that prettily faid now, fifter ?

Soph. The cafe is different——You owe me tribute
as your rightful conqueror ; and though I have declined
the taftelefs triumph of your homage, that's no remit-
tance of the duty : nor can you pay it to the ufurper of
my right, without rebellious perjury to me.

Fran. Hoyty ! toyty ! 'Egad there will be no end of
this——I muft even talk downright to her.   [*Afide.*

Soph. Oblations vow'd to a peculiar power, are to its
peculiar altars only due ; and though the offering might
be ill-received, yet fhould the murmuring fuppliant dare
to invoke another's aid, his vows are then become profane and impious to the Deity.

Char. So ! fince he would not make her a goddefs, I
find fhe's refolved to make one of herfelf.   [*Afide.*

Fran. Now really, Madam, if I were to put all this
into plain Englifh, the tranflation would amount to no
more than this, that your offended deity is a mere dog
in a manger : what the deuce, becaufe you don't love
oats, muft nobody elfe eat them ! Ha, ha !

Char. Ha ! ha ! ha !

Soph. Amazement ! horror ! I am fhocked and fhivered
to a thoufand atoms ! Oh, my violated ears !

Fran. Ay, ay ! Madam, you may give yourfelf as
many romantic airs as you pleafe ; but, in fhort, I can
play the civil hypocrite no longer.

Soph. Ye powers above, he triumphs in brutality !

Fran. That is, Madam, becaufe you will always take
civility,

civility for adoration. But however, to clear up this whole matter; if, for once, you can reduce yourself from a deity to what nature has made you, a woman of sense, I'll beg pardon for my brutality, and speak to you like a gentleman.

Soph. You may suppose me then to have the sense you speak of.

Fran. Why then I own, Madam, when first I came from travel, my good father, on whom I then depended, recommended me to an alliance in this family : I thought myself honoured in his commands; ' and being equally ' a stranger to you and your sister, I judged, as being the ' elder, you had a natural right to the preference of my ' addresses :' I saw you, saw your person lovely, adorned with all those charms that usually inspire the lover's tongue to bend the ear of beauty————

Char. How she drops her eyes at it !   [*Aside.*

Fran. But on a nearer converse, I found you scarce a mortal in your sentiments; ' so utter a disdain of love ' had you imbibed from your romantic education : no won- ' der I succeeded not : I shall not reproach you with my ' peculiar treatment : you pleased yourself, and I re- ' treated.' On this I thought my heart at liberty to try its better fortune here. Here I am fix'd, and justify my love ; where then is the injury to you, in laying at your sister's feet a heart, which your disdain rejected !

Soph. 'Tis true, while offered with impure desires : while sensually, and as a woman only, you pursued me : but had you greatly sought the marriage of the mind, the social raptures of the soul ; I might perhaps have cherished an intellectual union.

Fran. Ah ! but dear, dear Madam, those raptures in the air would not do my business ; I want an heir to my family, and in plain terms my case requires one that will give a little bodily help to it.

Soph. Nay then again, I must disclaim you; a heart so tainted would but sully the receiver : the shrine's disho- noured by a polluted sacrifice.

Char. So ! she's at her old flights again.   [*Aside.*

Soph. Thus then I fly for ever from your hopes————

Thus

Thus Daphne triumph'd o'er Apollo's flame,
And to his heav'n prefer'd a virgin's name :
The vanquifh'd God purfu'd, but to defpair,
While deathlefs laurels crown'd the flying fair.

[*Exit.*

Fran. So! there's one plague over ; I have difcharged my confcience upon her at leaft.

Char. Ha! ha! what a pretty way, though, my good fifter has, of turning a flight into a triumph! But fhe has a great heart.

Fran. O! 'twould be hard to deny her that fatisfaction; ' befide, the greateft heart in the world did juft the fame : ' we have known the late *grand monarque* lofe many a ' Battle ; but it was bloody hard to beat him out of a *Te* ' *Deum*.'

Char. Well, but now, how fhall we manage my father ?

Fran. Here he comes.

Enter Sir Gilbert.

Sir. Gilb. So, Mr. Frankly! you fee I give you fair play——and, troth, I have a great refpect for you—— But——a——a bargain's a bargain ; if another man has really paid for my confent, you muft not take it ill, if I don't refufe him.

Fran. I can't pretend to afk it, Sir : I think it favour enough, if you don't oblige your daughter to refufe me.

Sir Gilb. Not I, not I, man ; that's out of the queftion : fhe may pleafe herfelf, and if Witling fhould not pleafe her ; troth ! I cannot fay it would not pleafe me too : in fhort, if you two have wit enough to make up the difference, and bring me off——why there's no more to be faid——If not——accounts muft be made up——I have taken the premium, and muft ftand to my contract : for let me tell you, Sir, we citizens, are as tender of our credit in Change-Alley, as you fine gentlemen are of your honour at court.

Fran. Sir, depend upon it, your credit fhall not fuffer by me, whatever it may by your comparifon.

Sir Gilb. Why, what ails the comparifon ? Sir, I think the credit of the city may be compared to that of any body of men in Europe.

Fran.

Fran. Yes, Sir; but you miſtake me : I queſtion if any bodies may be compared to that of the city.

Sir Gilb. O ! your humble ſervant, Sir ; I did not take you————ay, ay, you're right ! you're right ! Ay, ay, ay, live and learn, Mr. Frankly : you'll find 'tis not your court, but city politicians muſt do the nation's buſineſs at laſt. Why, what did your courtiers do all the laſt reigns, but borrow money to make war, and make war to make peace, and make peace to make war ; and then to be bullies in one, and bubbles in t'other ? A very pretty account truly ; but we have made money, man : money ! money ! there's the health and life-blood of a government : and therefore I inſiſt upon it, that we are the wiſeſt citizens in Europe ; for we have coined more caſh in an hour, than the tower of London in twenty years.

Fran. Nay, you govern the world now, its plain, Sir, and truly that makes us hope it's upon the mending hand : for ſince our men of quality are got ſo thick into Change-Alley, who knows but in time a great man's word may go as far as a tradeſman's ?

Sir Gilb. Ah ! a wag, a wag ! In troth, Mr. Frankly, the more I know you, the more I like you : I ſee you know the world, you judge of men by their intrinſic value ; and you're right ! you're right ! titles are empty things. A wiſe man will always be a wiſe man, whether he has any title or no.

Fran. Ay, ay, Sir, and when a fool gets one, he's only known to be a greater fool.

Sir Gilb. You're right again : beſides, Sir, ſhall any man value himſelf upon a thing that another may buy for his money as well as he ? Ridiculous————a very pretty buſineſs truly, to give ten or twenty thouſand pounds, only to be called out of one's name : Ha, ha, ha !

Fran. Nay, Sir, and perhaps too, loſing the privilege of a private ſubjeçt, that of being beliçved upon your honour, or truſted upon your word.

Sir Gilb. Honour's a joke ! Is not every honeſt man a man of honour ?

Fran. Ay, but the beſt joke is, that every man of honour is not an honeſt man, Sir.

Sir Gilb. Odſbodlikins, Mr. Frankly, you are an ingenious gentleman, and I muſt have you into my family,
                                        though

though it coſt me twenty thouſand pounds to keep that pragmatical fellow out on't.

Fran. ‘ If I have any pretence to your favour, Sir, I ‘ will take care your family ſhall not ſuffer by my coming ‘ into it : for if the worſt muſt happen,’ 'tis but waiting till the other half year of Witling's contract is expired. I dare anſwer your daughter won't run away with him in the mean time.

Sir Gilb. Ay, but there's the queſtion : is the girl ſtaunch ? Are you ſure now, that like a young hound, ſhe may not gallop away with the rank ſcent of a coxcomb, and ſo ſpoil your ſport ?

Fran. ‘ I dare ſay ſhe will take this fear for a favour’— beſt examine her yourſelf, Sir.

Sir Gilb. Come hither, Charlotte.

Char. Your pleaſure, Sir ?

Sir Gilb. Are you ſure you are as wiſe as other fine ladies of your age, that know more of mankind than their fathers, and conſequently have a natural averſion to all huſbands of their chooſing ? In ſhort have you learnt enough of the world, to be heartily diſobedient upon occaſion ?

Char. When you pleaſe to give me the occaſion, Sir, I will try what I can do.

Sir Gilb. Humh ! ſhe promiſes fair. [*To* Frankly *aſide.*] The girl has wit——But now, child, the queſtion is whether you have common ſenſe or no (for they don't always go together.) Are you ſmoky ? Have you all your eye-teeth yet ? Are you peery, as the cant is ? In ſhort do you know what I would be at now ?

Char. Will you give me leave to gueſs, Sir ?

Sir Gilb. Out with it.

Char. Why then, (I hope at leaſt, Sir) you have a mind to make Witling believe, you are doing all in your power to bring his bargain to bear : and at the ſame time wiſh I would do all in my power to bring it to nothing.

Sir Gilb. [*Aſide.*] It will do ! it will do ! Mr. Frankly ; tell her ſhe's right ; you know it is not honeſt for me to ſay ſo : a hum !

Char. In ſhort, Sir, if you'll leave the matter to my diſcretion, I'll engage to bring you off.

Sir Gilb. Bring me off, huſſy ! why ; have you the

E confi-

confidence to fuppofe I won't do the fair thing by the
gentleman?

Char. I have not the confidence to fuppofe you would
do a hard thing by this gentleman, indeed papa!

[*Takes* Frankly's *hand.*

Sir Gilb. ' D'ye hear! d'ye hear!' what a fenfible affurance the flut has! Ah! it's a **wheedling toad**! [*Afide.*]
Adod! I'll have a little more of her————but do you
know, lady, that Mr. Witling has demanded my confent,
and that it will coft me above twenty thoufand pounds to
refufe it?

Char. Yes, Sir, I do know it; and if I were to give
him my confent, I know that I fhould have much the
worft bargain of the two.

Sir Gilb. Your confent! Why fure, Madam, when I
fay, do fo, do you pretend to have a will of your own?

Char. Umh! a little! a fmall pulfe, you know, papa.

[*Fawning on* Sir Gilb.

Sir Gilb. Ah, the coaxing gipfey! why, you confident,
abominable——Odfheart! I could kifs her————

Fran. Faith, do, Sir; that's no breach of your contract.

Sir Gilb. No! no! that's not fair neither; I am to be
angry with her——befides I don't keep my word, if I
don't fpeak a good one for him.

Char. That's not in your power, Sir; 'tis impoffible
any body can give him a good word, at leaft to me.

Sir Gilb. How! how! will not a handfome young
fellow, with an hundred thoufand pounds in his pocket, go
down with you? Will not a full plumb melt in your
mouth, miftrefs Dainty?

Char. Thank you, Sir; but I don't love trafh!

Sir Gilb. Trafh! Mr. Witling trafh!

Char. A coxcomb.

Sir Gilb. I fay he is——

Char. My averfion.

Sir Gilb. Bear witnefs, Mr. Frankly, fhe refufes him;
you fee all I fay fignifies nothing: but I fay again and
again, that I am refolved, Madam, you fhall mary him,
and that articles fhall be drawn this very morning.

Char. But do you think you can't perfuade him to ftay
a little, Sir?

Sir Gilb. Stay! yes; yes; a reafonable time, that is.

Char.

Char. You'll think it a reasonable one, I am sure, Sir, *Sir Gilb.* Well! well! how long?

Char. Only till I have done hating him, that's all.

Sir Gilb. Pshah! fiddle faddle! Marry him first, and you'll have time enough to hate him afterwards.

Char. Well, Sir, then I have but one favour to beg of you————

Sir Gilb. Come, what is't, what is't?

Char. Only, Sir, that in the draught of the articles, you will be pleased to leave a blank for the gentleman's name; and if I don't fill it up to your mind, say I know nothing of my own.

Sir Gilb. Fy! fy! you wicked thing you————Mr. Frankly, it will do! it will do! the girl has all her goings! keep her right, keep her right, and tight; and I'll warrant thee all safe, boy.

Fran. Never fear, Sir————now there's but one difficulty behind; were it but possible to make my lady our friend in this matter————

Sir Gilb. Pshaw! waw! never mind her; am not I master of my own family? Does she not know that my will's a law? and if I once say the word————

Fran. That's true, Sir; ' but you know, one would ' not make her a needless enemy:' she'll think herself affronted, take it as an insult to her understanding, not to be let into the secret at all.

Char. Indeed, Sir, I am afraid we shall have a foul house, if she is not consulted in the business.

Sir Gilb. Nay, nay, with all my heart, but the foolish woman alway loves to dispute about nothing; and such a spirit of contradiction runs away with her, I had as lief sit in the stocks as talk to her; however, for your private satisfaction————

Fran. Indeed, Sir, I think it will be better so.

Sir Gilb. Well, well, then I'll tell her my resolution instantly.

Char. Ah, poor papa! What a wicked distress have we brought him to! Now will he rather run upon the mouth of a cannon, than let us see he is afraid of gunpowder.

Fran. How my lady will bounce when he mentions it.

[*Aside.*

Sir Gilb. Oh, here's my Lady; I'll speak to her now.

Fran.

Fran. If you pleafe, we'll retire, that you may have no interruption.

Sir Gilb. Do fo, you're right. [*Exeunt* Fran. *and* Char.
Enter Lady Wrangle, *driving a Maid Servant in before her.*

L. Wrang. Out of my doors, you dunce ! you illite-rate monfter ! What ! could you not read ? Could not you fpell ? Where were your eyes, you brainlefs ideot ?

Sir Gilb. Hey-day ! hey-day ! What's the matter now ?

L. Wrag. Go, you eleventh plague of Egypt.

Maid. Indeed, Madam, I did not know it was of any ufe, it was fo blotted and blurred, I took it for wafte paper.

L. Wrang. Blurred ! you driveler ! Was ever any piece perfect, that had not corrections, rafures, interline-ations, and improvements ? Does not the very original fhew, that when the mind is warmeft, it is never fatisfied with its words ?

Incipit, & dubitat ; fcribit, damnatque tabellas,
Et notat, & delet ; mutat, culpatque probatque.

Sir Gilb. Oh, Lord ! Now the learned fit's upon her, the devil won't be able to deal with her.   [*Afide.*

L. Wrang. What have you done with it, you dolt-head ? Where is it ? Fetch it ; let me fee it, I fay.

Sir Gilb. Pray, my Lady Wrangle, what is all this rout about ?

L. Wrang. Oh, nothing, to be fure ! I am all always unreafonable.

Sir Gilb. Why, look you now, did I fay any fuch thing ?

L. Wrang. I don't care if you did.

Sir Gilb. It's very hard a man may not afk a civil quef-tion in his own houfe.

L. Wrang. Ay, do, fide with her, take her part; do, do, uphold her in her impudence.

Sir Gilb. Why, my Lady, did I fay a word to her ?

L. Wrang. Pray, Mr. Wrangle, give me leave to go-vern my own fervants. Don't you know, when I am out of temper, I won't be talk'd to ?

Sir Gilb. *Very true, my Lady.*

L. Wrang. Have not I plague enough here, do you think ?

Sir Gilb. Why ay, that's true too—Why, you confi-dent jade ! how dare you put my lady into fuch a violent paffion ?

Maid. Indeed, Sir, I don't know, not I. [*Whimpering.*
                                              L. Wrang.

L. Wrang. Pray, Mr. Wrangle, meddle with your own bufinefs; the fault's to me, and fure I am old enough to correct her myfelf.

Sir Gilb. Why, what a dickens, may'nt I be of your mind neither ? 'Sheart ! I can't be in the wrong on both fides.

L. Wrang. I don't know any bufinefs you have on either fide.

Sir Gilb. Nay, if a man muft not fpeak at all, it's another cafe.

L. Wrang. Lord ! you are ftrangely teizing—well, come fpeak—what, what, what is't you would fay now ?

Sir Gilb. Nay, nothing, not I ; I only afked what's the matter ?

L. Wrang. I can't tell you, the provocation's too great for words.

Sir Gilb. Well, well, well.

L. Wrang. What here ftill ? Am I to have no account of it then ? What have you done with it, you monfter ?

Maid. Madam, the cook took it out of my hand, as I was coming down ftairs with it ; he faid he wanted it.

L. Wrang. The cook ! run, fly, and bid the villain fend it me this moment.   [*Exit Maid.*

Sir Gilb. Why, what the dickins ! the fenfelefs jade has not given him a Flanders' lac'd head to boil his cabbage in, has fhe ?

L. Wrang. Pfhah ! Do you ever fee me concern'd for fuch trifles ?

Sir Gilb. Or has fhe let the rafcal finge his fowls with a bank bill ?

L. Wrang. If fhe had, do you think I would give myfelf fuch pain about either ?

Sir Gilb. Hah ! this muft be fome abominable thing indeed then.

L. Wrang. The lofs, for ought I know, may be irreparable.

Sir Gilb. Oh ! then fhe has loft your diamond necklace, I fuppofe.

L. Wrang. Pray don't plague me ; 'tis impoffible to exprefs the wickednefs of it.

Sir Gilb. What, the devil ! the cook has not got the flut with child, has he ?

L. Wrang. Worfe! worfe a thoufand times!

Sir Gilb. Worfe! What than playing the whore, or thief? Then the jade has certainly committed murder.

L. Wrang. The moft barbarous that ever was——

Sir Gilb. Hoh! then fhe has broke pug's neck, to be fure. [*Afide.*

L. Wrang. The changeling innocent has given that favage beaft, the cook, my whole new tranflation of the paffion of Byblis, for wafte paper, to be torn or tortur'd to a thoufand fordid ufes.

Sir Gilb. Nay then——

L. Wrang. And I have not another copy in the world, if it were to fave mankind from extirpation.

Sir Gilb. I'm glad on't, with all my heart; now could I laugh, if I durft, moft immoderately. [*Afide.*

L. Wrang. Now, miftrefs, have you brought it?
[*Re-enter Maid.*

Maid. Madam, the cook fays, he has fkewer'd it on to the roaft-beef, and he can't take it off: he won't burn his meat for nobody, not he, he fays.

L. Wrang. Here! call the footman. He won't! Bid them drag the rafcal hither by the ears, or I'll have them nailed down to the dreffer for his impudence—I'll turn the villain out of my houfe this moment.
[*Exit Maid.*

Sir Gilb. Come, come, my Lady, don't be in a heat about a trifle; I am glad to find it's no worfe.

L. Wrang. Worfe! had he robb'd the houfe, and after fired it, I could fooner have forgiven him.

Sir Gilb. Hah! thank you for that, Madam; but I fhould not.

L. Wrang. You! you fhould not! What would be your injury compared with mine? What I'm concern'd for, the whole learned world, even to pofterity, may feel the lofs of.

Sir Gilb. Well, well; have a little patience; may be fhe may get it again. And now you talk of pofterity, my lady Wrangle, I have fome thoughts of marrying my daughter Charlotte; as for Sophronia, you know——

L. Wrang. I know, that one won't, and t'other fhan't marry; fhe is a pert forward thing, and has difobliged me, and therefore I'll punifh her as I think fit. I defire
you

you won't name her to me, you fee I have other things in my head—all greas'd, and burnt to afhes, I fuppofe.

Sir Gilb. I had better talk to her another time, I believe.

Enter the Maid with the Cook.

L. Wrang. Oh! are you come at laft, Sir? Pray, how durft you fend me fuch an impudent anfwer?

Cook. I did not fend an impudent anfwer, Madam; I only faid the meat would be fpoil'd: but here fhe comes, and makes a noife, and a rout, and a clatter about nothing at all—and fo every impertinent jade here takes upon her—Oons! a man can't do his bufinefs in quiet for them.

L. Wrang. Hold your nonfenfical tongue, Sir, and give me the paper I fent for.

Cook. Paper! This is what fhe gave me.

[*Holds it on a fkewer, all greafy.*

L. Wrong. Oh my heavens! what a fpectacle! not one line legible, though an empire were to purchafe it. Look, look, look, you monfter! [*Holding him.*

Sir Gilb. So! here will be rare doings.

Cook. Oons! what a life's here about a piece of foul paper?

L. Wrang. A life, you villain! your whole life can't make amends for what you have done. I'll have you beat out of this houfe, till every bone in your body is broken for this, firrah.

Cook. Beat, Madam! Blood! I won't be beat. I did not come here for that: I'll be out of your houfe prefently; I'll fee who will break my bones then; and fo there's one of your napkins, Madam: as for your fheet of paper, there's a half-penny for't; and now take your courfe. I know how to get my wages, I'll warrant you—There's a law for fervants as well as other people.

[*Exit Cook.*

Sir Gilb. Go, go, mind your bufinefs, you filly Tom Ladle you.

L. Wrong. Ay; this is always the effect of your indulgence; no wonder I have no power over them. If you had the leaft grain of fpirit, you would have broke the rafcal's head for me.

Sir Gilb. Pfhah! there's no occafion for it—let's fee, let's let's fee! [*Takes up the paper.*] Come, come, this matter may be made up without bloodfhed ftill—ay, here; umh! umh!—by the way, I believe this beef's enough, it fmells bravely of the gravy.

L. Wrang. What! then I am your jeft, it feems.

Sir Gilb. Pooh! pry'thee be quiet; I tell you, I am ferious——ay, it's plain to be read ftill. [*Reads.*

All a poor maid could do (the gods, I'm fure,

Can tell) I've fuffer'd to compleat my cure—Cure! Ah, poor foul—— got the foul difeafe, I fuppofe.

L. Wrang. Your obfcene comment, Mr. Wrangle, is more provoking than the infolence of your fervants: but I muft tell you, Sir, I will never eat or fleep in your houfe more, if that rafcal is not turned out of it this moment.

Maid. I hope your Ladyfhip is not in earneft, Madam.

L. Wrang. What do you prate, Mrs. Minx?

Maid. Indeed, Madam, if John's to be turn'd away, I fhan't ftay in the family: for though he is fometimes a little hafty to a body, yet I have reafon to know he is an honeft-hearted man in the main; and I have too much kindnefs for him to ftay in any fervice, where he is to be abus'd.

L. Wrang. What, you are in love with him, Mrs. Trollop, are you? [*Cuffs her.*

Maid. Ods my life! Madam, I won't be ftruck by no body: and if I do love him, what's that to any body? and I don't know why poor folks mayn't be in love as well their betters.

Sir Gilb. Come, come, hold your tongue, huffy.

Maid. Sir, I can't hold my tongue; though I can't fay but your worfhip's a very kind mafter: but as for my Lady, the devil would not live with her; and fo, Madam, I defire you will provide yourfelf. [*Flings off.*

Sir Gilb. Odzines, Madam, at this rate I fhall have neither dinner to eat, nor bed to lie on. What fervants will bear this life, do you think? You have no more temper than a——Why how fhould a filly wench know what your impertinent poetry was good for?

L. Wrang. Impertinent! I'd have you know, Mr. Ignorant, there's not a line in the whole, that has not the true Attic falt in it.

Sir

Sir Gilb. Well, and now there's Englifh falt in it ; and I think the relifh of one's as good as t'other.

L. Wrang. Mr. Wrangle, if you have no fenfe of the foul's diviner faculties, know, I have, and can refent thefe vulgar infults. You fhall find, Sir, that a fuperior underftanding has a proportion'd fpirit to fupport its dignity. Let me have inftant reparation, or, by my injured genius, I'll fet you houfe and family in a blaze.

[*Exit L.* Wrang.

Sir Gilb. Why then blaze and burn by yourfelf; for I'll go out of the houfe. [*Going.*

Enter Frankly *and* Charlotte.

Fran. Have you feen my Lady, Sir ?

Sir Gilb. Yes, yes, I have feen her—but—I don't know——fhe——fhe——

Fran. Don't come into it, I fuppofe.

Sir Gilb. Umh ! no, not readily——in fhort, the houfe is all untiled.

Char. Lord, Sir ! what filthy thing's this ?

[*Seeing the Paper.*

Sir Gilb. Ay, there's the bufinefs——a brat of my Lady's brain, that has got a mifchance : that's all.

Fran. Some roafted poetry, I prefume.

Sir Gilb. Ay, ay ; the, the, the paffion of Bibble Babble ; I don't know what fhe calls it : but fhe has been in fuch a fume here, that half the fervants are going to leave the houfe about it. Charlotte, you can wheedle upon occafion ; pry'thee ftep into the hall, and fee if you can make up this matter among them.

Char. I'll do my beft, Sir. [*Exit* Char.

Fran. Poor Lady ! fhe is a little apt to be over-concerned for her poetry.

Sir Gilb. Concern'd ! Odfblews ! if a line on't happens to be miflaid, fhe's as mad as a blind mare that has loft her foal ; fhe'll run her head againft a ftone-wall to recover it. All the ufe I find of her learning is, that it furnifhes her with more words to fcold with.

Enter a Servant.

Serv. Sir, Mr. Grainger's come, and Mr. Witling.

Sir Gilb. Oh, that's well. Come, Mr. Frankly, let's all go into the dining-room together ; mayhap fhe may be afham'd to be in a paffion before company.

Fran.

Fran. At leaſt we may keep her within bounds, Sir.

Sir Gilb. You're right! you're right! Ah! its a very hard cafe! there's no condition of life without plague and trouble——Why, moſt people think now I have fortune enough to make ten men of quality happy——

And yet you fee how odly things are carried ;

'Tis true, I'm worth a million, but I'm married.

[*Excunt.*]

A C T   IV.

Granger *and* Frankly.

FRANKLY.

IN one word, Granger, thou art a very dangerous fellow ; ' I did not believe it poſſible thy blunt humour could have concealed ſo exquiſite a flatterer :' why thou art more in my lady's favour in half an hour, than all my art could make me in half a year.

Gran. Have I not always told you, Frankly, that one civil thing from a downright dealer, goes farther than a thouſand from a man of general complaiſance ? ' How do ' you think I firſt gain'd credit with Sophronia ? Not (as ' you expected to do it) by an implicit admiration ; but ' the contrary, inſolently laughing at her pretending to ' principles, which I would not allow her capable to com- ' prehend or practiſe. Now this naturally piqued her in- ' to an impatience to mend my opinion of her ; ſo the ' more difficult I ſeemed to be convinced of her virtues, ' the more eaſy I made it to mend her opinion of me.'

Fran. And if thou haſt not done it effectually, I know nothing of the fex : why, ſhe bluſh'd, man, like a damaſk roſe, when you firſt came into the room.

Gran. Did not I tell you too, her quarrel and ſpleen to you would be of ſervice to me ?

Fran. O! palpably ! I was ready to burſt to ſee her bridle, and ſmile at me, upon your growing particular to her.

Gran. And what pains ſhe took, to make you obſerve, that ſhe overlooked you ? ha ! ha !

' *Fran.* Yes, I did obſerve, indeed, that the whole
' dinner-

' dinner-time she was never two minutes without stealing
' a glance at you.

' *Gran.* O bless me! I can't bear the insolence of my
' own imagination! What a dear confusion will she feel?
' What a vermilion shame will spread through all that
' lovely form——if ever her flesh and blood should hap-
' pen to mutiny?

' *Fran.* Which, to tell you the truth, I think it does
' already.'

Gran. But the misfortune is, I have flatter'd my lady
into so good a humour, by engaging to make out a fair
copy of her basted verses there, that I doubt, she won't
be able to leave me alone with Sophronia.

Fran. Never fear; her malice is too busy, in setting
Witling against me, to interrupt you.

Gran. There, indeed, I have some hopes.

Fran. I believe I shall be able to assist them, and in
part to return the favour you have done me with Sir Gilbert.

Gran. Any thing in my power you may be sure of——
but see, he's here!

Enter Sir Gilbert.

Sir Gilb. O! your servant, gentlemen; I thought we
had lost you.

Gran. Your pardon, Sir, we had only a word or two
in private,

Fran. We were just coming into the company.

Sir Gilb. In troth, I can tell you, the sooner the better: for there's my lady and Charlotte are going to play
all the game upon us.

Fran. Never fear, Sir; as long as you have given me
leave to go Charlotte's halves, she'll make the most of her
cards, I'll warrant you.

Sir Gilb. I don't know that, but I am sure Witling
yonder is making the most of his time: his wit, or his
impudence have got him into such high favour with my
lady, that she is railing at you like a fury, and crying
him up for an angel: in short, Charlotte has discovered
all your affair with her, and has plainly told him you are
his rival. But it seems, Sir, your pretensions are so
ridiculous, that they are all three cracking their sides in a
full chorus of laughing at you.

Fran. Sir, I am obliged to you for your concern; but in all this, Charlotte is acting no wrong part, I can affure you.

Sir Gilb. No wrong part! Odfheart! I tell you fhe's coquetting to him, with every wicked limb about her — and is as full of her airs there, as a handfome widow to a young lord in the Lobby, when fhe has a fuit depending in the Houfe of Peers.

Fran. Better ftill, the more likely to carry her caufe, Sir.

Sir Gilb. Carry her caufe! carry her coxcomb, Sir; for, you'll fee, that will be the end on't : fhe'll be carry'd off herfelf, Sir. Why, man, he is going to beleaguer her with a whole army of fidlers yonder; ' there ' are fix coach loads of them now at the door, all ftow'd ' fore and aft, with nothing but cafes of inftruments :' Such a concourfe of cat-guts, you'd fwear one of their fqualling eunuchs were roafting alive here.

Fran. Believe me, Sir, there is no terror in all this preparation; ' for fince you are pleafed to think Mr. ' Granger's fecurity and mine fufficient againft any da- ' mage you can fuffer from your contract with Witling,' do you but ftand it out ftoutly with my lady, and I'll engage to difmount his mufical battery with a child's whiftle.

Sir Gilb. My lady! Pfhaw waw? What doft thou talk of her, man? Why I tell you, I'll put her into a moufe-hole, provided you engage to bring me off with Witling.

Gran. Your fecurity fhall be figned the minute it can be drawn, Sir.

Sir Gilb. That's enough; ' I have ordered my lawyer ' to fend his clerk with it, before he brings the deed of ' confent that I am to fign to Witling, :' but give me leave to tell you again, gentlemen, I really don't underftand the girl's way of proceeding all this while.

Fran. Why, Sir——don't you know that Witling is the vaineft togue upon earth.

Sir Gilb. I grant it.

' *Fran.* And confequently, that the pride of outwit- ' ting you in your daughter, gives him more pleafure than ' either her perfon or her portion?

' *Sir Gilb.* Not unlikely.

' *Fran.*

' *Fran.* And can you think, that from the same natural
' insolence, he would not rather seem to owe his triumph
' over a rival too, rather to his own merit, than any ac-
' cident of fortune ?

' *Sir Gilb.* I grant you that too.'

Fran. Why, Sir, then, if Charlotte were to despise
him, we are sure he would then insist upon his bargain ;
but while she flatters him, and you and I only laugh at
him, he may be vain enough to trust his triumph to her
choice and inclination only.

Sir Gilb. O ! now I begin to take you : so that, if he
is rightly handled among us, you propose that Charlotte
will be able to coquette him out of his contract.

Fran. Nay, it's her own project, Sir : and I cannot
really think we have an ill chance for it at worst : but we
must leave it all to her now. In love affairs, you know,
Sir, women have generally wiser heads than we.

Sir Gilb. Troth ! I don't wholly dislike it ; and if I
don't handle him roundly on my part—

Gran. Hush ! my lady——

Fran. Anon I'll tell tell you more, Sir.

Enter Lady Wrangle *and* Sophronia.

L.Wrang. Well, Sophronia, since I see this giddy girl is
neither to be formed by precept or example ; it is at least
some consolation, to find her natural inconstancy so effectually mortifies that vile apostate, Frankly.

Soph. Yet I am amazed he should not be more moved at
her infidelity.

L. Wrang. You know he's vain, and thinks his merit
may sleep in full security. But now ! to rouse him from
his dream—— Oh, Mr. Granger ! I am sorry you left
us ; I am perfectly killed with laughing ! There's Mr.
Witling has had such infinite humour ! He has entertain'd
as more than ten comedies.

Gran O ! Pray, Madam, let us go in and participate.

L. Wrang. By no means ; he's now alone with his
mistress, and 'twould be barbarous to interrupt them.

Gran. His mistress, Madam !

L. Wrang. Ay ! with Charlotte ; and, you know,
lovers so near their happiness are apt to like no company
so well as their own.

F *Fran.*

Fran. D'ye hear, Sir ?   [*To Sir* Gilb. *apart.*

Sir Gilb. I told you how it was.   [*To* Fran. *apart.*

L. Wrang. Befide, he is to give us a little mufic ; and I think this room will be more convenient.

Gran. He is a fortunate man indeed, Madam, to be fo well with the young lady already.

L. Wrang. There's no accounting for that idle paffion in uncultivated minds : I am not furprifed at her for-wardnefs, confidering the vulgar education Mr. Wrangle has given her.

Sir Gilb. Odfheart, Madam ! don't difparage my girl : fhe has had a more ufeful education than your ladyfhip.

L. Wrang. O ! no doubt ! fhe has fhewn moft hopeful effects on it, indeed ! by hanging upon every young fel-low's neck, that does but afk her the queftion.

Fran. Whatever faults Charlotte may have, Madam, I never knew her take pleafure in expofing thofe of other people.

' *L. Wrang.* O ! cry you mercy, Sir ; you have great
' reafon to defend her, I don't queftion : fhe is a faint in
' your eye, to be fure.

' *Fran.* Were fhe weak enough to imagine a fuperficial
' learning could make her one, 'tis poffible, her failings
' then, like other people's, might have been more con-
' fpicuous.'

L. Wrang. What do you mean, Sir ?

Fran. I mean, Madam, that as fhe does not read Ari-otle, Plato, Plutarch, or Seneca, fhe is neither roman-tic or vain of her pedantry ; and as her learning never went higher than Bickerftaff's Tatlers, her manners are confequently natural, modeft, and agreeable.

Sir Gilb. Ah ! well faid Frankly.   [*Afide.*

L. Wrang. Since I am told you were once in love with her, I fhall fay no more, but leave her own immediate behaviour to confirm your good opinion of her virtues. Ha, ha !   [*Exit.*

' *Gran.* While the lovers of this age, Madam, have
' fo deprav'd a tafte, we muft not wonder, if our modern
' fine ladies are apt to run into coquettry : they are now
' forced to it in their defence ; if they don't make
' advances, they ftand as lonely and ufelefs as untenan-
' ted houfes : fo that coquetry, it feems, is no more than
                ' fetting

' fetting a bill upon their door, that lovers in diſtreſs
' may read as they paſs——Here are night's lodgings to
' be let.

' *L. Wrang.* O! they are moſt hoſpitable dames in-
' deed: after this, methinks, the more proper appella-
' tion for coquets ſhould be that of landladies.

       [A ſervant whiſpers L. Wrang.

' I'll come and give orders myſelf.   *[Exit.*

Soph. I don't know any man alive, that looks upon the
degeneracy of mankind with ſo diſcerning an eye as Mr.
Granger; but I am afraid it will therefore draw him into
my misfortune, of being as odious to the illiterate of his
ſex, as I am to thoſe of mine.

Gran. If that were as juſt a reaſon, Madam, for your
having a favourable opinion of me, as it is for my perfect
admiration of you, we ſhould each of us have ſtill as many friends as any wife man or woman ought to deſire.

 Fran. Do you mind that, Sir?   *[Apart.*

Sir Gilb. A ſly rogue! he knows how to tickle her up,
I ſee.   *[Apart.*

Soph. And yet the rude world will ſay, perhaps, that
our mutual enmity to them has reduced us to a friendſhip
for one another.

Gran. That's a reproach can never reach you, Madam;
ſo much beauty cannot but have its choice of friends and
admirers: a form ſo bright and perfect, like a comet in
the hemiſphere, where'er it comes, muſt ſet mankind a
gazing.

 Soph. Fye! Mr. Granger!

Sir Gilb. What, a dickens! will ſhe ſwallow that bla-
zing ſtar now?   *[Apart.*

Fran. Ay, as he has dreſs'd it, and drink after it too,
Sir.   *[Apart.*

 Soph. I mind not multitudes.

Gran. Pardon me, I know you have a ſoul above them;
and I really think it the misfortune of your perſon, to
have been ſo exquiſitely fair, that where your virtue would
preſerve, your eyes deſtroy; they give involuntary love;
where'er you paſs, in ſpite of all your innocence, they
wound—— *Juvenumque prodis publicâ cura.*

Soph. Alas! my eyes are turn'd upon myſelf: ' and ſo
' little do I mind the follies of other people, that I ſome-

' times find myfelf alone in the midft of a public circle.

' *Gran.* I cannot wonder at that, Madam, fince our beft
' affemblies are generally made up of illiterate beings, that
' when they are alone, find themfelves in the worft com-
' pany, and fo are reduced to come abroad, though mere-
' ly to meet, and hate one another.'

Soph. What charms, then, can you fuppofe I could
have for a world, that has fo few for me ? Befide, at moft,
the men of modern gallantry gaze upon a woman of real
virtue, only as atheifts look into a fine church, from curiofity, not devotion : ' they may admire its ornaments and
' architecture ; but have neither grace nor faith for far-
' ther adoration.'

Gran. All men are not infidels ; of me, at leaft, you
have a convert : and tho' the fenfual practice of the
world had made me long defpair of fuch perfection in a
mortal mold ; yet when the rays of truth celeftial broke
in upon my fenfe, my confcious heart at once confefs'd
the deity ; I proftrate fell a profelyte to virtue ; and
now its chafte defires enlarge my foul, and raife me to feraphic joy.

Soph. Harmonious founds, celeftial tranfports ! [*Afide.*

Sir Gilb. Oh, dear ! Oh, dear ! was ever fuch a wicked
thief ? Odfheart, he'll make her go to prayers with him,
prefently !   [*Afide.*

Soph. No more ; we are obferved. Thefe heaven-born
emanations of the foul defire not vulgar ears. Some fitter
time may offer—till when———

Gran. Till then, be hufh'd our joys.

[Gran. *leaves her, and joins the men, while* Soph. *walks
apart, mufing.*

Soph. Our joys indeed ! Such was, in Paradife, our firft
parents joy, before they fell from innocence to fhame.

Fran. [*To* Gran.] Why did you not go on with her ?
We thought you were in a fine way. Sir Gilbert and I
were juft going to fteal off.

Gran. Soft and fair, Sir. A lady of her delicacy muft
be carried, like a taper new-lighted, gently forward ; if
you hurry her, out fhe goes.

Sir Gilb. You're right, you're right. Now you fhall
fee me manage her a little : I'll fpeak a good word for you
—a-hum—

Gran.

Gran. Hufh ! not for the world, Sir——Death, you'll fpoil all ! Don't you fee fhe is in contemplation ?

Sir Gilb. What if fhe be, man ? We muft not humour her till fhe is ftark mad, neither. Sophronia, how doft thou do, child ?

Soph. [*Repeating.*]——————The earth
   Gave fign of gratulation, and each hill :
   Joyous the birds ; frefh gales and gentle airs
   Whifper'd it to the woods, and from their wings
   Flung rofe, flung odours, from the juicy fhrub
   Difporting——

Sir Gilb. Very pretty, I proteft ; very pretty. Thefe amorous fcraps of fancy in thy head, make me hope that love is not far from thy heart, Sophy.

Soph. Love, Sir, was ever in my heart ; but fuch a love, as the blind Homer of this Britifh ifle, in rhymelefs harmony, fublimely fings——

Sir Gilb. Well, and, pr'ythee, what does he fay of it ?
Soph. ——————Love refines
   The thought, and heart enlarges ; has his feat
   In reafon, and is judicious, is the fcale,
   By which to heavenly love thou mayft afcend.

Sir Gilb. Very good again ; and troth, I'm glad to hear thou art fo heartily reconciled to it.

Soph. Eafier than air with air, if fpirits embrace,
   Total they mix, union of pure with pure
   Defiring——

Sir Gilb. Ah ! there, I doubt, we are a little crazy.
              [*Afide.*

Soph. This iron age, fo fraudulent and bold,
   Touch'd with this love, would be an age of gold.

Sir Gilb. Oh, lud ! Oh, lud ! this will never do. [*Afide.*

Gran. So, fhe has given the old gentleman his belly-full, I fee. Well, Sir, how do you find her ?

Sir Gilb. Ah, poor foul, piteous bad ! all upon the tantivy again ! You muft e'en undertake her yourfelf ; for I can do no good upon her. But here comes love of another kind.

   Enter Charlotte, Witling, *and Lady* Wrangle.

Char. Oh, fifter ! hete's Mr. Witling has writ the pretieft cantata, fure, that ever made mufic enchanting.

               Soph.

Soph. I am glad, fister, you are reconciled to any of his performances.

Wit. Oh, fie! Madam, fhe only rallies——A mere trifle.

Fran. That I dare fwear it is.

Wit. Ha, ha! no doubt on't; if you could like it, it muft be an extraordinary piece, indeed, Tom. You fee, my little rogue, we have crabbed him already.

[*Afide, to* Char.

L. Wrang. Mr. Frankly is a mere modern critic, that makes perfonal inclination the rule of his judgment; but to condemn what one never faw, is making fhort work, indeed.

Fran. With fubmiffion, Madam, I can fee no great rafhnefs in prefuming that a magpye can't fing like a nightingale.

Wit. No, nor an owl look like a peacock, neither. Ha, ha!

L. Wrang. and Char. Ha, ha, ha!

L. Wrang. Perfectly pleafant.

Char. Oh, wit to an infinity!

Fran. Much good may do you with your Canary-bird, Madam. [*To* Char.

Char. Oh, Sir, I am forry you are exhaufted! but when wit is upon the lee, no wonder it runs into rudenefs.

' *Fran.* I don't wonder at my not hitting your tafte, ' Madam, when fuch ftuff as this can go down with you.

' *Wit.* My ftuff, dear Tom, was compofed purely for ' the entertainment of this lady; and fince fhe likes it, I ' will allow, that you, of all mankind, have moft reafon ' to find fault with it. Ha, ha!

' *Char.* Nay, if he fhould like it, even I will then give ' it up to the world as good for nothing.

' *Fran.* Then it's in danger, I can tell you, Madam; ' for I fhall certainly like it; becaufe I am fure it will ' be good for nothing.

' *Char.* A pleafant paradox.

' *Fran.* None at all, Madam; for fince I find your ' heart is, like ftock, to be transferred upon a bargain, it ' will be fome pleafure, at leaft, to fee the groffnefs of ' your choice revenge me on your infidelity.

[*Ex. Wit.*

' *Wit.* Poor Tom ! What, are the grapes four, my
' dear ? Ha, ha, ha !

' *Char.* Pſhah ! never mind him. The cantata, dear
Mr. Witling, the cantata.

L. Wran. Oh, by all means ! ' Pray oblige us, Sir.

' *Wit.* Immediately, Madam ; but all things in order.
' Firſt give me leave to regale the good company with a
' ſmall craſh of inſtrumental.

' *L. Wrang.* As you pleaſe, Sir.

' *Wit.* Hey, Signor Carbonelli ! *Vi pace d'intrare !*
[*The muſic enter.*

' *L. Wrang.* Mr. Granger, won't you pleaſe to ſit ?

' *Sir Gilb.* Ay, ay, come, gentlemen ; but, in earneſt,
' does this puppy really pretend to ſing ?

' *Fran.* Much as he pretends to wit, Sir ; he can
' make a noiſe, at leaſt.

' *Sir Gilb.* But the whelp has no voice.

' *Fran.* Oh, Sir, that's out of faſhion ! Your beſt ma-
' ſters ſeldom have any.

' *Sir Gilb.* Then I would not give a fig for their mu-
' ſic, Sir ; I would as lief ſee a cripple dance. But let's
' hear what the fiddles can do. [*They play a ſonata.*]
' Well, and what, we are to ſuppoſe this is very fine,
' now, ha ?

Fran. No doubt on't, Sir ; at leaſt it will not be ſafe
' to ſay the contrary.

' *Sir Gilb.* Well, well, for a quiet life, then, very fine
' let it be ; but I wiſh I could hear a Lancaſhire horn-
' pipe for all that.'

L. Wrang. Come, dear Sir, no more apologies.
[*To* Witling.

Gran. See, Sir, Mr. Witling is going to entertain us.

Sir Gilb. Ay, that muſt be rare ſtuff indeed.

' *Wit.* Upon my life, Madam, I have no more voice
' than a kettle-drum ; beſide, this is for a treble, and out
' of my compaſs.

' *Char.* Oh, no matter ? feign it, dear Mr. Witling.

' *Wit.* I would fain oblige you, Madam ; but yet, me-
' thinks, nothing done to pleaſe you ſhould be feign'd,
' neither, Madam.

' *Fran.* Ha ! He would fain be witty, I ſee ; but don't
' trouble yourſelf, Madam ; he has as much mind to ſing
' as

'as you have to hear him: tho', Heaven knows, his voice
'is like his modefty, utterly forced; nature has nothing
'to do with either of them.

'*Wit.* Whatever my modefty is, dear Tom, thy unea-
'finefs I am fure is natural; that comes from thy heart,
'I dare anfwer for it. Ha, ha, ha!

'*Fran.* Oh, thou happy rogue!'

Wit. But, Madam, if I fing, you fhall promife me to
dance, then.

Char. Oh, any compofition! I'll do it with all my
heart.

L. Wrang. But the words 'firft, dear Sir, read them
'out.'

Wit. Well, ladies, fince you will have it——

Sir Gilb. He is a curfed while about it, methinks——

Wit. You muft know, then, this cantata is of a different
fpecies from the paffion generally expreffed in our modern
operas; for there you fee your lover ufually approaches
the fair lady with fighs, tears, torments, and dying. Now,
here I fhew you the way of making love like a pretty fellow; that is, like a man of fenfe, all life, and gaiety——
As for example——

Char. Pray, mind.

Wit. [*Reading.*]

> Thus to a penfive fwain,
> Who long had lov'd in vain,
> Thyrfis, the fecret arts
> Of gaining hearts
> From cold difdain,
> To his defpairing friend imparts.

So far recitative—Now for the air—A-hum, hum!

'*Soph.* Don't you think, Mr. Granger, that the double
'dative cafes of "to a penfive fwain, to his defpairing
'friend," almoft reduce this to nonfenfe?

'*Gran.* Juftly obferved, Madam; but, you know,
'nonfenfe and harmony are reconciled of late.'

> *Wit.* Would you woo her
> With fuccefs?
> Up to her,
> Purfue her
> With life and addrefs.

If gay,
Shew her play;
If colder,
Be bolder:

Now feize her,
And teize her,
And kifs her,
And pleafe her;
Till ripe for the joy,
You warm her,
Alarm her,
Difarm her,
You charm her,
I warrant thee, boy.

Part II.

But to pine and languifh,
Or figh your anguifh.
To the air,
Is fruitlefs pain,
Endur'd in vain:
Silent woes, and looks of care,
Will never, never win the fair.

End with the firft ftrain.

Ah, you little rogue! [*To* Charlotte.

L. Wrang. Infinitely pretty! ' Nothing, fure, was ever
' fo mufical.

' *Char.* Sing it, fing, it, dear Mr. Witling. I am on
' tiptoe to hear it.

' *Wit.* Well, Madam, if you can bear it in a falfetto.
[*He fings.*

' *Char.* O caro! caro!

' *Wit. Anima mia——*

Soph. [*To* Gran.] How happy are the felf-conceited!
' and yet, if he had not fung, now, this wretch's folly
' and ignorance had been lefs confpicuous.

' *Gran.* Right, Madam; but, you know, a man muft
' have variety of parts, to make an accomplifhed cox-
' comb.

' *Soph.*

' *Soph.* I fcarce think poetry is more abufed than mu-
' fic, by its vain pretenders.

' *Gran.* And yet it is hard to fay, Madam, whether
' thofe pretenders, or the falfe tafte of our modern ad-
' mirers, have more contributed to the abufe of either.'

Wit. But come, Madam, now your promife ; ' your
' airs only' [*To* Char.] can give a *bonne bouche* to our
entertainment.

Char. Well, fince I gave my word, I'll ufe no ceremony.

Soph. ' What, more folly ?' I grow tired. Shall we walk
into my library ? There we may raife our thoughts.

Gran. You charm me, Madam ; I thirft, methinks,
for a clear draught of Helicon.

Soph. Take no leave, but follow me. [*Ex.* Soph. & Gr.

Wit. ' *E ben fonate.*' [Charlotte *dances.*] ' *Eh ! viva !*
' *viva !*' All enchantment, Madam ! no ten thoufand
angels ever came up to it.

L. Wrang. It cannot be denied but Charlotte has an external genius; fhe wants no perfonal accomplifhments ; but
'tis great pity the application they have coft her, was not
laid out upon the improvement of her underftanding.

Wit. Oh, pardon me, Madam ! as long as there is a
good underftanding between her and me, what matter's
which of us has it, you know.

Sir Gilb. Ay, but there's the queftion, which of you
'tis that has it ; for if one of you has it, I am fure you
two will never come together.

Fran. Well faid ! at him, Sir. [*Afide.*

Wit. Look you, Sir Gilbert ; you may fancy your fair
daughter and I are a couple of fools, if you pleafe ; but if
one of us had not been wifer than the father, we could
never have had a right to come together, in fpite of his
teeth, that's certain. Ha, ha, ha !

L. Wrang. Pardon me, Mr. Witling, you under-rate
your merit ; for you had been fure of my confent without
your contract.

Wit. Ay, Madam, that was only a foolifh modefty that
I could not fhake off ; therefore I hope you will excufe
me, if durft not think merit alone was a fufficient bait to
bob Sir Gilbert out of his confent. Ha, ha, ha !

Sir Gilb. You are a very merry grig, Sir ; but have a
care you are not bobb'd yourfelf. Stay till you win, before
you laugh ; for you are not yet married, I prefume.

Wit.

Wit. Why no, nor you have not supped yet; yet I hold gold to silver, we both eat before we sleep.

Sir Gilb. Why! dost thou think the girl is in haste to marry thee to night!

Wit. I don't say that neither: but, Sir, as long as I have a sufficient deposit of the lady's inclinations, to answer for the rest of her premises, you will give me leave not to be afraid of her looking out for a new chap in the mean time, Sir.

Sir Gilb. A deposit! why wouldst thou persuade me the girl can be fool enough to like thee?

Wit. 'Egad, I don't know how it is, but she has wit enough, it seems, to make me think so——but if you won't take my word, let her answer for herself.

Sir Gilb. Ay, that I would be glad to hear.

Wit. Ha, ha! 'Egad, this is a pleasant question indeed ——Madam, are not you willing, (as soon as the church-books can be open) to make a transfer of your whole stock of beauty for the conjugal uses of your humble servant?

Char. Indeed, papa, I won't suppose that can be a question.

Wit. A hum! your humble servant, Sir.

Char. Beside, are not you obliged to sign a further deed of consent to Mr. Witling?

Sir Gilb. Yes, child; but the same deed reserves to you a right of refusal, as well as to him.

Char. That I understand, Sir; and there's one can witness for whom I have reserved that right of refusal.

[*Pointing to* Fran.

Wit. Your humble servant, again, Sir; ha, ha, ha!

L. Wrang. I am amazed, Mr. Wrangle, you could think she could be under the least difficulty in the choice.

Fran. And yet, Madam, there are very innocent la-dies, that have made a difficulty of changing their incli-nations in half an hour.

L. Wrang. A woman of strict virtue, Sir, ought to have no inclinations at all: or, if any, those only of be-ing obedient to the will of her parents.

Wit. Oh, let him alone, Madam; the more he rails, the more I shall laugh, depend upon't: the pain of a rival is the pleasantest game in the world: his wishing me at the devil, is just the same thing as if he wished me joy! ha, ha, ha!

Sir Gilb. Well, Sir, all I fhall fay, is, that if the girl
has common fenfe, thy contract muft ftill be good for
nothing.

Wit. Right! and if you had common fenfe, I am
fure you would never have made it; not but to do you
juftice, Sir Gilbert, I muft own you have wit in your
way too, though it's of a very odd turn, I grant you.

' *Sir Gilb.* Sir, I difown my pretenfions to any, if ever
' you had fenfe enough to find it out.

' *Wit.* Sure you forget, my dear Sir Gilbert. Don't
' you remember once I did find it out? Did not I flily
' catch you in St. What-de-callum's churchyard, with
' your table book, taking dead people's names from the
' tomb-ftones, to fill up your lift of your third fubfcrip-
' tion, that you might be fure of thofe that would never
' come to claim it? and then pretended to all your
' friends you were full? There, at leaft, you had more
' wit to keep people out, than any man living had to
' get in: for I grant you, your lift was dead fure! ha,
' ha, ha!

' *Sir Gilb.* Why, ay, this nonfenfical ftory now paffes
' for wit, I warrant, among your cockade and velvet
' fparks at Garraway's; but much good may do you
' with your jeft, as long as we have your money among
' us: I believe it will be no hard matter to bite moft of
' your foft heads off before it be long; and if you
' drive on as you feem to do, we fhall make bold to fet
' fome of you down where we took you up, odfheart-
' likins.

' *Wit.* Nay, I grant you, to do your own bufinefs,
' you muft do other peoples too; but if all the young
' fellows of drefs and pleafure would follow me, I would
' undertake to lead you a dance for all that.

' *Sir Gilb.* And, pray, what would you have them
' do!

' *Wit.* Why, do as you do: nothing that you pre-
' tend to do; or do as I did, every thing as you whif-
' pered me not to do. I minded what your broker did,
' not what you faid, my dear! And if every gentle-
' man would but buy, when you advife him to fell; or
' fell when you advife him to buy, 'twould be impoffible
' to go out of the way: why, 'tis as plain road, man,
' a; from Hyde-Park corner to Kenfington.'

Sir

Sir Gilb. Sir, you take a great deal of liberty with me; infomuch, that I muſt tell you, I am not ſure I won't pay the forfeit of my contraƈt, rather than part with my daughter to a coxcomb——and ſo take it as you will.

L. Wrang. Mr. Wrangle! what do you mean by this brutality?

Fran. Mr. Witling, Madam, will take nothing ill, that I think fit to juſtify, I am ſure.

Wit. No, faith! you need not fear it; I'll marry before I'll fight, depend upon't. Ha, ha!

L. Wrang. Mr. Witling, I beg you come away this moment——I'll undertake to do your merit juſtice. I'll ſee who dares pretend to govern in this family beſide myſelf. Charlotte, give him your hand—Come, Sir——

[*Exit Lady* Wrangle.

Wit. I am all obedience, Madam—your humble ſervant, Mr. Frankly ——" Would you woo her——"

[*Exit, ſinging with* Charlotte.

Fran. Admirably well done, Sir! 'you have worked 'his inſolence to rare order.' Now, if you can but ſtand it out as ſtoutly with my lady, our buſineſs is done.

Sir Gilb. If!—Will you ſtand by me?

Fran. Will you give me your authority, Sir, to handle her roundly, and make her know who ought to be her maſter?

Sir Gilb. My authority! ay, and thanks into the bargain——Come along, I'll ſend for the lawyer now—— Mr. Frankly, my blood riſes at her; ſhe ſhall find I'll vindicate the honour of the city, and, from this moment, demoliſh her petticoat government.

Fran. Well ſaid; I'll warrant you, Sir.   [*Exeunt.*

END of the FOURTH ACT.

A C T   V.

Sir Gilbert *and* Frankly.

SIR GILBERT.

MY dear Frankly, I could not reſt till I had thee alone again; thou haſt gained upon me for ever: your vindicating the huſband's authority, and taking my

wife

wife a peg lower before my face, has tickled my fancy to that degree, that, odzooks! I could wifh in my heart thou hadft been married to her.

Fran. Oh, I fhould be loth to have robbed you, Sir, of that happinefs.

Sir Gilb. A hum! you are right, you are right; I did not think of that indeed. Well; it's a very odd thing now, that a wife will fooner be kept under by any man than her hufband: why the deuce can't I govern her fo?

Fran. There's no great fecret in the matter, Sir; for take any couple in Chriftendom, you will certainly find, that the more troublefome of the two is always head of the family.

Sir Gilb. By my troth, I believe you are right; and fince the war is begun, I'll make a fair pufh for't. I am refolved now to thwart her in every thing; and if Granger has but wit enough to talk Sophronia into her fenfes; that is, if he can but convince her that fhe is flefh and blood, and born to breed, like other women; odzooks! he fhall marry her immediately: I'll plague her Ladyfhip that way too.

' *Fran.* That way! Oh, ay, its true: for I think I
' have heard you fay, Sir, that if either of your daugh-
' ters die unmarried, my Lady is to inherit their fortunes.

' *Sir Gilb.* Ay, ay; there the fhoe pinches, man; fhe
' would be as much an enemy to Granger, as fhe is to
' you, if fhe could in the leaft fufpect he would ever make
' any thing of it with Sophronia.'

Fran. And, if I don't miftake, Sir, Granger is in a fair way there too; for, to my knowledge, he has been locked up with her this half hour, here in her library.

Sir Gilb. The dickens!

Fran. Did not you obferve them fteal off together, juft before the mufic?

Sir Gilb. I wondered, indeed, what was become of them; by the lord Harry I am glad of it——I muft have a peep at them. [*Goes to the key-hole.*] Odfo! they are juft a coming forth.

Fran. We had beft be out of the way then, that we may not difturb them.

Sir Gilb. No, no, I'll warrant you: pr'ythee, let us ftand ' behind this fkreen,' and obferve what paffes.

Fran.

Fran. **Q**uick! quickly then; here they come.

[*They retire.*

Enter Granger *with* Sophronia.

Soph. **Oh,** Granger! ftill preferve this purity,
And my whole foul will open to receive thee:
Forget, like me, thy fex, how fweetly may
We pafs our days in rational defire!
‘ Thou feeft, I own, without a blufh, my love,
‘ For blufhes only rife from guilty flames;
‘ When confcience driven, reluctant to the crime,
‘ Leaps to the face, and marks the cheek with fhame:
‘ But the chafte heart fublim’d by purer fires,
‘ Knowing no confcious fear, referve, or guile,
‘ Gives, with unbounded franknefs, all its ftore,
‘ And only blufhes—that it gives no more.’

Gran. Hear this, ye bright immortal choirs above,
And own that human fouls, like you, can love.

Sir Gilb. Heyday! this is downright love in a trage-
dy! Well; he’s a comical thief.

‘ *Fran.* Hufh! let him go on, Sir.

‘ *Soph.* Can you forgive the tedious banifhment,
‘ Which my diftruft and dread impos’d on you?

‘ *Gran.* Can I reproach you for fo juft, fo kind
‘ A fear? While through the general race of man,
‘ A fenfual and infectious paffion rages,
‘ Giving, from fex to fex, the mortal tainture;
‘ Can I complain, if, to preferve yourfelf
‘ From the contagion, you’ve perhaps enjoin’d
‘ The healthy to perform his quarantine?
‘ But landing thus, upon my native foil,
‘ I leave my fufferings paft behind, and think
‘ The prefent now is all that’s left of time,
‘ Or worth my care.

‘ *Soph.* Blufh! blufh! ye bafe degenerate world,
‘ That boaft the blifs of grefs connubial love:
‘ Can you wear human forms, yet fee the prone,
‘ The brute creation equal your defires?
‘ Had you or fouls or fenfe refin’d, you’d form
‘ Your wifhes worthy your fuperior being;
‘ Curb, with imperial reafon, lawlefs nature,
‘ And reach, like us, the joys of love feraphic.’

Gran. Oh, harmony of heart! Oh, fpotlefs paffion!

G 2 Here,

Here, on this hand, the altar of my vows,
I offer up my purer part, my foul
To thine, and fwear inviolable——

   Soph. ————————Hold!

Paffions, like ours, no formal vows require;
For vows fuppofe diftruft, or faithlefs love,
The frail fecurity of fenfual flames;
But where the pure, with the pure foul unites,
The fimple hand, thus given, and receiv'd, fuffices.

   Gran. Let then this hand my fpotlefs heart refign.

   Soph. Thus in exchange I blend my foul with thine.

   Sir Gilb. So; they are got to hand and heart already;
but now, now for a touch at the reft of her premifes.

   Fran. Nay, dear Sir, be eafy.

   Sir Gilb. Well! well! I will.

   Soph. And now, no more Sophronia, but thy friend;
Be both my name and fex from hence forgotten.

   Gran. No:

Let me remember ftill that thou art fair;
For were there no temptation in thy beauty,
Where were the merit of fuch hard refiftance?
Indeed, my friend, 'tis hard! 'tis hard refiftance!
' The organs of my fight, my ear, my feeling,
' As I am made of human mold, in fpite
' Of me, exert their functions, and are pleas'd:'
I view thee with delight, I hear with tranfport,
And thy touch——is rapture——

   ' *Soph.* How fares my friend?

   ' *Gran.* Like the poor wretch that parches in a fever,
' With fatal thirft, yet begs for prefent eafe
' To drink, and die——

   ' *Soph.* From whence this new diforder?

   ' *Gran.* Tell me, Sophronia, is my virtue blameful,
' Becaufe my fenfes act as nature bids them?
' Am I in fault, if the fharp winter's froft
' Can chill my limbs, or fummer's fun will fcorn them?
' What matter can refift the elements?
' Rivers will freeze, and folid mountains burn;
' What bodies will not change?—Thus the tall oak—
   ' Though from our meaner flames fecure,
   ' Muft that, which falls from heaven, endure.

   ' *Soph.* Where has he learned this art of unoffending
' flattery?   [*Afide.*

                                   ' *Gran.*

' *Grang.* Canſt thou reproach me then, if while thy
 beauties
' With ſuch a blaze of charms invade my ſenſe,
' My human heart's not proof againſt their pow'r ?
 ' *Soph.* Reproach thee ! No ; bodies are but the ſhells,
' Or huts, that cover in the ſoul, and are,
' Like other fabrics, ſubject to miſchance :
' The cells of hermits may be fir'd ; but none
' Reproach the wretch that ſuffers by the flame.'
 Gran. Oh, Sophronia ! canſt thou forgive me then,
That my material droſs thus burns before thee ?
That my whole frame thus kindles at thy beauty ?
And even warms my ſoul with fond deſire ?
' Like an impatient child it languiſhes,
' And pines for wants unknown, it ſighs, it pants,
' To be indulg'd upon thy friendly boſom,
' To fold thee in my tender arms, to talk,
' And gaze, with mutual ſoft benevolence
' Of eyes, as giving were our only pleaſure.'
 Sir Gilb. Adod ! I believe he's in earneſt, he makes
me half in love to hear him.
 Soph. Is it poſſible ? Can then
Such ſoftneſs mingle with corporeal paſſion ?   [*Apart.*
 Gran. But while the ſoul alone is ſuffered to
Poſſeſs, and bars my mortal part from joy ;
My poor repining ſenſes murmur at
Their fate, and call thy purity unjuſt,
' To ſtarve the body, while the mind knows plenty,
' Yet, like a churl, ingroſſes whole the feaſt,
' My ſenſes claim a ſhare from nature's law ;
' They think, with a more melting ſoftneſs, they
' Could love, and e'en inform the ſoul with rapture.'
 Sir Gilb. Ay ; now we begin to work her.
 ' *Gran.* Conſider then, as part of me, thy friend,
' Thy friend may ſure be truſted with your pity !
' Oh, relieve them ! give me ſome ſign at leaſt,
' One kind embrace, or a chaſte ſiſter's kiſs,
' In certain proof that thou art ſtill my friend,
' That yet thou hat'ſt me not——I aſk no more.
 ' *Soph. Pignora certa petis? do pignora certa--Timendo.*
 Gran. ' Does then thy fear alone refuſe me ?' Oh,
  Sophronia !

        Why,

Why, why muſt virtue be this foe to nature?
Why ſet our ſenſes with our ſouls at variance,
As Heav'n had form'd thee fair—to kill thy friend.

Soph. What means my throbbing heart? Oh, virtue!
Now ſave me from unequal nature's power !   [now,
Now guard me from myſelf——and hide my ſhame!

Gran. Muſt I then periſh? Will my friend forſake me?

Soph. Oh, Granger! I am loſt!—thou haſt undone
I am fallen, and thou wilt hate me now.   [me!

Gran. Oh, Sophronia!

Soph. ——Lend me thy arm, ſupport me!
Thy melting plaints have ſtole upon my heart,
And ſoften me to wiſhes never known before.

Gran. Oh, the tumultuous joy! [*She ſinks into his arms.*

Sir Gilb. Ah, dead! dead! We have her, boy! we
have her.

' *Gran.* See how ſhe pants!
' How, like a wounded dove, ſhe beats her wings,
' And trembling hovers to her mate for ſuccour.
' Oh, the dear confuſion! Awake, Sophronia!
' Now wake to new and unconceiv'd delights,
' Which faint philoſophy could never reach,
' Which nature gave thee charms to taſte and give.
  ' *Soph.* Oh, I cou'd wiſh, methinks, for ev'ry power,
' That might have charms for thee : thy words,
' Like Hybla drops, diſtil upon my ſenſe,
' And I could hear thee talk for ever.'
  Gran. ' Oh, be but thus for ever kind, thy eyes
' Will find new ſubjects for eternal talk,
' And everlaſting love :' bluſh not, my fair,
That thou art kind : thy heart has only paid
To love, the tribute due from nature's whole creation :
' For wiſdom to his power oppos'd, is folly :'
Hear how the Britiſh Virgil ſings his ſway ;
  " Thus every creature, and of every kind,
  The ſecret joys of mutual paſſion find ;
  Not only man's imperial race, but they
  That wing the liquid air, or ſwim the ſea,
  Or haunt the deſert, ruſh into the flame ;
  For love is lord of all, and is in all the fame."
                   [*Exeunt* Gran. *and* Soph.
                             Sir

Sir Gilb. Oh, rare philofophy! Oh, fine philofophy! dainty philofophy! ho! [*Singing.*

Fran. Ha, ha, ha! that muſt be a pleaſant ſort of philoſophy indeed, Sir, that pretends to be wiſer than nature. Platonic love is a mere philoſopher's ſtone; when different ſexes once come to lay their heads together about it, the projection's ſure to fly *in fumo.*

Sir Gilb. Fumo! Ay, I warrant you. A handſome wench, that ſhuts herſelf up two or three hours with a young fellow, only out of friendſhip, is making a hopeful experiment in natural philoſophy indeed —— Why it's juſt like ſpreading a bag of gunpowder before a great fire, only to dry it; ha, ha, ha!

' *Fran.* Right, Sir—It puts me in mind of the Iriſh
' ſoldier, who, to ſteal powder out of a full barrel, cun-
' ningly bored a hole in it with a red hot poker.

' *Sir Gilb.* Ah, very good! ha, ha, ha! As you ſay,
' it's hard luck indeed, that her firſt touch of his hand
' ſhould blow up all the reſt of her body.

' *Fran.* But to do her juſtice, Sir, ſhe was not won
' without a good deal of art neither: a plain battery of
' love would have done nothing upon her; you ſee, he
' was forced to ſap her with his ſelf reproaches, and put
' it all upon the point of her compaſſion to his ſenſes.

' *Sir Gilb.* Nay, the toad did worm her nicely, that I
' muſt needs ſay.'

Fran. Ha, ha, ha! what a rare welcome too this news will have with my Lady! How ſhe will fume at the diſappointment!

Sir Gilb. Nay, I have nothing to do with that, you know; this was none of my doing: let every tub ſtand upon its own bottom; ' I ſhall e'en leave her Ladyſhip
' to his management: all I can promiſe him is, not to
' hinder the matter.

' *Fran.* That's all he will deſire, I dare ſay, Sir: be
' you but as a paſſive in his affair as mine, I'll warrant
' we will find courage enough between us to maintain
' our pretenſions.

Enter a Servant.

Serv. Sir, here's Mr. Delay, the lawyer.

Sir Gilb. Odſo! that's well! Now, Mr. Frankly——

Fran.

Fran. I believe, Sir, you had beſt keep him out of my Lady's fight, till matters are ripe for execution.

Sir Gilb. You are right, you are right ; ſay no more, I'll do it. *Ah, the ſly rogue ! how he tickled her up !*

Fran. *But harkee, harkee, Sir Gilbert—don't flinch now ; don't be a craven ; be ſure to ſtand it out ſtoutly with my Lady.*

Sir Gilb. *Will you and Granger continue to ſtand by me ?*

Fran. *To the laſt drop of our amorous blood to your daughters, and our amiable blood to you.*

Sir Gilb. *Why then, if I don't ſquabble it out with her Ladyſhip to the laſt drop of a huſband's authority,* may I live and die the cock of the hen-peck'd corporation.

                                   [*Exit.*

Fran. So ; thus far we ſtand fair : we have nothing now to combat but my Lady ; and Granger's ſuccefs with Sophronia, at this time, will naturally ſtrengthen our alliance againſt her. As for my friend Witling, his own aſſurance and vanity will partly do his buſineſs : ' but, ' however, in the mean while, it will not be amiſs to ' keep him warm and ripe for our deſign'——*à-propos !* here he comes.

Enter Witling.

Wit. Ha, ha, ha·! dear Tom ! I am glad I have found thee, faith ! I have a favour to beg of thee.

Fran. Why then, I am glad you have found me too ——becauſe, I believe, I ſhall not grant it.

Wit. Ha, ha ! what crabbed ſtill, my dear ! But I come to thee from a fair lady, child ; and 'tis for her ſake I am going to be obliged to thee.

Fran. I am glad of that too. A woman of ſenſe, I warrant her, by her ſending thee on a fool's errand.

' *Wit.* Ay, but my dear ! the errand happens to be ' her's now ; and ſo thou haſt civilly put the fool upon ' the woman of ſenſe. Good again ! one of thy old blun- ' ders, Tom ! for, I think thou haſt but curſed luck in ' making thy way to the women.

' *Fran.* When you tell me the lady you come from, ' I ſhall be better able to gueſs, whether ſhe takes me or ' you for a fool.'

Wit. Suppoſe then it were from a lady, Tom, that de-
                                           figns

figns to take either you or me for a hufband ? What doft thou think of my little Charlotte, my dear Tommy ?

Fran. Why, if fhe takes thee for a hufband, I fhall think her a fool ; and if I fhould take thee for a wit, fhe would think me a fool : but by her fending thee to afk a favour of me, it's a fign fhe thinks thee a fool.

Wit. Ha, ha ! a very pretty parcel of crofs purpofes ; a fool and wit, and wit and fool ; and fhe, and thee, and me ! What ! art thou playing at huftle-cap with thy words, child ? ' Thou doft not expeft I fhould take all ' thy jingle jumble for wit, doft thou ?

' *Fran.* No, faith ! if it be wit, I expeft thou fhouldft ' not take it.

' *Wit.* With all my heart—Come, come, it fhall be ' wit then ; I will miftake it for once.'—But to bufinefs— the fair lady, my dear Tom—

Fran. Ay, what of her ?

' *Wit.* Why, poor foul, fhe defir'd me to come to ' you, and——

' *Fran.* And leave her to better company, ha !

' *Wit.* Look you, Tom, I know lofers ought to have ' leave to fpeak, and therefore, at prefent, you fhall have ' all the wit to yourfelf, my dear : but don't be uneafy ' at my happinefs, dear Tom ; for to tell you the truth, ' the creature is fo curfed fond of me, that fhe begins ' to grow troublefome already. Ha, ha, ha !

' *Fran.* Why don't you make yourfelf eafy then, and ' give her up to me ?

' *Wit.* No no ; I muft not break the poor fool's heart ' neither:' for you muft know, fhe is in a terrible taking about me.

Fran. How fo, Sir ?

Wit. Why fhe faid, juft now, fhe was afraid to marry me fo foon as to-night upon thy account.

Fran. Good ! then there may be hopes fhe will not marry thee upon any account.

Wit. No, don't flatter thyfelf neither, my dear Tommy ; for her concern at the bottom was all upon my account.

Fran. How does that appear ?

Wit. Why you know, fays fhe, after all, poor Frankly has fome fort of pretenfions to me : I don't know how it

was

was, fays fhe; but fome way or other he got in with my father: fo I durft not wholly difcourage his addreffes. Now, Frankly's of a furly temper, 'fays fhe? and, ' if I fhould marry you, in the heat of his difappoint- ' ment, he may fay or do fome rafh thing upon't:' and I know, fays fhe, Mr. Witling, you are violent in your nature too; and if matters fhould rife to a quarrel, no- body knows where the mifchief may end; the world will certainly lay it all at my door——I fhould be the mife- rableft creature alive —— therefore I beg you, fays fhe, go to him from me, and try to make an amicable end of the bufinefs; and the moment poor Frankly's made eafy, fays fhe, I'll marry you the next hour, without any referve in the whole world.

Fran. Why then, without any referve in the whole world, pray tell the lady, that fhe may depend upon it I am certainly eafy——becaufe I am fure fhe impofes upon you.

Wit. Impofe upon me, child! ha, ha! that's pleafant enough, ha, ha!

Fran. That is, fhe let's you impofe upon yourfelf, which is the fame thing.

Wit. That may be, Tom; but the devil take me if I can find it out: ' but, however, I am mighty glad you ' do, becaufe then I am fure, as long as you are eafy, ' you can't take it ill, if I fhould burft my ribs with ' laughing at your fancy.

' *Fran.* Oh, not in the leaft! and to increafe your ' mirth, Sir, I will be farther bold to tell you, fhe has as ' hearty a contempt for you, if poffible, as I have.

' *Wit.* Good again! Ha, ha, ha!

' *Fran.* Thou art a thing fo below all human confide- ' ration, thou haft not wherewithal to give a Spaniard ' jealoufy.

' *Wit.* Ah, poor Tom, if thou didft but know all now! ' Ha, ha!

' *Fran.* But to think thyfelf agreeable to her, thou muft ' have the impudence of a French Harlequin.

' *Wit.* Ah, dear Tom, thou charmeft me! for fince I ' find thou art not, in the leaft, uneafy at her engage- ' ment with me, to tell thee the truth. I have nothing ' elfe at prefent that can poffibly retard my happinefs.

' *Fran.*

' *Fran.* Why then, Sir, be as happy as you deferve;
' and pray let the lady know, as to any favour fhe defigns
' you, I am in perfect peace of mind and tranquility.

' *Wit.* And you really give me leave to tell her fo?

' *Fran.* Tell her, I am more eafy than fhe herfelf will
' be, when fhe has married you.

' *Wit.* Why then' perifh me, if thou art not one of the
beft-bred rivals in the whole world! ha, ha, ha! and
here fhe comes, faith, to thank thee for her part of the
confolation. Ha, ha!

Fran. Ha, ha!

Enter Charlotte.

Char. So, gentlemen, I am glad to find you in fuch
good humour.

Wit. O! Madam, the deareft friends in the world:
I have obey'd your commands, and here's honeft Tom is
fo far from being uneafy at our marriage, that 'egad I
can't get him to believe it will ever come to any thing.

Char. O! as to that, Mr. Frankly may think as he
pleafes; but if he is not uneafy upon your account, that's
all I pretend to defire of him.

Wit. No, no, honeft Tom will give us no trouble, depend upon it.

Fran. Not I, upon my honour, Madam, ' for though
' I might be provoked to cut another man's throat, that
' fhould pretend to you, yet the value I have for Mr.
' Witling, fecures him from my leaft refentment.

' *Wit.* Look you there, Madam! you fee your fears
' are all over; I don't find we have any thing to do now,
' but to fend for the parfon.

' *Char.* Ay, but I don't well underftand him; for he
' feems to be neither jealous of your merit, nor my in-
' clination: and that I can fcarce think poffible.

' *Fran.* You may, upon my foul, Madam: for I have
' fo juft a fenfe of both, that if it had not been in re-
' gard to your father's contract, I am convinced you
' would never have endured the fight of him.

' *Wit.* Ah! poor Tom! he has much ado to fmother
' it. [*Apart.*

' *Char.* Very pretty! fo you think that my admitting
' his addreffes is mere grimace, and that I am all this
' while taking pains only to deceive Mr. Witling.

' *Fran.* Alas! you need not do that, Madam; he takes fo
' much

' much to deceive himfelf, he really gives you no trouble
' about it.

' *Wit.* You fee, child, we may put any thing upon
' him.

' *Char.* Right! you take it as I could wifh! Let me
' alone with him. And fo, Sir, you really expect I fhould
' be pleafed with your having this free opinion of my
' conduct ?'

Fran. I muft be pleafed with every thing you undertake in my favour, Madam.

Wit. How vain the rogue is too !   *[Afide.*

Char. I am amaz'd ! but how naturally a coxcomb
fhews himfelf.   *[Afide.*

Wit. Ay, that's when he is in your hands, Madam ;
' Ha, ha ! 'Egad fhe plays him nicely off.   *[Afide.*

' *Char.* After this, one fhould wonder at nothing!
' Nay, there are fome fools, I fee, whofe vanity is fo far
' from being offenfive, that they become diverting even
' to a rival.

' *Fran.* Mr. Witling is always entertaining, Madam.

' *Wit.* Hah, prodigious ! 'Egad he thinks you mean me
' all this while. Ha, ha, ha !   *[Apart.*

' *Char.* Well, fure there never was fo bright a cox-
' comb !   *[Apart.*

' *Wit.*' 'Egad I'll humour him : Ha, ha ?   *[Apart.*

Char. By all means, you will make him fhine to a miracle.   *[Apart.*

Wit. Why then, perifh me Tom, if ever I was fo well
diverted at a French comedy.   *[Shakes his hand.*

Fran. That may very well be, Sir; for fools are apt
to be fond of their own parts.   *[Shakes Witling's hand.*

Char. Ha, ha !

Wit. Ay ! fo they are, the devil take me ; for, I fee,
there's no beating thee out of thine.

Fran. How fhould I be out, when you play all the
fcene yourfelf !

Wit. No, no, Tom, I only laugh all ; but 'tis your
part that makes me, child.

Fran. Right ! If you did not laugh, where the devil
fhould the jeft be ?

Wit. Why, then, you fee, I do the fool juftice, Tom,
Ha, ha !

Fran.

Fran. Ay, the devil take me, doſt thou; I never ſaw him better acted.

‘ *Wit.* Ah! but you don’t know, my dear, that to
‘ make a coxcomb ſhine, requires a little more wit than
‘ thou art aware of.

‘ *Fran.* I know that he who has leaſt wit of us two,
‘ has enough to do that, my dear.

‘ *Wit.* Ay, that is when a coxcomb ſhows himſelf,
‘ Tom.

‘ *Fran.* Nay, in that I grant no mortal can come up
‘ to thee.

‘ *Wit.* Ha, ha, ha! Oh, dear rogue, I muſt kiſs
‘ thee.

‘ *Omnes.* Ha, ha, ha!

Enter Lady Wrangle.

L. Wrang. Your ſervant, your ſervant, good people; whence all this mighty mirth, pray?

Wit. O, Madam, here has been ſuch a ſcene! ſuch hit and daſh upon one another; in ſhort, ſuch brightneſs o’both ſides, the full moon, in a froſty night, never came up to it.

Char. I muſt needs ſay, I never ſaw Mr. Witling ſhine ſo before.

‘ *Fran.* No, Madam? Why, he always talks like a lu-
‘ natic, as you now may judge by his ſimilies.

‘ *Wit.* Ah, poor Tom! thy wit indeed is, like the
‘ light of the moon, none of thy own: if I don’t miſ-
‘ take, my dear, I was forced to ſhine upon thee, before
‘ thou wert able to make one reflection.

‘ *Fran.* There you are once in the right: for I certain-
‘ ly could not have laughed, if you had not given me a
‘ hearty occaſion.

‘ *Wit.* Ay, but the cream of the jeſt is, Tom, that at
‘ the ſame time I really gave thee no occaſion at all.

‘ *Fran.* Right again, my dear: for your not knowing
‘ that, is the only jeſt that’s worth laughing at.

‘ *Both.* Ha, ha, ha!’

L. Wrang. This muſt be ſome extraordinary miſtake indeed; for I have no notion that Mr. Frankly and you can have reaſon to laugh upon the ſame occaſion.

Wit. Why, faith! the occaſion is a little extraordi-

H nary;

nary ; for you muſt know, Madam, that honeſt Tom and
I here, are both going to be married to this lady.

L. Wrang. Both !

Wit. Ay both, Madam ; for, it ſeems, ſhe has not
been able to convince us, that either of us muſt go without her.

L. Wrang. That's ſo like Mr. Frankly's vanity, that
cannot think his miſtreſs loſt, though he ſees her juſt falling into the arms of his rival.

Fran. My vanity and yours, Madam, are much upon
a foot; tho' I think you happened to be firſt cured of it.

L. Wrang. What do you mean, Sir ?

Fran. That by this time you are convinced I was never
in love with your ladyſhip.

L. Wrang. I am convinced, that a very little trouble
would have made you ſo.

‘ *Fran.* It muſt have been a good deal more than it coſt
‘ me, to make you believe ſo.

‘ *L. Wrang.* If you have ſtill hopes of marrying
‘ Charlote, Sir, I don't wonder at your believing any
‘ thing. Ha, ha, ha !

‘ *Fran.* Laugh when you ſee me deſpair, Madam.

‘ *L. Wrang.* I need not ſtay for that ; your hope, is
‘ ridiculous enough, and I laugh becauſe you can't ſee.'

Fran. ‘ Yes, yes, I can ſee,' Madam : I have ſeen all
this day what 'tis you drive at : in ſhort, Madam, you
have no mind that either of Sir Gilbert's daughters ſhould
marry ; becauſe if they die maids, you have ſecured the
chance of ſucceeding to their fortunes.

‘ *L. Wrang.* Ay, do make the world believe that, if
‘ you can : perſuade Mr. Witling that I have no mind
‘ Charlotte ſhould marry him.

‘ *Fran.* What Mr. Witling thinks, is out of the queſ-
‘ tion, Madam ; but you are ſure that ſhe never deſigns to
‘ marry him : ſo that your ſetting up his pretenſions is
‘ not with the leaſt view of doing him good, but of doing
‘ me harm ; or rather, that while you manage the diſ-
‘ pute well on both ſides, neither of us may have her.

‘ *L. Wrang.* He has gueſs'd the ſecret ; but that ſhall
‘ not hinder my proceeding. [*Aſide.*] You are in the right
‘ to hope as long as you can, Sir ; but I preſume you
　　　　　　　　　　　　　　　　　　　　　‘ don't

' don't do it from my friendſhip, nor Mr. Wrangle's con-
' ſent, or Charlotte's inclination.

' *Fran.* Be what it will, Madam, it has a better foun-
' dation, than your hope of ſuceeding either to her's or
' Sophronia's fortune: for,' ſhall I tell you another ſecret, Madam? Sophronia is going to be married to
Granger; ſo that you are equally like to be diſappointed
there too.

L. Wrang. Sophronia married!

Fran. Ay, ay, married, married, Madam: wedded,
bedded, made a mere wife of: 'tis not half an hour ago
ſince I ſaw her ſink, and melt into his boſom, with all
the yielding fondneſs of a milk-maid.

L. Wrang. Sophronia, do this?

Fran. Sophronia, Madam; nay, Sir Gilbert was, at
the ſame time, a ſecret witneſs of all; and was glad, glad
of it, Madam: ' and to my certain knowledge, reſolves,
' that Granger ſhall marry her inſtantly:' and ſo, Madam,
all that fantaſtic fort philoſophy, that you have been
building in her brains for ſeven years together, is (with
one honeſt attack of mere fleſh and blood) fairly demoliſh-
ed, and brought to nothing.

L. Wrang. I'll not believe it; I know your ears deceiv'd
you; he might perhaps tranſport her, but never to a ſenſual thought.

' *Fran.* Oons! Madam, I tell you, I heard and ſaw it
' all; myſelf, ſaw her ſighing, bluſhing, panting in his
' arms, with mortal, ſenſual, amorous deſire: all her
' romantic pride reduced, and humbled to the obedience
' of that univerſal monarch of mankind, Love, Madam;
' plain, naked, natural Love, Love, Madam.

' *L. Wrang.* I am confounded! If this be true, his
' triumph is inſupportable. [*Aſide.*] Ha! what do I ſee!'
                Enter Granger, *leading* Sophronia.

' *Fran.* Dear Granger, I congratulate thy happineſs!

' *Gran.* My happineſs indeed! for till I was victorious,
' I knew not half the value of my conqueſt.

' *Fran.* [*To* Sophronia.] Give me then leave to hope,
' Madam, that our former difference is forgot; ſince the
' more elevated paſſion of my friend has now convinced
' me of my own unworthineſs.

' *Soph.*

' *Soph.* I cannot difavow my tendereft fenfe of Gran-
' ger's merit, give it what name you pleafe; I own 'tis
' fomething——*Quod nequeo dicere, & fentio tantum :*
' but am proud that love alone, unaffifted by philofophy,
' could never have fubdued me.

' *L. Wrang.*' Is it poffible !

By your leave, Madam,

[*She breaks through the company, and takes* Soph. *apart.*

' *Fran.* Heyday ! what's to do now ?

' *Gran.* O Frankly ! I have fuch a melting ⎫
' fcene to tell thee !   ⎪
' *Fran.* You may fpare yourfelf the trouble, ⎪
' Sir Gilbert and I over-heard every word of it. ⎬ [*Afide.*
' But I allow you an artift.   ⎪
' *Gran.* Was it not very whimfical ?   ⎪
' *Fran.* Hufh !   ⎭

' *L. Wrang.* [*To* Soph.'] Look in my face—full upon
me.

Soph. Why that fevere look, Madam ?

L. Wrang. To make you blufh at your apoftafy.

Soph. Converts to truth are no apoftates, Madam.

L. Wrang. Is this your felf-denial ! This your diftafte
of odious man ?

Soph. Madam, I have confider'd well my female ftate,
and am now a profelyte to that philofophy, which fays,

Nature makes nought in vain.

L. Wrang. What's then become of your Platonic
fyftem ?

Soph. Diffolved, evaporated, impracticable, and falla-
cious all : you'll own I have labour'd in the experiment,
but found at laft, that to try gold in a crucible of virgin-
wax, was a mere female folly.

L. Wrang. But how 'durft you, Madam, entertain a
thought of marriage without acquainting me ?

Soph. Madam, I am now under this gentleman's protection ; and from henceforth, think my actions only cog-
nizable to him.

L. Wrang. Very fine !

Fran. Ay, ay, Madam, 'tis but fretting your fpleen
to no purpofe ; you have no right to difpofe of either of
thofe ladies : Sir Gilbert's confent is what we depend
upon : and as far as that can go, we fhall make bold to
infift

infift upon them both, Madam : and fo you may as well put your paffion in your pocket, Madam.

L. Wrang. Infupportable!   [*Walks in anger.*

Wit. Ha, ha! well faid, Tommy! What, art thou crack-brained ftill, my dear? How the devil didft thou come by Sir Gill's confent? What, he has not mortgag'd it twice over, has he? But if he has, with all my heart; I fancy we fhall find a way to make his firft deed ftand good, however; and that, I am fure, I have here fafe in my pocket, child.

Fran. Oh, that fhall be tried prefently, Sir; and here he comes with the lawyer, for the purpofe.

Enter Sir Gilbert, *with a Lawyer.*

L. Wrang. Mr. Wrangle, what do you mean by this ufage? How dare you affront me thus?

Sir Gilb. I affront you, my Lady!

L. Wrang. Ay, Sir, by bringing thefe royfters here, to infult me in my own family.

Sir Gilb. Frankly—ftand by me.

Gran. Royfters, Madam!

L. Wrang. Sir, I am not fpeaking to you. I fay, Mr. Wrangle, how dare you do this?

Sir Gilb. Do, Madam! I don't do any thing, not I. If the gentlemen have done any harm, you had beft talk to them; I believe they have both tongues in their heads, and will be able to anfwer you.

Fran. Ay, ay, Madam, if you have received any injury from either of us, we are the proper perfons to talk with you.

L. Wrang. What, will you ftand by, and tamely fee me abufed in my own houfe?

Sir Gilb. Odzines, Madam, don't abufe yourfelf! the gentlemen are civil gentlemen, and men of honour; but if you don't know how to behave yourfelf to them, that's none of their fault.

L. Wrang. Prodigious! behave myfelf! Do you prefume to teach me, you rude, illiterate monfter?

Sir Gilb. Hold her faft, pray, gentlemen.

Gran. [*Interpofing.*] Come, come, be compofed, Madam. Confider how thefe violent emotions difhonour your philofophy.

Sir

Sir Gilb. Ay, Madam, if you are a philofopher, now, let's fee a fample of it.

L. Wrang. Yes, Sir, I'll give you one inftance of it immediately ; before you ftir out of this room, I'll make you do juftice to this gentleman ; I'll make you keep your contract, Sir.

Sir Gilb. Why, Madam, you need not be in a paffion about that ; I don't defign any other ; I'll do him juftice immediately.

L. Wrang. Oh, will you fo ? Come, then, where's the deed, Sir ?

Wit. A-hum ! Your humble fervant ! How doft thou do now, my little Tommy ?

Fran. I'll tell you prefently, Sir.

Wit. Ha, ha ! 'Egad, thou art refolved to die hard, I find.

Law. Here, Madam, this is the deed ; there is nothing wanting but the blanks to be filled up with the bridegroom's name.   Pray, which is the gentleman ?

L. Wrang. Here, Sir, this is he——Put in William Witling, efq.

Sir Gilb. Hold, Madam, two words to that bargain ? that is not the gentleman I have refolved upon.

L. Wrang. Come, come, Mr. Wrangle, don't be a fool, I fay.

Sir Gilb. And, pray, Madam, don't you pretend to be wifer than I am.

L. Wrang. What ftupid fetch have you got in your head now ?

Wit. Heyday ! what time of the moon is this ? Why, have not I your contract here in my hand, Sir Gilbert ?

Sir Gilb. With all my heart ; make your beft on't ; I'll pay the penalty ; and what have you to fay now ? And fo, Sir, [*To the Lawyer.*] I fay, put me in Thomas Frankly, efq.

L. Wrang. Mr. Wrangle, don't provoke me.   Do you know that the penalty of your refufing Mr. Witling, is above fix-and-twenty thoufand pounds difference, Sir ?

Sir Gilb. Yes, Madam ; but to let you fee that I am not the fool you take me for, neither ; there's that will fecure me againft paying a farthing of it.

[*Sir* Gilbert *fhews a bond.*
                                        L. Wrang.

2

L. Wrang. What do you mean?

Sir Gilb. Why, that this, Madam, is a joint bond from Mr. Granger and Frankly, to indemnify me from all demands, costs, and consequences of Mr. Witling's contract.

[*Lady* Wrangle *peruses the bond.*

Char. Now, Mr. Witling, you see upon what a shallow foundation Frankly built all his vanity and assurance. But, poor man! he did not consider it was still in my power to marry you, tho' you had no contract at all with my father.

Wit. Right, my pretty soul—I suppose he thought the merit and frank air of this bond, forsooth, would have made you cock sure to him; but I'll let him see, presently, that I know how to pay a handsome compliment to a fair lady, as well as himself. 'Egad, I will bite his head off.

Char. Ay, do, Mr. Witling; you touch my heart with the very thought of it.

Wit. Ah, you charming devil!

L. Wrang. [*To Sir* Gilbert.] Is this, then, your expedient? Is this your sordid way of evading all right and justice? Go, you vile scandal to the board you sit at! But you shall find that I have a superior sense of honour: and thus, thus, thus, I'll force you to be just.

[*Tears the bond.*

Fran. Confusion!

Sir Gilb. Oons, Madam! what do you mean by this outrage?

L. Wrang. Now, where's your security? Where is your vile evasion now, Sir? What trick, what shift have you now to save you?

Sir Gilb. Frankly——stand by me.

'*Fran.* Was ever such a devil?'

Gran. Fear nothing; I'll warrant you; come, Sir, don't be disheartened; your security shall be renewed to your content. Let the lawyer draw it up this instant, and I'll give my word and honour to sign it again before all this company.

Sir Gilb. Say'st thou so, my lad? Why, then, odsheartlikins——Frankly, stand by me.

Fran. Generous Granger!

L. Wrang. Let the lawyer draw up any such thing in my house, if he dares. *Gran.*

Gran. Nay, then, Madam, I'll fee who dares moleft him.

Fran. 'Egad, whoever does, fhall have more than one to deal with.

Sir Gilb. Well faid; ftand your ground—Write away, man. [*To the Lawyer.*

Char. Now, Mr. Witling——

Wit. Nay, nay, if that's your play, gentlemen—Come, come, I'll fhew you a fhorter way to make an end of this matter——and to let you fee you are all in the wrong box, and that now I am fecure of the lady's inclination, I think it a difhonour to her beauty to make ufe of any other advantage, than the naked merit of her humble fervant. There, Sir Gilbert, there's your contract back again; tear it, cancel it, or light your pipe with it—And Madam—— [*To* Char.

Char. Ay, now, Mr. Witling, you have made me the happieft creature living. And now, Mr. Lawyer——

Wit. Ay, now, gentlemen——

Char. Put in Thomas Frankly, efq.

Wit. Fire and brimftone!

Fran. Ay, now Mr. Witling——

Sir Gilb. Odfheart, in with him——

L. Wrang. Come, come, Mr. Wrangle——

Sir Gilb. Oons, wife, be quiet!

L. Wrang. Wife! What, am I abufed, infulted, then?

Sir Gilb. Ah, Charlotte, let me hug thee, and bufs thee, and blefs thee to death! But, here, huffy, here's a pair of lips that will make better work with thee.

Wit. Bit, by the powers!

Char. Nay, don't fay that of me, Mr. Witling; 'twas even all your own doing: for you can't reproach me with having once told you I ever loved, or liked you. How then could you think of marrying me?

Wit. Not reproach you, Madam? Oons, and death! did you not as good as ——

Fran. Hold, Sir; when you fpeak to my wife, I muft beg you to foften the tone of your voice a little.

Wit. Heyday! what a pox, muft not lofers have leave to fpeak, neither?

Fran. No, no, my dear Billy, thou art no lofer at all;
for

for you have made your call, you fee, and now have fairly had your refufal too.

Wit. Ha, ha! that's pleafantly faid, however, 'egad! I can't help laughing at a good thing, though, tho' I am half ready to hang myfelf.

Fran. Nay, then, Witling, henceforth I'll allow thee a man of parts; ' tho', at the fame time, you muft grant ' me, there are no fools like your wits.' But fince thou haft wit enough to laugh at thyfelf, I think nobody elfe ought to do it.

' *Wit.* Why, then, dear Tom, I give you joy; for, to ' fay the truth, I believe I was a little over-hafty in this ' matter. But, as thou fayeft, he that has not wit ' enough to find himfelf fometimes a fool, is in danger of ' being fool enough to have nobody think him a wit but ' himfelf.'

Fran. [*To L.* Wrang.] And now, Madam, were it but poffible to deferve your pardon——

L. Wrang. I fee you know my weaknefs——Submiffion muft prevail upon a generous nature—I forgive you.

Sir Gilb. Why, that's well faid of all fides. And, now you are part of my family, gentlemen, I'll tell you a fecret that concerns your fortunes——Hark you—in one word——fell——fell out as faft as you can; for (among friends) the game's up——afk no queftions—— but, I tell you, the jeft is over——But money down, (d'ye obferve me?) money down. Don't meddle for time; for the time's a coming, when thofe that buy will not be able to pay. And fo, the devil take the hindmoft; and Heaven blefs you all together.

Gran. And now, Sophronia, fet we forward to the promifed land of love.

Soph. In vain, againft the force of nature's law,
 Would rigid morals keep our hearts in awe;
 All our loft labours of the brain but prove,
 In life there's no philofophy like love.

END of the FIFTH ACT.

EPILOGUE.

THE time is come the Roman bard foretold,
   A brazen year succeeds an age of gold;
An age ⸻
When specious books were open'd for undoing,
And English hands, in crouds, subscrib'd their ruin.
Some months ago, whoever could suppose,
A goosequill race of rulers should have rose, ⎫
T'have made the warlike Britons groan beneath their blows? ⎭
Evils, that never yet beheld the sun, ⎫
To foreign-arms, or civil jars, unknown, ⎬
These trembling miscreants, by their wiles have done. ⎭
Thus the fierce lion, whom no force could foil,
By village-curs is baited in the toil.
Forgive the muse then, if her scenes were laid
Before your fair possessions were betray'd;
She took the flitting form as fame then ran,
While a director seem'd an honest man:
But were she from his present form to take him,
What a huge gorging monster must she make him?
How would his paunch with golden ruin swell?
Whole families devouring at a meal?
What motley humour in a scene might flow,
Were we these upstarts in their arts to show?
When their high betters at their gates have waited,
And all to beg the favour to be cheated;
Even that favour, (or they're by fame bely'd)
To raise the value of the cheat, deny'd.
And while Sir John was airing on his prancers,
He'as left his cookmaid to give peers their answers.
Then clerks in Berlins, purchas'd by their cheats,
That splash their walking betters in the streets.
And while, by fraud, their native country's sold,
Cry, Drive, you dog, and give your horses gold:
Even Jews no bounds of luxury refrain,
But boil their Christian hams in pure Champain.
Till then, the guilty, that have caus'd these times,
Feel a superior censure for their crimes,
Let all, whose wrongs the face of mirth can bear,
Enjoy the muse's vengeance on them here.

Robert del.   *Published for Bells British Theatre April 5 1777.*   *I. Thornthwaite Sculp.*

M.ʳ BADDELEY *in the Character of* PETULANT.

Carry your Mistress's Monkey a Spider,
go flea Dogs and read romances,
I'll go to bed to my Maid.

BELL'S EDITION.

THE

WAY OF THE WORLD.

A COMEDY,

As written by WILLIAM CONGREVE.

DISTINGUISHING ALSO THE

VARIATIONS OF THE THEATRE,

AS PERFORMED AT THE

Theatre-Royal in Drury-Lane.

Regulated from the Prompt-Book,

By PERMISSION of the MANAGERS,

By Mr. HOPKINS, Prompter.

Audire est operæ pretium, procedere rectè
Qui mæchis non vultis.——
——Metuat doti deprensa.——

HOR. sat. 2. l. 1.
IBID.

LONDON:
Printed for JOHN BELL, near *Exeter-Exchange,* in the *Strand.*

MDCCLXXVII.

To the Right Honourable

R A L P H,

EARL of MONTAGUE, &c.

My Lord,

WHETHER the world will arraign me of vanity or not, that I have presumed to dedicate this comedy to your Lordship, I am yet in doubt; though it may be it is some degree of vanity even to doubt of it. One who has at any time had the honour of your Lordship's conversation, cannot be supposed to think very meanly of that which he would prefer to your perusal: yet it were to incur the imputation of too much sufficiency, to pretend to such a merit as might abide the test of your Lordship's censure.

Whatever value may be wanting to this play while it is mine, will be sufficiently made up to it, when it is once become your Lordship's: and it is my security, that I cannot have over-rated it more by my dedication, than your Lordship will dignify it by your patronage.

That it succeeded on the stage, was almost beyond my expectation; for but little of it was prepared for that general taste which seems now to be predominant in the palates of our audience.

Those characters which are meant to be ridiculed in most of our comedies, are of fools so gross, that, in my humble opinion, they should rather disturb than divert the well-natured and reflecting part of an audience; they are rather objects of charity than contempt; and instead of moving our mirth, they ought very often to excite our compassion.

A 2   This

This reflection moved me to defign fome characters, which fhould appear ridiculous, not fo much through a natural folly (which is incorrigible, and therefore not proper for the ftage) as through an affected wit; a wit, which, at the fame time that it is affected, is alfo falfe. As there is fome difficulty in the formation of a character of this nature, fo there is fome hazard which attends the progrefs of its fuccefs upon the ftage; for many come to a play, fo over-charged with criticifm, that they very often let fly their cenfure, when, through their rafhnefs, they have miftaken their aim. This I had occafion, lately, to obferve; for this play had been acted two or three days, before fome of thefe hafty judges could find the leifure to diftinguifh betwixt the character of a Witwoud and a Truewit.

I muft beg your Lordfhip's pardon for this digreffion from the true courfe of this epiftle; but that it may not feem altogether impertinent, I beg that I may plead the occafion of it, in part of that excufe of which I ftand in need, for recommending this comedy to your protection. It is only by the countenance of your Lordfhip, and the few fo qualified, that fuch who write with care and pains can hope to be diftinguifhed: for the proftituted name of poet, promifcuoufly levels all that bear it.

Terence, the moft correct writer in the world, had a Scipio and a Lelius, if not to affift him, at leaft to fupport him in his reputation: and, notwithftanding his extraordinary merit, it may be, their countenance was not more than neceffary.

The purity of his ftile, the delicacy of his turns, and the juftnefs of his characters, were all of them beauties, which the greater part of his audience were incapable of tafting. Some of the coarfeft ftrokes of Plautus, fo feverely cenfured by Horace, were more likely to affect the multitude; fuch who come with expectation to laugh at the laft act of a play, and are better entertained with two or three unfeafonable jefts, than with the artful folution of the fable.

As Terence excelled in his performances, fo had he great advantages to encourage his undertakings; for he built moft on the foundations of Menander: his plots were generally modelled, and his characters ready drawn to his hand. He copied Menander; and Menander had

no

no lefs light in the formation of his characters, from the obfervations of Theophraſtus, of whom he was a difciple; and Theophraſtus, it is known, was not only the difciple, but the immediate fucceffor of Ariſtotle, the firſt and greateſt judge of poetry. Thefe were great models to defign by; and the further advantage which Terence poffeffed, towards giving his plays the due ornaments of purity of ſtile, and juſtnefs of manners, was not lefs confiderable, from the freedom of converfation which was permitted him with Lelius and Scipio, two of the greateſt and moſt polite men of his age. And, indeed, the privilege of fuch a converfation, is the only certain means of attaining to the perfection of dialogue.

If it has happened in any part of this comedy, that I have gained a turn of ſtile, or expreſſion more correct, or at leaſt more corrigible, than in thofe which I have formerly written, I muſt, with equal pride and gratitude, afcribe it to the honour of your Lordſhip's admitting me into your converfation, and that of a fociety where every body elfe was fo well worthy of you, in your retirement, laſt fummer, from the town; for it was immediately after that this comedy was written. If I have failed in my performance, it is only to be regretted, where there were fo many, not inferior either to a Scipio or a Lelius, that that there ſhould be one wanting equal in capacity to a Terence.

If I am not miſtaken, poetry is almoſt the only art which has not yet laid claim to your Lordſhip's patronage. Architecture and painting, to the great honour of our country, have flouriſhed under your influence and protection. In the mean time, Poetry, the eldeſt fiſter of all arts, and parent of moſt, feems to have refigned her birthright, by having neglected to pay her duty to your Lordſhip; and by permitting others of a later extraction to prepoffefs that place in your eſteem, to which none can pretend a better title. Poetry, in its nature, is facred to the good and great; the relation between them is reciprocal, and they are ever propitious to it. It is the privilege of poetry to addrefs to them, and it is their prerogative alone to give it protection.

This received maxim is a general apology for all writers who confecrate their labours to great men: but I

could

could wifh, at this time, that this addrefs were exempted from the common pretence of all dedications; and as I can diftinguifh your Lordfhip even among the moft deferving, fo this offering might become remarkable by fome particular inftance of refpect, which fhould affure your Lordfhip, that I am, with all due fenfe of your extreme worthinefs and humanity,

My Lord,

Your Lordfhip's moft obedient,

And moft obliged humble fervant,

WILLIAM CONGREVE.

T O

Mr. *C O N G R E V E*;

OCCASIONED BY HIS

C   O   M   E   D   Y,

CALLED THE

WAY   OF   THE   WORLD.

WHEN pleasure's falling to the low delight,
    In vain the joys of the uncertain fight;
No fense of wit when rude fpectators know,
But in diftorted gefture, farce and fhow:
How could, great author, your afpiring mind
Dare to write only to the few refin'd;
Yet tho' that nice ambition you purfue,
'Tis not in Congreve's power to pleafe but few.
Implicitly devoted to his fame,
Well-drefs'd barbarians know his awful name;
Tho' fenfelefs they're of mirth, but when they laugh,
As they feel wine, but when till drunk, they quaff.
    On you, from fate, a lavifh portion fell,
In ev'ry way of writing to excel.
Your mufe applaufe to Arabella brings,
In notes as fweet as Arabella fings.
Whene'er you draw an undiffembled woe,
With fweet diftrefs your rural numbers flow.
Paftora's the complaint of ev'ry fwain,
Paftora ftill the echo of the plain!
Or if your mufe defcribe, with warming force,
The wounded Frenchman falling from his horfe;

And

And her own William glorious in the ſtrife,
Beſtowing on the proſtrate foe his life :
You the great aĉt as gen'rouſly rehearſe,
And all the Engliſh fury's in your verſe.
By your ſeleĉted ſcenes, and handſome choice,
Ennobled Comedy exalts her voice ;
You check unjuſt eſteem, and fond deſire,
And teach to ſcorn what elſe we ſhould admire ;
The juſt impreſſion taught by you we bear.
The player aĉts the world, the world the play'r ;
Whom ſtill that world unjuſtly diſeſteems,
Tho' he, alone, profeſſes what he ſeems :
But when your muſe aſſumes her tragic part,
She conquers and ſhe reigns in ev'ry heart ;
To mourn with her men cheat their private woe,
And gen'rous pity's all the grief they know.
The widow, who impatient of delay,
From the town-joys muſt maſk it to the play,
Joins with your Mourning Bride's refiſtleſs moan,
And weeps a loſs ſhe ſlighted, when her own.
You give us torment, and you give us eaſe,
And vary our affliĉtions as you pleaſe.
Is not a heart ſo kind as yours in pain,
To load your friends with cares you only feign ;
Your friends in grief, compos'd yourſelf, to leave ?
But 'tis the only way you'll e'er deceive.
Then ſtill, great Sir, your moving pow'r employ,
To lull our ſorrow, and correĉt our joy.

R. STEELE.

PROLOGUE.

OF those few fools who with ill stars are curst,
   Sure scribbling fools, call'd poets, fare the worst ;
For they're a set of fools which Fortune makes,
And after she has made them fools, forsakes.
With Nature's oafs 'tis quite a diff'rent case,
For Fortune favours all her ideot-race ;
In her own nest the cuckoo-eggs we find,
O'er which she broods to hatch the changeling-kind.
No portion for her own she has to spare,
So much she doats on her adopted care.

   Poets are bubbles, by the town drawn in,
Suffer'd at first some trifling stakes to win :
But what unequal hazards do they run !
Each time they write, they venture all they've won :
The 'squire that's butter'd still, is sure to be undone.
This author, heretofore, has found your favour ;
But pleads no merit from his past behaviour.
To build on that might prove a vain presumption,
Should grants, to poets made, admit resumption :
And in Parnassus he must lose his seat,
If that be found a forfeited estate.

   He owns with toil he wrought the following scenes ;
But if they're naught, ne'er spare him for his pains :
Damn him the more ; have no commiseration
For dulness on mature deliberation.
He swears he'll not resent one hiss'd-off scene,
Nor, like those peevish wits, his play maintain,
Who, to assert their sense, your taste arraign.
Some plot we think he has, and some new thought ;
Some humour too, no farce ; but that's a fault.
Satire, he thinks, you ought not to expect ;
For so reform'd a town, who dares correct ?
To please, this time, has been his sole pretence ;
He'll not instruct, lest it should give offence.
Should he, by chance, a knave or fool expose,
That hurts none here—sure here are none of those.
In short, our play shall (with your leave to shew it)
Give you one instance of a passive poet,
Who to your judgments yields all resignation,
To save or damn, after your own discretion.

                           DRA.

DRAMATIS PERSONÆ.

M E N.

	Drury-Lane.	*Covent-Garden.*
Fainall, in love with Mrs. *Marwood*,	Mr. Reddifh.	Mr. Wroughton.
Mirabell, in love with Mrs. *Millamant*,	Mr. Smith.	Mr. Lewis.
Witwoud, { follow- } ers of { *Petulant*, } Mill.	Mr. King. Mr. Baddeley.	Mr. Lee Lewes. Mr. Woodward.
Sir Wilful Witwoud, halfbrother to *Witwoud*, and nephew to Lady *Wishfort*.	Mr. Yates.	Mr. Dunftall.
Waitwell, fervant to *Mirabell*,	Mr. Parfons.	Mr. Wilfon.

W O M E N.

Lady *Wishfort*, enemy to *Mirabell*, for having falfely pretended love to her,	Mrs. Hopkins.	Mrs. Pitt.
Mrs. *Millamant*, a fine lady, niece to Lady *Wishfort*, and loves *Mirabell*,	Mrs. Abington.	Mrs. Barry.
Mrs. *Marwood*, friend to Mr. *Fainall*, and likes *Mirabell*.	Mifs Sherry.	Mrs. Mattocks.
Mrs. *Fainall*, daughter to Lady *Wishfort*, and wife to *Fainall*,	Mrs. Greville.	Mrs. Whitefield.
Foible, woman to Lady *Wishfort*,	Mifs Pope.	Mrs. Green.
Mincing, woman to Mrs *Millamant*,	Mifs Platt.	Mrs. Pouffin.

Dancers, Footmen, and Attendants.

S C E N E, *L O N D O N.*

The Time equal to that of the Prefentation.

T H E

T H E

WAY OF THE WORLD.

⁎ *The lines distinguished by inverted comas, ‘ thus,’ are omitted in the Representation, and those printed in Italics are the additions of the Theatre.*

A C T   I.

SCENE I. *A Chocolate-house.*

Mirabell *and* Fainall [*rising from cards*] Betty *waiting.*

MIRABELL.

YOU are a fortunate man, Mr. Fainall.

Fain. Have we done?

Mira. What you please. I'll play on to entertain you.

Fain. No, I'll give you your revenge another time, when you are not so indfferent; you are thinking of something else now, and play too negligently; the coldness of a losing gamester, lessens the pleasure of the winner. I'd no more play with a man that slighted his ill fortune, than I'd make love to a woman who undervalued the loss of her reputation.

Mira. You have a taste extremely delicate, and are for refining your pleasures.

Fain. Pr'ythee, why so reserv'd? Something has put you out of humour.

Mira. Not at all: I happen to be grave to-day; and you are gay; that's all.

Fain. Confess, Millamant and you quarrell'd last night, after I left you; my fair cousin has some humours that would tempt the patience of a stoick. What, some coxcomb came in, and was well received by her, while you were by.

Mira. Witwoud and Petulant: and what was worse,

2   her

her aunt, your wife's mother, my evil genius; or to
fum up all in her own name, my old lady Wifhfort came
in.——

Fain. O there it is then——She has a lafting paffion
for you, and with reafon——What, then my wife was
there?

Mira. Yes, and Mrs. Marwood, and three or four
more, whom I never faw before; feeing me, they all
put on their grave faces, whifper'd one another; then
complain'd aloud of the vapours, and after fell into a profound filence.

Fain. They had a mind to be rid of you.

Mira. For which reafon I refolv'd not to ftir. At laft
the good old lady broke through her painful taciturnity,
with an invective againft long vifits. I would not have
underftood her, but Millamant joining in the argument,
I rofe, and with a conftrained fmile told her, I thought
nothing was fo eafy as to know when a vifit began to be
troublefome; fhe reddened and I withdrew, without ex-
pecting her reply.

Fain. You were to blame to refent what fhe fpoke only in compliance with her aunt.

Mira. She is more miftrefs of herfelf than to be under
the neceffity of fuch refignation.

Fain. What! tho' half her fortune depends upon her
marrying with my lady's approbation?

Mira. I was then in fuch a humour, that I fhould
have been better pleafed if fhe had been lefs difcreet.

Fain. Now I remember, I wonder not they were
weary of you; laft night was one of their cabal nights;
they have them three times a week, and meet by turns,
at one another's apartments, where they come together
like the coroner's inqueft, to fit upon the murder'd reputations of the week. You and I are excluded; and it was
once propofed that all the male fex fhould be excepted;
but fomebody moved, that to avoid fcandal, there might
be one man of the community; upon which motion Witwood and Petulant were enrolled members.

Mira. And who may have been the foundrefs of this
fect? My Lady Wifhfort, I warrant, who publifhes her
deteftation of mankind; and full of the vigour of fifty-
five,

five, declares for a friend and ratafia ; and let poſterity ſhift for itſelf, ſhe'll breed no more.

Fain. The diſcovery of your ſham addreſſes to her, to conceal you love to her niece, has provoked this ſeparation : had you diſſembled better, things might have continued in the ſtate of nature.

Mira. I did as much as man could, with any reaſonable conſcience ; I proceeded to the very laſt act of flattery with her, and was guilty of a ſong in her commendation.   Nay, I got a friend to put her into a lampoon, and compliment her with the imputation of an affair with a young fellow, which I carried ſo far, that I told her the malicious town took notice that ſhe was grown fat of a ſudden ; and when ſhe lay in of a dropſy, perſuaded her ſhe was reported to be in labour.   The devil's in't if an old woman is to be flattered farther, unleſs a man ſhould endeavour downright perſonally to debauch her ; and that my virtue forbade me.   But for the diſcovery of this amour, I am indebted to your friend, or your wife's friend, Mrs. Marwood.

Fain. What ſhould provoke her to be your enemy, unleſs ſhe has made you advances which you have ſlighted ? Women do not eaſily forgive omiſſions of that nature.

Mira. She was always civil to me, till of late ; I confeſs I am not one of thoſe coxcombs who are apt to interpret a woman's good manners to her prejudice ; and think that ſhe who does not refuſe 'em ev'ry thing, can refuſe 'em nothing.

Fain. You are a gallant man, Mirabell ; and tho' you may have cruelty enough not to ſatisfy a lady's longing ; you have too much generoſity, not to be tender of her honour.   Yet you ſpeak with an indifference which ſeems to be affected ; and confeſſes you are conſcious of a negligence.

Mira. You purſue the argument with a diſtruſt that ſeems to be unaffected, and confeſs you are conſcious of a concern for which the lady is more indebted to you, than is your wife.

Fain. Fy, fy, friend, if you grow cenſorious, I muſt leave you——I'll look upon the gameſters in the next room.

Mira. Who are they ?

B

Fain.

Fain. Petulant and Witwood—Bring me fome chocolate.   [*Exit.*

Mira. Betty, what fays our clock?

Bet. Turn'd of the laft canonical hour, Sir.

Mira. How pertinently the jade anfwers me! Ha!
almoft one o'clock! [*Looking on his watch*] Oh, y'are
come——

Enter Footman.

Mira. Well; is the grand affair over? You have been
fomething tedious.

Serv. Sir, there's fuch coupling at Pancras, that they
ftand behind one another, as 'twere in a country dance.
Ours was the laft couple to lead up; and no hopes ap-
pearing of difpatch, befides, the parfon growing hoarfe,
we were afraid his lungs would have failed before it came
to our turn; fo we drove round to Duke's Place; and
there they were rivetted in a trice.

Mira. So, fo, you are fure they are married.

Serv. Married and bedded, Sir: I am witnefs.

Mira. Have you the certificate?

Serv. Here it is, Sir.

' *Mira.* Has the Taylor brought Waitwell's clothes
' home, and the new liveries?

' *Serv.* Yes, Sir.'

Mira That's well. Do you go home again, d'ye hear,
and adjourn the confummation 'till farther order; bid
Waitwell fhake his ears, and dame Partlet ruftle up her
feathers, and meet me at one o'clock by Rofamond's
pond; that I may fee her before fhe returns to her lady:
and, as you tender your ears, be fecret.   [*Exit* Footman.

Enter Fainall,

Fain. Joy of your fuccefs, Mirabell; you look pleas'd.

Mira. Ay; I have been engaged in a matter of fome
fort of mirth, which is not yet ripe for difcovery. I am
glad this is not a cabal-night. I wonder, Fainall, that
you who are married, and of confequence fhould be difcreet, will fuffer your wife to be of fuch a party.

Fain. Faith, I am not jealous. Befides, moft who are
engaged, are women and relations; and for the men,
they are of a kind too contemptible to give fcandal.

Mira. I am of another opinion. The greater the coxcomb, always the more the fcandal: for a woman who is not
a fool,

a fool, can have but one reason for affociating with a man who is one.

Fain. Are you jealous as often as you fee Witwoud entertained by Millamant ?

Mira. Of her underftanding I am, if not of her perfon.

Fain. You do her wrong; for to give her her due, fhe has wit.

Mira. She has beauty enough to make any man think fo ; and complaifarce enough not to contradict him who fhall tell her fo.

Fain. For a paffionate lover, methinks you are a man fomewhat too difcerning in the failings of your miftrefs.

Mira. And for a difcerning man, fomewhat too paffionate a lover ; for I like her with all her faults ; nay like her for her faults. Her follies are fo natural, or fo artful, that they become her ; and thofe affectations which in another woman would be odious, ferve but to make her more agreeable. I'll tell thee, Fainall, fhe once ufed me with that infolence, that in revenge I took her to pieces ; fifted her, and feparated her failings ; ' I ftudied 'em and ' got 'em by rote. The catalogue was fo large, that I ' was not without hopes, one day or other, to hate her ' heartily : to which end I fo ufed myfelf to think of 'em, ' that at length, contrary to my defign and expectation, ' they gave me every hour lefs and lefs difturbance; 'till ' in a few days it became habitual to me, to remember ' 'em without being difpleas'd.' They are now grown as familiar to me as my own frailties ; and in all probability in a little time longer, I fhall like 'em as well.

Fain. Marry her, marry her ; be half as well acquainted with her charms, as you are with her defects, and my life on't you are your own man again.

Mira. Say you fo ?

Fain. I, I, I have experience ; I have a wife, and fo forth.

Enter a Meffenger.

Meff. Is one fquire Witwoud here ?

Bet. Yes ; what's your bufinefs ?

Meff. I have a letter for him, from his brother Sir Wilful, which I am charged to deliver into his own hands.

Bet. He's in the next room, friend——That way.

[*Exit* Meffenger.

Mira.

Mira. What, is the chief of that noble family in town, Sir Wilful Witwoud ?

Fain. He is expected to-day. Do you know him ?

Mira. I have feen him, he promifes to be an extraordinary perfon; I think you have the honour to be related to him.

Fain. Yes ; he is half brother to this Witwoud by a former wife, who was fifter to my Lady Wifhfort, my wife's mother. If you marry Millamant, you muft call coufins too.

Mira. I had rather be his relation than his acquaintance.

Fain. He comes to town in order to equip himfelf for travel.

Mira. For travel ! Why the man that I mean is above forty.

Fain. No matter for that ; 'tis for the honour of England, that all Europe fhould know we have blockheads of all ages.

Mira. I wonder there is not an act of parliament to fave the credit of the nation, and prohibit the exportation of fools.

Fain. By no means, 'tis better as 'tis; 'tis better to trade with a little lofs, than to be quite eaten up with being overftocked.

Mira. Pray, are the follies of this knight-errant, and thofe of the fquire his brother, any thing related ?

Fain. Not at all ; Witwoud grows by the knight, like a medlar grafted on a crab. One will melt in your mouth, and t'other fet your teeth on edge; one is all pulp, and the other all core.

' *Mira.* So one will be rotten before he be ripe, and ' the other will be rotten without ever being ripe at all.'

Fain. Sir Wilful is an odd mixture of bafhfulnefs and obftinacy.—But when he's drunk, he's as loving as the monfter in the Tempeft; and much after the fame manner. To give t'other his due, he has fomething of good-nature, and does not always want wit.

Mira. Not always ; but as often as his memory fails him, and his common-place of comparifuns. He is a fool with a good memory, and fome few fcraps of other
folk's

folk's wit. He is one, whofe converfation can never be approved, yet it is now and then to endured. He has indeed one good quality, he is not exceptious; ' for he ' fo paffionately affects the reputation of underftanding ' raillery, that he will conftrue an affront into a jeft; and ' call downright rudenefs and ill language, fatire and ' fire.'

Fain. If you have a mind to finifh his picture, you have an opportunity to do it at full length. Behold the original.

Enter Witwoud.

Wit. Afford me your compaffion, my dears; pity me, Fainall; Mirabell, pity me.

Mira. I do from my foul.

Fain. Why, what's the matter?

Wit. No letters for me, Betty?

Bet. Did not a meffenger bring you one but now, Sir?

Wit. Ay, but no other?

Bet. No, Sir.

Wit. That's hard, that's very hard——A meffenger, a mule, a beaft of burden, he has brought me a letter from the fool my brother, as heavy as a panegyric in a funeral fermon, or a copy of commendatory verfes from one poet to another; and what's worfe, 'tis as fure a forerunner of the author, as an epiftle dedicatory.

Mira. A fool, and your brother, Witwoud!

Wit. Ay, ay, my half brother, my half brother; he is no nearer, upon honour.

Mira. Then 'tis poffible he may be but half a foul.

Wit. Good, good, Mirabell, *le drole!* Good, good; hang him, don't let's talk of him.—Fainall, how does your lady? Gad, I fay any thing in the world to get this fellow out of my head. I beg pardon that I fhould afk a man of pleafure, and the town, a queftion at once fo foreign and domeftic. But I talk like an old maid at a marriage; I don't know what I fay: but fhe's the beft woman in the world.

Fain. 'Tis well you don't know what you fay, or elfe your commendation would go near to make me either vain or jealous.

Wit. No man in town lives well with a wife but Fainall. Your judgment, Mirabell?

Mira.

Mira. You had better ftep and afk his wife, if you would be credibly informed.

Wit. Mirabell.

Mira. Ay.

Wit. My dear, I afk ten thoufand pardons :——Gad I have forgot what I was going to fay to you.

Mir. I thank you heartily, heartily.

Wit. No, but pr'ythee excufe me,—my memory is fuch a memory.

Mira. Have a care of fuch apologies, Witwoud ;— for I never knew a fool but he affected to complain, either of the fpleen or his memory.

Fain. What have you done with Petulant ?

Wit. He's reckoning his money,—my money it was ——I have no luck to-day.

Fain. You may allow him to win of you at play ;— for you are fure to be too hard for him at repartee : fince you monopolize the wit that is between you, the fortune muft be his of courfe.

Mira. I don't find that Petulant confeffes the fuperiority of wit to be your talent, Witwoud.

Wit. Come, come, you are malicious now, and would breed debates——Petulant's my friend, and a very ho-neft fellow, and a very pretty fellow, and has a fmatter-ing——Faith and troth, a pretty deal of an odd fort of a fmall wit : nay, I'll do him juftice. I'm his friend, I won't wrong him——And if he had any judgment in the world,—he would not be altogether contemptible. Come, come, don't detract from the merits of my friend.

Fain. You don't take your friend to be over-nicely bred.

Wit. No, no, hang him, the rogue has no manners at all, that I muft own——No more breeding than a bum-baily, that I grant you——'Tis pity ; the fellow has fire and life.

Mira. What, courage ?

Wit. Hum, faith I don't know as to that,—I can't fay as to that——Yes, faith, in controverfy, he'll contradict any body.

Mira. Though 'twere a man whom he feared, or a wo-man whom he loved.

Wit. Well, well, he does not always think before he fpeaks ;—we have all our failings : you are too hard upon him,

4

him, you are faith. Let me excuse him,——I can defend moſt of his faults, except one or two : one he has, that's the truth on't; if he were my brother, I could not acquit him—That indeed I could wiſh were otherwiſe.

Mira. Ay, marry ; what's that, Witwoud ?

Wit. Oh, pardon me——Expoſe the infirmities of my friend.—No, my dear, excuſe me there.

† *Fain.* What I warrant he's inſincere, or 'tis ſome ſuch trifle.

Wit. No, no, what if he be ? 'Tis no matter for that, his wit will excuſe that : a wit ſhould no more be ſincere, than a woman conſtant; one argues a decay of parts, as t'other of beauty.

Mira. May be you think him too poſitive ?

Wit. No, no, his being poſitive is an incentive to argument, and keeps up converſation.

Fain. Too illiterate.

Wit. That, that's his happineſs—His want of learning gives him the more opportunity to ſhew his natural parts.

Mira. He wants words.

Wit. Ay ; but I like him for that now ; for his want of words gives me the pleaſure very often to explain his meaning.

Fain. He's impudent.

Wit. No, that's not it.

Mira. Vain.

Wit. No.

Mira. What, he ſpeaks unſeaſonable truths ſometimes, becauſe he has not wit enough to invent an evaſion.

Wit. Truths ! Ha, ha, ha ! No, no ; ſince you will have it—I mean, he never ſpeaks truth at all—that's all. He will lie like a chamberbaid, or a woman of quality's porter. Now that is a fault.

Enter Coachman.

Coach. Is maſter Petulant here, miſtreſs ?

Bet. Yes.

Coach. Three gentlewomen in a coach would ſpeak with him.

Fain. Oh, brave Petulant ! Three !

Bet. I'll tell him.   [*Exit.*

' *Coach.* You muſt bring two diſhes of chocolate and
' a glaſs of cinnamon-water.   [*Exit.*

' *Wit.* That ſhould be fur two faſting ſtrumpets, and a
' bawd troubled with wind.   Now you may know what
' the three are.

' *Mira.* You are very free with your friend's acquaint-
' ance.

Wit. ' Ay, ay, friendſhip without freedom is as dull as
' love without enjoyment, or wine without toaſting ;
' but to tell you a ſecret,' theſe are trulls whom he allows coach hire, and ſomething more, by the week, to
call on him once a day at public places.

Mira. How !

Wit. You ſhall ſee he won't go to 'em, becauſe there's
no more company here to take notice of him.——Why
this is nothing to what he uſed to do :—before he found
out this way, I have known him call for himſelf——

Fain. Call for himſelf ! What doſt thou mean ?

Wit. Mean ! why he would ſlip you out of this cho-
colate-houſe, juſt when you had been talking to him—
As ſoon as your back was turned—whip he was gone ;
—then trip to his lodging, clap on a hood and ſcarf, and
a maſk, flap into a hackney-coach, and drive hither to
the door again in a trice ; where he would ſend in for
himſelf; that is, I mean, call for himſelf, wait for
himſelf; nay, and what's more, not finding himſelf,
ſometimes leave a letter for himſelf.

Mira. I confeſs this is ſomething extraordinary——I
believe he waits for himſelf now, he is ſo long a coming :
Oh, I aſk his pardon.

Enter Betty.

Bet. Sir, the coach ſtays.

Enter Petulant.

Pet. Well, well ; I come ;—'Sbud, a man had as good
be a profeſſed midwife, as a profeſſed whoremaſter, at
this rate ; to be knocked up, and raiſed at all hours, and
in all places.   Pox on them, I won't come—D'ye hear,
tell them I won't come——Let them ſnivel and cry their
hearts out.

Fain. You are very cruel, Petulant.

Pet. All's one, let it paſs————I have a humour to
be cruel.   *Mira.*

Mira. I hope they are not perfons of condition that you ufe at this rate.

Pet. Condition! condition's a dried fig, if I am not in humour——' By this hand, if they were your—a—a ' —your what-dee-call-'ems themfelves, they muft wait ' or rub off, if I want appetite.

' *Mira.* What-dee-call-'ems! What are they, Wit-' woud?

' *Wit.* Empreffes, my dear——By your what-dee-' call-'ems, he means Sultana queens.

' *Pet.* Ay, Roxana's.

' *Mira.* Cry your mercy.

' *Fain.* Witwoud fays they are——

' *Pet.* What does he fay they are?

' *Wit.* I! fine ladies, I fay.

' *Pet.* Pafs on, Witwoud——Harkee, by this light ' his relations—Two co-heireffes his coufins, and an old ' aunt, who loves catterwauling better than a conven-' ticle.

' *Wit.* Ha, ha, ha! I had a mind to fee how the rogue ' would come off—Ha, ha, ha! gad, I can't be angry ' with him, if he had faid they were my mother and my ' fifters.

' *Mira.* No.

' *Wit.* No; the rogue's wit and readinefs of inven-' tion charm me; dear Petulant.'

Bet. They are gone, Sir, in great anger.

Pet. Enough, let them trundle. Anger helps com-plexion, faves paint.

Fain. This continence is all diffembled; this is in or-der to have fomething to brag of the next time he makes court to Millamant, and fwear he has abandoned the whole fex for her fake.

Mira. Have you not left off your impudent pretenfion there yet? I fhall cut your throat, fome time or other, Petulant, about that bufinefs.

Pet. Ay, ay, let that pafs——There are other throats to be cut——

Mira. Meaning mine, Sir?

Pet. Not I—I mean nobody—I know nothing—— But there are uncles and nephews in the world—and they may be rivals—What then, all's one for that—

Mira.

Mira. Now, harkee, Petulant, come hither—Explain, or I fhall call your interpreter.

Pet. Explain ; I know nothing—— Why you have an uncle, have you not, lately come to town, and lodges by my lady Wifhfort's ?

Mira. True.

Pet. Why, that's enough—You and he are not friends ; and if he fhould marry and have a child, you may be difinherited, ha ?

Mira. Where haft thou ftumbled upon all this truth ?

Pet. All's one for that ; why then fay I know fomething.

Mira. Come, thou art an honeft fellow, Petulant, and fhalt make love to my miftrefs, thou fha't, faith. What haft thou heard of my uncle ?

Pet. I ! nothing I. If throats are to be cut, let fwords clafh ; fnug's the word, I fhrug and am filent.

Mira. Oh, raillery, raillery. Come, I know thou art in the women's fecrets—— What, you're a cabalift ; I know you flaid at Millamant's laft night, after I went. Was there any mention made of my uncle, or me ? Tell me. If thou hadft but good-nature equal to thy wit, Petulant, Tony Witwoud, who is now thy competitor in fame, would fhew as dim by thee as a dead whiting's eye by a pearl of orient ; he would no more be feen by thee, than Mercury is by the fun. Come, I'm fure thou wo't tell me.

Pet. If I do, will you grant me common fenfe then, for the future ?

Mira. Faith, I'll do what I can for thee, and I'll pray that Heaven may grant it thee in the mean time.

Pet. Well, harkee.

Fain. Petulant and you both will find Mirabell as warm a rival as a lover.

Wit. Pfha, pfha, that fhe laughs at Petulant is plain. And for my part—But that it is almoft a fafhion to admire her, I fhould—Harkee—To tell you a fecret, but let it go no farther—Between friends, I fhall never break my heart for her.

Fain. How !

Wit. She's handfome ; but fhe's a fort of an uncertain woman.

Fain.

Fain. I thought you had died for her.

Wit. Umph N——

Fain. She ha

Wit. 'Tis what she will hardly allow any body elfe—Now, demme, I fhould hate that, if fhe were as handfome as Cleopatra. Mirabell is not fo fure of her as he thinks for.

Fain. Why do you think fo?

Wit. We ftaid pretty late there laft night ; and heard fomething of an uncle to Mirabell, who is lately come to town,—and is between him and the beft part of his eftate ; Mirabell and he are at fome diftance, as my lady Wifhfort has been told ; and you know fhe hates Mirabell worfe than a Quaker hates a parrot, or than a fifh-monger hates a hard froft. Whether this uncle has feen Mrs. Millamant or not, I cannot fay ; but there were items of fuch a treaty being in embryo ; and if it fhould come to life, poor Mirabell would be in fome fort unfortunately fobbed, i'faith.

Fain. 'Tis impoffible Millamant fhould hearken to it.

Wit. Faith, my dear, I can't tell; fhe's a woman, and a kind of a humourift.

Mira. And this is the fum of what you could colleᵭ laft night.

Pet. The quinteffence. May be Witwoud knows more, he ftayed longer——Befides, they never mind him ; they fay any thing before him.

Mira. I thought you had been the greateft favourite.

Pet. Ay, *tête-à-tête* ; but not in public, becaufe I make remarks.

Mira. You do?

Pet. Ay, ay ; pox, I'm malicious, man. Now he's foft, you know ; they are not in awe of him——The fellow's well bred ; he's what you call a——What-dee-call-'em, a fine gentleman : but he's filly withal.

Mira. I thank you, I know as much as my curiofity requires. Fainall, are you for the Mall?

Fain. Ay, I'll take a turn before dinner.

Wit. Ay, we'll all walk in the park ; the ladies talked of being there.

Mira. I thought you were obliged to watch for your brother, Sir Willful's arrival.

Wit.

Wit. No, no; he comes to his aunt's, my lady Wish-fort: pox on him, I shall be troubled with him too; what shall I do with the fool?

Pet. Beg him for his estate, that I may beg you after-wards; and so have but one trouble with you both.

Wit. Oh, rare Petulant; thou art as quick as fire in a frosty morning; thou shalt to the Mall with us, and we'll be very severe.

Pet. Enough, I'm in a humour to be severe.

Mira. Are you? Pray then walk by yourselves—Let not us be accessary to your putting the ladies out of coun-tenance with your senseless ribaldry, which you roar out aloud as often as they pass by you; and when you have made a handsome woman blush, then you think you have been severe.

Pet. What, what? Then let them either shew their innocence by not understanding what they hear, or else shew their discretion by not hearing what they would not be thought to understand.

Mira. But hast not thou then sense enough to know that thou oughtest to be most ashamed thyself, when thou hast put another out of countenance?

Pet. Not I, by this hand ——— I always take blush-ing either for a sign of guilt or ill breeding.

Mira. I confess you ought to think so. You are in the right, that you may plead the error of your judg-ment in defence of your practice.

> Where modesty's ill-manners, 'tis but fit
> That impudence and malice pass for wit.

END of the FIRST ACT.

ACT II.

SCENE, St. James's Park.

Mrs. Fainall and Mrs. Marwood.

Mrs. FAINALL.

AY, ay, dear Marwood, if we will be happy, we must find the means in ourselves, and among ourselves. Men are ever in extremes; either doating, or averse. While they are lovers, if they have fire and sense, their

jealousies

jealoufies are infupportable : and when they ceafe to love
(we ought to think at leaft) they loathe ; they look upon
us with horror and diftafte ; they meet us like the ghofts
of what we were, and as from fuch, fly from us.

Mrs. Mar. True, 'tis an unhappy circumftance of life,
that love fhould ever die before us ; and that the man fo
often fhould outlive the lover.   But fay what you will,
'tis better to be left than never to have been lov'd.   To
pafs our youth in dull indifference, to refufe the fweets
of life, becaufe they once muft leave us, is as prepofte-
rous, as to wifh to have been born old, becaufe we one
day muft be old.   For my part, my youth may wear and
wafte, but it fhall never ruft in my poffeffion.

Mrs. Fain. Then it feems you diffemble an averfion to
mankind, only in compliance to my mother's humour.

Mrs. Mar. Certainly.   To be free ; I have no tafte of
thofe infipid dry difcourfes, with which our fex of force
muft entertain themfelves, apart from men.   We may
affect endearments to each other, profefs eternal friendfhips, and feem to doat like lovers ; but 'tis not in our
natures long to perfevere.   Love will refume his empire
in our breafts, and every heart, or foon or late, receive
and re-admit him as its lawful tyrant.

Mrs. Fain. Blefs me, how have I been deceived !
Why you profefs a libertine.

Mrs. Mar. You fee my friendfhip by my freedom.
Come, be as fincere, acknowledge that your fentiments
agree with mine.

Mrs. Fain. Never.

Mrs. Mar. You hate mankind ?

Mrs. Fain. Heartily, inveterately.

Mrs. Mar. Your hufband ?

Mrs. Fain. Moft tranfcendently ; ay, though I fay it,
meritorioufly.

Mrs. Mar. Give me your hand upon it.

Mrs. Fain. There.

Mrs. Mar. I join with you ; what I have faid has been
to try you.

Mrs. Fain. Is it poffible ? Doft thou hate thofe vipers,
men ?

Mrs. Mar. I have done hating 'em, and am now come

C   to

to defpife 'em; the next thing I have to do, is eternally
to forget 'em.

Mrs. Fain. There fpoke the fpirit of an Amazon, a
Penthefilea.

Mrs. Mar. And yet I am thinking fometimes to carry
my averfion farther.

Mrs. Fain. How?

Mrs. Mar. Faith, by marrying; ' if I could but find
' one that loved me very well, and would be thoroughly
' fenfible of ill ufage, I think I fhould do myfelf the
' violence of undergoing the ceremony.

' *Mrs. Fain.* You would not make him a cuckold?

' *Mrs. Mar.* No; but I'd make him believe I did, and
' that's as bad.

' *Mrs. Fain.* Why had you not as good do it?

' *Mrs. Mar.* Oh, if he fhould ever difcover it, he
' would then know the worft, and be out of his pain;
' but I would have him ever to continue upon the rack of
' fear and jealoufy.

' *Mrs. Fain.* Ingenious mifchief!' Would thou wert
married to Mirabell.

Mrs. Mar. Would I were.

Mrs. Fain. You change colour.

Mrs. Mar. Becaufe I hate him.

Mrs. Fain. So do I; but I can hear him named. But
what reafon have you to hate him in particular?

Mrs. Mar. I never loved him; he is, and always was,
infufferably proud.

Mrs. Fain. By the reafon you give for your averfion,
one would think it diffembled; for you have laid a fault
to his charge, of which his enemies muft acquit him.

Mrs. Mar. Oh, then it feems you are one of his favourable enemies. Methinks you look a little pale, and now
you flufh again.

Mrs. Fain. Do I? I think I am a little fick o' the fudden.

Mrs. Mar. What ails you?

Mrs. Fain. My hufband. Don't you fee him? He
turned fhort upon me unawares, and has almoft overcome
me.

Enter Fainall *and* Mirabell.

Mrs. Mar. Ha, ha, ha! he comes opportunely for you.

Mrs.

Mrs. Fain. For you, for he has brought Mirabell with him.

Fain. My dear.

Mrs. Fain. My foul.

Fain. You don't look well to-day, child.

Mrs. Fain. D'ye think fo ?

Mira. He's the only man that does, Madam.

Mrs. Fain. The only man that would tell me fo at leaft ; and the only man from whom I could hear it without mortification.

Fain. Oh, my dear, I am fatisfied of your tendernefs : I know you cannot refent any thing from me ; efpecially what is an effect of my concern.

Mrs. Fain. Mr. Mirabell, my mother interrupted you in a pleafant relation laft night, I would fain hear it out.

Mira. The perfons concerned in that affair, have yet a tolerable reputation.——I am afraid Mr. Fainall will be cenforious.

Mrs. Fain. He has a humour more prevailing than his curiofity, and will willingly difpenfe with the hearing of one fcandalous ftory, to avoid giving an occafion to make another, by being feen to walk with his wife. This way, Mr. Mirabell, and I dare promife you will oblige us both.　　　　　　[*Exeunt* Mira. *and Mrs.* Fain.

Fain. Excellent creature ! Well, fure if I fhould live to be rid of my wife, I fhould be a miferable man.

Mrs. Mar. Ay ?

Fain. For having only that one hope, the accomplifhment of it, of confequence, muft put an end to all my hopes ; and what a wretch is he who muft furvive his hopes ! Nothing remains, when that day comes, but to fit down and weep like Alexander, when he wanted other worlds to conquer.

Mrs. Mar. Will you not follow them.

Fain. Faith, I think not.

Mrs. Mar. Pray let us ; I have a reafon.

Fain. You are not jealous ?

Mrs. Mar. Of whom ?

Fain. Of Mirabell.

Mrs. Mar. If I am, is it inconfiftent with my love to you, that I am tender of your honour ?

　　　　　　　　　　　　　Fain.

Fain. You would intimate then, as if there were a fellow-feeling between my wife and him.

Mrs. Mar. I think she does not hate him to that degree she would be thought.

Fain. But he, I fear, is too infenfible.

Mrs. Mar. It may be you are deceived.

Fain. It may be fo. I do not now begin to apprehend it.

Mrs. Mar. What?

Fain. That I have been deceived, Madam, and you are falfe.

Mrs. Mar. That I am falfe! What mean you?

Fain. To let you know, I fee through all your little arts—Come, you both love him; and both have equally diffembled your averfion. Your mutual jealoufies of one another, have made you clafh till you have both ftruck fire. I have feen the warm confeffion reddening on your cheeks, and fparkling from your eyes.

Mrs. Mar. You do me wrong.

Fain. I do not——'Twas for my eafe to overfee and wilfully neglect the grofs advances made him by my wife; that by permitting her to be engaged, I might continue unfufpected in my pleafures; and take you oftener to my arms in full fecurity. But could you think, becaufe the nodding hufband would not wake, that e'er the watchful lover flept?

Mrs. Mar. And wherewithal can you reproach me?

Fain. With infidelity, with loving another, with love of Mirabell.

Mrs. Mar. 'Tis falfe. I challenge you to fhew an inftance that can confirm your groundlefs accufation. I hate him.

Fain. And wherefore do you hate him? He is infenfible, and your refentment follows his neglect. An inftance! The injuries you have done him are a proof: your interpofing in his love. What caufe had you to make difcoveries of his pretended paffion? to undeceive the credulous aunt, and be the officious obftacle of his match with Millamant?

Mrs. Mar. My obligations to my lady urged me: I had profeffed a friendfhip to her; and could not fee her eafy nature fo abufed by that diffembler.

Fain.

Fain. What, was it confcience then? Profeffed a friendfhip! Oh, the pious friendfhips of the female fex!

Mrs. Mar. More tender, more fincere, and more enduring, than all the vain and empty vows of men, whether profeffing love to us, or mutual faith to one another.

Fain. Ha, ha, ha! you are my wife's friend too.

Mrs. Mar. Shame and ingratitude! Do you reproach me? You, you, upbraid me! Have I been falfe to her, through ftrict fidelity to you, and facrificed my friendfhip to keep my love inviolate? And have you the bafenefs to charge me with the guilt, unmindful of the merit? To you it fhould be meritorious, that I have been vicious: and do you reflect that guilt upon me, which fhould lie buried in your bofom?

Fain. You mifinterpret my reproof. I meant but to remind you of the flight account you once could make of ftricteft ties, when fet in competition with your love to me

Mrs. Mar. 'Tis falfe, you urged it with deliberate malice—' I was fpoke in fcorn, and I never will forgive it.

Fain. Your guilt, not your refentment, begets your rage. If yet you loved, you could forgive a jealoufy: but you are ftung to find you are difcovered.

Mrs. Mar. It fhall be all difcovered. You too fhall be difcovered; be fure you fhall. I can but be expofed— If I do it myfelf I fhall prevent your bafenefs.

Fain. Why, what will you do?

Mrs. Mar. Difclofe it to your wife; own what has paft between us.

Fain. Frenzy!

Mrs. Mar. By all my wrongs I'll do't——I'll publifh to the world the injuries you have done me, both in my fame and fortune: with both I trufted you, you bankrupt, in honour, as indigent of wealth.

Fain. Your fame I have preferved. Your fortune has been beftowed as the prodigality of your love would have it, in pleafures which we both have fhared. Yet, had not you been falfe, I had ere this repaid it——' Tis true—— had you permitted Mirabell with Millamant to have ftolen their marriage, my lady had been incenfed beyond all means of reconcilement: Millamant had forfeited the moiety of her fortune, which then would have defcended

to

to my wife ;———and wherefore did I marry, but to make lawful prize of a rich widow's wealth, and fquander it on love and you?

Mrs. Mar. Deceit and frivolous pretence.

Fain. Death, am I not married? What's pretence? Am I not imprifoned, fettered? Have I not a wife? Nay, a wife that was a widow, a young widow, a hand-fome widow; and would be again a widow, but that I have a heart of proof, and fomething of a conftitution to buft'e through the ways of wedlock, and this world. Will you yet be reconciled to truth and me?

Mrs. Mar. Impoffible! Truth and you are inconfiftent ———— I hate you, and fhall for ever.

Fain. For loving you?

Mrs. Mar. I loathe the name of love after fuch ufage; and next to the guilt with which you would afperfe me, I fcorn you moft. Farewel.

Fain. Nay, we muft not part thus.

Mrs. Mar. Let me go.

Fain. Come, I'm forry.

Mrs. Mar. I care not——Let me go——Break my hands, do——I'd leave them to get loofe.

Fain. I would not hurt you for the world. Have I no other hold to keep you here?

Mrs. Mar. Well, I have deferved it all.

Fain. You know I love you.

Mrs. Mar. Poor diffembling! Oh, that——Well, it is not yet————

Fain. What? What is it not? What is it not yet? It is not yet too late————

Mrs. Mar. No, it is not yet too late————I have that comfort.

Fain. It is, to love another.

Mrs. Mar. But not to loathe, deteft, abhor mankind, myfelf, and the whole treacherous world.

Fain. Nay, this is extravagance——Come, I afk your pardon——No tears——I was to blame; I could not love you, and be eafy in my doubts—Pray forbear—— I believe you; I'm convinced I've done you wrong; and any way, every way will make amends;——— I'll hate my wife yet more; damn her, I'll part with her, rob her of all fhe's worth, and we'll retire fomewhere,

any

any where, to another world—I'll marry thee—Be paci-
fied—'Sdeath, they come! hide your face, your tears—
You have a mask, wear it a moment. This way, this
way, be persuaded. [*Exeunt.*

Enter Mirabel *and Mrs.* Fainwell.

Mrs. Fain. They are here yet.

Mira. They are turning into the other walk.

Mrs. Fain. While I only hated my husband, I could
bear to see him; but since I have despised him, he's too
offensive.

Mira. Oh, you should hate with prudence.

Mrs. Fain. Yes, for I have loved with indiscretion.

Mira. You should have just so much disgust for your
husband, as may be sufficient to make you relish your
lover.

Mrs. Fain. You have been the cause that I have loved
without bounds, and would you set limits to that aversion of which you have been the occasion? Why did you
make me marry this man?

Mir. ' Why do we daily commit disagreeable and dan-
' gerous actions? To save that idol reputation. If the
' familiarities of our loves had produced that conse-
' quence, of which you were apprehensive, where could
' you have fixed a father's name with credit, but on a
' husband? I knew Fainall to be a man lavish of his mo-
' rals, an interested and professing friend, a false and a
' designing lover; yet one whose wit and outward fair
' behaviour have gained a reputation with the town,
' enough to make that woman stand excused, who has
' suffered herself to be won by his addresses. A better
' man ought not to have been sacrificed to the occasion;
' a worse had not answered to the purpose.' When you
are weary of him, you know your remedy.

Mrs. Fain. I ought to stand in some degree of credit
with you, Mirabell.

Mira. ' In justice to you,' I have made you privy to
my whole design, and put it in your power to ruin or advance my fortune.

Mrs. Fain. Whom have you instructed to represent
your pretended uncle?

Mira. Waitwell, my servant.

Mrs. Fain. He is an humble servant to Foible, my mother's woman, and may win her to your interest.

Mira.

Mira. Care is taken for that——She is won and worn by this time. They were married this morning.

Mrs. Fain. Who?

Mira. Waitwell and Foible. I would not tempt my servant to betray me, by trusting him too far. If your mother, in hopes to ruin me, should consent to marry my pretended uncle, he might, like Mosca in the Fox, stand upon terms, so I made him sure before-hand.

Mrs. Fain. So, if my poor mother is caught in a contract, you will discover the imposture betimes; and release her, by producing the certificate of her gallant's former marriage.

Mira. Yes, upon condition that she consent to my marriage with her niece, and surrender the moiety of her fortune in her possession.

Mrs. Fain. She talk'd last night of endeavouring at a match between Millamant and your uncle.

Mira. That was by Foible's direction, and my instruction, that she might seem to carry it more privately.

Mrs. Fain. Well, I have an opinion of your success; for I believe my lady will do any thing to get an husband; and when she has this, which you have provided for her, I suppose she will submit to any thing to get rid of him.

Mira. Yes, I think the good lady wou'd marry any thing that resembled a man, though 'twere no more than what a butler could pinch out of a napkin.

Mrs. Fain. Female frailty! ' We must all come to it, ' if we live to be old, and feel the craving of a false appetite, when the true is decayed.

' *Mira.* An old woman's appetite is depraved like that ' of a girl—'Tis the green-sickness of a second child-' hood; and, like the taint offer of a latter spring, serves ' but to usher in the fall; and withers in an affected ' bloom.

' *Mrs. Fain.*' But here's your mistress.

Enter Mrs. Millamant, Witwoud, *and* Mincing.

Mira. Here she comes i'faith, full sail, with her fan spread and streamers out, and a shoal of fools for tenders ——Ha, no, I cry her mercy.

Mrs. Fain. I see but one poor empty sculler; and he tows her woman after him.

Mira.

Mira. You feem to be unattended, Madam,——You us'd to have the *beau monde* throng after you ; and a flock of gay fine perukes hovering round you.

Wit. Like moths about a candle——I had like to have loft my comparifon for want of breath.

Milla. O I have deny'd myfelf airs to-day. I have walk'd as faft through the crowd——

Wit. As a favourite juft difgraced ; and with as few followers.

Milla. Dear Mr. Witwoud, truce with your fimilitudes : for I am as fick of 'em——

Wit. As a phyfician of a good air——I cannot help it, Madam, tho' 'tis againft myfelf.

Milla. Yet, again ; Mincing, ftand between me and his wit.

Wit. Do, Mrs. Mincing, like a fkreen before a great fire. I confefs I do blaze to-day, I am too bright.

Mrs. Fain. But, dear Millamant, why were you fo long ?

Milla. Long ! Lord, have I not made violent hafte ? I have afk'd ev'ry living thing I met for you ; I have enquir'd after you, as after a new fafhion.

Wit. Madam, truce with your fimilitudes————No, you met her hufband, and did not afk him for her.

Mira. By your leave, Witwoud, that were like enquiring after an old fafhion, to afk a hufband for his wife.

Wit. Hum, a hit, a hit, a palpable hit, I confefs it.

Mrs. Fain. You were dreffed before I came abroad.

Milla. Ay, that's true——O but then I had——Mincing, what had I ? Why was I fo long ?

Minc. O, Mem, your Lafhip ftaid to perufe a pacquet of letters.

Milla. O ay, letters—I had letters—I am perfecuted with letters—I hate letters—Nobody knows how to write letters ; and yet one has 'em one does not know why— They ferve one to pin up one's hair.

Wit. Is that the way ? Pray, Madam, do you pin up your hair with all your letters ? I find I muft keep copies.

Milla. Only with thofe in verfe, Mr. Witwoud. I never pin up my hair with profe. I think I try'd once, Mincing.

Minc.

Minc. O, Mem, I ſhall never forget it.

Milla. Ay, poor Mincing tift and tift all the morning.

Minc. 'Till I had the cramp in my fingers, I'll vow, Mem, and all to no purpoſe. But when your Laſhip pins it up with poetry, it fits ſo pleaſant the next day as any thing, and is ſo pure and ſo crips.

Wit. Indeed ! ſo crips ?

Minc. You're ſuch a critic, Mr. Witwoud.

Milla. Mirabell, did you take exceptions laſt night ? O ay, and went away—Now I think on't, I'm angry ?—No, now I think on't I am pleas'd—For I believe I gave you ſome pain.

Mira. Does that pleaſe you ?

Milla. Infinitely ; I love to give pain.

Mira. You would affect a cruelty which is not in your nature ; your true vanity is in the power of pleaſing.

Milla. O, I aſk your pardon for that—One's cruelty is one's power, and when one parts with one's cruelty one parts with one's power : and when one has parted with that, I fancy one's old and ugly.

Mira. Ay, ay ; ſuffer your cruelty to ruin the object of your power, to deſtroy your lover—And then how vain, how loſt a thing you'll be ? Nay, 'tis true : you are no longer handſome when you have loſt your lover ; your beauty dies upon the inſtant : for beauty is the lover's gift ; 'tis he beſtows your charms——Your glaſs is all a cheat. The ugly and the old, whom the looking-glaſs mortifies, yet after commendation can be flattered by it, and diſcover beauties in it : for that reflects our praiſes, rather than your face.

Milla. O the vanity of theſe men ! Fainall, d'ye hear him ? If they did not commend us, we were not hand-ſome ! Now you muſt know they could not commend one, if one was not handſome. Beauty the lover's gift, —Lord, what is a lover that it can give ? Why one makes lovers as faſt as one pleaſes, and they live as long as one pleaſes, and they die as ſoon as one pleaſes : and then, if one pleaſes, one makes more.

Wit. Very pretty. Why you make no more of making of lovers, Madam, than of making ſo many card-matches.

Milla.

Milla. One no more owes one's beauty to a lover, than one's wit to an echo: they can but reflect what we look and fay; vain empty things, if we are filent or unfeen, and want a being.

Mira. Yet, to thofe two vain empty things, you owe too the greateft pleafures of your life.

Milla. How fo ?

Mira. To your lover you owe the pleafure of hearing yourfelves prais'd ; and to an echo the pleafure of hearing yourfelves talk.

Wit. But I know a lady that loves talking fo inceffant-ly, fhe won't give an echo fair play ; fhe has that ever-lafting rotation of tongue, that an echo muft wait 'till fhe dies, before it can catch her laft words.

Milla. O fiction ; Fainall, let us leave thefe men.

Mira. Draw off Witwoud.   [*Afide to* Mrs. Fainall.

Mrs. Fain. Immediately ; I have a word or two for Mr. Witwoud.   [*Exeunt* Mrs. Fain. *and* Witwoud.

Mira. I would beg a little private audience too——You had the tyranny to deny me laft night ; though you knew I came to impart a fecret to you that concern'd my love.

Milla. You faw I was engag'd.

Mira. Unkind. You had the leifure to entertain a herd of fools : things who vifit you from their exceffive idle-nefs ; beftowing on your eafinefs that time, which is the incumbrance of their lives. How can you find delight in fuch fociety ? It is impoffible they fhould admire you, they are not capable : or if they were, it fhou'd be to you as a mortification ; for fure to pleafe a fool is fome degree of folly.

Milla. I pleafe myfelf——Befides, fometimes to con-verfe with fools is for my health.

Mira. Your health ! Is there a worfe difeafe than the converfation of fools ?

Milla. Yes, the vapours ; fools are phyfic for it, next to *affa foetida.*

Mira. You are in a courfe of fools.

Milla. Mirabell, if you perfift in this offenfive free-dom——you'll difpleafe me——I think I muft refolve, after all, not to have you——We fhan't agree.

Mira. Not in our phyfic it may be.

Milla.

Milla. And yet our diftemper in all likelihood will be the fame ; for we fhall be fick of one another. I fhan't endure to be reprimanded, nor inftructed, 'tis fo dull to act always by advice, and fo tedious to be told of one's faults——I can't bear it. Well, I won't heve you Mira- bell——I'm refolv'd——I think——You may go—— Ha, ha, ha! What would you give that you could help loving me ?

Mira. I would give fomething that you did not know I could not help it.

Milla. Come, don't look grave then. Well, what do you fay to me ?

Mira. I fay that a man may as foon make a friend by his wit, or a fortune by his honefty, as win a woman with plain-dealing and fincerity.

Milla. Sententious Mirabell ! Prithee don't look with that violent and inflexible wife face, like Solomon at the dividing of the child in an old tapeftry hanging.

Mira. You are merry, Madam ; but I would perfuade you for a moment to be ferious.

Milla. What, with that face ? No, if you keep your countenance, 'tis impoffible I fhould hold mine. Well, after all, there is fomething very moving in a love-fick face. Ha, ha, ha—Well I won't laugh, don't be peevifh. ——Heigho ! Now I'll be melancholy, as melancholy as a watch-light. Well, Mirabell, if ever you will win me, woo me now——Nay, if you are fo tedious, fare you well ? I fee they are walking away.

Mira. Can you find, in the variety of your difpofition, one moment——

Milla. To hear you tell me Foible's married, and your plot like to fpeed—No.

Mira. But how you come to know it ——

Milla. Without the help of the devil, you can't ima- gine, unlefs fhe fhould tell me herfelf. Which of the two it may have been, I will leave you to confider ; and when you have done thinking of that, think of me.

[*Exit.*

Mira. I have fomething more—Gone—Think of you ! To think of a whirlwind, though 'twere in a whirlwind, were a cafe of more fteady contemplation ; ' a very ' tranquility of mind and manfion. A fellow that lives in

' a wind-mill,

‘ a windmill, has not a more whimsical dwelling than the
‘ heart of a man that is lodged in a woman. There is no
‘ point of the compass to which they cannot turn, and by
‘ which they are not turn'd ; and by one as well as ano-
‘ ther ; for motion, not method, is their occupation. To
‘ know this, and yet continue to be in love, is to be made
‘ wise from the dictates of reason, and yet persevere to play
‘ the fool by the force of instinct'—Oh, here come my pair
of turtles.—What, billing so sweetly ! Is not Valentine's
day over with you yet?

Enter Waitwell *and* Foible.

Mira. Sirrah, Waitwell, why sure you think you were
marry'd for your own recreation, and not for my conve-
niency.

Wait. Your pardon, Sir. With submission, we have
indeed been solacing in lawful delights ; but still with an
eye to business, Sir ; I have instructed her as well as I
could. If she can take your directions as readily as my
instructions, Sir, your affairs are in a prosperous way.

Mira. Give you joy, Mrs. Foible.

Foib. O-la, Sir, I'm so asham'd— I'm afraid my lady
has been in a thousand inquietudes for me. But I protest,
Sir, I made as much haste as I could.

Wait. That she did, indeed, Sir. It was my fault that
she did n t make more.

Mira. That I believe.

Foib. But I told my lady, as you instructed me, Sir,
that I had a prospect of seeing Sir Rowland your uncle ;
and that I would put her ladyship's picture in my pocket
to shew him ; which I'll be sure to say has made him so
enamour'd with her beauty, that he burns with impatience to lie at her ladyship's feet, and worship the original.

Mira. Excellent Foible ! Matrimony has made you
eloquent in love.

Wait. I think she has profited, Sir, I think so.

Foib. You have seen Madam Millamant, Sir ?

Mira. Yes.

Foib. I told her, Sir, because I did not know that you
might find an opportunity ; she had so much company
last night.

Mira.

Mira. Your diligence will merit more——in the mean time—— [*Gives money.*

Foib. O dear Sir, your humble fervant.

Wait. Spoufe.

Mira. Sand off, Sir, not a penny——Go on and pro-fper, Foible——The leafe fhall be made good, and the farm ftock'd, if we fucceed.

Foib. I don't queftion your generofity, Sir; and you need not doubt of fuccefs. If you have no more commands, Sir, I'll be gone; I'm fure my lady is at her toilet, and can't drefs 'till I come——O dear, I'm fure that [*looking out.*] was Mrs. Marwood, that went by in a mafk, if fhe has feen me with you I'm fure fhe'll tell my lady. I'll make hafte home and prevent her. Your fervant, Sir. B'w'y Waitwell. [*Exit.*

Wait. Sir Rowland, if you pleafe. The jade's fo pert upon her preferment fhe forgets herfelf.

Mira. Come, Sir, will you endeavour to forget your-felf——and transform into Sir Rowland.

Wait. Why, Sir, it will be impoffible I fhould remember myfelf——Marry'd, knighted, and attended, all in one day! 'Tis enough to make a man forget himfelf. ' The difficulty will be how to recover my acquaintance ' and familiarity with my former felf; and fall from my ' transformation to a reformation into Waitwell. Nay, ' I fhan't be quite the fame Waitwell neither,' and now I remember, I'm marry'd, and can't be my own man again.

Ay, there's my grief; that's the fad change of life;
To lofe my title, and yet keep my wife.

END of the SECOND ACT.

ACT III.

SCENE, *A room in* Lady Wifhfort's *houfe.*

Lady Wifhfort *at her toilet,* Peg *waiting.*

LADY WISHFORT.

MErciful! no news of Foible yet?

Peg. No, Madam.

Lady W. I have no more patience—If I have not fretted

ted myfelf till I am pale again, there's no veracity in me·
Fetch me the red—the red, do you hear, fweetheart?
An errant afh-colour, as I'm a perfon. Look you how
this wench ftirs! Why doft thou not fetch me a little
red? Didft thou not hear me, Mopus?

Peg. The red ratafia does your ladyfhip mean, or the
cherry-brandy?

Lady W. Ratafia, fool! no, fool, not the ratafia, fool.
Grant me patience! I mean the Spanifh paper, ideot,
complexion. Darling paint, paint, paint; doft thou underftand that, changeling, dangling thy hands, like bob-
bins, before thee? Why doft thou not ftir, puppet? thou
wooden thing upon wires!

Peg. Lord, Madam, your ladyfhip is fo impatient!—
I cannot come at the paint, Madam; Mrs. Foible has
locked it up, and carried the key with her.

Lady W. A pox take you both! Fetch me the cherry-
brandy, then.   [*Exit* Peg.
I'm as pale and as faint—I look like Mrs. Qualmfick, the
curate's wife, that's always breeding. Wench, come,
come, wench; what art thou doing; Sipping, tafting?
Save thee, doft thou not know the bottle?

Re-enter Peg, *with a bottle and China cup.*

Peg. Madam, I ftaid to bring your ladyfhip a cup.

Lady W. A cup, fave thee! and what a cup haft
thou brought? Doft thou take me for a fairy, to drink
out of an acorn? Why didft thou not bring thy thimble?
Haft thou ne'er a brafs thimble clinking in thy pocket,
with a bit of nutmeg? I warrant thee. Come, fill, fill—
So—again. See who that is. [*One knocks.*] Set down
the bottle firft. Here, here, under the table——What,
wouldft thou go with the bottle in thy hand, like a tap-
fter? As I'm a perfon, this wench has lived in an inn
upon the road, before fhe came to me, 'like Maritornes,
'the Afturian, in Don Quixote.' No Foible yet?

Peg. No, Madam, Mrs. Marwood.

Lady W. Oh, Marwood! let her come in. Come in,
good Marwood.

Enter Mrs. Marwood.

Mrs. Mar. I'm furprized to find your ladyfhip in difha-
bille at this time of day.

Lady W. Foible's a loft thing; has been abroad fince
morning and never heard of fince.

Mrs. Mar.

Mrs. Mar. I faw her but now, as I came mafk'd through the Park, in conference with Mirabell.

Lady W. With Mirabell! You call my blood into my face, with mentioning that traitor. She durft not have the confidence. I fent her to negociate an affair, in which, if I'm detected, I'm undone. If that wheedling villain has wrought upon Foible to detect me, I'm ruin'd. Oh, my friend, I'm a wretch of wretches, if I'm detected!

Mrs. Mar. Oh, Madam, you cannot fufpect Mrs. Foible's integrity.

Lady W. Oh, he carries poifon in his tongue, that would corrupt integrity itfelf! If fhe has given him an opportunity, fhe has as good as put her integrity into his hands. Ah, dear Marwood! what's integrity to an opportunity?—Hark! I hear her. Dear friend, retire into my clofet, that I may examine her with more freedom. You'll pardon me, dear friend, I can make bold with you. There are books over the chimney; Quarles and Pryn, and the Short View of the Stage, with Bunyan's Works, to entertain you.—Go, you thing, and fend her in. [*To* Peg.

Enter Foible.

Lady W. Oh, Foible! where haft thou been? What haft thou been doing?

Foib. Madam, I have feen the party.

Lady W. But what haft thou done?

Foib. Nay, 'tis your ladyfhip has done, and are to do; I have only promifed. But a man fo enamoured——fo tranfported! Well, if worfhipping of pictures be a fin— Poor Sir Rowland, I fay.

Lady W. The miniature has been counted like. But haft thou not betrayed me, Foible? Haft thou not detected me to that faithlefs Mirabell? What hadft thou to do with him in the Park? Anfwer me, has he got nthing out of thee?

Foib. So, the devil has been beforehand with me. What fhall I fay?——Alas, Madam, could I help it, if I met that confident thing? Was I in fault? If you had heard how he ufed me, and all upon your ladyfhip's account, I am fure you would not fufpect my fidelity. Nay, if that had been the worft, I could have borne; but he had a fling at your ladyfhip too; and then I could not hold: but, i'faith, I gave him his own.

Lady W.

Lady W. Me! What did the filthy fellow fay?

Foib. Oh, Madam, 'tis a fhame to fay what he faid!—
With his taunts, and his fleers, toffing up his nofe——
Humph, (fays he) what, are you hatching fome plot,
(fays he) you are fo early abroad? Or catering (fays he)
ferreting for fome difbanded officer, I warrant. Half-pay
is but thin fubfiftence (fays he)—Well, what penfion does
your lady propofe?—Let me fee (fays he)——what, fhe
muft come down pretty deep, now; fhe's fuperannuated,
(fays he) and——

Lady W. Ods my life! I'll have him—I'll have him
murdered, I'll have him poifoned. Where does he eat?
I'll marry a drawer, to have him poifoned in his wine.
I'll fend for Robin from Locket's immediately.

Foib. Poifon him! poifoning's too good for him. Starve
him, Madam, ftarve him; marry Sir Rowland, and get
him difinherited. Oh, you would blefs yourfelf to hear
what he faid!

Lady W. A villain! Superannuated!

Foib. Humph, (fays he) I hear you are laying defigns
againft me too, (fays he) and Mrs. Millamant is to marry
my uncle; (he does not fufpect a word of your ladyfhip)
but (fays he) I'll fit you for that, I warrant you (fays he).
I'll hamper you for that, (fays he) and you and your old
frippery too (fays he). I'll handle you——

Lady W. Audacious villain! handle me! Would he
durft—Frippery! old frippery! Was there ever fuch a
foul-mouth'd fellow? I'll be marry'd to-morrow; I'll be
contracted to-night.

Foib. The fooner the better, Madam.

Lady W. Will Sir Rowland be here, fay'ft thou?
When, Foible?

Foib. Incontinently, Madam. No new fheriff's wife
expects the return of her hufband, after knighthood, with
that impatience with which Sir Rowland burns for the
dear hour of kiffing your ladyfhip's hand after dinner.

Lady W. Frippery! fuperannuated frippery! I'll frippery the villain; I'll reduce him to frippery and rags; a
tatterdemalion. Yes, he fhall have my niece, with her
fortune, he fhall.

Foib. He! I hope to fee him lodge in Ludgate firft,

D 3 and

and angle into Black Friars for brafs farthings, with an old mitten.

Lady W. Ay, dear Foible ; thank thee for that, dear Foible. He has put me out of all patience. I fhall never recompofe my features to receive Sir Rowland with any œconomy of face. This wretch has fretted me, that I am abfolutely decayed. Look, Foible.

Foib. Your ladyfhip has frowned a little too rafhly, indeed, Madam. There are fome cracks difcernible in the white varnifh.

Lady W. Let me fee the glafs—Cracks, fay'ft thou ? Why, I am errantly flead. I look like an old peel'd wall. Thou muft repair me, Foible, before Sir Rowland comes, or I fhall never keep up to my picture.

Foib. I warrant you, Madam : a little art once made your picture like you ; and now, a little of the fame art muft make you like your picture. Your picture muft fit for you, Madam.

Lady W. But art thou fure Sir Rowland will not fail to come ? Or will he not fail when he does come ; Will he be importunate, Foible, ' and pufh ?' For if he fhould not be importunate, I fhall never break decorums. I fhall die with confufion, if I am forced to make advances. ' Oh, no, I can never advance. I fhall fwoon, if he fhould ' expect advances.' No, I hope Sir Rowland is better bred, than to put a lady to the neceffity of breaking her forms. I won't be too coy, neither ; I won't give him de- fpair. But a little difdain is not amifs ; a little fcorn is alluring.

Foib. A little fcorn becomes your ladyfhip.

Lady W. Yes, but tendernefs becomes me beft—A fort of a dyingnefs. You fee that picture has a fort of a—— Ha, Foible ! a fwimmingnefs in the eyes——Yes, I'll look fo——My niece affects it ; but fhe wants features. Is Sir Rowland handfome ? Let my toilet be removed ; I'll drefs above. I'll receive Sir Rowland here. Is he handfome ? Don't anfwer me ; I won't know ; I'll be furprifed ; be taken by furprife.

Foib. By ftorm, Madam. Sir Rowland's a brifk man.

Lady W. Is he ? Oh, then, he'll importune, if he's a brifk man. I fhall fave decorums, if Sir Rowland im- portunes. I have a mortal terror at the apprehenfion of
offending

offending againſt decorums. Oh, I'm glad he's a briſk man! Let my things be removed, good Foible. [*Exit.*

Enter Mrs. Fainall.

Mrs. Fain. Oh, Foible! I have been in a fright, leſt I ſhould come too late. That devil, Marwood, ſaw you in the Park with Mirabell, and, I'm afraid, will diſcover it to my Lady.

Foib. Diſcover what, Madam ?

Mrs. Fain. Nay, nay, put not on that ſtrange face. I am privy to the whole deſign, and know that Waitwell, to whom thou wert this morning married, is to perſonate Mirabell's uncle, and, as ſuch, winning my Lady, to involve her in thoſe difficulties from which Mirabell only muſt releaſe her, by his making his conditions to have my couſin and her fortune left to her own diſpoſal.

Foib. Oh, dear Madam, I beg your pardon ! It was not my confidence in your ladyſhip that was deficient; but I thought the former good correſpondence between your ladyſhip and Mr. Mirabell, might have hindered his communicating this ſecret.

Mrs. Fain. Dear Foible, forget that.

Foib. Oh, dear Madam, Mr. Mirabell is ſuch a ſweet, winning gentleman ! But your ladyſhip is the pattern of generoſity. Sweet lady, to be ſo good ! Mr. Mirabell cannot chooſe but be grateful. I find your ladyſhip has his heart ſtill. Now, Madam, I can ſafely tell your ladyſhip our ſucceſs. Mrs. Marwood has told my Lady; but I warrant I managed myſelf, I turned it all for the better. I told my Lady, that Mr. Mirabell railed at her ; I laid horrid things to his charge, I'll vow ; and my Lady is ſo incenſed, that ſhe'll be contracted to Sir Rowland to-night, ſhe ſays. I warrant I worked her up, that he may have her for aſking for, ' as they ſay of a Welch ' maidenhead.'

Mrs. Fain. Oh, rare Foible !

Foib. Madam, I beg your ladyſhip to acquaint Mr. Mirabell of his ſucceſs. I would be ſeen as little as poſſible to ſpeak to him ; beſides, I believe Madam Marwood watches me. She has a month's mind; but I know Mr. Mirabell can't abide her—[*Calls.*]—John, remove my Lady's toilet. Madam, your ſervant. My Lady is ſo impatient, I fear ſhe'll come for me, if I ſtay.

Mrs.

Mrs. Fain. I'll go with you up the back ſtairs, leſt I
ſhould meet her. [*Exeunt.*

Enter Mrs. Marwood.

Mrs. Mar. Indeed, Mrs. Engine ! is it thus with you ?
Are you become a go-between of this importance ? Yes,
I ſhall watch you. ' Why, this wench is the *paſs-par-*
' *tout*, a very maſter-key to every body's ſtrong box.'
My friend, Fainall, have you carried it ſo ſwimmingly ?
' I thought there was ſomething in it : but it ſeems it's
' over with you. Your loathing is not from a want of
' appetite, then, but from a ſurfeit ; elſe you could ne-
' ver be ſo cool to fall from a principal to be an aſſiſtant ;
' to procure for him ! a pattern of generoſity that, I con-
' feſs. Well, Mr. Fainall, you have met with your
' match. Oh, man, man ! woman, woman ! The de-
' vil's an aſs. If I were a painter I would draw him like
' an ideot, a driveler, with bib and bells. Man ſhould
' have his head and horns, and woman the reſt of him.
' Poor ſimple fiend !'—Madam Marwood has a month's
mind ; but he can't abide her. 'Twere better for him
you had not been his confeſſor in that affair, without you
could have kept his counſel cloſer. ' I ſhall not prove
' another pattern of generoſity. He has not obliged me
' with thoſe exceſſes of himſelf ; and now I'll have none
' of him. Here comes the good lady, panting ripe ; with
' a heart full of hope, and a head full of care, like any
' chymiſt upon the day of projection.

' *Enter Lady* Wiſhfort.

' *Lady W.* Oh, dear Marwood! what ſhall I ſay for
' this rude forgetfulneſs ? But my dear friend is all
' goodneſs.

' *Mrs. Mar.* No apologies, dear Madam ; I have been
' very well entertained.

' *Lady W.* As I'm a perſon, I am in a very chaos, to
' think I ſhould ſo forget myſelt ; but I have ſuch an olio
' of affairs, really I know not what to do——[*Calls.*]——
' Foible!——I expect my nephew, Sir Wilfull, every
' moment, too——Why, Foible!——He means to tra-
' vel for improvement.

' *Mrs. Mar.* Methinks Sir Wilfull ſhould rather think
' of marrying than travelling, at his years. I hear he is
' turned of forty.

' *Lady*

' *Lady W.* Oh, he's in less danger of being spoiled by
' his travels. I am against my nephew's marrying too
' young. It will be time enough when he comes back,
' and has acquired discretion to choose for himself.

' *Mrs. Mar.* Methinks Mrs. Millamant and he would
' make a very fit match. He may travel afterwards.
' 'Tis a thing very usual with young gentlemen.

' *Lady W.* I promise you, I have thought on't ; and
' since 'tis your judgment, I'll think on't again. I assure
' you, I will ; I value your judgment extremely. On my
' word, I'll propose it.

' *Enter* Foible.

' Come, come, Foible—I had forgot my nephew will be
' here before dinner—I must make haste.

' *Foib.* Mr. Witwoud and Mr. Petulant are come to
' dine with your ladyship.

' *Lady W.* Oh, dear ! I can't appear till I'm dress'd.
' Dear Marwood, shall I be free with you again, and beg
' you to entertain them ? I'll make all imaginable haste.
' Dear friend, excuse me.   [*Ex.* Foible *and Lady* W.'

Enter Mrs. Millamant *and* Mincing.

Milla. Sure never any thing was so unbred as that
odious man——Marwood, your servant.

Mrs. Mar. You have a colour ; what's the matter ?

Milla. That horrid fellow, Petulant, has provoked me
into a flame——I have broke my fan——Mincing, lend
me yours. Is not all the powder out of my hair ?

Mrs. Mar. No. What has he done ?

Milla. Nay, he has done nothing ; he has only talked
—Nay, he has said nothing, neither ; but he has contra-
dicted every thing that has been said. For my part, I
thought Witwoud and he would have quarrelled.

Minc. I vow, Mem, I thought once they would have fit.

Milla. Well, 'tis a lamentable thing, I swear, that one
has not the liberty of choosing one's acquaintance, as one
does one's cloaths.

' *Mrs. Mar.* If we had that liberty, we should be as
' weary of one set of acquaintance, tho' never so good,
' as we are of one suit, tho' never so fine : a fool and a
' doily stuff would now and then find days of grace, and
' be worn for variety.

' *Milla.* I could consent to wear them, if they would
' wear

' wear alike ; but fools never wear out—They are fuch
' *drap-de-berry* things ! Without one could give them to
' one's chambermaid, after a day or two.'

Mrs. Mar. ' 'Twere better fo indeed. Or what think
' you of the play-houfe? A fine, gay, gloffy fool fhould
' be given there, like a new mafking habit after the maf-
' querade is over, and we have done with the difguife ;
' for a fool's vifit is always a difguife, and never admitted
' by a woman of wit, but to blind her affair with a lover
' of fenfe.' If you would but appear barefaced now, and
own Mirabell, you might as eafily put off Petulant and
Witwoud, as your hood and fcarf. And indeed 'tis time ;
for the town has found it : ' the fecret is grown too big
' for the pretence : 'tis like Mrs. Primley's great belly ;
' fhe may lace it down before, but it burnifhes on her
' hips. Indeed, Millamant, you can no more conceal it,
' than my Lady Strammel can her face, that goodly face,
' which, in defiance to her Rhenifh-wine tea, will not be
' comprehended in a mafk.'

Milla. I'll take my death, Marwood, you are more
cenforious than a decayed beauty, or a difcarded toaft—
Mincing, tell the men they may come up. My aunt is
not dreffing here. Their folly is lefs provoking than your
malice.   [*Exit* Minc.
The town has found it ! What has found it ? That Mirabell loves me is no more a fecret, than it is a fecret that
you difcovered it to my aunt, or than the reafon why you
difcovered it is a fecret.

Mrs. Mar. You are nettled.

Milla. You are miftaken. Ridiculous!

Mrs. Mar. Indeed, my dear, you'll tear another fan,
if you don't mitigate thofe violent airs.

Milla. Oh, filly ! Ha, ha, ha ! I could laugh immo-
deraly. Poor Mirabell ! his conftancy to me has quite
deftroyed his complaifance for all the world befide. I
fwear, I never enjoin'd it him to be fo coy. If I had the
vanity to think he would obey me, I would command him
to fhew more gallantry. 'Tis hardly well bred, to be fo
particular on one hand, and fo infenfible on the other.
But I defpair to prevail ; fo let him follow his own way.
Ha, ha, ha ! Pardon me, dear creature, I muft laugh ;
                                             ha,

ha, ha, ha! tho', I grant you, 'tis a little barbarous, ha, ha, ha!

' *Mrs. Mar.* What pity 'tis, fo much raillery, and de-
' livered with fo fignificant gefture, fhould be fo unhappi-
' ly directed to mifcarry !

' *Milla.* Ha! dear creature, I afk your pardon; I
' fwear, I did not mind you.'

Mrs. Mar. Mr. Mirabell and you both may think it a thing impoffible, when I fhall tell him by telling you——

Milla. Oh, dear! what? For it is the fame thing if I hear it. Ha, ha, ha!

Mrs. Mar. That I deteft him, hate him, Madam.

Milla. Oh, Madam! why, fo do I. And yet the creature loves me, ha, ha, ha! How can one forbear laughing to think of it? I am a Sybil, if I am not amazed to think what he can fee in me. I'll take my death, I think you are handfomer, and within a year or two as young. If you could but ftay for me, I fhould overtake you—But that cannot be—Well, that thought makes me melancholic—Now I'll be fad.

Mrs. Mar. Your merry note may be changed fooner than you think.

Milla. D'ye fay fo? ' Then I'm refolved I'll have a
' fong, to keep up my fpirits.'—*But here come the gentlemen.*
' *Enter* Mincing.

' *Minc.* The gentlemen ftay but to comb, Madam;
' and will wait on you.

' *Milla.* Defire Mrs. ——, that is in the next room, to
' fing the fong I would have learnt yefterday——You
' fhall hear it, Madam—Not that there's any great mat-
' ter in it; but 'tis agreeable to my humour.

' S O N G.

' Love's but the frailty of the mind,
' When 'tis not with ambition join'd;
' A fickly flame, which, if not fed, expires;
' And feeding, waftes in felf-confuming fires.

' 'Tis not to wound a wanton boy
' Or am'rous youth, that gives the joy;
' But 'tis the glory to have pierc'd a fwain,
' For whom inferior beauties figh'd in vain.

' Then

' Then I alone the conqueſt prize,
' When I inſult a rival's eyes :
' If there's delight in love, 'tis when I ſee
' That heart which others bleed for, bleed for me.
 Enter Petulant *and* Witwoud.

Milla. Is your animoſity compos'd, gentlemen ?

Wit. Raillery, raillery, Madam ; we have no animoſity—We hit off a little wit now and then, but no animoſity—The falling out of wits is like the falling out of
lovers———We agree in the main, like treble and baſe.
Ha, Petulant ?

Pet. Ay, in the main——But when I have a humour
to contradict———

Wit. Ay, when he has a humour to contradict, then
I contradict too. What, I know my cue. Then we
contradict one another like two battle-dores : for contra-
dictions beget one another like Jews.

Pet. If he ſays black's black—if I have a humour to
ſay 'tis blue——Let that paſs——All's one for that. If
I have a humour to prove it, it muſt be granted.

Wit. Not poſitively muſt——— But it may———
may.

Pet. Yes, it poſitively muſt, upon proof poſitive.

Wit. Ay, upon proof poſitive it muſt ; but upon proof
preſumptive it only may. That's a logical diſtinction
now, Madam.

Mrs. Mar. I perceive your debates are of importance,
and very learnedly handled.

Pet. Importance is one thing, and learning's another ;
but a debate's a debate, that I aſſert.

Wit. Petulant's an enemy to learning ; he relies altogether on his parts.

Pet. No, I'm no enemy to learning ; it hurts not me.

Mrs. Mar. That's a ſign indeed 'tis no enemy to you.

Pet. No, no; 'tis no enemy to any body, but them
that have it.

Milla. Well, an illiterate man's my averſion : I wonder at the impudence of any illiterate man, to offer to
make love.

Wit. That I confeſs I wonder at too.

Milla. Ah ! to marry an ignorant ! that can hardly read
or write.

            Pet.

Pet. Why fhould a man be any farther from being married, tho' he can't read, than he is from being hang'd. The ordinary's paid for fetting the pfalm, and the parifh-prieft for reading the ceremony. And for the reft which is to follow in both cafes, a man may do it without book————So all's one for that.

Milla. D'ye hear the creature ? Lord, here's company, I'll be gone.   [*Exit.*

Enter Sir Wilfull Witwoud, *in a riding-drefs, and a Footman.*

Wit. In the name of Bartholomew and his fair, what have we here ?

Mrs. Mar. 'Tis your brother, I fancy. Don't you know him ?

Wit. Not I————Yes, I think it is he————I've almoft forgot him ; I have not feen him fince the coronation.

Foot. Sir, my lady's dreffing. Here's company; if you pleafe to walk in, in the mean time.

Sir Wil. Dreffing ! What, 'tis but morning here, I warrant, with you in London : we fhou'd count it towards afternoon in our parts, down in Shropfhire————Why then belike my aunt han't din'd yet————Ha, friend !

Foot. Your aunt, Sir ?

Sir Wil. My aunt, Sir ! yes, my aunt, Sir, and your lady, Sir ; your lady is my aunt, Sir—Why, what doft thou not know me, friend ? Why then fend fome body hither that does. How long haft thou lived with thy lady, fellow, ha ?

Foot. A week, Sir ; longer than any body in the houfe, except my lady's woman.

Sir Wil. Why then belike thou doft not know thy lady, if thou feeft her, ha, friend ?

Foot. Why truly, Sir, I cannot fafely fwear to her face in the morning, before fhe is drefs'd ; 'Tis like I may give a fhrewd guefs at her by this time.

Sir Wil. Well, pr'ythee try what thou canft do, if thou canft not guefs, enquire her out, doft hear, fellow ? And tell her, her nephew, Sir Wilfull Witwoud, is in the houfe.

Foot. I fhall, Sir.

Sir Wil. Hold ye, hear me, friend ; a word with you in your ear ; pr'ythee who are thefe gallants ?

E

Foot.

Foot. Really, Sir, I can't tell; here come fo many here, 'tis hard to know 'em all.   [*Exit.*

Sir Wil. Oons this fellow knows lefs than a ftarling; I don't think a'knows his own name.

Mrs. Mar. Mr. Witwoud, your brother is not behind-hand in forgetfulnefs—I fancy he has forgot you too.

Wit. I hope fo——The devil take him that remembers firft, I fay.

Sir Wil. Save you, gentlemen and lady.

Mrs. Mar. For fhame, Mr. Witwoud: why won't you fpeak to him ?——And you, Sir.

Wit. Petulant, fpeak.

Pet. And you, Sir.

Sir Wil. No offence, I hope.   [*Salutes* Marwood.

Mrs. Mar. No fure, Sir.

Wit. This is a vile dog, I fee that already. No of-fence ! Ha, ha, ha! to him ; to him, Petulant; fmoke, him.

Pet. It feems as if you had come a journey, Sir; hem, hem.   [*Surveying him round.*

Sir Wil. Very likely, Sir, that it may feem fo.

Pet. No offence, I hope, Sir.

Wit. Smoke the boots, the boots : Petulant, the boots; ha, ha, ha !

Sir Wil. May be not, Sir; thereafter as 'tis meant, Sir.

Pet. Sir, I prefume upon the information of your boots.

Sir Wil. Why, 'tis like you may, Sir : if you are not fatisfy'd with the information of my boots, Sir, if you will ftep to the ftable, you may enquire further of my horfe, Sir.

Pet. Your horfe, Sir ! Your horfe is an afs, Sir ?

Sir Wil. Do you fpeak by way of offence, Sir ?

Mrs. Mar. The gentleman's merry, that's all, Sir— S'life we fhall have a quarrel betwixt an horfe and an afs, before they find one another out. [*Afide.*] You muft not take any thing amifs from your friends, Sir. You are among your friends here, though it may be you don't know it—If I am not miftaken, you are Sir Wilfull Wit-woud.

Sir Wil. Right, Lady ; I am Sir Wilfull Witwoud ;
                                          fo

fo I write myfelf ; no offence to any body, I hope ; and nephew to the lady Wifhfort of this manfion.

Mrs. Mar. Don't you know this gentleman, Sir ?

Sir Wil. Hum ! What, fure 'tis not——Yea, by'r lady, but 'tis—'Sheart I know not whether 'tis or no—Yea, but 'tis, by the Wrekin. Brother Antony ! what Tony, i'faith ! What doft thou not know me ? By'r lady nor I thee, thou art fo becravatted, and fo beperiwig'd——— 'Sheart why doft not fpeak ? Art thou overjoy'd ?

Wit. Odfo, brother, is it you ? Your fervant, brother.

Sir Wil. Your fervant ! Why yours, Sir. Your fervant again—'Sheart, and your friend and fervant to that —And a— [*pugh*] and flap dragon for your fervice, Sir : and a hare's foot, and a hare's fcut for your fervice, Sir ? an you be fo cold and fo courtly !

Wit. No offence, I hope, brother.

Sir Wil. 'Sheart, Sir, but there is, and much offence —A pox ! is this your inns o'court-breeding, not to know your friends and your relations, your elders, and your betters ?

Wit. Why, brother Wilfull of Salop, you may be as fhort as a Shrewfbury cake, if you pleafe. But I tell you 'tis not modifh to know relations in town. You think you're in the country, where great lubberly brothers flabber and kifs one another when they meet, like a call of ferjeants—'Tis not the fafhion here ; 'tis not indeed, dear brother.

Sir Wil. The fafhion's a fool, and you're a fop, dear brother. 'Sheart, I've fufpected this—By'r lady I conjectur'd you were a fop, fince you began to change the ftile of your letters, and write in a fcrap of paper gilt round the edges, no bigger than a Subpœna. I might expect this when you left off, Honoured brother ; and hoping you are in good health, and fo forth—To begin with a, Rat me, knight, I'm fo fick of laft night's debauch, —Ods heart, and then tell a familiar tale of a cock and a bull, and a whore and a bottle, and fo conclude ——— You could write news before you were out of your time, when you liv'd with honeft Pumple-nofe the attorney of Furnival's Inn——You cou'd intreat to be remember'd then to your friends round the Wrekin. We could have

Gazettes then, and Dawk's letter, and the weekly bill, 'till of late days.

Pet. 'Slife, Witwoud, were you ever an attorney's clerk? Of the family of the Furnivals. Ha, ha, ha!

Wit. Ay, ay, but that was but for a while. Not long, not long. Pshaw, I was not in my own power then. An orphan, and this fellow was my guardian. Ay, ay, I was glad to confent to that, man, to come to London. He had the difpofal of me then. If I had not agreed to that, I might have been bound 'prentice to a felt-maker in Shrewfbury; this fellow would have bound me to a maker of felts.

Sir Wil. 'Sheart, and better than to be bound to a maker of fops; where, I fuppofe, you have ferv'd your time; and now you may fet up for yourfelf.

Mrs. Mar. You intend to travel, Sir, as I'm inform'd.

Sir Wil. Belike I may, Madam. I may chance to fail upon the falt feas, if my mind hold.

Pet. And the wind ferve.

Sir Wil. Serve or not ferve, I fhan't afk licence of you, Sir; nor the weather-cock your companion. I direct my difcourfe to the lady, Sir; 'tis like my aunt may have told you, Madam————Yes, I have fettled my concerns, I may fay now, and am minded to fee foreign parts. If an how the peace holds, whereby that is taxes abate.

Mrs. Mar. I thought you had defigned for France at all adventures.

Sir Wil. I can't tell that; 'tis like I may, and 'tis like I may not. I am fomewhat dainty in making a refolution—becaufe when I make it I keep it. I don't ftand, fhill I fhall I, then; if I fay't, I'll do't: but I have thoughts to tarry a fmall matter in town, to learn fomewhat of your Lingo firft, before I crofs the feas. I'd gladly have fpice of your French, as they fay, whereby to hold difcourfe in foreign countries.

Mrs. Mar. Here's an academy in town for that ufe.

Sir Wil. Is there? 'Tis like there may.

Mrs. Mar. No doubt you will return very much improv'd.

Wit. Yes, refin'd like a Dutch fkipper from a whale-fifhing.

Enter

Enter ‘ Lady Wishfort *and*’ Fainall.

‘ *Lady W.* Nephew, you are welcome.

‘ *Sir Wil.* Aunt, your servant.

‘ *Fain.* Sir Wilfull, your most faithful servant.

‘ *Sir Wil.* Cousin Fainall, give me your hand.

‘ *Lady W.* Cousin Witwoud, your servant ; Mr. Pe-
‘ tulant, your servant—Nephew, you are welcome
‘ again. Will you drink any thing after your journey,
‘ nephew, before you eat ? Dinner's almost ready.

‘ *Sir Wil.* I'm very well, I thank you, aunt—However,
‘ I thank you for your courteous offer. 'Sheart I was
‘ afraid you wou'd have been in the fashion too, and have
‘ remember'd to have forgot your relations. Here's your
‘ cousin Tony, belike, I mayn't call him brother for fear
‘ of offence.

‘ *Lady W.* O he's a railer, nephew—My cousin's a
‘ wit : and your great wits always rally their best friends
‘ to choose. When you have been abroad, nephew,
‘ you'll understand raillery better.

‘ [Fain. *and* Mrs. Marwood *talks apart.*

‘ *Sir Wil.* Why then let him hold his tongue in the
‘ mean time, and rail when that day comes.’

Enter Mincing.

Minc. Gentlemen, I come to acquaint you that dinner is impatient, and my lady waits.

Sir Wil. Impatient ! Why then belike it won't stay 'till
I pull off my boots. Sweetheart, can you help me to a
pair of slippers ?——My man's with his horses, I warrant.

Mincing. Fy, fy, Sir, you wou'd not pull off your
boots here ; you must go down into the hall.

‘ *Lady W.* Dinner shall stay for you. My nephew's
‘ little unbred, you'll pardon him. Gentlemen, will you
‘ walk ? Marwood ?’

Mrs. Mar. I'll follow you, Madam, before Sir Wilfull is ready.   [*Exeunt.*

Fain. Why then Foible's a bawd, an errant, rank,
match-making bawd. And I, it seems, I am a husband, a
rank-husband ; and my wife a very errant, rank-wife,—
all in the Way of the World. 'Sdeath, to be a cuckold by
anticipation, a cuckold in embryo ! ‘ Sure I was born
‘ with budding antlers, like a young satyr, or a citizen's

E 3   ‘ child.’

' child.' 'Sdeath to be out-witted, to be out-jilted——
out-matrimony'd——If I had kept my fpeed like a ftag,
'twere fomewhat——but to crawl after, with my horns
like a fnail, and be out-ftripp'd by my wife——'tis
fcurvy wedlock.

Mrs. Mar. Then fhake it off, you have often wifh'd
for an opportunity to part ;—and now you have it.   But
firft prevent their plot——the half of Millamant's fortune is too confiderable to be parted with to a foe, to Mirabell.

Fain. Damn him, that had been mine——had you
not made that fond difcovery————That had been forfeited, had they been married. My wife had added luftre
to my horns, by that increafe of fortune ; I cou'd have
worn 'em tipt with gold, tho' my forehead had been furnifh'd like a deputy-lieutenant's hall.

Mrs. Mar. They may prove a cap of maintenance to
you ftill, if you can away with your wife ; ' and fhe's
' no worfe than when you had her. I dare fwear fhe had
' given up her game before fhe was married.

'   *Fain.* Hum !—That may be.

'   *Mrs. Mar.* You married her to keep you ; and if you
' can contrive to have her keep you better than you ex-
' pected, why fhould you not keep her longer than you
' intended.'

Fain. The means ! the means !

Mrs. Mar. Difcover to my lady your wife's conduct ;
threaten to part with her——My lady loves her, and
will come to any compofition to fave her reputation.
Take the opportunity of breaking it, juft upon the difcovery of this impofture.   My lady will be enraged beyond bounds, and facrifice niece, and fortune, and all
at that conjuncture. And let me alone to keep her warm ;
if fhe fhould flag in her part, I will not fail to prompt
her.

Fain. Faith, this has an appearance.

Mrs. Mar. I'm forry I hinted to my lady to endeavour a match between Millamant and Sir Wilfull, that
may be an obftacle.

Fain. Oh, for that matter, leave me to manage him ;
I'll difable him for that. He will drink like a Dane : after
dinner, I'll fet his hand in.

Mrs.

' *Mrs. Mar.* Well, how do you ftand affected towards
' the lady ?

' *Fain.* Why faith, I'm thinking of it—Let me fee—
' I am married already, fo that's over—My wife has
' played the jade with me—Well, that's over too—I
' never loved her, or if I had, why that would have been
' over too by this time—Jealous of her I cannot be, for
' I am certain ; fo there's an end of jealoufy—Weary
' of her I am, and fhall be—No, there's no end of that ;
' no, no, that were too much to hope—Thus far con-
' cerning my repofe—Now for my reputation—As to
' my own, I married not for it; fo that's out of the
' queftion—And as to my part in my wife's—Why, fhe
' had parted with her's before ; fo bringing none to me,
' fhe can take none from me ; 'tis againft all rule of
' play, that I fhould lofe to one who has not where-
' withal to ftake.

' *Mrs. Mar.* Befides, you forget; marriage is ho-
' nourable.

' *Fain.* Hum ! faith, and that's well thought on ;
' marriage is honourable, as you fay ; and if fo, where-
' fore fhould cuckoldom be a difcredit, being derived
' from fo honourable a root ?

' *Mrs. Mar.* Nay, I know not ; if the root be honour-
' able, why not the branches ?

' *Fain.* So, fo ; why this point's clear'—Well, how
do we proceed ?

Mrs. Mar. I will contrive a letter, which fhall be delivered to my lady at the time when that rafcal, who is
to act Sir Rowland, is with her. It fhall come as from
an unknown hand——for the lefs I appear to know of
the truth, the better I can play the incendiary. Befides,
I would not have Foible provoked, if I could help it——
becaufe you know fhe knows fome paffages——Nay, I
expect all will come out——But let the mine be fprung
firft, and then I care not if I am difcovered.

Fain. If the worft come to the worft—I'll turn my
wife to grafs—I have already a deed of fettlement of the
beft part of her eftate ; which I wheedled out of her ;
and that you fhall partake at leaft.

Mrs. Mar. I hope you are convinced that I hate Mirabell now : you'll be no more jealous ?

4

Fain.

Fain. Jealous, no——by this kiſs——let huſbands be jealous; but let the lover ſtill believe; ' or, if he doubt, ' let it be only to endear his pleaſure, and prepare the ' joy that follows, when he proves his miſtreſs true : but ' let huſband's doubts convert to endleſs jealouſy ; or, if ' they have belief, let it corrupt to ſuperſtition, and blind ' credulity ;' I am ſingle, and will herd no more with them. True, I wear the badge, but I'll diſown the order. And ſince I take my leave of them, I care not if I leave them a common motto to their common creſt.

All huſbands muſt, or pain, or ſhame, endure ;
The wife too jealous are, fools too ſecure.

END of the THIRD ACT.

ACT IV.

SCENE *continues.*

Lady Wiſhfort *and* Foible.

LADY WISHFORT.

IS Sir Rowland coming, ſay'ſt thou, Foible? and are things in order ?

Foib. Yes, Madam. I have put wax lights in the ſconces ; and placed the footmen in a row in the hall, in their beſt liveries, with the coachman and poſtillion to fill up the equipage.

Lady W. Have you pulvilled the coachman and po-ſtillion, that they may not ſtink of the ſtable, when Sir Rowland comes by ?

Foib. Yes, Madam.

' *Lady W.* And are the dancers and the muſic ready, ' that he may be entertained in all points with corre-' ſpondence to his paſſion ?

' *Foi.* All is ready, Ma'am.'

Lady W. And——well——and how do I look, Foible ?

Foi. Moſt killing well, Madam.

Ladp W. Well, and how ſhall I receive him ? In what figure ſhall I give his heart the firſt impreſſion ? There is a great deal in the firſt impreſſion. Shall I ſit ?——No, I won't ſit——I'll walk——ay, I'll walk from the door
upon

upon his entrance; and then turn full upon him——
No, that will be too fudden—I'll lie, ay, I'll lie down
—I'll receive him in my little dreffing-room, there's a
couch——Yes, yes, I ll give the firſt impreffion on a
couch——I won't lie neither, but loll and lean upon one
elbow; with one foot a little dangling off, jogging in a
thoughtful way——Yes—— and then as foon as he appears, ſtart; ay, ſtart, and be ſurpriſed, and riſe to meet
him in a pretty diſorder——Yes——Oh, nothing is more
alluring than a levee from a couch in ſome confuſion
——It ſhews the foot to advantage, and furniſhes with
bluſhes, and recompofing airs beyond compariſon. Hark !
There's a coach.

Foib. 'Tis he, Madam.

Lady W. Oh, dear, has my nephew made his addreffes
to Millamant ? I ordered him.

Foib. Sir Wilfull is fet in to drinking, Madam, in the
parlour.

Lady W. Od's my life, I'll fend him to her. Call her
down, Foible; bring her hither. I'll fend him as I go.
When they are together, then come to me, Foible, that I
may not be too long alone with Sir Rowland.

[*Exit Lady* W.

Enter Mrs. Millamant *and Mrs.* Fainall.

Foib. Madam, I ſtayed here, to tell your ladyſhip that
Mr. Mirabell has waited this half hour for an opportunity to talk with you. Though my lady's orders were to
leave you and Sir Wilfull together. Shall I tell Mr. Mirabell that you are at leiſure ?

Milla. No——What would the dear man have ? I am
thoughtful, and would amuſe myſelf——Bid him come
another time.

    There never yet was woman made,
    Nor ſhall, but to be curs'd.

[*Repeating and walking about.*
That's hard !

Mrs. Fain. You are very fond of Sir Jack Suckling to-
day, Millamant, and the poets.

Milla. He ? Ay, and filthy verſes——So I am.

Foib. Sir Wilfull is coming, Madam. Shall I ſend Mr.
Mirabell away ?

Milla. Ay, if you pleaſe, Foible, ſend him away——

Or

Or fend him hither——juſt as you will, dear Foible——
I think I'll fee him—Shall I ? Ay, let the wretch come.

Thyrfis, a youth of the infpired train. [*Repeating*.
Dear Fainall, entertain Sir Wilfull——Thou haſt philofophy to undergo a fool ; thou art married and haſt patience——— I would confer with my own thoughts.

Mrs. Fain. I am obliged to you, that you would make
me your proxy in this affair; but I have bufinefs of my
own.

Enter Sir Wilfull.

Mrs. Fain. Oh, Sir Wilfull ; you are come at the critical inſtant. There's your miſtrefs up to the ears in love
and contemplation ; purfue your point, now or never.

Sir Wil. Yes ; my aunt will have it fo——I would
gladly have been encouraged with a bottle or two, becaufe I'm fomewhat wary at firſt, before I'm acquainted :
[*This while* Millamant *walks about repeating to herfelf.*]
——But I hope, after a time, I ſhall break my mind—
that is, upon further acquaintance—So for the prefent,
coufin, I'll take my leave——If fo be, you'll be fo kind
to make my excufe ; I'll return to my company——

Mrs. Fain. Oh, fy, Sir Wilfull ? What, you muſt not
be daunted

Sir Wil. Daunted ! No, that's not it; it is not fo much
for that—for if fo be that I fet on't, I'll do't. But only
for the prefent, 'tis fufficient 'till further acquaintance,
that's all——your fervant.

Mrs. Fain. Nay, I'll fwear you ſhall never lofe fo favourable an opportunity, if I can help it. I'll leave you
together, and lock the door. [*Exit* Fain.

Sir Wil. Nay, nay, coufin—I have forgot my gloves
—What d'ye do ? 'Sheart a'has locked the door indeed,
I think——Nay, coufin Fainall, open the door——
Pſha ! what a vixen trick is this?——Nay, now a'has
feen me too—Coufin, I made bold to pafs through as it
were——I think this door's inchanted——

Milla. [*Repeating.*]

    I pr'ythee fpare me, gentle boy,

    Prefs me no more for that flight toy.

Sir Wil. Anan ? Coufin, your fervant.

Milla. That foolifh trifle of a heart—Sir Wilfull ?

Sir Wil. Yes——your fervant. No offence, I hope,
coufin.   *Milla.*

Milla. [*Repeating.*]
　I fwear it will do its part,
　　Tho' thou doft thine, employ'ft thy power and art.
Natural, eafy Suckling !

Sir Wil. Anan ! Suckling ! No fuch fuckling neither,
coufin, nor ftripling : I thank Heaven, I'm no minor.

Milla. Ah, ruftic, ruder than Gothic.

Sir Wil. Well, well, I fhall underftand your Lingo one
of thefe days, coufin ; in the mean while I muft anfwer
in plain Englifh.

Milla. Have you any bufinefs with me, Sir Wilfull ?

Sir Wil. Not at prefent, coufin——Yes, I made bold
to fee, to come and know, if that how you were difpofed
to fetch a walk this evening, if fo be that I might not be
troublefome, I would have fought a walk with you.

Milla. A walk ? What then ?

Sir Wil. Nay, nothing——Only for the walk's fake,
that's all——,

Milla. I naufeate walking ; 'tis a country diverfion ;
I loathe the country, and every thing that relates to it.

Sir Wil. Indeed ! Hah ! Look ye, look ye, you do ?
Nay, 'tis like you may——Here are choice of paftimes
here in town, as plays and the like, that muft be confeffed indeed——

Milla. Ah, *l'etourdie !* I hate the town too.

Sir Wil. Dear heart, that's much —- Hah ! that you
fhould hate 'em both ! Hah ! 'tis like you may ; there
are fome can't relifh the town, and others can't away with
the country—'tis like you may be one of thofe, coufin.

Milla. Ha, ha, ha ! Yes, 'tis like I may—You have
nothing further to fay to me ?

Sir Wil. Not at prefent, coufin——'Tis like when I
have an opportunity to be more private—I may break
my mind in fome meafure——I conjecture you partly
guefs——However, that's as time fhall try——But fpare
to fpeak and fpare to fpeed, as they fay.

Milla. If it is of no great importance, Sir Wilfull,
you will oblige me to leave me : I have juft now a little
bufinefs.—

Sir Wil. Enough, enough, coufin : yes, yes, all a cafe
—— When you're difpofed, when you're difpofed. Now's
as well as another time ; and another time as well as now.
　　　　　　　　　　　　　　　　　　　　　All's

All's one for that—Yes, yes, if your concerns call you, there's no haste; it will keep cold as they say—Coufin, your fervant——I think this door's locked.

Milla. You may go this way, Sir.

Sir Wil. Your fervant, then with your leave I'll return to my company.

Milla. Ay, ay; ha, ha, ha!   [*Exit Sir* Wil.
Like Phœbus fung the no lefs am'rous boy.

Enter Mirabell.

Mira.—Like Daphne fhe, as lovely and as coy. Do you lock yourfelf up from me, to make my fearch more curious? Or, is this pretty artifice contrived, to fignify that here the chace muft end, and my purfuit be crowned, for you can fly no farther?——

Milla. Vanity! No——I'll fly and be followed to the laft moment; though I am upon the very verge of matrimony, I expect you fhould folicit me as much as if I were wavering at the gate of a monaftery, with one foot over the threfhold. I'll be folicited to the very laft, nay, and afterwards.

Mira. What, after the laft?

Milla. 'Oh, if I fhould think I was poor, and had no' thing to beftow, if I were reduced to an inglorious' eafe, and freed from the agreeable fatigues of folicita-' tion.

' *Mir.* But don't you know, that when favours are' conferred upon inftant and tedious folicitation, that' they diminifh in their value, and that both the giver' lofes the grace, and the receiver leffens his pleafure.

· ' *Milla.* It may be in things of common application; ' but never fure in love'—Oh, I hate a lover that can dare to think he draws a moment's air, independent on the bounty of his miftrefs. There is not fo impudent a thing in nature, as the faucy look of an affured man, confident of fuccefs. The pedantic arrogance of a very hufband has not fo pragmatical an air. Ah, I'll never marry, unlefs I am firft made fure of my will and pleafure.

Mira. Would you have 'em both before marriage? Or will you be contented with the firft now, and ftay for the other 'till after grace?

Milla. Ah! don't be impertinent——My dear liberty,

berty, fhould I leave thee? My faithful folitude, my
darling contemplation, muft I bid you then adieu? Ah!
adieu—My morning thoughts, agreeable wakings, indo-
lent flumbers, ye *douceurs*, ye *fommeils du matin* adieu.—
I can't doubt, 'tis more than impoffible——Pofitively,
Mirabell, I'll lie a-bed in a morning as long as I pleafe.

Mira. Then I'll get up in a morning as early as I
pleafe.

Milla. Ay! idle creature, get up when you will——
And, d'ye hear, I won't be call'd names after I'm married, pofitively I won't be called names.

Mira. Names!

Milla. Ay; as wife, fpoufe, my dear, joy, jewel,
love, fweet-heart, and the reft of that naufeous cant, in
which men and their wives are fo fulfomely familiar—I
fhall never bear that——Good Mirabell, don't let us be
familiar or fond, nor kifs before folks, like my lady Faddle and Sir Francis: nor go to Hyde Park together the
firft Sunday in a new chariot, to provoke eyes and
whifpers, and then never be feen there together again;
as if we were proud of one another the firft week, and
afhamed of one another ever after. Let us never vifit
together, nor go to a play together; but let us be very
ftrange and well-bred: let us be as ftrange as if we had
been married a great while; and as well-bred as if we
were not married at all.

Mir. Have you any more conditions to offer? Hitherto your demands are pretty reafonable.

Milla. Trifles—As liberty to pay and receive vifits to
and from whom I pleafe; to write and receive letters,
without interrogatories or wry faces on your part; to
wear what I pleafe; and choofe converfation with regard
only to my own tafte; to have no obligation upon me to
converfe with wits that I don't like, becaufe they are
your acquaintance; or to be intimate with fools, becaufe
they may be your relations. Come to dinner when I
pleafe; dine in my dreffing-room when I'm out of humour, without giving a reafon. To have my clofet inviolate; to be fole emprefs of my tea-table, which you
muft never prefume to approach without firft afking
leave. And laftly, wherever I am, you fhall always knock
at the door before you come in. Thefe articles fub-

F   fcribed,

fcribed, if I continue to endure you a little longer, I may by degrees dwindle into a wife.

Mira. Your bill of fare is fomething advanced in this latter account. Well, have I liberty to offer conditions ——That when you are dwindled into a wife, I may not be beyond meafure enlarged into a hufband.

Milla. You have free leave; propofe your utmoft, fpeak and fpare not.

Mira. I thank you. *Imprimis* then, I covenant that your acquaintance be general; that you admit no fworn confident, or intimate of your own fex; 'no fhe friend 'to fkreen her affairs under your countenance, and tempt 'you to make trial of a mutual fecrecy;' no decoy-duck to wheedle you a fop-fcrambling to the play in a mafk ——Then bring you home in a pretended fright, when you think you fhall be found out——And rail at me for miffing the play, and difappointing the frolic which you had to pick me up and prove my conftancy.

Milla. Deteftable *imprimis!* I go to the play in a mafk!

Mira. *Item,* I article, that you continue to like your own face, as long as I fhall: and while it paffes current with me, that you endeavour not to new-coin it. To which end, together with all the vizards for the day, I prohibit all mafks for the night, made of oiled fkins, and I know not what—— Hogs bones, hare's gall, pig water, and the marrow of a roafted cat. *Item,* I fhut my doors againft all bawds with bafkets, and penny-worths of muflin, china, fans, Atlaffes, &c. ——*Item,* when you fhall be breeding ————

Milla. Ah, name it not.

Mira. Which may be prefumed, with a bleffing on our endeavours ————

Milla. Odious endeavours!

Mira. I denounce againft all ftraight lacing, fqueezing for a fhape, till you mould my boy's head like a fugar-loaf; and inftead of a man child make me father to a crooked-brat. Laftly, to the dominion of the tea table I fubmit——But with provifo, that you exceed not in your province: but reftrain yourfelf to native and fimple tea-table drinks, as tea, chocolate, and coffee. As like-wife to genuine and authorized tea-table talk—Such as
                                                                    mending

mending of fashions, spoiling reputations, railing at absent friends, and so forth——But that on no account you encroach upon the men's prerogative, and presume to drink healths, or toast fellows; for prevention of which I banish all foreign forces, all auxiliaries to the tea table, as orange brandy, all anniseed, cinnamon, citron and Barbadoes waters, together with ratafia, and the most noble spirit of clary.——But for cowslip wine, poppy water, and all dormitives, those I allow—These proviso's admitted, in other things I may prove a tractable and complying husband.

Milla. Oh, horrid proviso's! filthy strong waters! I toast fellows! Odious men! I hate your odious proviso's.

Mira. Then we're agreed. Shall I kiss your hand upon the contract? And here comes one to be a witness to the sealing of the deed.

Enter Mrs. Fainall.

Milla. Fainall, what shall I do? Shall I have him? I think I must have him.

Mrs. Fain. Ay, ay, take him, take him; what should you do?

Milla. Well then——I'll take my death, I'm in a horrid fright——Fainall, I shall never say it——Well——I think——I'll endure you.

Mrs. Fain. Fy, fy, have him, have him, and tell him so in plain terms: for I am sure you have a mind to him.

Milla. Are you? I think I have——and the horrid man looks as if he thought so too——Well, you ridiculous thing you, I'll have you——I won't be kissed, nor I won't be thanked——Here, kiss my hand though ——So, hold your tongue now, don't say a word.

Mrs. Fain. Mirabell, there's a necessity for your obedience;——' You have neither time to talk nor stay:
' my mother is coming; and in my conscience, if she
' should see you, would fall into fits, and may be not
' recover time enough to return to Sir Rowland, who
' as Foible tells me, is in a fair way to succeed.' Therefore spare you extasies for another occasion, and slip down the back stairs, where Foible waits to consult you.

Milla. Ay, ay, go. In the mean time I'll suppose you have said something to please me.

Mira.

Mira. I am all obedience. [*Exit.*

Mrs. Fain. Yonder Sir Wilfull's drunk, and fo noify, that my mother has been forced to leave Sir Rowland to appeafe him ; but he anfwers her only with finging and drinking——What they may have done by this time I know not ; but Petulant and he were upon quarrelling as I came by.

Milla. Well, if Mirabell fhould not make a good hufband, I am a loft thing——for I find I love him violently.

Mrs. Fain. So it feems ; for you mind not what's faid to you.——If you doubt him, you had beft take up with Sir Wilfull.

Milla. How can you name that fuperannuated lubber ? Foh !

Enter Witwoud *from drinking.*

Mrs. Fain. So, is the fray made up, that you have left them ?

Wit. Left them ! I could ftay no longer——I have laughed like ten chriftenings—I am tipfy with laughing ——If I had ftaid any longer I fhould have burft —— I muft have been let out and pieced in the fides like an unfized camblet——Yes, yes, the fray is compofed ; my lady came in like a *noli profequi*, and ftopped the proceedings.

Milla. What was the difpute ?

Wit. That's the jeft ; there was no difpute. They could neither of 'em fpeak for rage, and fo fell a fputtering at one another like two roafting apples.

Enter Petulant *drunk.*

Now, Petulant, all's over, all's well. Gad, my head begins to whim it about——Why doft thou not fpeak ? Thou art both as drunk and as mute as a fifh.

Pet. Look you, Mrs. Millamant——if you can love me, dear nymph—fay it—and that's the conclufion—— Pafs on, or pafs off——that's all.

Wit. Thou haft uttered volumes, folios, in lefs than *decimo fexto*, my dear Lacedemonian. Sirrah, Petulant, thou art an epitomizer of words.

Pet. Witwoud——You are an annihilator of fenfe.

Wit. Thou art a retailer of phrafes ; and doft deal in remnants of remnants, like a maker of pincufhions ——

Thou

Thou art, in truth, (metaphorically fpeaking) a fpeaker of fhort hand.

Pet Thou art (without a figure) juft one half of an afs, and Baldwin yonder, thy half brother, is the reft — A Gemini of affes fplit wou'd make juft four of you.

Wit. Thou doft bite, my dear muftard-feed; kifs me for that.

Pet. Stand off ——I'll kifs no more males —— I have kifs'd your twin yonder in a humour of reconciliation, till he *(hiccups)* rifes upon my ftomach like a raddifh.

Milla. Eh ! filthy creature—What was the quarrel?

Pet. There was no quarrel ————There might have been a quarrel.

Wit. If there had been words enow between 'em to have exprefs'd provocation, they had gone together by the ears like a pair of caftanets.

Pet. You were the quarrel.

Milla. Me !

Pet. If I have a humour to quarrel, I can make lefs matters conclude premifes—If you are not handfome, what then ; if I have a humour to prove it ? If I fhall have my reward, fay fo ; if not, fight for your face the next time yourfeif ————— I'll go fleep.

Wit. Do, wrap thyfelf up like a wood-loufe, and dream revenge————And, hear me, if thou canft learn to write by to-morrow morning, pen me a challenge———— I'll carry it for thee

Pet. Carry your miftrefs's monkey a fpider——go flea dogs, and read romances—I'll go to bed to my maid.

Mrs. Fain. He's horridly drunk———How came you all in this pickle ?

Wit. A plot, a plot, to get rid of the knight———— Your hufband's advice. but he fneak'd off.

-     *Enter* Sir Wilfull *drunk; and* Lady Wifhfort.

Lady W. Out upon't ! out upon't ! at years of difcretion, and comport yourfelf at this rantipole rate.

Sir Wil. No offence, aunt.

Lady W. Offence ! As I'm a perfon, I'm afham'd of you——Fough ! how you ftink of wine ! D'ye think my niece will ever endure fuch a Borachio ! you're an abfolute Borachio !

Sir Wil.

Sir Wil. Borachio!

Lady W. At a time when you fhou'd commence an amour, and put your beft foot foremoft.———

Sir Wil. 'Sheart, an you grudge me your liquor, make a bill——— Give me more drink, and take my purfe.

S O N G.

Pry'thee fill me the glafs
'Till it laugh in my face,
With aie that is potent and mellow ;
He that whines for a lafs
Is an ignorant afs,
For a bumper has not its fellow.

But if you wou'd have me marry my coufin——Say the word, and I'll do't—— Wilfull will do't, that's the word ———Wilfull will do't, that's my creft———my motto I have forgot.

Lady W. My nephew's a little overtaken, coufin—but 'tis with drinking your health———O' my word you are oblig'd to him.

Sir Wil. In vino veritas, aunt : ——— If I drink your health ,to-day, coufin—I am a Borachio. But if you have a mind to be married, fay the word, and fend for the piper ; Wilfull will do't. If not, duft it away, and let's have t'other round ——Tony! Ods heart where's Tony ?—Tony's an honeft fellow, but he fpits after a bumper, and that's a fault.

Sings. We'll drink and we'll never have done, boys,
Put the glafs then around with the fun, boys,
Let Apollo's example invite us ;
For he's drunk ev'ry night,
And that makes him fo bright,
That he's able next morning to light us.

The fun's a good pimple, an honeft foaker, he has a cellar at your Antipodes. If I travel, aunt, I touch at the Antipodes—your Antipodes are a good rafcally fort of topfy-turvy fellows—If I had a bumper I'd ftand upon my head and drink a health to 'em—A match or no match, coufin, with the hard name—Aunt, Wilfull will do't. ' If fhe has her maidenhead, let her
' look

' look to't ; if fhe has not, let her keep her own coun-
' fel in the mean time, and cry out at the nine month's
' end.'

Milla. Your pardon, Madam, I can ftay no longer—
Sir Wilfull grows very powerful. Egh ! how he fmells !
I fhall be overcome if I ftay. Come, coufin.

[*Exeunt* Milla. *and* Mrs. Fain.

Lady W. Smells ! he would poifon a tallow-chandler
and his family. Beaftly creature ! I know not what to do
with him.—Travel, quotha ! ay, travel, travel, get thee
gone ; get thee but far enough ; to the Saracens or the
Tartars, or the Turks, for thou are't not fit to live in a
Chriftian commonwealth, thou beaftly Pagan.

Sir Wil. Turks ! no, no, Turks, aunt ; your Turks
are Infidels, and believe not in the grape ; your Mahometan, your Muffulman is a dry ftinkard—No offence,
aunt. My map fays, that your Turk is not fo honeft a
man as your Chriftian. I cannot find by the map, that
your Mufti is orthodox ; whereby it is a plain cafe, that
orthodox is a hard word, aunt, and *(hiccups)* Greek for
claret.

Sings. To drink is a Chriftian diverfion
　　　　Unknown to the Turk and the Perfian ;
　　　　　　Let Mahometan fools
　　　　　　Live by Heathenifh rules,
　　　　And be damn'd over tea-cups and coffee.
　　　　　　But let Britifh lads fing
　　　　　　Crown a health to the King,
　　　　And a fig for your Sultan and Sophy.

Ah, Tony !

[*Enter* Foible *and whifpers* Lady Wifhfort.

Lady W. Sir Rowland impatient ! Good lack ! what
fhall I do with this beaftly tumbril ?——Go lie down and
fleep, you fot—Or, as I'm a perfon, I'll have you bafti-
nado'd with broom-fticks. Call up the wenches with
broom-fticks.

Sir Wil. Ahey ! wenches : where are the wenches ?

Lady W. Dear coufin Witwoud : get him away, and
you will bind me to you inviolably. I have an affair of
moment that invades me with fome precipitation——
You will oblige me to all futurity.

Wit.

Wit. Come, knight——Pox on him, I don't know what to fay to him——Will you go to a cock-match ?

Sir Wit. With a wench, Tony ? Is fhe a fhake-bag, firrah ? Let me bite your cheek for that.

Wit. Horrible ! he has a breath like a bagpipe—Ay, ey, come, will you march, my Salopian ?

Sir Wil. Lead on, little Tony -- I'll follow thee, my Anthony, my Tantony. Sirrah, thou fhalt be my Tantony, and I'll be thy Pig.

——And a fig for your Sultan and Sophy.

[*Exeunt* Sir Wil. *and* Wit.

Lady W. This will never do. It will never make a match :— at leaft before he has been abroad.

Enter Waitwell *difguis'd as for* Sir Rowland.

Dear Sir Rowland, I am confounded with confufion at the retrofpection of my own rudenefs—I have more pardons to afk than the Pope diftributes in the year of Jubilee. But I hope where there is likely to be fo near an alliance—we may unbend the feverity of decorum—and difpenfe with a litle ceremony.

Wait. My impatience, Madam, is the effect of my tranfport — And till I have the poffeffion of your adorable perfon, I am tantaliz'd on the rack ; and do but hang, Madam, on the tenter of expectation.

Lady W. You have excefs of gallantry, Sir Rowland ; and prefs things to a conclufion, with a moft prevailing vehemence.—But a day or two for decency of marriage——

Wait. For decency of funeral, Madam. The delay will break my heart——or, if that fhould fail, I fhall be poifoned. My nephew will get an inkling of my defigns, and poifon me ---- and I would willingly ftarve him before I die——I would gladly go out of the world with that fatisfaction———That would be fome comfort to me, if I could but live fo long as to be reveng'd on that unnatural viper.

Lady W. Is he fo unnatural, fay you ? Truly, I would contribute much both to the faving of your life, and the accomplifhment of your revenge——Not that I refpect myfelf ; tho' he has been a perfidious wretch to me.

Wait. Perfidious to you !

Lady W.

Lady W. O Sir Rowland, the hours that he has died away at my feet, the tears that he has fhed, the oaths that he has fworn, the palpitations that he has felt, the trances and the tremblings, the ardours and the extafies, the kneelings and the rifings, the heart-heavings and the hand-gripings, the pangs and the pathetic regards of his protefting eyes! Oh, no memory can regifter.

Wait. What, my rival! Is the rebel my rival? a' dies.

Lady W. No don't kill him at once, Sir Rowland, ftarve him gradually inch by inch.

Wait. I'll do't. In three weeks he fhall be barefoot; in a month out at knees with begging an alms——He fhall ftarve upward and upward, 'till he has nothing living but his head, and then go out in a ftink like a candle's end upon a fave-all.

Lady W. Well, Sir Rowland, you have the way—— You are no novice in the labyrinth of love—You have the clue——But as I am a perfon, Sir Rowland, you muft not attribute my yielding to any finifter appetite ——I hope you do not think me prone to any iteration of nuptials.

Wait. Far be it from me——

Lady W. If you do, I proteft I muft recede——or think that I have made a proftitution of decorum; but in the vehemence of compaffion, and to fave the life of a perfon of fo much importance.

Wait. I efteem it fo.

Lady W. Or elfe you wrong my condefcenfion.——

Wait. I do not, I do not ————

Lady W. Indeed you do.

Wait. I do not, fair fhrine of virtue.

Lady W. If thou think the leaft fcruple of carnality was an ingredient————

Wait. Dear Madam, No. You are all camphire and frankincenfe, all chaftity and odour.

Lady W. Or that————

Enter Foible.

Foib. Madam, ' The dancers are ready, and' there's one with a letter, who muft deliver it into your own hands.

Lady W.

Lady W. Sir Rowland, will you give me leave ? Think favourably, judge candidly, and conclude you have found a perfon who would fuffer racks in honour's caufe, dear Sir Rowland, and will wait on you inceffantly.

[*Exit* Lady W.

Wait. Fy, fy !—What a flavery have I undergone ? fpoufe, haft thou any cordial ? I want fpirits.

Foib. What a wafhy rogue art thou, to pant thus for a quarter of an hour's lying and fwearing to a fine lady ?

Wait. O, fhe is the antidote to defire. ' Spoufe, thou ' wilt fare the worfe for't——I fhall have no appetite to ' iteration of nuptials—this eight and forty hours.' By this hand, I'd rather be a chairman in the dog-days, than act Sir Rowland till this time to-morrow.

Re-enter Lady Wifhfort, *with a letter.*

Lady W. ' Call in the dancers ;—Sir Rowland, we'll ' fit, if you pleafe, and fee the entertainment. [*Dance.*' Now, with your permiffion, Sir Rowland, I will perufe my letter——I would open it in your prefence, becaufe I would not make you uneafy. If it fhould make you un-eafy, I would burn it——fpeak, if it does——but you may fee the fuperfcription is like a woman's hand.

Foib. By heaven ! Mrs. Marwood's, I know it—my heart akes——Get it from her—— [*To him.*

Wait. A woman's hand ! No, Madam, that's no wo-man's hand, I fee that already. That's fome body whofe throat muft be cut.

Lady W. Nay, Sir Rowland, fince you give me a proof of your paffion, by your jealoufy, I promife you I'll make a return, by a frank communication——you fhall fee it— we'll open it together——look you here. [*Reads*] " Ma-dam, though unknown to you," Look you there, 'tis from no body that I know.——" I have that honour for your character, that I think myfelf obliged to let you know you are abufed. He who pretends to be Sir Row-land, is a cheat and a rafcal." Oh heavens ! what's this ?

Foib. Unfortunate, all's ruin'd.

Wait. How, how, let me fee, let me fee—[*Reading,*] " A rafcal, and difguis'd and fuborn'd for that impo-fture"——O villany ! O villany ! " by the contrivance of"——

Lady W.

Lady W. I shall faint, I shall die, oh!

Foib. Say 'tis your nephew's hand—Quickly, his plot, swear, swear it.———   [*To him.*

Wait. Here's a villain, Madam, don't you perceive it, don't you see it?

Lady W. Too well, too well. I have seen too much.

Wait. I told you at first I knew the hand—A woman's hand! The rascal writes a sort of a large hand; your Roman hand——I saw there was a throat to be cut presently. If he were my son, as he is my nephew, I'd pistol him———

Foib. O treachery! But are you sure, Sir Rowland, it is his writing?

Wait. Sure! Am I here? do I live? Do I love this pearl of India? I have twenty letters in my pocket from him, in the same character.

Lady W. How!

Foib. O what luck it is, Sir Rowland, that you were present at this juncture! This was the business that brought Mr. Mirabell disguis'd to Madam Millamant this afternoon. I thought something was contriving, when he stole by me, and would have hid his face.

Lady W. How, how——I heard the villain was in the house, indeed; and now I remember, my niece went away abruptly, when Sir Wilfull was to have made his addresses.

Foib. Then, then Madam, Mr. Mirabell waited for her in her chamber; but I would not tell your ladyship to discompose you when you were to receive Sir Rowland.

Wait. Enough, his date is short.

Foib. No, good Sir Rowland, don't incur the law.

Wait. Law! I care not for law. I can but die, and 'tis in a good cause—— My lady shall be satisfied of my truth and innocence, though it cost me my life.

Lady W. No, dear Sir Rowland, don't fight; if you should be killed, I must never shew my face; ' O con-
' sider my reputation, Sir Rowland.—No, you shan't
' fight, I'll go in and examine my niece; I'll make her
' confess.'—I conjure you, Sir Rowland, by all your love, not to fight.

Wait.

Wait. I am charmed, Madam ; I obey. But fom^e proof you muft let me give you. I'll go for a black box' which contains the writings of my whole eftate, and deliver that into your hands.

Lady W. Ay, dear Sir Rowland, that will be fome comfort ; bring the black box.

Wait. And may I prefume to bring a contract, to be figned this night ? May I hope fo far ?

Lady W. Bring what you will ; but come alive. Pray, come alive. ' Oh, this is a happy difcovery !'

Wait. Dead or alive, I'll come ; and married we will be, in fpite of treachery ; ay, and get an heir that fhall defeat the laft remaining glimpfe of hope in my abandoned nephew. Come, my buxom widow :

Ere long you fhall fubftantial proof receive

That I'm an arrant knight————.

Foib. ————Or arrant knave.

[*Exeunt.*

END of the FOURTH ACT.

ACT   V.

SCENE   *continues.*

Enter Lady Wifhfort *and* Foible.

LADY WISHFORT.

OUT of my houfe, out of my my houfe, thou viper, thou ferpent, that I have foftered ; thou bofom traitrefs, that I raifed from nothing——Begone, begone, begone, go, go—that I took from wafhing of old gauze, and weaving of dead hair, with a bleak blue nofe, over a chafing-difh of ftarv'd embers, and dining behind a traverfe-rag, in a fhop no bigger than a bird-cage. Go, go, ftarve again ; do, do.

Foib. Dear Madam, I'll beg pardon on my knees.

Lady W. Away, out, out ; go, fet up for yourfelf again, do ; drive a trade, do, with your three-pennyworth of fmall ware, flaunting upon a pack-thread, under a brandy-feller's bulk, or againft a dead wall, by a ballad-monger. Go, hang out an old frifoneer gorget, with a yard of yellow colberteen again, do ; an old

4   gnawed

gnawed maſk, two rows of pins, and a child's fiddle; a glaſs necklace, with the beads broken, and a quilted night-cap, with one ear; go, go, drive a trade. Theſe were your commodities, you treacherous trull; this was the merchandiſe you dealt in, when I took you into my houſe, placed you next myſelf, and made you governante of my whole family. You have forgot this, have you, now you have feathered your neſt?

Foib. No, no, dear Madam. Do but hear me; have but a moment's patience; I'll confeſs all. Mr. Mirabell ſeduced me. I am not the firſt that he has wheedled with his diſſembling tongue: your ladyſhip's own wiſdom has been deluded by him; then how ſhould I, a poor igno-rant, defend myſelf? Oh, Madam, if you knew but what he promiſed me, and how he aſſured me your ladyſhip ſhould come to no damage! or elſe the wealth of the In-dies ſhould not have bribed me to conſpire againſt ſo good, ſo ſweet, ſo kind a lady as you have been to me.

Lady W. No damage! What, to betray me, to marry me to a caſt ſerving-man; to make me a receptacle, an hoſpital for a decayed pimp! No damage! Oh, thou frontleſs impudence, ' more than a big-bellied actreſs!'

Foib. Pray, do but hear me, Madam. He could not marry your ladyſhip. Madam: no, indeed, his marriage was to have been void in law; for he was married to me firſt, to ſecure your ladyſhip. He could not have bedded your ladyſhip; for if he had conſummated with your la-dyſhip, he muſt have run the riſque of the law, and been put upon his clergy—Yes, indeed, I enquired of the law, in that caſe, before I would meddle or make.

Lady W. What, then, I have been your property, have I? I have been convenient to you, it ſeems, while you were catering for Mirabell. I have been broker for you. What, have you made a paſſive bawd of me? This exceeds all precedent. I am brought to fine uſes, to be-come a botcher of ſecond-hand marriages between Abi-gails and Andrews. I'll couple you; yes, I'll baſte you together, you and your Philander. I'll Duke's-Place you, as I'm a perſon. Your turtle is in cuſtody already: you ſhall coo in the ſame cage, if there be conſtable or warrant in the pariſh. *[Exit.*

G *Foib.*

Foib. Oh, that ever I was born! Oh, that ever I was married!—A bride! ay, I fhall be a Bridewell bride. Oh!

Enter Mrs. Fainall.

Mrs. Fain. Poor Foible! what's the matter?

Foib. Oh, Madam, my Lady's gone for a conftable! I fhall be had to a juftice, and put to Bridewell, to beat hemp. Poor Waitwell's gone to prifon already.

Mrs. Fain. Have a good heart, Foible; Mirabell is gone to give fecurity for him. This is all Marwood's and my hufband's doing.

Foib. Yes, I know it, Madam; fhe was in my Lady's clofet, and overheard all that you faid to me before dinner. She fent the letter to my Lady; and that miffing effect, Mr. Fainall laid this plot to arreft Waitwell, when he pretended to go for the papers; and in the mean time, Mrs. Marwood declared all to my Lady.

Mrs. Fain. Was there no mention made of me in the letter? My mother does not fufpect my being in the confederacy : I fancy Marwood has not told her, tho' fhe has tola my hufband.

Foib. Yes, Madam; but my Lady did not fee that part : we ftifled the letter before fhe read fo far. Has that mifchievous devil told Mr. Fainall of your ladyfhip, then?

Mrs. Fain. Ay, all's out, my affair with Mirabell, every thing difcovered. This is the laft day of our living together, that's my comfort.

Foib. Indeed, Madam, and fo it is a comfort, if you knew all. He has been even with your ladyfhip; which I could have told you long enough fince; but I love to keep peace and quietnefs by my good will. I had rather bring friends together, than fet them at a diftance. But Mrs. Marwood and he are nearer related than ever their parents thought for.

Mrs. Fain. Sayft thou fo, Foible? Canft thou prove this?

Foib. I can take my oath of it, Madam, fo can Mrs. Mincing; we have had many a fair word from Madam Marwood, to conceal fomething that paffed in our chamber, one evening, when you were at Hyde Park; and we were thought to have gone a walking; but we went up unawares--Though we were fworn to fecrecy too; Madam
Marwood

Marwood took a book, and fwore us upon it ; but it was but a book of poems : fo long as it was not a bible-oath, we may break it with a fafe confcience.

Mrs. Fain. This difcovery is the moſt opportune thing I could wiſh. Now, Mincing——

Enter Mincing.

Minc. My Lady would fpeak with Mrs. Foible, Mem. Mr. Mirabell is with her : he has fet your fpoufe at liberty, Mrs. Foible, and would have you hide yourfelf in my Lady's clofet, till my old Lady's anger is abated. Oh, my old Lady is in a perilous paffion at fomething Mr. Fainall has faid——He fwears, and my old Lady cries. There's a fearful hurricane, I vow. He fays, Mem, how that he'll have my Lady's fortune made over to him, or he'll be divorced.

Mrs. Fain. Does your Lady, or Mirabell, know that ?

Minc. Yes, Mem ; they have fent me to fee if Sir Wilfull be fober, and to bring him to them. My Lady is refolved to have him, I think, rather than lofe fuch a vaſt fum as fix thoufand pounds. Oh, come, Mrs. Foible ; I hear my old Lady.

Mrs. Fain. Foible, you muſt tell Mincing, that fhe muſt prepare to vouch, when I call her.

Foib. Yes, yes, Madam.

Minc. Oh, yes, Mem, I'll vouch any thing for your ladyſhip's fervice, be what it will. [*Ex.* Foib. *and* Minc.

Enter Lady Wiſhfort *and* Marwood.

Lady W. Oh, my dear friend ! how can I enumerate the benefits that I have received from your goodnefs ? To you I owe the timely difcovery of the falfe vows of Mirabell ; to you I owe the detection of the impoſtor, Sir Rowland ; and now you are become an interceffor with my fon-in-law, to fave the honour of my houfe, and compound for the frailties of my daughter. Well, friend, you are enough to reconcile me to the bad world, or elfe I would retire to defarts and folitudes, and feed harmlefs fheep by groves and purling ſtreams. Dear Marwood, let us leave the world, and retire by ourfelves, and be ſhepherdeffes.

Mrs. Mar. Let us firſt difpatch the affair in hand, Madam ; we fhall have leifure to think of retirement afterwards. Here is one who is concerned in the treaty.

Lady

Lady W. Oh, daughter, daughter! is it poffible thou fhouldft be my child, bone of my bone, and flefh of my flefh, and, as I may fay, another Me, and yet tranfgrefs the moft minute particle of fevere virtue? ' Is it poffible ' you fhould lean afide to iniquity, who have been caft in ' the direct mould of virtue? I have not only been a ' mould, but a pattern for you, and a model for you, af- ' ter you were brought into the world.'

Mrs. Fain. I don't underftand your ladyfhip.

Lady W. Not underftand! Why, have you not been naught? Have you not been fophifticated? Not under- ftand! Here I am ruined to compound for your caprices and your cuckoldums. I muft pawn my plate and my jewels, and ruin my niece, and all little enough——

Mrs. Fain. I'm wronged and abufed, and fo are you. 'Tis a falfe accufation, as falfe as hell, as falfe as your friend there, ay, or your friend's friend, my falfe huf- band.

Mrs. Mar. My friend, Mrs. Fainall! Your hufband my friend! What do you mean?

Mrs. Fain. I know what I mean, Madam, and fo do you; and fo fhall the world, at a time convenient.

Mrs. Mar. I am forry to fee you fo paffionate, Madam. More temper would look more like innocence. But I have done. I am forry my zeal to ferve your ladyfhip and family, fhould admit of mifconftruction, or make me liable to affronts. You will pardon me, Madam, if I meddle no more with an affair, in which I am not per- fonally concerned.

Lady W. Oh, dear friend! I am fo afhamed that you fhould meet with fuch returns——You ought to afk par- don on your knees, ungrateful creature! fhe deferves more from you, than all your life can accomplifh. Oh, don't leave me deftitute in this perplexity. No, ftick to me, my good genius.

Mrs. Fain. I tell you, Madam, you're abufed. Stick to you! ay, like a leach, to fuck your beft blood—fhe'll drop off when fhe's full. Madam, you fhan't pawn a bod- kin, nor part with a brafs counter, in compofition for me. I defy them all. Let them prove their afperfions. I know my own innocence, and dare ftand a trial. [*Exit.*

Lady W. Why, if fhe fhould be innocent; if fhe fhould

be wronged after all, ha?———I don't know what
to think———' And, I promife you, her education
' has been very unexceptionable. I may fay it: for
' I chiefly made it my own care to initiate her very
' infancy in the rudiments of virtue, and to impreſs
' upon her tender years a young odium and averfion to
' the very fight of men——ay, friend, fhe would ha'
' fhriek'd, if fhe had but feen a man, till fhe was in her
' teens. As I'm a perfon, 'tis true. She was never fuf-
' fered to play with a male child, tho' but in coats; nay,
' her very babies were of the feminine gender. Oh, fhe
' never looked a man in the face, but her own father, or
' the chaplain, and him we made a fhift to put upon her
' for a woman, by the help of his long garments, and his
' fleek face, 'till fhe was going in her fifteen.

' *Mrs. Mar.* 'Twas much fhe fhould be deceived fo
' long.

' *Lady W.* I warrant you, or fhe would never have
' borne to have been catechized by him, and have heard
' his long lectures againft finging and dancing, and fuch
' debaucheries; and going to filthy plays, and profane
' mufic-meetings, where the lewd trebles fqueak nothing
' but bawdy, and the baffes roar blafphemy. Oh, fhe
' would have fwooned at the fight or name of an ob-
' fcene play-book! And can I think, after all this, that
' my daughter can be naught? What, a whore, and
' thought it excommunication to fet her foot within the
' door of a playhoufe?' Oh, dear friend, I can't believe
it! No, no, as fhe fays, let him prove it, let him prove it.

Mrs. Mar. Prove it, Madam! what, and have your
name proftituted in a public court: yours and your daughter's reputation worried at the bar, by a pack of bawling
lawyers? To be ufhered in with an O Yes of fcandal; ' and
' have your cafe opened by an old fumbling letcher in a
' coif, like a man-midwife, to bring your daughter's infamy
' to light; to be a theme for legal punfters, and quibblers
' by the ftatute; and become a jeft, againft a rule of court,
' where there is no precedent for a jeft in any record,
' not even in Doomfday-book; to difcompofe the gravity
' of the bench, and provoke naughty interrogatories in
' more naughty law Latin; while the good judge, tick-
' led with the proceeding, fimpers under a grey beard,

' and

' and fidges off and on his cuſhion, as if he had fwallowed
' cantharides, or fat upon cow-itch.'

Lady W. Oh, 'tis very hard!

' *Mrs. Mar.* And then to have my young revellers of
' the Temple take notes, like 'prentices at a conventicle,
' and after talk it over again in Commons, or before draw-
' ers in an eating-houfe.

' *Lady W.* Worfe and worfe!'

Mrs. Mar. Nay, this is nothing; if it would end here
'twere well. But it muft, after this, be configned by the
fhort-hand writers to the public prefs; and from thence
be transferred to the hands, nay, into the throats and
lungs of hawkers, ' with voices more licentious than the
' loud flounder-man's:' and this you muſt hear till you
are ftunned; nay, you muſt hear nothing elfe for fome
days.

Lady W. Oh, 'tis infupportable! No, no, dear friend,
make it up, make it up; ay, ay, I'll compound; I'll give
up all, myfelf and my all, my niece and her all; any thing,
every thing for compofition.

Mrs. Mar. Nay, Madam, I advife nothing; I only lay
before you, as a friend, the inconveniencies which, perhaps, you have overfeen. Here comes Mr. Fainall; if
he will be fatisfied to huddle up all in filence, I ſhall be
glad. You muſt think I would rather congratulate than
condole with you.

Enter Fainall.

Lady W. Ay, ay, I do not doubt it, dear Marwood.
No, no, I do not doubt it.

Fain. Well, Madam, I have fuffered myfelf to be overcome by the importunity of this lady, your friend; and
am content you ſhall enjoy your own proper eftate during
life, on condition you oblige yourfelf never to marry,
under fuch penalty as I think convenient.

Lady W. Never to marry!

Fain. No more ſir Rowlands—the next impofture may
not be fo timely detected.

' *Mrs. Mar.* That condition, I dare anfwer, my Lady
' will confent to, without difficulty; ſhe has already but
' too much experienced the perfidioufnefs of men. Be-
' fides, Madam, when we retire to our paftoral folitude,
' we ſhall bid adieu to all other thoughts.

' *Lady*

' *Lady W.* Ay, that's true ; but in cafe of neceffity,
' as of health, or fome fuch emergency————

' *Fain.* Oh, if you are prefcribed marriage, you fhall be
' confidered ; I will only referve to myfelf the power to
' choofe for you. If your phyfic be wholefome, it mat-
' ters not who is your apothecary.' Next, my wife fhall
fettle on me the remainder of her fortune, not made over
already ; and for her maintenance depend entirely on my
difcretion.

Lady W. This is moft inhumanly favage ; ' exceeding
' the barbarity of a Mufcovite hufband.'

Fain. ' I learned it from his Czarifh majefty's retinue,
' in a winter evening's conference, over brandy and pep-
' per, amongft other fecrets of matrimony and policy, as
' they are at prefent practifed in the northern hemifphere.
' But this muft be agreed unto, and that pofitively.'
Laftly, I will be endowed, in right of my wife, with that
fix thoufand pounds, which is the moiety of Mrs. Millamant's fortune in your poffeffion ; and which fhe has forfeited (as will appear by the laft will and teftament of your
deceafed hufband, Sir Jonathan Wifhfort) for her difobe-
dience, in contracting herfelf without your confent or
knowledge ; and by refufing the offered match with Sir
Wilfull Witwoud, which you, like a careful aunt, had
provided for her.

Lady W. My nephew was *non compos*, and could not
make his addreffes.

Fain. I come to make demands——I'll hear no ob-
jections.

Lady W. You will grant me time to confider ?

Fain. Yes, while the inftrument is drawing, to which
you muft fet your hand till more fufficient deeds can be
perfected ; which I will take care fhall be done with all
poffible fpeed. In the mean while, I will go for the faid
inftrument ; and, till my return, you may balance this
matter in your own difcretion. [*Exit.*

Lady W. This infolence is beyond all precedent, all
parallel ! Muft I be fubject to this mercilefs villain ?

Mrs. Mar. 'Tis fevere indeed, Madam, that you fhould
fmart for your daughter's wantonnefs.

Lady W. 'Twas againft my confent that fhe married
this barbarian ; but fhe would have him, tho' her year was
not

not out——— Ah, her firſt huſband, my ſon Languiſh, would not have carried it thus. Well, that was my choice, this is hers; ſhe is matched now with a witneſs——I ———ſhall be mad; dear friend, is there no comfort for me? Muſt I live to be confiſcated at this rebel-rate? ———Here come two more of my Egyptian plagues too.

Enter Millamant *and Sir* Wilfull.

Sir Wil. Aunt, your ſervant.

Lady W. Out, caterpillar, call not me aunt? I know you not.

Sir Wil. I confeſs I have been a little in diſguiſe, as they ſay——'Sheart, and I'm ſorry for't. What would you have? I hope I committed no offence, aunt———and if I did, I am willing to make ſatisfaction; and what can a man ſay fairer? If I have broke any thing I'll pay for't, an it coſt a pound. And ſo let that content for what's paſt, and make no more words. For what's to come, to pleaſure you I'm willing to marry my couſin. So pray let's all be friends, ſhe and I are agreed upon the matter before a witneſs.

Lady W. How's this, dear niece? Have I any comfort? Can this be true?

Milla. I am content to be a ſacrifice to your repoſe, Madam, and to convince you that I had no hand in the plot, as you are miſinformed, I have laid my commands on Mirabell to come in perſon, and be a witneſs that I give my hand to this flower of knighthood; and for the contract that paſſed between Mirabell and me, I have obliged him to make a reſignation of it in your Lady-ſhip's preſence——He is without, and waits your leave for admittance.

Lady W. Well, I'll ſwear I am ſomething revived at this teſtimony of your obedience; but I cannot admit that traitor——I fear I cannot fortify myſelf to ſupport his appearance. He is as terrible to me as a Gorgon; if I ſee him, I fear I ſhall turn to ſtone, petrify inceſſantly.

Milla. If you diſoblige him, he may reſent your re-fuſal, and inſiſt upon the contract ſtill. Then 'tis the laſt time he will be offenſive to you.

Lady

Lady W. Are you fure it will be the laft time?—If I were fure of that——fhall I never fee him again?

Milla. Sir Wilfull, you and he are to travel together, are you not?

Sir Wil. 'Sheart, the gentleman's a civil gentleman; aunt, let him come in; why we are fworn brothers and fellow travellers.——We are to be Pylades and Oreftes, he and I——He is to be my interpreter in foreign parts. He has been over-feas once already; and with provifo that I marry my coufin, will crofs 'em once again, only to bear me company.——'Sheart, I'll call him in——an I fet on't once, he fhall come in; and fee who'll hinder him. *[Goes to the door and hems.*

Mrs. Mar. This is precious fooling, if it would pafs; but I'll know the bottom of it.

Lady W. Oh, dear Marwood, you are not going?

Mrs. Mar. Not far, Madam; I'll return immediately. *[Exit Mrs. Mar.*

Sir Wil. Look up, man, I'll stand by you; 'fbud an fhe do frown, fhe can't kill you;——befides——harkee, fhe dare not frown defperately, becaufe her face is none of her own? 'Sheart, an fhe fhould, her forehead would wrinkle like the coat of a cream cheefe; but mum for that, fellow-traveller.

Mira. If a deep fenfe of the many injuries I have offered to fo good a lady, with a fincere remorfe, and a hearty contrition, can but obtain the leaft glance of compaffion, I am too happy——' Ah, Madam, there was a
' time—but let it be forgotten—I confefs I have defer-
' vedly forfeited the high place I once held of fighing at
' your feet; nay, kill me not, by turning from me in
' difdain—I come not to plead for favour; nay, not for
' pardon; I am fuppliant only for pity'—I am going where I never fhall behold you more——

Sir Wil. How, fellow-traveller?——You fhall go by yourfelf then.

Mira. Let me be pitied firft, and afterwards forgotten —I afk no more.

Sir Wil. By'r Lady, a very reafonable requeft, and will coft you nothing, aunt——Come, come, forgive and forget, aunt; why you muft an you are a Chriftian.

Mira. At leaft think it is punifhment enough, that I have loft what in my heart I hold moft dear; that to
your

your cruel indignation I have offered up this beauty, and
with her my peace and quiet; nay, all my hopes of fu-·
ture comfort.

Sir Wil. An he does not move me, would I may never·
be of the Quorum——An it were not as good a deed as
to drink, to give her to him again,——I would I might
never take fhipping—— Aunt, if you don't forgive quickly, I fhall melt, I can tell you that, my contract went
no farther than a little mouth-glue, and that's hardly
dry :——one doleful figh more from my fellow-traveller,
and 'tis diffolved.

Lady. Well, nephew, upon your account——Ah, he·
has a falfe infinuating tongue——Well, Sir, I will ftifle·
my juft refentment at my nephew's requeft ——I will
endeavour what I can to forget——but on provifo that·
you refign the contract with my niece immediately.

Mira. It is in writing, and with papers of concern;
but I have fent my fervant for it, and will deliver it to
you, with all acknowledgments for your tranfcendent
goodnefs.

' *L. W.* Oh, he has witchcraft in his eyes and tongue;
' when I did not fee him, I could have bribed a villain·
' to his affaffination; but his appearance rakes the em-·
' bers which have fo long lain fmothered in my breaft.'
                                        [*Afide,*

                Enter Mr. Fainall *and Mrs.* Marwood.

Fain. Your date of deliberation, Madam, is expired.
Here is the inftrument; are you prepared to fign?

Lady|W. If I were prepared, I am not impowered.
My niece exerts a lawful claim, having matched herfelf
by my directions to Sir Wilfull.

Fain. That fham is too grofs to pafs on me——though
'tis impofed upon you, Madam.

Milla. Sir, I have given my confent.

Mira. And, Sir, I have refigned my pretenfions.

Sir Wil. And, Sir, I affert my right; and will maintain it in defiance of you, Sir, and of your inftrument.
'Sheart an you talk of an inftrument, Sir, I have an old
fox by my thigh fhall hack your inftrument of ram vellum to fhreds, Sir. It fhall not be fufficient for a mitti-·
mus, or a taylor's meafure; therefore withdraw your
inftrument, or by'r Lady I fhall draw mine.

                                              Lady

Lady W. Hold, nephew, hold.

Milla. Good Sir Wilfull, refpite your valour.

Fain. Indeed! Are you provided of your guard, with your fingle beaf-eater there. But I'm prepared for you; and infift upon the firft propofal. You fhall fubmit your own eftate to my management, and abfolutely make over my wife's to my fole ufe; as purfuant to the purport and tenor of this other covenant—I fuppofe, Madam, your confent is not requifite in this cafe; nor, Mr. Mirabell, your refignation; nor, Sir Wilfull, your right. ——You may draw your fox if you pleafe, Sir, and make a bear-garden flourifh fomewhere elfe: for here it will not avail. This, my lady Wifhfort, muft be fubfcribed, or your darling daughter's turned a-drift, like a leaky hulk, to fink or fwim, as fhe and the current of this lewd town can agree.

Lady W. ' Is there no means, no remedy to ftop my ' ruin?' Ungraieful wretch! doft thou not owe thy being, thy fubfiftence, to my daughter's fortune?

Fain. I'll anfwer you when I have the reft of it in my poffeffion.

Mira. But that you would not accept of a remedy from my hands—' I own I have not deferved you fhould ' owe any obligation to me;' or elfe perhaps I could advife——

Lady W. Oh, what? what? To fave me and my child from ruin, from want, I'll forgive all that's paft; nay, I'll confent to any thing to come, to be delivered from this tyranny.

Mira. Ay, Madam: but that's too late, my reward is intercepted. You have difpofed of her, who only could have made me a compenfation for all my fervices:—— But be it as it may, I am refolved I'll ferve you; you fhall not be wronged in this favage manner.

Lady W. How! Dear Mr. Mirabell? Can you be fo generous at laft! But it is not poffible. Harkee, I'll break my nephew's match; you fhall have my niece yet, and all her fortune, if you can but fave me from this imminent danger.

Mira. Will you? I take you at your word. I afk no more. I muft have leave for two criminals to appear.

Lady W. Ay, ay, any body, any body.

Mira.

Mira. Foible is one, and a penitent.

Enter Mrs. Fainall, Foible, *and* Mincing.

Mrs. Mar. Oh, my fhame! Thefe corrupt things are brought hither to expofe me.   [*To* Fain.

[*Mira. and Lady go to Mrs.* Fain *and* Foib.

Fain. If it muft all come out, why let them know it; 'tis but the Way of the World. That fhall not urge me to relinquifh or abate one tittle of my terms; no, I will infift the more.

Foib. Yes indeed, Madam, I'll take my bible oath of it.

Min. And fo will I, Mem.

Lady W. Oh, Marwood, Marwood, art thou falfe? My friend deceive me! Haft thou been a wicked accomplice with that profligate man?

Mrs. Mar. Have you fo much ingratitude and injuftice, to give credit againft your friend to the afperfions of two fuch mercenary trulls?

Minc. Mercenary, Mem! I fcorn your words. 'Tis true we found you and Mr. Fainall in the blue garret; by the fame token, you fwore us to fecrecy upon Meffalina's poems. Mercenary! No, if we would have been mercenary, we fhould have held our tongues; you would have bribed us fufficiently.

Fain. Go, you are an infignificant thing ——Well, what are you the better for this? Is this Mr. Mirabell's expedient; I'll be put off no longer——You, thing, that was a wife, fhall fmart for this. I will not leave thee wherewithal to hide thy fhame: your body fhall be naked as your reputation.

Mrs. Fain. I defpife you, and defy your malice—You have afperfed me wrongfully—I have proved your falfehood—Go, you and your treacherous—I will not name it, but ftarve together —— Perifh.

Fain. Not while you are worth a groat, indeed, my dear. Madam, I'll be fool'd no longer.

Lady W. Ah, Mr. Mirabell, this is fmall comfort, the detection of this affair.

Mira. O, in good time——your leave for the other offender and penitent to appear, Madam.

Enter Waitwell, *with a box of writings.*

L. W. O, Sir Rowland——Well, rafcal.

4

Wait.

Wait. What your ladyſhip pleaſes—I have brought the black box at laſt, Madam.

Mira. Give it me. ' Madam, you remember your ' promiſe.

' *Lady W.* Ay, dear Sir.'

Mira. Where are the gentlemen ?

Wait. At hand, Sir, rubbing their eyes—juſt riſen from ſleep.

Fain. 'Sdeath, what's this to me ? I'll not wait your private concerns.

Enter Petulant *and* Witwoud.

Pct. How now ? What's the matter ? Whoſe hand's out ?

Wit. Hey·day ! what are you all got together, like players at the end of the laſt act ?

Mira. You may remember, gentlemen, I once requeſted your hands as witneſſes to a certain parchment.

Wit. Ay, I do, my hand I remember.—Petulant ſet his mark.

Mira. You wrong him, his name is fairly written, as ſhall appear——you do not remember, gentlemen, any thing of what the parchment contained——

[*Undoing the box.*

Wit. No.

Pct. Not I. I writ, I read nothing.

Mira. Very well, now you ſhall know—' Madam, your promiſe.

' *Lady W.* Ay, ay, Sir, upon my honour.'

Mira. Mr. Fainall, it is now time that you ſhould know, that your lady, while ſhe was at her own diſpoſal, and before you had by your inſinuations wheedled her out of a pretended ſettlement of the greateſt part of her fortune——

Fain. Sir ! pretended !

Mira. Yes, Sir. I ſay that this lady, while a widow, having, it ſeems, received ſome cautions reſpecting your inconſtancy and tyranny of temper, ' which from her ' own partial opinion and fondneſs of you, ſhe could ' never have ſuſpected,' ſhe did, I ſay, by the wholſome advice of friends, and of ſages learned in the laws of this land, deliver this ſame , as her act and deed, to me in truſt, and to the uſes within mentioned. You may read, if you

H   pleaſe

Pleafe——[*Holding out the parchment*] though perhaps what is written on the back may ferve your occafions.

Fain. Very likely, Sir. What's here? Damnation! [*Reads.*] " A deed of conveyance of the whole eftate real of Arabella Languifh, widow, in truft to Edward Mirabell." Confufion!

Mira. Even, fo, Sir, 'tis the Way of the World, Sir; of the widows of the world. I fuppofe this deed may bear an elder date than what you have obtained from your lady.

Fain. Perfidious fiend! then thus I'll be reveng'd——
{*Offers to run at* Mrs. Fain.

Sir Wil. Hold, Sir! now you may make your beargarden flourifh fomewhere elfe, Sir.

Fain. Mirabell, you fhall hear of this, Sir, be fure you fhall————Let me pafs, oaf.   [*Exit.*

Mrs. Fain. Madam, you feem to ftifle your refentment : you had better give it vent.

Mrs. Mar. Yes, it fhall have vent——and to your confufion, or I'll perifh in the attempt. [*Exit* Mrs. Mar.

Lady W. O daughter, daughter, 'tis plain thou haft inherited thy mother's prudence.

Mrs. Fain. Thank Mr. Mirabell, a cautious friend, to whofe advice all is owing.

Lady W. Well, Mr. Mirabell, you have kept your promife,—and I muft perform mine.——Firft, I pardon, for your fake, Sir Rowland there, and Foible——The next thing is to break the matter to my nephew—and how to do that ——

Mira. For that, Madam, give yourfelf no trouble,— let me have your confent—Sir Wilfull is my friend; he has had compaffion upon lovers, and generoufly engaged a volunteer in this action, for our fervice; and now defigns to profecute his travels.

Sir Wil. 'Sheart, aunt, I have no mind to marry. My coufin's a fine lady, and the gentleman loves her, and fhe loves him, and they deferve one another; my refolution is to fee foreign parts——I have fet on't—— and when I'm fet on't, I muft do't. And if thefe two gentlemen wou'd travel too, I think they may be fpared.

Pet. For my part, I fay little—I think things are beft off or not.

Wit.

Wit. I gad, I underſtand nothing of the matter—I'm in a maze yet, like a dog in a dancing-ſchool.

Lady W. Well, Sir, take her, and with her all the joy I can give you.

Milla. Why does not the man take me ? Would you have me give myſelf to you over again ?

Mira. Ay, and over and over again ; [*Kiſſes her hand.*] I would have you as often as poſſibly I can. Well heaven grant I love you not too well, that's all my fear.

Sir Wil. 'Sheart, you'll have time enough to toy after you're marry'd ; ' or if you will toy now, let us have a ' dance in the mean time ; that we who are not lovers ' may have ſome other employment beſides looking on.

' *Mira.* With all my heart, dear Sir Wilfull. What ' ſhall we do for muſic ?

' *Foib.* O, Sir, ſome that were provided for Sir Row- ' land's entertainment, are yet within call. [*A dance.*]

Lady W. As I am a perſon I can hold out no longer—I ' have waſted my ſpirits ſo to-day already, that I am ready ' to ſink under the fatigue ; and' I cannot but have ſome fear upon me yet, that my ſon Fainall, will purſue ſome deſperate courſe.

Mira. Madam, diſquiet not yourſelf on that account ; to my knowledge, his circumſtancs are ſuch, he muſt of force comply ; ' for my part I will contribute all ' that in me lies, to a re-union.' In the mean time, Madam, [*To* Mrs. Fain.] let me, before theſe witneſſes, reſtore to you this deed of truſt ; it may be a means, well managed, to make you live eaſily together.

From hence let thoſe be warn'd, who mean to wed ;
Leſt mutual falſhood ſtain the bridal-bed :
For each deceiver to his coſt may find,
That marriage-frauds, too oft are paid in kind.

[*Exeunt.*

END of the FIFTH ACT.

EPILOGUE.

AFTER our Epilogue this croud difmiffes,
  I'm thinking how this play'll be pull'd to pieces.
But pray confider, e're you doom its fall,
How hard a thing 'twould be, to pleafe you all.
There are fome critics fo with fpleen difeas'd,
They fcarcely come, inclining to be pleas'd:
And fure he muft have more than mortal fkill,
Who pleafes any one againft his will.
Then all bad poets, we are fure are foes,
And how their number's fwell'd, the town well knows;
In fhoals, I've mark'd 'em, judging in the pit;
Tho' they're on no pretence for judgment fit,
But that they have been damn'd for want of wit.
Since when, they, by their own offences taught,
Set up for fpies on plays, and finding fault.
Others there are, whofe malice we'd prevent;
Such, who watch plays, with fcurrilous intent
To mark out who by characters are meant:
And tho' no perfect likenefs they can trace;
Yet each pretends to know the copy'd face.
Thefe, with falfe gloffes, feed their own ill-nature,
And turn to libel, what was meant a fatire.
May fuch malicious fops this fortune find,
To think themfelves alone the fools defign'd:
If any are fo arrogantly vain,
To think they fingly can fupport a fcene,
And furnifh fool enough to entertain.
For well the learn'd and the judicious know,
That fatire fcorns to ftoop fo meanly low,
As any one abracted fop to fhew.
For, as when painters form a matchlefs face,
They from each fair one, catch fome diff'rent grace;
And fhining features in one portrait blend,
To which no fingle beauty muft pretend:
So poets oft, do in one piece expofe,
Whole belles affemblées of coquets and beaus.

J. Roberts del.   Publish'd for Bell's British Theatre April 25, 1777.   B. Reading sculp.

*M*r *QUICK, in the Character of* **JUDGE GRIPUS.**

'Tis my proper Chattel, and, I'll have it.

BELL'S EDITION.

AMPHITRYON:

OR, THE

TWO SOCIAS.

A COMEDY,

As altered from DRYDEN *by* Dr. HAWKESWORTH.

DISTINGUISHING ALSO THE

VARIATIONS OF THE THEATRE,

AS PERFORMED AT THE

Theatre-Royal in Drury-Lane.

Regulated from the Prompt-Book,

By PERMISSION *of the* MANAGERS,

By Mr. HOPKINS, Prompter.

LONDON:

Printed for JOHN BELL, near *Exeter-Exchange,* in the *Strand.*

MDCCLXXVII.

ADVERTISEMENT.

On comparing this play, as performed at the Theatres, with the original, it was found impracticable to restore it to its primitive state, without throwing the whole into confusion; the Editor, therefore, hopes the reasons assigned in the Preface for the alterations and additions, will render it more acceptable to the reader than the original, and exculpate him, for deviating from his general rule *of giving the author entire.*

P R E F A C E.

THE abilities of Dryden as a writer, are so generally and so justly acknowledged to be of the first
class, that it would be something worse than impropriety,
to alter any of his productions without assigning the reason. For the alteration of his Amphitryon, indeed, the
reason is evident; for it is so tainted with the profane-
ness and immodesty of the time in which he wrote, that
the present time, however selfish and corrupt, has too
much regard to external decorum, to permit the representation of it upon the stage, without drawing a veil, at
least, over some part of its deformity : the principal part
of the alterations, therefore, are made with a moral
view ; though some inaccuracies, which were remarked
on the examination which these alterations made necessary, are also removed, of which the following are the
chief.

In the scene between Sofia and Mercury, in the Second
Act, Amphitryon is supposed to have sent a buckle of
diamonds by Sofia, as a present to Alcmena ; for Sofia first
asks Mercury if *Amphitryon did send a certain servant with
a present to his wife* ; and soon after asks him, " what that
" present was ;" which, by Mercury's answer, appears
to be the diamond buckle : yet in the scene between Amphitryon and Alcmena, in the Third Act, when Alcmena asks him, as a proof of his having been with her
before, from whose hands she had the jewel, he cries out,
" This is amazing ; have I already given you those dia-
" monds ? *the present I reserved*——" And instead of
supposing that Sofia had delivered them as part of his
errand, which he pretended he could not execute, he
appeals to him for their being in safe custody, reserved
to be presented by himself. This is an inconsistency peculiar to Dryden, for neither Plautus nor Moliere any
where mention the present to have been sent by Sofia.

There

There is another inaccuracy of the fame kind, which occurs both in Plautus and Moliere. It appears in the Second Act, that one part of Sofia's errand was to give Alcmena a particular account of the battle; and Sofia's account of his being prevented, is fo extravagant and abfurd, that Amphitryon cannot believe it: yet, when Alcmena, in the Third Act, afks Amphitryon how fhe came to know *what he had fent* Sofia *to tell her*, Amphitryon, in aftonifhment, feems to admit that fhe could know thefe particulars *only from himfelf*, and does not confider her queftion as a proof that Sofia had indeed delivered his meffage, though for fome reafons he had pretended the contrary, and forged an incredible ftory to account for his neglect. As it would have been much more natural for Amphitryon to have fuppofed that Sofia had told him a lie, than that Alcmena had, by a miracle, learned what only he and Sofia could tell her, without feeing either of them; this inaccuracy is removed, by introducing fuch a fuppofition, and making the dialogue correfpond with it.

In the Second Act, Jupiter, in the character of Amphitryon, leaves Alcmena with much reluctance, pretending hafte to return to the camp, and great folicitude to keep his vifit to her a fecret from the Thebans: yet when he appears again in the Third Act, which he knew would be taken for the third appearance of Amphitryon, he does not account for his fuppofed fecond appearance at the return of the real Amphitryon, juft after his departure, which feems to be abfolutely neceffary to maintain his borrowed character confiftently; and without dropping the leaft hint of his being no longer folicitous to conceal his excurfion from the camp, he fends Sofia to invite feveral of the citizens to dinner.

Many other inaccuracies lefs confiderable, and lefs apparent, have been removed, which it is not neceffary to point out: whoever fhall think it worth while diligently to compare the play as it ftood, with the altered copy, can fcarce fail to fee the reafon of the alterations as they occur.

It muft be confeffed, that there are ftill many things in Amphitryon, which, though I did not obliterate, I would not have written; but I think none of thefe are
ex-

exceptionable in a moral view. There are many paſſages in which lord Amphitryon and lady Alcmena are treated by their ſervants with a familiarity, which is not now allowed on the greater ſtage of the living world; and, indeed, from this fault, I ſcarce know any comedy that is perfectly free: however, ſome of the groſſer freedoms that were taken by Phædra with the character of Judge Gripus, are rejected; and this was the more neceſſary, as Gripus was Alcmena's uncle; and, therefore, in her preſence, could not, without the utmoſt impropriety, be enquired after of Amphitryon himſelf, as a wretch who had grown old in the abuſe of his office as a magiſtrate, by ſelling juſtice, and ſwelling his purſe with bribes.

If, after all, it be aſked, why this play was altered at all, I anſwer, becauſe it might otherwiſe have been revived, either by other managers, or at another houſe, without being altered, otherwiſe than by being maimed: ſome parts, indeed would have been left out; but as nothing would have been ſubſtituted in the ſtead, it would have become imperfect, in proportion as it became leſs vicious ; and would ſtill have been ſo vicious in the very conſtituent parts, as to ſully, and, perhaps, corrupt almoſt every mind, before which it had been repreſented. But though I ſhould have been ſorry to ſee the joint work of Plautus, Moliere, and Dryden, ſo mutilated, as to loſe that proportion of parts by which alone thoſe parts can conſtitute a whole; yet my principal view was effectually to prevent the exhibition of it in a condition, in which it could not be ſafely ſeen: and this, I hope, will be admitted as a ſufficient apology, for my having thus employed ſome hours of that time which ſhall return no more, by thoſe who have little regard for Amphitryon as a piece of ancient humour, retouched and heightened by two of the moſt eminent maſters that modern times have produced.

The

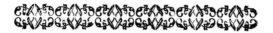

The Original PROLOGUE.

Written by Mr. DRYDEN.

THE lab'ring bee, when his sharp sting is gone,
  Forgets his golden work, and turns a drone :
Such is a satyr, when you take away
That rage, in which his noble vigour lay.
What gain you, by not suffering him to teize ye ?
He neither can offend you, now, nor please ye.
The honey-bag and venom lay so near,
That both together you resolv'd to tear ;
And lost your pleasure, to secure your fear.
How can he show his manhood, if you bind him
To box, like boys, with one hand ty'd behind him ?
This is plain levelling of wit ; in which
The poor has all th' advantage, not the rich.
The blockhead stands excus'd for wanting sense ;
And wits turn blockheads in their own defence.
Yet, though the stage's traffic is undone,
Still Julian's interloping trade goes on :
Though satyr on the theatre you smother,
Yet in lampoons, you libel one another.
The first produces still a second jig ;
You whip them out, like school-boys, till they gig :
And, with the same success, we readers guess ;
For, every one still dwindles to a less.
And much good malice, is so meanly drest,
That we wou'd laugh, but cannot find the jest.
If no advice your rhiming rage can stay,
Let not the ladies suffer in the fray.
Their tender sex is privileg'd from war ;
'Tis not like knights, to draw upon the fair.

What

What fame expect you from so mean a prize?
We wear no murd'ring weapons, but our eyes.
Our sex, you know, was after yours design'd;
The last perfection of the Maker's mind:
Heav'n drew out all the gold for us, and left your dross
  behind.
Beauty, for valour's best reward, he chose;
Peace, after war; and after toil, repose.
Hence, ye prophane, excluded from our sights,
And charm'd by day, with honour's vain delights,
Go, make your best of solitary nights.
Recant betimes, 'tis prudence to submit:
Our sex is still your overmatch in wit:
We never fail, with new successful arts,
To make fine fools of you, and all your parts.

PROLOGUE.

THIS night let busy man to pleasure spare:
   Far hence be searching thought, and pining care ;
Far hence whate'er can agonize the soul,
Grief, terror, rage, the dagger, and the bowl !
The comic muse, a gay propitious pow'r,
To dimpled laughter gives this mirthful hour.
The scenes which Plautus drew, to-night we shew
Touch'd by Moliere, by Dryden taught to glow.
Dryden !—in evil days his genius rose,
When wit and decency were constant foes :
Wit then defil'd in manners and in mind,
Whene'er he sought to please, disgrac'd mankind.
Freed from his faults, we bring him to the fair ;
And urge once more his claim to beauty's care.
That thus we court your praise, is praise bestow'd ;
Since all our virtue from your virtue flow'd.
But there are some—no matter where they sit—
Who smack their lips and hope the luscious bit.
These claim regard, deny it they that can——
" The prince of darkness is a gentleman !"
Yet why apologize, though these complain ;
They're free to all the rest of Drury-Lane.
To these bright rows we boast a kind intent ;
We sought their plaudit, and their pleasure meant.
Yet not on what we give, our fame must rise ;
In what we take away, our merit lies.
On no new force bestow'd we found our claim ;
To make wit honest, was our only aim :
If we succeed, some praise we boldly ask——
To make wit honest is no easy task.

DRAMATIS PERSONÆ.

MEN.

	Drury-Lane.	*Covent-Garden.*
Jupiter,	Mr. Reddish.	Mr. Lewis.
Mercury,	Mr. Jefferson.	Mr. Lee Lewes.
Phœbus,	Mr. Hurst.	Mr. Booth.
Amphitryon,	Mr. Aickin.	Mr. Wroughton.
Sofia,	Mr. King.	Mr. Woodward.
Gripus,	Mr. Parsons.	Mr. Quick.
Polidas,	Mr. Fawcett.	
Tranie,	Mr. Chaplin.	

WOMEN.

Alcmena,	Miss Younge.	Mrs. Hartley.
Phædra,	Miss Pope.	Mrs. Mattocks.
Bromia,	Mrs. Bradshaw.	Mrs. Pitt.
Night,	Miss Platt.	Mrs. Pouffin.

SCENE, *THEBES.*

AMPHITRYON.

AMPHITRYON.

⁂ The lines marked with inverted commas, 'thus,' are omitted in the representation.

ACT I.

Mercury *and* Phœbus *discovered.*

PHOEBUS.

KNOW you the reason of this present summons ?
'Tis neither council-day, nor is this heaven.
What business has our Jupiter on earth ?
Why more at Thebes than any other place ?
And why are we, of all the deities,
Selected out to meet him in consult ?
They call me God of Wisdom ; but the hind,
That, whistling, turns the furrow to my beams,
Knows full as much as I.

Merc. I have discharged my duty, which was to summon you, Phœbus. We shall know more anon, when the thunderer comes down. 'Tis our part to obey our father ; and here he is.

Jupiter *descends.*

Jup. No thoughts, not ev'n of gods, are hid from Jove.
Your doubts are all before me ; but my will,
In awful darkness wrapt, no eye can reach,
Till I withdraw the veil. Yet thus far know,
That, for the good of human kind, this night
I shall beget a future Hercules,
Who shall redress the wrongs of injur'd mortals,
Shall conquer monsters, and reform the world.

Phœb. Some mortal, we presume, of Cadmus' blood—
Some Theban beauty——

Jup. Yes, the fair Alcmena.
You two must be subservient to my purpose.

3   Amphitryon,

Amphitryon, the brave Theban general,
Has overcome his country's foes in fight,
And in a fingle duel flain their king.
His conquering troops are eager on their march,
Returning home ; while their young general,
More eager to review his beauteous wife,
Pofts on before, wing'd with impetuous love,
And, by to-morrow's dawn, will reach this town.

Phœb. Then how are we to be employ'd this evening ?
Time's precious, and thefe fummer nights are fhort ;
I muft be early up to light the world.

Jup. You fhall not rife ; there fhall be no to-morrow.

Merc. Then the world's to be at an end, I find.

Phœb. Or elfe a gap in nature, of a day.

Jup. The night, if not reftrain'd, too foon would pafs ;
Too foon the dawn would bring Amphitryon back,
Whofe place I mean to hold. And fure a day,
One day, will be well loft to bufy man.
Night fhall continue fleep, and care fufpend :
So, many men fhall live, and live in peace,
Whom funfhine had betray'd to envious fight,
And fight to fudden rage, and rage to death.

Phœb. I fhall be curs'd by all the lab'ring trades,
That early rife. But you muft be obey'd.

Jup. No matter for the cheating part of man ;
They have a day's fin lefs to anfwer for.

Phœb. When would you have me wake ?

Jup. Your brother Mercury fhall bring you word.
                    [*Exit* Phœbus *in his chariot.*

Now, Hermes, I muft take Amphitryon's form ;
Thou muft be Sofia, this Amphitryon's flave,
Who, all this night, is travelling to Thebes,
To tell Alcmena of her lord's approach,
And bring her joyful news of victory.

Merc. But why muft I be Sofia ?

Jup. Dull god of wit, thou ftatue of thyfelf !
Thou muft be Sofia, to keep out Sofia,
Whofe entrance well might raife unruly noife,
And fo diftract Alcmena's tender foul,
She would not meet, with equal warmth, my love.

Merc. Let me alone ; I'll cudgel him away ;
But I abhor fo villainous a fhape.

                                    Jup.

Jup. Take it; I charge thee, on thy duty, take it;
Nor dare to lay it down, till I command thee.

        Night *appears above in her chariot.*

Look up; the Night is in her silent chariot,
And rolling just o'er Thebes. Bid her drive flowly,
Or make a double turn about the world;
While I drop Jove, and take Amphitryon's drefs,
To be the greater, while I feem the lefs.   [*Exit* Jup.

Merc. [*To* Night.] Madam Night, a good even to you.
Fair and foftly, I befeech you, Madam: I have a word
or two to you, from no lefs a god than Jupiter.

Night. Oh, my induftrious and rhetorical friend, is it
you? What makes you here upon earth at this unfeafonable hour?

Merc. Why, I'll tell you prefently; but firft let me fit
down; for I'm confoundedly tired.

Night. Fie, Mercury! fure your tongue runs before
your wit, now. Does it become a god, think you, to
fay that he is tired?

  Merc. Why, do you think the Gods are made of iron?

Night. No; but you fhould always keep up the decorum of divinity in your converfation, and leave to mankind the ufe of fuch vulgar words as derogate from the
dignity of immortality.

Merc. Ay, 'tis fine talking, faith, in that eafy chariot
of yours: you have a brace of fine geldings before you,
and have nothing to do, but to touch the reins with your
finger or thumb, throw yourfelf back in your feat, and enjoy your ride wherever you pleafe: but 'tis not fo with
me; I, who am the meffenger of the gods, and traverfe
more ground, both in heaven and earth, than all of them
put together, am, thanks to Fate, the only one that is
not furnifhed with a vehicle.

Night. But if Fate has denied you a vehicle, fhe has
beftowed wings upon your feet.

Merc. Yes, I thank her, that I might make the more
hafte; but does making more hafte, keep me from being
tired, d'ye think?

Night. Well, but to the bufinefs. What have you to
fay to me?

Merc. Why, as I told you, I have a meffage from Jupiter; it is his will and pleafure, that you muffle up this

part of the world in your dark mantle, fomewhat longer than ufual at this time of the year.

Night. Why, what is to be done now?

Merc. Done! why, he is this night to be the progenitor of a demigod, who fhall deftroy monfters, humble tyrants, and redrefs the injured; men are to become happy by his labours, and heroic by his example.

Night. Jupiter is very gracious indeed to mankind; but I am not much obliged to him for the honourable employment he has been pleafed to affign me in this bufinefs.

Merc. Not obliged to him, Madam! why fo? You was always a friend to mankind; and he might reafonably think you would take pleafure in deferving their homage upon fo important an occafion.

Night. Pleafure! What, in taking upon me the moft odious character; a character that————

Merc. Come, come, Madam; that is good of which good comes: this is a fafe principle for us deities, whatever it is for mortals, who can no more fee the confequences of their own actions, than what is doing behind your curtain.

Night. Sir, I beg pardon—I acknowledge, Sir, that you are much better acquainted with thefe affairs than I am; and therefore will e'en accept of my employment, relying wholly upon your judgment.

Merc. Not fo faft, good Madam Night; none of your innuendo's, if you pleafe: you are reported not to be fo fhy as you pretend; and I know that you are the trufty confident of many a private treaty, and have as little to boaft of, in fome particulars, as I.

Night. Well, well, do not let us expofe ourfelves to the malicious laughter of mankind, by our quarrels.

Merc. About your bufinefs, then; put a fpoke into your chariot-wheels, and order the feven ftars to halt, while I put myfelf into the habit of a ferving-man, and drefs up a falfe Sofia, to wait upon a falfe Amphitryon. Good night, Night.

Night. My fervice to Jupiter. Farewel, Mercury.

[Night *goes backward.* *Exit* Merc.

SCENE,

SCENE, Amphitryon's *Palace.*

Enter Alcmena.

Alc. Why was I marry'd to the man I love ?
For, had he been indifferent to my choice,
Or had been hated, abfence had been pleafure ;
But now I fear for my Amphitryon's life.
At home, in private, and fecure from war,
I am amidft an hoft of armed foes ;
Suftaining all his cares, pierc'd with his wounds ;
And, if he falls, (which, Oh, ye gods, avert !)
Am in Amphitryon flain. Would I were there,
And he were here ! fo might we change our fates,
That he might grieve for me, and I might die for him !

Enter Phædra, *running.*

Phæd. Good news, good news, Madam !—Oh, fuch
admirable news, that, if I kept it in a moment, I fhould
burft with it !

Alc. Is it from the army ?

Phæd. No matter.

Alc. From Amphitryon ?

Phæ. No matter, neither.

Alc. Anfwer me, I charge thee, if thy good news be
any thing relating to my Lord ; if it be, affure thyfelf
of a reward.

Phæd. Ay, Madam, now you fay fomething to the matter. You know the bufinefs of a poor waiting-woman
here upon earth, is to be fcraping up fomething againft a
rainy day, called the day of marriage ; every one in our
own vocation. But what matter is it to me if my Lord
has routed the enemy, if I get nothing of their fpoils ?

Alc. Say, is my Lord victorious ?

Phæd. Why, he is victorious. Indeed, I prayed de-
voutly to Jupiter for a victory ; by the fame token, that
you fhould give me ten pieces of gold, if I brought you
news of it.

Alc. They are thine ; fuppofing he be fafe too.

Phæd. Nay, that's a new bargain ; for I vowed to
Jupiter, that then you fhould give me ten pieces more.
But I do undertake for my Lord's fafety, if you will
pleafe to difcharge Jupiter of the debt, and take it upon
you to pay.

B 2

Alc. When he returns in safety, Jupiter and I will pay your vow.

Phæd. And I am sure I articled with Jupiter, that if I brought you news, that my Lord was upon return, you should grant me one small favour more, that will cost you nothing.

Alc. Make haste, thou torturer; is my Amphitryon upon return?

Phæd. Promise me that I shall be your bedfellow to-night, as I have been ever since my Lord's absence —— unless I shall be pleased to release you of your word.

Alc. That's a small request; 'tis granted.

Phæd. But, swear, by Jupiter.

Alc. I swear, by Jupiter.

Phæd. Then, I believe he is victorious; and I know he is safe; for I looked through the key-hole, and saw him knocking at the gate.

Alc. And wouldst thou not open to him? Oh, thou traitress!

Phæd. No, I was a little wiser. I left Sofia's wife to let him in; for I was resolved to bring the news, and make my pennyworths out of him, as time shall show.

Enter Jupiter *in the shape of* Amphitryon, *with* Sofia's *wife,* Bromia. *He kisses and embraces* Alcmena.

Jup. Oh, let me live for ever on those lips!
The nectar of the gods to these is tasteless.
I swear, that were I Jupiter, this night
I would renounce my Heav'n to be Amphitryon.

Alc. Then, not to swear beneath Amphitryon's oath,
(Forgive me, Juno, if I am profane)
I swear, I would be what I am this night,
And be Alcmena, rather than be Juno.

Brom. Good, my Lord, what's become of my poor bedfellow, your man, Sofia? What, I say, tho' I am a poor woman, I have a husband as well as my Lady.

Phæd. And what have you done with your old friend, and my old sweetheart, Judge Gripus? If he be rich, I'll make him welcome, like an honourable magistrate; but if not——

Alc. My Lord, you tell me nothing of the battle.
Is Thebes victorious? Are our foes destroy'd?

For,

For, now I find you fafe, I fhould be glad
To hear you were in danger.

Brom. [*Pulling him on one fide.*] I afked the firft queftion ; anfwer me, my Lord.

Phæd. [*Pulling him on t'other fide.*] Peace ! mine's a lover, and yours but a hufband ; and my Judge is my Lord too ; the title fhall take place, and I will be anfwered.

Jup. Sofia is fafe—Gripus is rich—both coming——
I rode before them with a lover's hafte.——

Alc. Then I, it feems, am laft to be regarded ?

Jup. Not fo, my love, but thefe obftreperous tongues
Have fnatch'd their anfwers firft—they will be heard.
Let us retire where none fhall interrupt us ;
I'll tell thee there the battle and fuccefs.
But I fhall oft begin, and then break off ;
For love will often interrupt my tale,
And make fo fweet confufion in our talk,
That thou fhalt afk, and I fhall anfwer things,
That are not of a piece, but patch'd with kiffes ;
And nonfenfe fhall be eloquent in love.

Alc. I am the fool of love, and find within me
The fondnefs of a bride, without the fear.
My whole defires and wifhes are in you.
Great Juno ! thou, whofe holy care prefides
O'er wedded love, thy choiceft bleffings pour
On this aufpicious night.

Jup. Juno may grudge ; for fhe may fear a rival
In thofe bright eyes : but Jupiter will grant,
And doubly blefs this night.

Phæd. [*Afide.*] But Jupiter fhould afk my leave firft.

Alc. Bromia, prepare the chamber ;
The tedious journey has difpos'd my Lord
To feek his needful reft.   [*Exit* Bromia.

Phæd. 'Tis very true, Madam ; the poor gentleman muft needs be weary : and, therefore, 'twas not ill contrived, that he muft lie alone to-night.

Alc. [*To* Jup.] I muft confefs, I made a kind of promife.

Phæd. [*Almoft crying.*] A kind of promife, do you call it ? I fee you would fain be coming off. I am fure you fwore to me, by Jupiter, that I fhould be your bedfellow ; and I'll accufe you to him too, the firft prayers I make ; and I'll pray on purpofe too, that I will.

Jup.

Jup. Oh, the malicious hilding!

Alc. I did fwear, indeed, my Lord.

Jup. Forfwear thyfelf; for Jupiter but laughs
At lovers perjuries.

Phæd. The more fhame for him, if he does.

Jup. Alcmena, come——

Alc. [*Sighing.*] She has my oath;
And fure fhe may releafe it, if fhe pleafes——

Phæd. Why, truly, Madam, I am not cruel, in my nature, to poor diftreffed lovers; for it may be my own
cafe another day: and therefore, if my Lord pleafes to
confider me——

Jup. Any thing, any thing! but name thy wifh, and
have it——

Phæd. Ay, now you fay, any thing, any thing! but
you would tell me another ftory to-morrow morning.
Look you, my Lord, here's a hand open to receive: you
know the meaning of it.

Jup. Thou fhalt have all the treafury of heaven.

Phæd. Yes, when you are Jupiter to difpofe of it. You
have got fome part of the enemies fpoil, I warrant you——
I fee a little trifling diamond upon your finger; and I am
proud enough to think it would become mine too.

Jup. Here, take it.
         [*Taking a ring off his finger, and giving it.*
This is a very woman:
Her fex is avarice, and fhe, in one,
Is all her fex.

Phæd. Ay, ay, 'tis no matter what you fay of us. Go,
get you together, you naughty couple——To-morrow
morning I fhall have another fee for parting you.
         [Phædra *goes out before* Alcmena *with a light.*

Jup. Now, for one night, I leave the world to Fate;
Love is alone my great affair of ftate.
This night let all my altars fmoke in vain,
And man, unheeded, praife me, or complain.
Yet if in fome fhort intervals of reft,
By fome fond youth, an am'rous vow's addreft,
His pray'r is in an happy hour preferr'd;
And when Jove loves, a lover fhall be heard.   [*Exit.*

END of the FIRST ACT.

A C T

ACT II.

A Night-Scene of a Palace.

Sofia *with a dark-lanthorn*: Mercury, *in* Sofia's *shape, with a dark-lanthorn also.*

SOSIA.

WAS not the devil in my master, to send me out this dreadful dark night, to bring the news of his victory to my Lady ? And was not I possessed with ten devils, for going on his errand, without a convoy for the safeguard of my person ? Lord how am I melted into sweat with fear ! I am diminished of my natural weight above two stone. I shall not bring half myself home again, to my poor wife and family. Well, the greatest plague of a serving-man is to be hired to some great lord. They care not what drudgery they put upon us, while they lie lolling at their ease a-bed, and stretch their lazy limbs in expectation of the whore which we are fetching for them. The better sort of them will say, Upon my honour, at every word : yet ask them for our wages, and they plead the privilege of their honour, and will not pay us ; nor let us take our privilege of the law upon them. These are a very hopeful sort of patriots, to stand up as they do, for liberty and property of the subject. There's conscience for you !

Merc. [*Aside.*] This fellow has something of the republican spirit in him.

Sof. [*Looking about him.*] Stay; this, methinks, should be our house. And I should thank the gods now, for bringing me safe home. But I think I had as good let my devotions alone, till I have got the reward for my good news, and then thank them once for all ; for, if I praise them before I am safe within doors, some damn'd mastiff dog may come out and worry me ; and then my thanks are thrown away upon them.

Merc. [*Aside.*] Thou art a wicked rogue, and wilt have thy bargain before-hand : therefore thou get'st not into the house this night ; and thank me accordingly as I use thee.

Sof. Now I am to give my Lady an account of my Lord's victory ; 'tis good to exercise my parts before-hand, and file my tongue into eloquent expressions; to tickle her ladyship's imagination.

Mercs.

Merc. [*Afide.*] Good! and here's the god of eloquence to judge of thy oration.

Sof. [*Setting down his lanthorn.*] This lanthorn, for once, fhall be my Lady; becaufe fhe is the lamp of all beauty and perfection.

Merc. Excellent!

Sof. Then thus I make my addreffes to her. [*Bows.*] Madam, my Lord has chofen me out, as the moft faithful, though the moft unworthy of his followers, to bring your ladyfhip this following account of our glorious expedition. —Then fhe—Oh, my poor Sofia, [*In a fhrill tone.*] how am I overjoyed to fee thee!—She can fay no lefs——— Madam, you do me too much honour, and the world will envy me this glory—Well anfwered on my fide——And how does my Lord Amphitryon?——Madam, he always does like a man of courage, when he is called by honour —There, I think, I nick'd it——But, when will he return?——As foon as poffibly he can; but not fo foon as his impatient heart could wifh him with your ladyfhip.

Merc. [*Afide.*] When Thebes is an univerfity, thou deferveft to be their orator.

Sof. But what does he do, and what does he fay? Pr'ythee, tell me fomething more of him—— He always fays lefs than he does, Madam; and his enemies have found it to their coft—Where the devil did I learn thefe elegancies and gallantries?

Merc. So; he has all the natural endowments of a fop, and only wants the education.

Sof. [*Staring up to the fky.*] What, is the devil in the night? She's as long as two nights. The feven ftars are juft where they were feven hours ago. High day—high night, I mean, by my favour. What, has Phœbus been playing the good-fellow, and over-flept himfelf, that he forgets his duty to us mortals?

Merc. How familiarly the rafcal treats us gods! but I fhall make him alter his tone immediately.

[*Mercury comes nearer, and ftands juft before him.*

Sof. [*Seeing him, and ftarting back. Afide.*] How now! What, do my eyes dazzle, or is my dark lanthorn falfe to me? Is not that a giant before our door, or a ghoft of fomebody flain in the late battle? If he be, 'tis uncon-fcionably done, to fright an honeft man thus, who never
drew

drew weapon wrathfully in all his life. Whatever wight he be, I am devilishly afraid, that's certain ; but 'tis discretion to keep my own counsel. I' lsing, that I may seem valiant.

[Sofia *sings* ; *and as* Mercury *spea*   *little and little drops* *his voice.*

Merc. What saucy companion is this, that deafens us with his hoarse voice ? What midnight ballad-finger have we here ? I shall teach the villain to leave off catterwawling.

Sof. I would I had courage for his sake ; that I might teach him to call my singing catterwawling—An illiterate rogue ; an enemy to the muses and to music.

Merc. There is an ill favour that offends my nostrils ; and it wafteth this way.

Sof. He has smelt me out. My fear has betrayed me into this favour—I am a dead man—The bloody villain is at his fee, fa, fum, already.

Merc. Stand ; who goes there ?

Sof. A friend.

Merc. What friend ?

Sof. Why, a friend to all the world that will give me leave to live peaceably.

Merc. I defy peace and all its works—My arms are out of exercise ; they have mauled nobody these three days : I long for an honourable occasion to pound a man, and lay him asleep at the first buffet.

Sof. [*Aside.*] That would almost do me a kindness ; for I have been kept waking, without tipping one wink of sleep, these three nights.

Merc. Of what quality are you, fellow ?

Sof. Why, I am a man, fellow—Courage, Sofia !——

Merc. What kind of man ?

Sof. Why, a two-legged man ; what man should I be ? [*Aside.*] I must bear up to him ; he may prove as errant a milksop as myself.

Merc. Thou art a coward, I warrant thee ; do I not hear thy teeth chatter in thy head ?

Sof. Ay, ay, that's only a sign they would be snapping at thy nose—[*Aside.*] Bless me, what an arm and fist he has ! with great thumbs too, and golls and knuckle-bones of a very butcher.

Merc.

Merc. Sirrah, from whence come you, **and whither go**
you ? Anfwer me directly, upon pain of affaffination.

Sof. I am coming from whence I came, and am going
whither I go ; that's directly home. Tho' this is fomewhat an uncivil manner of proceeding, at the firft fight
of a man, let me tell you.

Merc. Then, to begin our better acquaintance, let me
firft make you a fmall prefent of this box o' th' ear——
                                             [*Strikes him.*

Sof. If I were as choleric a fool as you are, now, here
would be fine work betwixt us two ; but I am a little better bred, than to difturb the fleeping neighbourhood ;
and fo, good night, friend——   [*Going.*

Merc. [*Stopping him.*] Hold, Sir ; you and I muft not
part fo eafily.   Once more, whither are you going ?

Sof. Why, I am going as faft as I can, to get out of the
reach of your clutches.   Let me but only knock at that
door there.

Merc. What bufinefs have you at that door, firrah ?

Sof. This is our houfe ; and when I'm got in I'll tell
you more.

Merc. Whofe houfe is this, faucinefs, that you are fo
familiar with, to call it ours ?

Sof. 'Tis mine, in the firft place ; and next, my mafter's ;
for I lie in the garret, and he lies under me.

Merc. Have your mafter and you no names, firrah ?

Sof. His name is Amphitryon—Hear that, and tremble.

Merc. What, my lord general ?

Sof. Oh ! has his name mollified you ? I have brought
you down a peg lower already, friend.

Merc. And your name is———

Sof. Lord, friend, you are fo very troublefome—What
fhould my name be, but Sofia ?

Merc. How, Sofia, fay you ; How long have you taken up that name, firrah ?

Sof. Here's a fine queftion ! Why, I never took it up,
friend ; it was born with me.

Merc. What, was your name born Sofia ? Take this remembrance for that lie.   [*Beats him.*

Sof. Hold, friend ; you are fo very flippant with your
hands, you won't hear reafon. What offence has my name
done you, that you fhould beat me for it ? S. O. S. I. A.
                                                    they

they are as civil, honeſt, harmleſs letters, as any are in the whole alphabet.

Merc. I have no quarrel to the name, but that 'tis e'en too good for you, and 'tis none of yours.

Sof. What, am not I Soſia, ſay you?

Merc. No.

Sof. I ſhould think you are ſomewhat merrily diſpoſed, if you had not beaten me in ſuch ſober ſadneſs. You would perſuade me out of my heathen name, would you?

Merc. Say you are Soſia again, at your peril, ſirrah.

Sof. I dare ſay nothing; but thought is free. But, whatever I am called, I am Amphitryon's man, and the firſt letter of my name is S too. You had beſt tell me that my maſter did not ſend me home to my lady, with news of his victory.

Merc. I ſay he did not.

Sof. Lord, lord, friend, one of us two is horribly given to lying!—but I do not ſay which of us, to avoid con‑ tention.

Merc. I ſay my name is Soſia, and yours is not.

Sof. I would you could make good your words; for then I ſhould not be beaten, and you ſhould.

Merc. I find you would be Soſia, if you durſt—' but ' if I catch you thinking ſo——

' *Sof.* I hope I may think I was Soſia; and I can find ' no difference between my former ſelf, and my preſent ' ſelf; but that I was plain Soſia before, and now I am ' lac'd Soſia.'

Merc. Take this, for being ſo impudent to think ſo.

[*Beats him.*

Sof. [*Kneeling.*] Truce a little, I beſeech thee. I would be a ſtock or a ſtone, now, by my good will, and would not think at all, for ſelf-preſervation. But will you give me leave to argue the matter fairly with you, and promiſe me to depoſe that cudgel, if I can prove myſelf to be that man that I was before I was beaten.

' *Merc.* Well, proceed in ſafety. I promiſe you I will ' not beat you.

' *Sof.* In the firſt place, then, is not this town called ' Thebes?

' *Merc.* Undoubtedly.

' *Sof.* And is not this houſe Amphitryon's?

2

' *Merc,*

' *Merc.* Who denies it ?

' *Sof.* I thought you would have denied that too ; for
' all hang upon a ſtring. Remember then, that theſe
' two preliminary articles are already granted. In the
' next place, did not the aforeſaid Amphitryon beat the
' Teleboans, kill their king, Pterelas, and ſend a certain
' ſervant, meaning ſomebody, that for ſake's-ſake ſhall be
' nameleſs, with news of his victory, and of his reſolution
' to return to-morrow ?

' *Merc.* This is all true, to a very tittle : but who is
' that certain ſervant ? there's all the queſtion.

' *Sof.* Is it peace or war betwixt us ?

' *Merc.* Peace.

' *Sof.* I dare not wholly truſt that abominable cudgel.
' But 'tis a certain friend of yours and mine, that had a
' certain name, before he was beaten out of it. But if
' you are a man that depend not altogether upon force
' and brutality, but ſomewhat alſo upon reaſon, now do
' you bring better proofs that you are that ſame cer-
' tain man ; and in order to it, anſwer me to certain
' queſtions.

' *Merc.* I ſay I am Sofia, Amphitryon's man. What
' reaſon have you to urge againſt it ?

' *Sof.* What was your father's name ?

' *Merc.* Davus ; who was an honeſt huſbandman, whoſe
' ſiſter's name was Harpage, that was married and died in
' a foreign country.

' *Sof.* So far you are right, I muſt confeſs ; and your
' wife's name is——

' *Merc.* Bromia—a deviliſh ſhrew of her tongue, and a
' vixen of her hands, that leads me a miſerable life——

' *Sof.* By many a ſorrowful token. This muſt be I.

' *Merc.* I was once taken upon ſuſpicion of burglary,
' and was whipped through Thebes, and branded for my
' pains.

' *Sof.* Right me again. But if you are I, as I begin to
' ſuſpect, that whipping and branding might have been
' paſſed over in ſilence, for both our credits.'——And yet,
now I think on't, if I am I, (as I am I) he cannot be I.
All theſe circumſtances he might have heard ; but I will
now interrogate him upon ſome private paſſages. [*Aſide.*]
What was Amphitryon's ſhare of the booty ?

Merc.

Merc. A buckle of diamonds, confifting of five large ftones, which was worn as an ornament by Pterelas.

Sof. What does he intend to do with it?

Merc. To prefent it to his wife, Alcmena.

Sof. And where is it now?

Merc. In a cafe, fealed with my mafter's coat of arms.

Sof. This is prodigious, I confefs!—but yet 'tis nothing, now I think on't; for fome falfe brother may have revealed it to him. [*Afide.*]—But I have another queftion to afk you, of fomewhat that paffed only betwixt myfelf and me—If you are Sofia, what were you doing in the heat of battle?

Merc. What a wife man fhould, that has a refpect for his own perfon. I ran into our tent, and hid myfelf amongft the baggage?

Sof. [*Afide.*] Such another cutting anfwer, and I muft provide myfelf of another name. [*To him.*] And how did you pafs your time in that fame tent?—You need not anfwer to every circumftance fo exactly now; you muft lie a little, that I may think you the more me.

Merc. That cunning fhall not ferve your turn, to circumvent me out of my name. I am for plain naked truth——There ftood a hogfhead of old wine, which my Lord referved for his own drinking——

Sof. [*Afide.*] Oh, the devil! As fure as death, he muft have hid himfelf in that hogfhead, or he could never have known that.

Merc. And by that hogfhead, upon the ground, there lay the kind inviter and provoker of good drinking——

Sof. Nay, now I have caught you—there was neither inviter nor provoker; for I was all alone.

Merc. A lufty gammon of ——

Sof. Bacon!——That word has quite made an end of me——Let me fee—This muft be I, in fpite of me—— But let me view him nearer.

[*Walks about* Mercury *with his dark lanthorn.*

Merc. What are you walking about me for, with your dark lanthorn?

Sof. No harm, friend; I am only furveying a parcel of earth here that I find we two are about to bargain for. [*Afide.*] He's damnable like me, that's certain. —*Imprimis*, there's the patch upon my nofe, with a pox to him——

C   *Item,*

Item, A very foolish face, with a long chin at the end on't—*Item*, one pair of shambling legs, with two splay feet belonging to them. And—*summa totalis*, from head to foot, all my bodily apparel——[*To Merc.*] Well, you are Sofia; there's no denying it. But what am I, then? for my mind misgives me, I am somebody still, if I knew but who I were.

Merc. When I have a mind to be Sofia no more, then thou may'st be Sofia again.

Sof. I have but one request more to thee—that, tho' not as Sofia, yet as a stranger, I may go into that house, and carry a civil message to my Lady.

Merc. No, sirrah; not being Sofia, you have no message to deliver, nor lady in this house.

Sof. Thou canst not be so barbarous, to let me lie in the streets all night, after such a journey, and such a beating; and therefore I am resolved to knock at the door in my own defence.

Merc. If you come near the door, I recall my word, and break off the truce——and then expect————

[*Holds up his cudgel.*

Sof. No, the devil take me, if I do expect—I have felt too well what sour fruit that crab-tree bears: I'll rather beat it back upon the hoof to my Lord Amphitryon, to see if he will acknowledge me for Sofia: if he does not, then I am no longer his slave; there's my freedom dearly purchased with a sore drubbing: if he does acknowledge me, then I am Sofia again; so far 'tis tolerably well: but then I shall have a second drubbing for an unfortunate ambassador as I am; and that's intolerable. [*Exit.*

Merc. I have fobbed his excellency pretty well. Now let him return, and make the best of his credentials. But here comes Jupiter.

Enter Jupiter, *leading* Alcmena, *followed by* Phædra. *Pages with torches before them,*

Jup. Those torches are offensive; stand aloof:

[*To the Pages.*

For tho' they bless me with thy heav'nly sight, [*To her.* They may disclose the secret I would hide. The Thebans must not know I have been here; Detracting crouds would blame me, that I stole These happy moments from my public charge,

To

To confecrate to thee ; and I could wifh
That none were witnefs of the theft, but fhe
By whom it is approv'd——

Alc. So long an abfence, and fo fhort a ftay !
What, but one night ! One night of joy and love,
Could only pay one night of cares and fears ;
And all the reft are an uncancell'd fum.

Jup. Alcmena, I muft go.

Alc. Not yet, my Lord.

Jup. Indeed, I muft.

Alc. Indeed, you fhall not go.

Jup. Behold the ruddy ftreaks o'er yonder hill !
Thofe are the blufhes of the breaking morn,
That kindle day-light to this nether world.

Alc. No matter for the day ; it was but made
To number out the hours of bufy men.
Let them be bufy ftill, and ftill be wretched ;
And take their fill of anxious drudging day :
But you and I will draw our curtains clofe,
Extinguifh day-light, and fhut out the fun.
Stay, then, my Lord—I'll bribe you with this kifs.

' *Merc.* [*Afide.*] That's a plaguy little devil. What a
' roguifh eye fhe has ! I begin to like her ftrangely.
' She's the perquifite of my place too; for my Lady's
' waiting-woman is the proper fees of my Lord's chief
' gentleman.'

Jup. A bribe, indeed, that foon will bring me back ;
Though now it is not poffible to ftay.

Alc. Not poffible ! Alas, how fhort is life,
If we compute alone thofe happy hours
In which we wifh to live ! ' Our feventy years
' Are fill'd with pains, difeafes, wants and woes,
' And only dafh'd with love; a little love !
' Sprinkled by fits, and with a fparing hand.
' Count all our joys, from childhood ev'n to age,
' They would but make a day of ev'ry year.
' Oh, would the gods comprife the quinteffence
' In feventy days, and take the reft away !'

Jup. By heav'n, thy ev'ry word and look, Alcmena,
Fans the fierce flame thy charms have kindled here.
My love, encreas'd by thine, as fire by fire,
Mounts with more ardour in a brighter blaze.

But

But yet one fcruple pains me at my parting;
I love fo nicely, that I cannot bear
To owe my pleafures to fubmiffive duty:
Tell me, and footh my paffion, that you give them
All to the lover, and forget the hufband.

     ' *Alc.* And yet, my Lord, the hufband's right alone
' Can juftify the love that burns for you:
' Nor do I fuffer ought that would fuggeft
' The fcruple which your fond defire has rais'd.
     ' *Jup.* Oh, that you lov'd like me! then you would
' A thoufand thoufand niceties in love.   [find
' The common love of fex to fex is brutal:
' But love refin'd will fancy to itfelf
' Millions of gentle cares, and fweet difquiets.
' The being happy is not half the joy;
' The manner of the happinefs is all.
     ' *Alc.* Confeffing that you love and are belov'd,
' Reft happy in that thought, nor wifh to lofe
' The right that confecrates the lover's joy.
     ' *Jup.* I am at once a lover and an hufband;
' But as a lover only I am happy:
' A lover, jealous of a hufband's right,
' By which he fcorns to claim; whofe tend'reft joy
' Muft all be giv'n, not paid. Oh, my Alcmena,
' Indulge the lover's wifhes, thus refin'd,
' Divide him from the hufband, give to each
' What each requires, thy virtue to the hufband,
' And on the lover lavifh all thy love!'

    Alc. I comprehend not what you mean, my Lord:
But only love me ftill, and love me thus,
And think me fuch as beft may pleafe your thought.

    Jup. There's myftery of love in all I fay:
But duty, cruel duty, tears me from thee.
Howe'er, indulge at leaft this fmall requeft——
When next you fee your hufband, dear Alcmena,
Think of your lover then.

    Alc. Oh, let me ne'er divide what Heav'n has join'd!
Hufband and lover both are dear to me.

    Jup. Farewel——

    Alc. Farewel——But will you foon return?

    Jup. I will, believe me, with a lover's hafte.

    [*Exeunt* Jup. *and* Alc. *feverally:* Phæd. *follows her.*
                         Mer.

Merc. Now I fhould follow him ; but Love has laid a lime-twig for me, and made a lame god of me. Yet why fhould I love this Phædra ? She's mercenary, and a jilt into the bargain. Three thoufand years hence, there will be a whole nation of fuch women, in a certain country that will be called France ; and there's a neighbour ifland too, where the men will be all intereft. Oh, what a precious generation will that be, which the men of the ifland fhall propagate out of the women of the continent !

Re-enter Phædra.

And fo much for prophecy ; for fhe's here again, and I muft love her, in fpite of me.

Phæd. Well, Sofia, and how go matters ?

Merc. Our army is victorious.

Phæd. And my fervant, Judge Gripus ?

Merc. A voluptuous gormand.

Phæd. But has he gotten wherewithal to be voluptuous ? Is he wealthy ?

Merc. He fells juftice as he ufes, fleeces the rich rebels, and hangs up the poor.

Phæd. Then, while he has money he may make love to me. Has he fent me no token ?

Merc. Yes, a kifs ; and by the fame token, I am to give it you, as a remembrance from him.

Phæd. How now, impudence ! A beggarly ferving-man prefume to kifs me !

Merc. Suppofe I were a god, and fhould make love to you ?

Phæ. I would firft be fatisfied whether you were a poor god or a rich god.

Merc. Suppofe I were Mercury, the god of merchandife ?

Phæd. What, the god of fmall wares and fripperies, of pedlars and pilferers ?

Merc. [*Afide.*] How the gipfy defpifes me !

Phæd. I had rather you were Plutus, the god of money, or Jupiter in a golden fhower. There was a god for us women ! He had the art of making love. Doft thou think that kings, or gods either, get miftreffes by their good faces ? No, 'tis the gold and the prefents they can make : there's the prerogative they have over their fair fubjects.

Merc.

Merc. All this notwithſtanding, I muſt tell you, pretty Phædra, I am deſperately in love with you.

Phæd. And I muſt tell thee, ugly Sofia, thou haſt not wherewithal to be in love.

Merc. Yes, a poor man may be in love, I hope.

Phæd. I grant, a poor rogue may be in love; but he can never make love   Alas, Sofia! thou haſt neither face to invite me, nor youth to pleaſe me, nor gold to bribe me; and, beſides all this, thou haſt a wife—Poor, miſerable Sofia!——What, ho, Bromia!

Merc. Oh, thou mercileis creature! why doſt thou conjure up that ſprite of a wiſe?

Phæd. To rid myſelf of that devil of a poor lover. Since you are ſo lovingly diſpoſed, I'll put you together. What, Bromia, I ſay, make haſte.

Merc. Since thou wilt call her, ſhe ſhall have all the cargo I have gotten in the wars.

Phæd. Why, what have you gotten, good gentleman ſoldier, beſides a legion of——   [*Snaps her fingers.*

Merc. When the enemy was routed, I had the plundering of a tent.

Phæd. That's to ſay, a houſe of canvas, with moveables of ſtraw——Make haſte, Bromia——

Merc. But it was the general's own tent.

Phæd. You durſt not fight, I'm certain; and therefore came laſt in, when the rich plunder was gone beforehand. Will you come, Bromia?

Merc. Pr'ythee, do not call ſo loud——A great goblet, that holds a gallon.

Phæd. Of what was that goblet made? Anſwer quickly; for I am juſt calling very loud——Bro——

Merc. Of beaten gold. Now call aloud, if thou doſt not like the metal.

Phæd. Bromia!   [*Very ſoftly.*

Merc. That ſtruts in this faſhion, with his arms a-kimbo, like a city magiſtrate; and a great bouncing belly, like a hoſteſs with child of a kilderkin of wine. Now what ſay you to that preſent, Phædra?

Phæd. Why, I am conſidering——

Merc. What, I pr'ythee?

Phæd. Why, how to divide the buſineſs equally; to
take

take the gift, and refuse the giver, thou art so damnably ugly and so old.

Merc. [*Afide.*] Oh, that I was not confined to this ungodly shape to-day! But Gripus is as old and as ugly too.

Phæd. But Gripus is a person of quality, and my lady's uncle; and if he marries me, I shall take place of my lady. Hark, your wife! she has sent her tongue before her. I hear the thunder-clap already; there's a storm approaching.

Merc. Yes, of thy brewing, I thank thee for it: Oh, how I should hate thee now, if I could leave loving thee!

Phæd. Not a word of the dear golden goblet, as you hope for——you know what, Sofia.

Merc. You give me hope then——

Phæd. Not absolutely hope neither: but gold is a great cordial in love matters; and the more you apply of it, the better.——[*Afide.*] I am honest, that's certain; but when I weigh my honesty against the goblet, I am not quite resolved on which side the scale will turn.

[*Exit* Phædra.

Merc. [*Aloud.*] Farewel, Phædra; remember me to my wife, and tell her——

Enter Bromia.

Brom. Tell her what? Traitor! that you are going away without seeing her.

Merc. That I am doing my duty, and following my master.

Brom. Umph——so brisk too! Your master could leave his army in the lurch, and come galloping home at midnight, and steal to bed as quietly as any mouse, I warrant you: my master knew what belonged to a married life; but you, sirrah——You trencher-carrying rascal, you worse than dunghill-cock! that stood clapping your wings and crowing without doors, when you should have been at roost, you villain!——

Merc. Hold your peace, dame Partlet, and leave your cackling: my master charged me to stand centry without doors.

Brom. My master! I dare swear thou bely'st him; my master's more a gentleman than to lay such an un-

rea-

reafonable command upon a poor diftreffed married
couple, and after fuch an abfence too. No, there's no
comparifon between my mafter and thee, thou fneakfby.

Merc. No more than there is betwixt my lady and you,
Bromia. You and I have had our time in a civil way,
fpoufe, and much good love has been betwixt us : but
we have been married fifteen years, I take it; and that
hoighty toighty bufinefs ought, in confcience, to be
over.

Brom. Marry come up, my faucy companion ! I am
neither old, nor ugly enough, to have that faid to me.

Merc. But will you hear reafon, Bromia ? My lord
and my lady are yet in a manner bride and bridegroom :
—do but think in decency, what a jeft it would be to the
family, to fee two venerable old married people, ogling
and leering, and fighing out fine tender things to one
another !

Brom. How now, traitor ! dareft thou maintain that I
am paft the age of having fine things faid to me ?

Merc. Not fo, my dear ; but certainly I am paft the
age of faying them.

Brom. Thou deferveft not to be yoked with a woman
of honour, as I am, thou perjured villain !

Merc. Ay, you are too much a woman of honour, to
my forrow ; many a poor hufband would be glad to compound for lefs honour in his wife, and more quiet. Be
honeft and continent in thy tongue, and do thy worft
with every thing elfe about thee.

Brom. Thou wouldft have me a woman of the town,
wouldft thou ! to be always fpeaking my hufband fair,
to make him digeft his cuckoldom more eafily : wouldft
thou be a wittal, with a vengeance to thee? I am refolved I'll fcour thy hide for that word.

[*Holds up her ladle at him.*

Merc. Thou wilt not ftrike thy lord and hufband,
wilt thou ? [*She courfes him about* ; Mercury *running about.*]
[*Afide.*] Was ever poor deity fo hen-pecked as I am !—
Nay, then 'tis time to charm her afleep with my en-
chanted rod,—before I am difgraced or ravifhed——

[*Plucks out his caduceus, and ftrikes her upon the fhoulder
with it.*

Brom. What, art thou rebelling againft thy anointed
wife !

wife ! I'll make thee——How now !——What, has
the rogue bewitched me ! I grow dull and ftupid on the
fudden——I can neither ftir hand nor foot——[*Yawn-
ing.*]——I can't fo much as wag my tongue—neither;
and that's the laft live—ing part about a——woman——
[*Falls down.*

Merc. [*Alone.*] Lord, what have I fuffered, for being
but a counterfeit married man one day ! If ever I come
to his houfe, as a hufband again——then—— And yet
that then was a lie too—For while I am in love with this
young gipfy, Phædra, I muft return——But lie thou
there, thou type of Juno ; thou that wanteft nothing of
her tongue, but the immortality. If Jupiter ever let
thee fet foot where fhe is, Juno will have a rattling
fecond of thee.

For two fuch tongues will break the poles afunder;
And, hourly fcolding, make perpetual thunder.
[*Exit* Mercury.

End of the Second Act.

ACT III.

SCENE, *before* Amphitryon's *Palace.*

Amphitryon *and* Sofia.

Amphitryon.

NOW, firrah, follow me into the houfe—thou fhalt
be convinced at thy own coft, villain ! What horrible lies haft thou told me ! fuch improbabilities, fuch
ftuff, fuch nonfenfe!——

Sof. I am but a flave, and you are mafter ; and a poor
man is always to lie, when a rich man is pleafed to contradict him : but as fure as this is our houfe——

Am. So fure 'tis thy place of execution.

Sof. Hold, dear Sir ! if I muft have a fecond beating,
in confcience let me ftrip firft, that I may fhow you the
black and blue ftreaks upon my fides and fhoulders. I am
fure I fuffered them in your fervice.

Am. To what purpofe wouldft thou fhow them ?

Sof. Why, to the purpofe that you may not ftrike me
upon

upon the fore places; and that as he beat me the laſt night croſs-ways, ſo you would pleaſe to beat me long-ways, to make clean work on't, that at leaſt my ſkin may look like chequer-work.

Am. This requeſt is too reaſonable to be refuſed : but, that all things may be done in order, tell me over again the ſame ſtory, with all the circumſtances of thy com-miſſion; that a blow may follow in due form for every lie. To repetition, rogue, to repetition.

Sof. No, it ſhall be all lie if you pleaſe, and I'll eat my words to ſave my ſhoulders.

Am. Ay, ſirrah, now you find you are to be diſproved; but 'tis too late : to repetition, rogue, to repetition.

Sof. With all my heart, to any repetition but the cudgel. But would you be pleaſed to anſwer me one civil queſtion; Am I to uſe complaiſance to you, as to a great perſon, that will have all things ſaid your own way; or, am I to tell you the naked truth alone, with-out the ceremony of a farther beating ?

Am. Nothing but the truth, and the whole truth; ſo help thee cudgel.

Sof. That's a damned concluſion of a ſentence : but ſince it muſt be ſo——Back and ſides, at your own peril——I ſet out from the port in an unlucky hour; I went darkling, and whiſtling, to keep myſelf from be-ing afraid; mumbling curſes betwixt my teeth, for be-ing ſent at ſuch an unnatural time of night.

Am. How, ſirrah, curſing and ſwearing againſt your lord and maſter! take—— [*Going to ſtrike.*

Sof. Hold, Sir—pray conſider, if this be not unreaſo-able, to ſtrike me for telling the whole truth, when you commanded me : I'll fall into my old dog-trot of lying again, if this muſt come of plain dealing.

Am. To avoid impertinences, make an end of your journey; and come to the houſe : what found you there ?

Sof. I found before the door a ſwinging fellow, with all my ſhapes and features, and accoutered alſo in my habit.

' *Am.* Who was that fellow ?

' *Sof.* Who ſhould it be, but another Sofia ! a certain ' kind of another me : who knew all my unfortunate

' com-

' commiffion, precifely to a word, as well as I Sofia; as
' being fent by yourfelf from the port, upon the fame
' errand to Alcmena.

' *Am.* What grofs abfurdities are thefe?

' *Sof.* Oh, lord, Oh, lord! what abfurdities? as plain
' as any packftaff. That other me, had pofted himfelf
' there before me, me.—You won't give a man leave to
' fpeak poetically now; or, elfe I would fay, that I was
' arrived at the door, before I came thither.

' *Am.* This muft either be a dream, or drunkennefs,
' or madnefs in thee. Leave your buffooning and ly-
' ing, I am not in humour to bear it, firrah.

' *Sof.*' I would you fhould know I fcorn a lie, and am
a man of honour in every thing, but juft fighting. I tell
you once again, in plain fincerity and fimplicity of heart,
that, before laft night, I never took myfelf but for one
fingle individual Sofia; but, coming to our door, I found
myfelf, I know not how, divided, and, as it were, fplit
into two Sofias.

Am. Leave buffooning: I fee you would make me
laugh; but you play the fool fcurvily.

Sof. That may be: but if I am a fool, I am not the
only fool in this company.

Am. How now, impudence! I fhall———

Sof. Be not in wrath, Sir: I meant not you. I cannot
poffibly be the only fool; for if I am one fool, I muft
certainly be two fools; becaufe, as I told you, I am
double.

Am. That one fhould be two is very probable!—A
man had need of patience to endure this gibberifh—be
brief, and come to a conclufion———

Sof. What would you have, Sir? I came thither, but
the t'other I was there before me; for that there were
two I's, is as certain, as that I have two eyes in this
head of mine. This I, that am here, was weary: the
t'other I was frefh: this I was peaceable, and t'other I
was a hectoring bully I.

' *Am.* And thou expecteft I fhould believe thee?

' *Sof.* No, I am not fo unreafonable; for I could
' never have believed it myfelf, if I had not been well
' beaten into it: but a cudgel, you know, is a con-
' vincing argument in a brawny fift. What fhall I fay,
' but

' but that I was compelled at laſt to acknowledge my-
' ſelf? I found that he was very I, without fraud, cozen,
' or deceit. Beſides, I viewed myſelf, as in a mirror,
' from head to foot—he was handſome, of a noble pre-
' ſence, a charming air, looſe and free in all his mo-
' tions—and ſaw he was ſo much I, that I ſhould have
' reaſon to be better ſatisfied with my own perſon, if his
' hands had not been a little of the heavieſt.'

Am. Once again to a concluſion: ſay you paſſed by
him, and entered into the houſe.

Soſ. I am a friend to truth, and ſay no ſuch thing : he
defended the door, and I could not enter.

Am. How, not enter !

Soſ. Why, how ſhould I enter ? unleſs I were a ſprite
to glide by him, and ſhoot myſelf through locks, and
bolts, and two-inch boards ?

Am. Oh, coward ! Didſt thou not attempt to paſs ?

Soſ. Yes; and was repulſed, and beaten for my pains.

Am. Who beat thee ?

Soſ. I beat me.

Am. Didſt thou beat thyſelf?

Soſ. I don't mean I, here : but the abſent me beat me
here preſent.

Am. There's no end of this intricate piece of nonſenſe.

Soſ. 'Tis only nonſenſe, becauſe I ſpeak it who am a
poor fellow ; but it would be ſenſe, and ſubſtantial ſenſe,
if a great man ſaid it, that was backed with a title, and
the eloquence of ten thouſand pounds a year.

Am. No more—but let us enter. Hold; my Alcmena
is coming out, and has prevented me ! How ſtrangely will
ſhe be ſurprized to ſee me here, ſo unexpectedly !

Enter Alcmena *and* Phædra.

Alc. [*To* Phæd.] Make haſte after me to the temple ;
that we may thank the gods for this glorious ſucceſs,
which Amphitryon has had againſt the rebels. Oh,
heaven ! [*Seeing him.*

Am. Thoſe heav'ns, and all the bleſt inhabitants,
[*Saluting her.*

Grant, that the ſweet rewarder of my pains
May ſtill be kind, as on our nuptial night.

Alc. So ſoon return'd !

3 *Am.*

Am. So foon return'd! Is this my welcome home?
　　　　　　　　　　　　　　[Stepping back.
So foon return'd, fays I am come unwifh'd!
This is no language of defiring love:
Love reckons hours for months, and days for years;
And every little abfence is an age.

　Alc. What fays, my lord?

　Am. No, my Alcmena, no:
True love by its impatience meafures time,
And the dear object never comes too foon.

　Alc. Nor ever came you fo, nor ever fhall:
But you yourfelf are chang'd from what you were,
' Pall'd in defires, and furfeited of blifs;'
Not fuch as when laft night at your return
I flew with tranfport to your clafping arms.

　Am. How's this?

　Alc. Did you not read your welcome in my eyes?
Did you not hear it in my falt'ring voice?
Did not the pleafing tumult fhake my frame,
Nature's fpontaneous proof of fudden joy,
Which no falfe love can feign!

　Am. What's this you tell me?

　Alc. Far fhort of truth, by Heav'n!
My proofs of joy, with joy you then receiv'd,
And gave with ufury back. At break of day
You left me with a figh; you now return,
Though not unwifh'd, yet furely unexpected;
And why fhou'd my furprife be thought a crime?

　Am. I left you with a figh at break of day!——

　Alc. Yes, for the camp,——have you forgot, Am-

　Am. Or, have you dream'd, Alcmena?　[phitryon?
Perhaps fome kind, revealing deity,
Has whifper'd, in your fleep, the pleafing news
Of my return; and you believ'd it real!

　Alc. Some melancholy vapour, fure, has feiz'd
Your brain, Amphitryon, and difturb'd your fenfe:
Or yefternight is not fo long a time,
But you might fpare my blufhes, and remember
How kind a welcome to my arms I gave you.

　Am. I thank you for my melancholy vapour.

　Alc. 'Tis but a juft requital for my dream.

　　　　　　　　D　　　　　　　　　　　*Phæd.*

Phæd. If my mafter thinks fit thus to angle for a quarrel, I think he had no great reafon to come back.

[In the mean time Amph. *and* Alc. *walk by themfelves, and frown at each other as they meet.*

Am. You dare not juftify it to my face.

Alc. Not what ?

Am. That I return'd before this hour.

Alc. You dare not, fure, deny you came laft night, And ftaid till break of day.

Am. Oh, impudence !——Why, Sofia !

Sof. Nay, I fay nothing ; for all things here may go by enchantment (as they did with me) for ought I know.

Alc. Speak, Phædra, was he here ?

Phæd. You know, Madam, I am but a chambermaid ; and by my place, I am to forget all that was done over night in love-matters,——unlefs my mafter pleafe to rub up my memory with another diamond.

Am. Now in the name of all the gods, Alcmena, A little recollect your fcatter'd thoughts, And weigh what you have faid.

Alc. I weigh'd it well, Amphitryon, e'er I fpoke ; And fhe, and Bromia, all the flaves and fervants, Can witnefs they beheld you when you came : If other proof be wanting, tell me how I came to know your fight, your victory, The death of Pterelas in fingle combat ?——

Am. [*Turning angrily to* Sofia.] Now, rafcal !—you did not get into the houfe And deliver my meffage, did you ? [*Going to ftrike him.*

Sof. Hold, Sir, for the fake of truth and mercy !—— Dear Madam ! [*To* Alcmena.] as your gentle nature is a friend to diftreffed innocence, interpofe in my behalf.

Alc. [*To* Amph.] Why will you not, Amphitryon, anfwer me ?

What in my queftion can have turn'd your rage On this poor flave ?

Am. What but grofs falfhoods, which he forg'd to mock me :

And you abet him——But for this——

[*Is again going to ftrike* Sofia.

Sof. Nay, dear Sir, do not punifh me unheard.

Am. Did you not tell me——

Sof.

Sof. Yes, I did tell you—and I told you truly, that when I would have gone into the houfe I was beaten away.

Am. Well, firrah, and don't it now appear by what Alcmena fays, that you did get in? How elfe could fhe know the news I fent you with, rafcal?

Sof. And don't it appear by my back and fhoulders, that I was beaten away? But you will not let a man produce his witneffes——

Am. Did you not get in? Anfwer me that, rogue, directly, and without equivocation.

Sof. Why, yes, it is true—and I muft confefs that in fome fenfe, it may be faid, I did get it; though it may alfo, in a certain fenfe, be truly faid, that I was beaten away.

Am. Why thou impudent, prevaricating——

Sof. Sir, let me befeech you, that reafon may predominate for my fake, and that you would make fuch diftinctions as the nature of my cafe requires: it is true that I did get in, and it is true that I did not get in ; this I, that is here now, did not get in, but was beaten away by t'other I; but that other I did get in, and was not beaten away ;—there is a me me, and there is a he me——

Am. Audacious flave! 'twere infamy to fpare thee.

Phæd. Do, my Lord; pray fpare him till he has told the reft of his ftory; it is but beating him a little the more when he has done.

Sof. [*Earneftly to* Phædra.] It was at that very door, there it is—here was one I, and there was t'other.

Phæd. What, you mean that you fquinted, and looked two ways at once.

Sof. I mean no fuch thing—[*He now turns from her and addreffes* Alcmena.] ' It is not eafy to make one felf ' underftood in thefe nice cafes: but I fay——hem! I ' fay, that I being become the duplicate of myfelf, ' as to the body, and the underftanding, did notwith- ' ftanding find that there was a diverfity of the will, and ' that both in action and in fufferance——'

Am. [*Fiercely pulling him away.*] Begone——thy folly tortures me to madnefs.

D. 2   *Alc.*

Alc. [*Interpofing.*] The fame ftrange phrenfy has pof-
fefs'd you both ;

It was from you, not him, I heard the news.

Am. From me !

Alc. From you—and when you told me Pterelas's death,
You gave this jewel, which he ufed to wear.

Am. This is amazing !

Have I already given you thofe diamonds,
The prefent I referv'd ?

Alc. 'Tis an odd queftion :
You fee I wear 'em ; look.

Am. Now anfwer, Sofia.

Sof. Yes, now I can anfwer with a fafe confcience, as
to that point ; all the reft may be art magic—but, as for
the diamonds, here they are, under fafe cuftody.

Alc. Then what are thefe upon my arm ? [*To* Sofia.

Sof. Flints, or pebbles, or fome fuch trumpery of en-
chanted ftones. Yet now I think on't, Madam, did not a
certain friend of mine prefent them to you ?

Alc. What friend ?

Sof. Why, another Sofia ; one that made himfelf Sofia in my defpire, and alfo unfofiated me.

Am. Sirrah, leave your naufeous nonfenfe ; break open
the feal, and take out the diamonds.

Sof. More words than one to a bargain, Sir, I thank
you : that's no part of prudence for me to commit burglary upon the feals. Do you look firft upon the fignet,
and tell me in your confcience, whether the feals be not
as firm as when you clapped the wax upon them.

Am. The fignature is firm.   [*Looking.*

Sof. Then take the fignature into your own cuftody,
and open it ; for I will have nothing done at my proper
peril.   [*Giving him the cafket.*

Am. Oh, heavens ! here's nothing but an empty fpace,
the neft where they were laid.   [*Breaking open the feal.*

Sof. Then if the birds are flown, the fault's not mine.
Here has been fine conjuring work ; or elfe the jewel,
knowing to whom it fhould be given, took occafion to
fteal out, by a natural inftinct, and tied itfelf to that
pretty arm.

Am. Can this be poffible !

Sof. Yes, very poffible : you, my lord Amphitryon,
                                                   may

may have brought forth another you my lord Amphitryon ; as well as I Sofia have brought forth another me
Sofia ; and our diamonds may have procreated thefe diamonds ; and fo we are all three double.

Phæd. If this be true, I hope my golden goblet has
gigged another golden goblet ; and then they may carry
double upon all four. [*Afide.*

Alc. My Lord, I have ftood filent, out of wonder
What you cou'd wonder at.

Am. A chilling fweat, a damp of jealoufy, [*Afidc.*
Hangs on my brows, and clams upon my limbs.
I fear, and yet I muft be fatisfy'd :
And to be fatisfy'd, I muft diffemble.

Alc. Why mufe you fo, and murmur to yourfelf ?
If you repent your bounty, take it back.

Am. Not fo ; but, if you pleafe, relate what paft
At our laft interview.

Alc. That queftion wou'd infer you were not here.

Am. I fay not fo ;
I only would refrefh my memory,
And have my reafons to defire the ftory.

Alc. The ftory is not long : you know I met you,
Kifs'd you, and prefs'd you clofe within my arms,

Am. I cou'd have fpar'd that kindnefs. [*Afide.*
And what did I ? [*To her.*

Alc. With equal love return'd my warm embrace.

Am. Go on——
And ftab me with each fyllable thou fpeak'ft. [*Afide.*

Alc. I have no more to fay.

' *Am.* Why, went we not to bed ?

' *Alc.* Why not ?

' Is it a crime for hufband and for wife
' To go to bed, my lord ?'

Am. Perfidious woman !

Alc. Ungrateful man !

Am. She juftifies it too !

Alc. I need not juftify : of what am I accus'd ?

Am. Of that prodigality of kindnefs
Giv'n to another, and ufurp'd from me.
So blefs me heav'n, if fince my firft departure,
I ever fet my foot upon this threfhold.

Alc. Then I, it feems, am falfe !

Am.

Am. As furely falfe, as what thou fay'ft is true.

Alc. I have betray'd my honour, and my love!
And am a foul adultrefs!

Am. What thou art,
Thou ftand'ft condemn'd to be, by thy relation.

Alc. Go, thou unworthy man; for ever go:
No more my hufband! Go, thou bafe impoftor;
Who tak'ft a vile pretence to taint my fame;
And, not content to leave, wouldft ruin me.
Enjoy thy wifh'd divorce: I will not plead
My innocence of this pretended crime:
I need not: do thy worft, I fear thee not:
For know, the more thou wou'dft expofe my virtue,
Like pureft linen laid in open air,
'Twill bleach the more, and whiten to the view.

Am. 'Tis well thou art prepar'd for thy divorce:
For, know thou too, that after this affront,
This foul indignity, done to my honour,
Divorcement is but petty reparation.
But, fince thou haft, with impudence, affirm'd
My falfe return, and brib'd my flaves to vouch it,
The truth fhall, in the face of Thebes, be clear'd;
Thy uncle, the companion of my voyage,
And all the crew of fea-men, fhall be brought,
Who were embark'd and came with me to land,
Nor parted, till I reach'd this curfed door:
So fhall this vifion of my late return
Stand a detected lie; and woe to thofe
Who thus betray'd my honour.

Sof. Sir, fhall I wait on you?

Am. No, I will go alone: expect me here.

[*Exit* Amphitryon.

Phæd. Pleafe you——that I—— [*To* Alcmena.

Alc. Oh, nothing now can pleafe me:
Darknefs, and folitude, and fighs, and tears,
And all th' infeparable train of grief,
Attend my fteps for ever—— [*Exit* Alcmena.

Sof. What if I fhould lie now, and fay we have been
here before? I never faw any good that came of telling
truth. [*Afide.*

Phæd. He makes no more advances to me: I begin a
little

little to fufpect, that my gold goblet will prove but
coppér.   [*Afide.*

Sof. Yes, 'tis refolv'd—I will lie abominably, againſt
the light of my own confcience. For fuppofe the other
Sofia has been here ; perhaps that ſtrong dog has not only
beaten me, but alſo has miſuſed my wife ! Now, by
aſking certain queſtions of her, with a fide-wind, I may
come to underſtand how fquares go ; and whether my
nuptial bed be violated.   [*Afide.*

Phæd. Moſt certainly he has learned impudence of
his maſter, and will deny his being here ; but that ſhall
not ſerve his turn, to cheat me of my preſent !—[*Afide.*]
Why, Sofia ! What in a brown ſtudy ?

Sof. A little *cogitabund*, or fo, concerning this diſmal
revolution in our family.

Phæd. But that ſhould not make you neglect your
duty to me, your miſtreſs.

Sof. Pretty foul : I would thou wert; upon condition
that old Bromia were fix foot under ground.

Phæd. What ! is all your hot courtſhip to me dwindled
into a poor unprofitable wiſh ? You may remember, I did
not bid you abſolutely deſpair.

Sof. No, for all things yet may be accommodated, in
an amicable manner, betwixt my maſter and my lady.

Phæd. I mean, to the buſineſs, betwixt you and me—
Sof. Why, I hope, we two never quarrelled.

Phæd. Muſt I remember you of a certain promiſe
that you made me at our laſt parting ?

Sof. Oh, when I went to the army ; that I ſhould ſtill
be praiſing thy beauty to Judge Gripus, and keep up his
affections to thee.

Phæd. No, I mean the buſineſs betwixt you and me
this morning—that you promiſed me——

Sof. That I promiſed thee——I find it now : that
ſtrong dog, my brother Sofia, has been here before me,
and made love to her.   [*Afide.*

Phæd. You are confidering, whether or no you ſhould
keep your promiſe——

Sof. No, ſweet creature, the promiſe ſhall not be
broken ; but what I have undertaken, I will perform like
a man of honour.

                                              Phæd,

Phæd. Then you remember the preliminaries of the
prefent——

Sof. Yes, yes, in grofs I do remember fomething; but
this difturbance of the family has fomewhat ftupified my
memory: fome pretty *quelque chofe*, I warrant thee; fome
acceptable toy, of fmall value.

Phæd. You may call a gold goblet, a toy: but I put a
greater value upon your prefents.

Sof. A gold goblet, fay'ft thou! Yes, now I think
on't, it was a kind of a gold goblet; as a gratuity—

Phæd. No, no; I had rather make fure of one bribe
before-hand, than be promifed ten gratuities.

Sof. Yes, now I remember, it was, in fome fenfe, a
gold goblet, by way of earneft; and it contained——

Phæd. One large——

Sof. How, one large——

Phæd. Gallon.

Sof. No; that was fomewhat too large, in confcience:
it was not a whole gallon; but it may contain, reafonably
fpeaking, one large——thimble-full. ' But gallons and
' thimble-fulls are fo like, that, in fpeaking, I might
' eafily miftake them.'

Phæd. Is it come to this? Out, traitor!

' *Sof.* I had been a traitor, indeed, to have betrayed
' thee to the fwallowing of a gallon; but a thimble-full
' of cordial-water is eafily fipt off: and then, this fame
' goblet is fo very light too, that it will be no burden to
' carry it about with thee in thy pocket.

' *Phæd.*' Oh, apoftate to thy love! Oh, perjured villain!

Enter Bromia.

What are you here, Bromia! I was telling him his own:
I was giving him a rattle for his treacheries to you, his
love: you fee I can be a friend, upon occafion.

Brom. Ay, chicken, I never doubted of thy kindnefs: but, for this fugitive——this rebel——this mif-
creant——

Sof. A kind welcome to an abfent lover, as I have
been.

Brom. Ay; and a kind greeting you gave me, at your
return; when you ufed me fo barbaroufly this morning.

Sof. Ay, the t'other Sofia has been with her too; and
has ufed her barbaroufly: barbaroufly, that is to fay,
un-

uncivilly; and uncivilly, I am afraid that means too civilly. [*Aside.*

Phæd. You had beſt deny you were here this morning! And by the ſame token——

Sof. Nay, no more tokens, for heaven's ſake, dear Phædra. Now muſt I again ponder with myſelf a little, whether it be better for me to have been here, or not to have been here, this morning. [*Aside.*

Enter a Servant.

Serv. Phædra, my Lord's without; and will not enter till he has firſt ſpoken with you. [*Exit Servant.*

Phæd. [*To him in private.*] Oh, that I could ſtay to help to worry thee for this abuſe; but the beſt on't is, I leave thee in good hands—Farewel, thimble—To him, Bromia. [*Exit* Phædra.

Brom. No; to be ſure you did not beat me, and put me into a ſwoon, and deprive me of the natural uſe of my tongue for a long half hour: you did not beat me down with your little wand: but I ſhall teach you to uſe your rod another time——I ſhall.

Sof. Put her into a ſwoon, with my little wand, and ſo forth: that's more than ever I could do. Theſe are terrible circumſtances, that ſome Sofia or other has been here. [*Aside.*] Well, but Bromia—if I did beat thee down with my little wand, I warrant I was monſtrous kind to thee afterwards.

Brom. Yes, monſtrous kind indeed! You never ſaid a truer word; for, when I came to kiſs you, you pulled away your mouth, and turned your cheek to me.

Sof. Good.

Brom. How, good! Here's fine impudence: what, do you inſult upon me too?

Sofia. No, I do not inſult upon you:—but, for a certain reaſon, that I beſt know, I am glad that matter ended ſo fairly and peaceably betwixt us.

Brom. Yes, 'twas very fair and peaceably; to ſtrike a woman down, and beat her moſt outrageouſly.

Sofia. Is it poſſible that I drubbed thee?

Brom. I find your drift——You would fain be provoking me to a new trial now: but, i'faith, you ſhall bring me to no more handy-blows—I ſhall make bold to truſt to my tongue hereafter. You never durſt have

offered

offered to hold up a finger againſt me, till you went a trooping.

Sofia. Then I am conqueror; and I laud my own courage. This renown I have achieved by ſoldierſhip and ſtratagem. Know your duty, ſpouſe, henceforward, to your ſupreme commander. [*Strutting.*

Enter Jupiter *and* Phædra.

Phæd. Indeed, I wondered at your quick return.

Jup. Ev'n ſo almighty love wou'd have it, Phædra;
' And the ſtern goddeſs of ſweet bitter cares,
' Who bows our necks beneath her brazen yoke.'
I would have mann'd my heart, and held it out:
But, when I thought of what I had poſſeſs'd;
Thoſe joys, that never end but to begin,
My duty ſoon was overborne; I ſcorn'd
The buſy malice of cenſorious tongues,
And, careleſs to conceal my ſtolen journey,
Determin'd one day more to ſpend in Thebes.

Phæd. And yet a ſecond time you left Alcmena,
With looks unkind that threaten'd longer abſence.
'Twas but ev'n now ———

Jup. Wou'd it had never been!
I die to make my peace.

Phæd. 'Tis difficult.

Jup. But nothing is impoſſible to love;
To love like mine : for I have prov'd its force.
If I ſubmit, there's hope.

Phæd. It is poſſible I may ſolicit for you.

Jup. But wilt thou promiſe me to do thy beſt?

Phæd. Why, I promiſe nothing—unleſs you begin
To promiſe firſt. [*Curt'ſying.*

Jup. I wo'not be ungrateful.

Phæd. Well; I'll try to bring her to you.

Jup. That's all I aſk:
And I will ſo reward thee, gentle Phædra ——

Phæd. What with the ſweet ſound of " gentle Phædra, and my kind advocate."—

Jup. No, there's a ſound will pleaſe thee better.
[*Throwing her a purſe.*

Phæd. Ay, there's ſomething of melody in this ſound.
I could dance all day, to the muſic of chink, chink.
[*Exit* Phæd.
Jup.

Jup. Go, Sofia,
To Polidas, to Tranio, and to Gripus,
Companions of our war : invite 'em all
To join their pray'rs to fmooth Alcmena's brow ;
And, with a folemn feaft, to crown the day.

Sofia. [*Taking* Jupiter *about the knees.*] Let me embrace you, Sir.—[Jupiter *pufhes him away.*] Nay, you muft give me leave to exprefs my gratitude. I have not eaten, to fay eating, nor drank, to fay drinking, never fince our villainous encamping fo near the enemy.

Jup. You, Bromia, fee that all things be prepar'd
With that magnificence, as if Jove himfelf
Were gueft, or mafter here.

Sofia. Or, rather, as much as if twenty Joves were to be guefts, or matters here.

Brom. That you may eat for to-day and to-morrow.

Sofia. Or, rather again, for to-day and yefterday ; and as many months backward, as I am indebted to my own belly.

Jup. Away, both of you.

[*Exeunt* Sofia *and* Bromia *feverally.*
Now I have pack'd him hence ; thou, other Sofia,
(Who though thou art not prefent, hear'ft my voice)
Be ready to attend me at my call,
And to fupply his place.

Enter Mercury *to* Jupiter ; Alcmena *and* Phædra *alfo enter, but* Alcmena *feeing* Jupiter, *turns back, and retires frowning.*

Jup. See, fhe appears !   [*Seeing* Alcmena.
Oh, ftay.

Merc. She's gone ; and feem'd to frown at parting.

Jup. Follow, and thou fhalt fee her foon appeas'd ;
For I, who made her, know her inward ftate :
No woman, once well-pleas'd, can throughly hate.
I gave 'em beauty, to fubdue the ftrong ;
(A mighty empire, but it lafts not long.)
I gave 'em pride, to make mankind their flave ;
But, in exchange, to men I flattery gave.
Th' offending lover, when he loweft lies,
Submits, to conquer ; and but kneels, to rife.

End of the Third Act.

ACT

A C T IV.

Jupiter *following* Alcmena; Mercury *and* Phædra.

JUPITER.

OH, ftay, my dear Alcmena! hear me fpeak.
 Alc. No, I would fly thee to the ridge of earth,
And leap the precipice, to 'fcape thy fight.
 Jup. For pity——
 Alc. Leave me, thou ungrateful man!
I hate myfelf, for having lov'd thee once.
 Jup. Hate not the beft and faireft of your kind:
Nor can you hate your lover, tho' you would.
Your tears, that fall fo gently, are but grief:
There may be anger; but there muft be love.
The dove that murmurs at her mate's neglect,
But counterfeits a coynefs to be courted.
  ' *Alc.* Courtfhip from thee, and after fuch affronts!
  ' *Jup.* Is this that everlafting love you vow'd laft night?
  ' *Alc.* Think what thou wert, and who could fwear too
   much?
 ' Think what thou art, and that abfolves the oath.
  ' *Jup.* Can you forfake me for fo fmall a fault?
 ' 'Twas but a jeft, perhaps too far purfu'd;
 ' 'Twas but, at moft, a trial of your faith,
 ' How you could bear unkindnefs:
 ' 'Twas but to get a reconciling kifs,
 ' A wanton ftratagem of love.
  ' *Alc.* See how he doubles, like a hunted hare:
 ' A jeft, and then a trial, and a bait——'
 Jup. Think me jealous, then.
 Alc. Oh, that I could! for that's a noble crime;
And which a lover can, with eafe, forgive:
 ' 'Tis the high pulfe of paffion in a fever;
 ' A fickly draught but fhews a burning thirft:'
Thine was a furfeit, not a jealoufy;
And in that loathing of thy fatiate love,
Thou faw'ft the odious object with difdain.
 Jup. Oh, think not that! for you are ever new——
 ' Your fruits of love, like thofe of endlefs fpring
 ' In happy climes, where fome are in the bud,
 ' Some green, and ripening fome, while others fall.

      2   ' *Alc.*

' *Alc.* Ay, now you tell me this. Your puny paſſion,
' Like the deprav'd deſires of fretful ſickneſs,
' Raves in ſhort fits of craving and diſguſt.
' This morn, at break of day, you would be gone;
' Then chang'd your purpoſe, and came back; then rag'd,
' Becauſe th' effect of chance was not foreſeen;
' Then left me in diſguſt, with inſult too;
' And now, return'd again, you talk of love.
' But never hope to be receiv'd again!
' You would again deny you were receiv'd,
' And brand my ſpotleſs fame.'

 Jup. I will not dare to juſtify my crime:
No, I confeſs I have deſerv'd your hate.
Too charming fair, I kneel for your forgiveneſs:
I beg, by thoſe fair eyes,   [*Kneeling.*
Which gave me wounds that time can never cure,
Receive my ſorrows, and reſtore my joys.

 ' *Alc.* Unkind and cruel! I can ſpeak no more.

 ' *Jup.* Oh, give it vent, Alcmena, give it vent;
' I merit your reproach, I would be curs'd:
' Let your tongue curſe me, while your heart forgives.'

 Alc. Can I forget ſuch uſage?

 Jup. Can you hate me?

 Alc. I'll do my beſt; for ſure I ought to hate you.

 Jup. That word was only hatch'd upon your tongue,
It came not from your heart. But try again;
And if once more, you can but ſay, I hate you,
My ſword ſhall do you juſtice.

 Alc. Then——I hate you——

 Jup. Then you pronounce the ſentence of my death.

 Alc. I hate you much—but yet I love you more.

 Jup. To prove that love, then ſay, that you forgive
For there remains but this alternative;   [me:
Reſolve to pardon, or to puniſh me.

 Alc. Alas! what I reſolve appears too plain:
In ſaying that I cannot hate, I pardon:

 Jup. But what's a pardon worth, without a ſeal?
Permit me, in this tranſport of my joy— [*Kiſſes her hand.*

 Alc. Forbear; I am offended with myſelf,
    [*Putting him gently away with her hand.*
That I have ſhewn this weakneſs ——Let me go
' Where I may bluſh alone——'
     [*Going, and looking back on him.*
    E   But

But come not you ;
Left I fhould fpoil you with excefs of fondnefs,
And take you to my heart again.   [*Exit* Alc.

Jup. Forbidding me to follow, fhe invites me.   [*Afide.*
This is the mould of which I made the fex :
I gave them but one tongue, to fay us nay,
And two kind eyes, to grant. Be fure that none [*To* Mer.
Approach, to interrupt us.   [*Exit* Jup. *after* Alc.

Merc. Your Lady has made the challenge of reconciliation to my Lord. Here's a fair example for us two,
Phædra.

Phad. No example at all, Sofia ; for my Lady had the
diamonds beforehand, and I have none of the gold goblet.

Merc. The goblet fhall be forth-coming, if thou wilt
give me weight for weight.

Phæd. Yes, and meafure for meafure too, Sofia ; that
is, for a thimble-full of gold, a thimble-full of love.

Merc. What think you now, Phædra ? Here's a
weighty argument of love, for you !
          [*Pulling out the goblet in a cafe from under his cloak.*

Phæd. Now, Jupiter, of his mercy, let me kifs thee,
Oh, thou dear metal !   [*Taking it in both hands.*

Merc And Venus, of her mercy, let me kifs thee,
dear, dear Phædra !

Phæd. Not fo faft, Sofia ; there's an unlucky proverb
in your way--Many things happen betwixt the cup and
the lip, you know.

Merc. Why, thou wilt not cheat me of my goblet ?

Phæd. Yes, as fure as you would cheat me of my virtue. I am yet but juft even with you, for the laft trick you
played me. And, befides, this is but a bare retaining fee ;
you muft give me another, before the caufe is opened.

Merc Shall I not come to your bed-fide to-night ?

Phæd. No, nor to-morrow night, neither : but this
fhall be my fweetheart in your place : 'tis a better bedfellow, and will keep me warmer in cold weather. [*Exit.*

Merc. Now, what's the god of wit in a woman's hand ?
This very goblet I ftole from Gripus ; and he got it out
of bribes too. But this is the common fate of ill-gotten
goods, that, as they came in by covetoufnefs, they go out
by extravagance――

                                                  Enter

Enter Amphitryon.

Oh, here's Amphitryon again ! but I'll manage him above
in the balcony.   [*Exit* Merc.

Am. Not one of thofe I look'd for, to be found !
Has fome enchantment hid them from my fight ?
Perhaps, as Sofia fays, 'tis witchcraft all.
Seals may be open'd, diamonds may be ftol'n ;
But how I came, in perfon, yefterday,
And gave that prefent to Alcmena's hands,
That which I never gave, nor ever came,
Oh, there's the rock on which my reafon fplits !
Would that were all ! I fear my honour too !
I'll try her once again : fhe may be mad——
A wretched remedy ! but all I have,
To keep me from defpair.
How now ! what means the locking up of my
Doors at this time of day ?   [*Knocks.*

Merc. [*Above.*] Softly, friend, foftly. You knock as
loud, and as faucily, as a lord's footman, that was fent before him, to warn the family of his lordfhip's vifit. Sure
you think the doors have no feeling. What the devil are
you, that rap with fuch authority ?

Am. Look out, and fee : 'tis I.

Merc. You ! what you ?

Am. No more, I fay, but open.

Merc. I'll know to whom firft.

Am. I am one that can command the doors open.

Merc. Then you had beft command them, and try whether they will obey you.

Am. Doft thou not know me ?

Merc. Pr'ythee, how fhould I know thee ? Doft thou
take me for a conjurer ?

Am. What's this, Midfummer-moon ? Is all the world
gone a madding ? Why, Sofia !

Merc. That's my name indeed : didft thou think I had
forgot it ?

Am. Doft thou fee me ?

Merc. Why, doft thou pretend to go invifible ? If thou
haft any bufinefs here, difpatch it quickly ; I have no
leifure to throw away upon fuch prattling companions.

Am. Thy companion, flave ! How dar'ft thou ufe this
infolent language to thy mafter ?

Merc. How! thou my mafter? By what title? I never had any other mafter but Amphitryon.

Am. Well, and for whom doft thou take me?

Merc. For fome rogue or other; but what rogue I know not.

Am. Doft thou not know me for Amphitryon, flave?

Merc. How fhould I know thee, when I fee thou doft not know thyfelf? Thou Amphitryon! In what tavern haft thou been, and how many bottles did thy bufinefs, to metamorphofe thee into my Lord?

Am. I will fo drub thee for this infolence ――

Merc. How now, Impudence! are you threatening your betters? I fhould bring you to condign punifhment, but that I have a great refpect for the good wine, tho' I find it in a fool's noddle.

Am. What, none to let me in? Why Phædra! Bromia!

Merc. Peace, fellow; if my wife hears thee, we are both undone. At a word, Phædra and Bromia are very bufy; and my Lady and my Lord muft not be difturbed.

Am. Amazement feizes me!

Merc. At what art thou amazed? My Lord Amphitryon and my Lady Alcmena had a falling out, and are retired, without feconds, to decide the quarrel. If thou wert not a meddlefome fool, thou would not be thrufting thy nofe into other people's matters. Get thee about thy bufinefs, if thou haft any; for I'll hear no more of thee.
[Exit Mercury *from above.*

Am. Brav'd by my flave, difhonour'd by my wife!
To what a defp'rate plunge am I reduc'd,
If this be true the villain fays? But why
That feeble if? It muft be true; fhe owns it.
Now, whether to conceal or blaze th' affront?
One way, I fpread my infamy abroad;
And t'other, hide a burning coal within,
That preys upon my vitals. I can fix
On nothing, but on vengeance.

Enter Sofia, Polidas, Gripus, *and* Tranio.

Grip. Yonder he is, walking haftily to and fro before his door, like a citizen clapping his fides before his fhop, in a frofty morning: 'tis to catch a ftomach, I believe.

Sof. I begin to be afraid that he has more ftomach to my fides and fhoulders, than to his own victuals. How
he

he ſhakes his head, and ſtamps, and what ſtrides he
fetches! He's in one of his damn'd moods again. I don't
like the looks of him.

Am. Oh, my mannerly, fair-ſpoken, obedient ſlave, are
you there? I can reach you now, without climbing. Now
we ſhall try who's drunk, and who's ſober.

Sof. Why, this is as it ſhould be. I was ſomewhat ſuſ-
picious that you were in a peſtilent humour. Yes, we
will have a craſh at the bottle, whenever your Lordſhip
pleaſes. I have ſummon'd them, you ſee; and they are
notable topers, eſpecially Judge Gripus.

Grip. Yes, faith, I never refuſe my glaſs, in a good
quarrel.

Am. [*To* Sof.] Why, thou inſolent villain! I'll teach
a ſlave how to uſe his maſter thus.

Sof. Here's a fine buſineſs towards! I am ſure I ran as
faſt as ever my legs could carry me, to call them. Nay,
you may truſt my diligence in all affairs belonging to the
belly.

Grip. He has been very faithful to his commiſſion, I'll
bear him witneſs.

Am. How can you be witneſs where you were not preſent? The balcony, ſirrah, the balcony!

Sof. Why, to my beſt remembrance, you never invited
the balcony.

Am. What nonſenſe doſt thou plead for an excuſe of
thy foul language, and thy baſe replies!

Sof. You fright a man out of his ſenſes firſt, and blame
him afterwards for talking nonſenſe. But 'tis better for
me to talk nonſenſe, than for ſome to do nonſenſe; I will
ſay that, whatever comes on't. Pray, Sir, let all things
be done decently. What, I hope, when a man is to be
hanged, he is not truſs'd upon the gallows, like a dumb
dog, without telling him wherefore.

Am. By your pardon, gentlemen; I have no longer
patience to forbear him.

Sof. Juſtice, juſtice, my Lord Gripus! as you are a true
magiſtrate, protect me. Here's a proceſs of beating going
forward, without ſentence given.

Grip. My Lord Amphitryon, this muſt not be. Let
me firſt underſtand the demerits of the criminal.

Sof. Hold you to that point, I beſeech your honour,

E 3

as you commiferate the cafe of a poor, innocent male-factor.

Am. To fhut the door againft me, in my very face! to deny me entrance! to brave me from the balcony! to laugh at me! to threaten me! What proofs of innocence call you thefe? But if I punifh not this infolence——

[*Is going to beat him, and is held by* Polidas *and* Tranio.

I beg you, let me go——

Sof. I charge you, in the king's name, hold him faft; for you fee he's bloodily difpofed.

Grip. Now, what haft thou to fay for thyfelf, Sofia?

Sof. I fay, in the firft place——Be fure you hold him, gentlemen; for I fhall never plead worth one farthing, while I am bod.ly afraid.

Pol. Speak boldly; I warrant thee.

Sof. Then, if I may fpeak boldly, under my Lord's fa-vour—I do not fay he lies neither; no, I am too well bred for that; but his lordfhip fibbs moft abominably.

Am. Do you hear his impudence? Yet will you let me go?

Sof. No impudence at all, my Lord; for how could I, naturally fpeaking, be in the balcony and affronting you, when, at the fame time, I was in every ftreet in Thebes, inviting thefe gentlemen to dinner?

Grip. Hold a little. How long fince was it, that he fpoke to you from the faid balcony?

Am. Juft now; not a minute before he brought you hither.

Sof. Now fpeak, my witneffes.

Grip. I can anfwer for him, for this laft half hour.

Pol. And I.

Tran. And I.

Sof. Now, judge equitably, gentlemen, whether I was not a civil, well-bred perfon, to tell my Lord he fibbs only.

Am. Who gave you that order to invite them?

Sof. He that beft might, yourfelf. By the fame token, you bid old Bromia provide an 'twere for a god; and I put in for a brace, or a leafh; no, now I think on't, it was for ten couple of gods, to make fure of plenty.

Am. When did I give thee this pretended commiffion?

Sof. Why, you gave me this pretended commiffion juft

after

after you had given Phædra a purse of gold to bring you and my Lady together, that you might try to make up matters with her after your quarrel.

Am. Where, in what place, did I give this order?

Sof. Here, in this place, in the presence of this very door, and of that balcony; and if they could speak, they would both justify it.

Am. Oh, Heaven! these accidents are so surprising, the more I think of them the more I am lost in my imagination.

Grip. Nay, he has told us some passages, as he came along, that seem to surpass the power of nature.

Sof. What think you now, my Lord, of a certain twin brother of mine, called Sofia? 'Tis a sly youth. Pray Heaven, you have not just such another relation within doors, called Amphitryon. It may be it was he that put upon me, in your likeness; and perhaps he may have put something upon your lordship too, that may weigh heavy upon the forehead.

Am. [*To those who hold him.*] Let me go—Sofia may be innocent, and I will not hurt him—Open the door; I'll resolve my doubts immediately.

Sof. The door is peremptory that it will not be opened without keys; and my brother, on the inside, is in possession, and will not part with them.

Am. Then 'tis manifest that I am affronted. Break open the door there.

Grip. Stir not a man of you to his assistance.

Am. Dost thou take part with my adultress too, because she is thy niece?

Grip. I take part with nothing but the law; and to break the doors open, is to break the law.

Am. Do thou command them, then.

Grip. I can command nothing without my warrant; and my clerk is not here, to take his fees for drawing it.

Am. [*Aside.*] The devil take all justice-brokers ——I curse him too, when I have been hunting him all over the town, to be my witness——But I'll bring soldiers to force open the door by my own commission.

[*Exit* Amphitryon.

Sof. Pox o' these forms of law, to defeat a man of a dinner, when he's sharp set! 'Tis against the privilege of
a free-

a free-born ſtomach; and is no leſs than ſubverſion of fundamentals.

Jupiter *appears above in the balcony.*

Jup. Oh, my friends, I am ſorry I have made you wait ſo long! You are welcome; and the door ſhall be opened to you immediately.   [*Exit* Jup.

Grip. Was not that Amphitryon?

Sof. Why, who ſhould it be elſe?

Grip. In all appearance it was he. But how got he thither?

Pol. In ſuch a trice too!

Tran. And after he had juſt left us!

Grip. And ſo much altered, for the better, in his humour?

Sof. Here's ſuch a company of fooliſh queſtions, when a man's hungry. You had beſt ſtay dinner, till he has proved himſelf to be Amphitryon in form ot law. But I'll make ſhort work of that buſineſs; for I'll take mine oath 'tis he.

Grip. I ſhould be glad it were.

Sof. How, glad it were! with your damn'd interrogatories—when you ought to be thankful that ſo it is.

Grip. [*Aſide.*] That I may ſee my miſtreſs, Phædra, and preſent her with my great gold goblet.

Sof. If this be not the true Amphitryon, I with I may be kept without doors, faſting, and biting my own fingers for want of victuals; and that's a dreadful imprecation. I am for the inviting, eating, and treating Amphitryon; I am ſure 'tis he that is my lawfully begotten lord: and if you had an ounce of the juſtice in you, you ought to have laid hold on t'other Amphitryon, and committed him for a rogue, and an impoſtor, and a vagabond.

[*The door is opened;* Mercury *from within.*

Merc. Enter quickly, maſters. The paſſage on the right hand leads to the gallery, where my Lord expects you——For I'm called another way.

[Gripus, Tranio, *and* Polidas *go into the houſe.*

Sof. I ſhould know that voice, by a ſecret inſtinct. 'Tis a tongue of my family, and belongs to my brother, Sofia. It muſt be ſo; for it carries a cudgelling kind of ſound in it. But, put the worſt—let me weigh this matter wiſely—Here's a beating and a belly-full, againſt no

beating

beating and no belly-full. The beating is bad; but the dinner is good. Now, not to be beaten, is but negatively good; but, not to fill my belly, is positively bad. Upon the whole matter, my final resolution is, to take the good and the bad as they come together.

        [*Is entering*; Mercury *meets him at the door.*

Merc. Whither now, you kitchen-scum? From whence this impudence, to enter here without permission?

Sof. Most illustrious Sir, my ticket is my hunger. Shew the full bowels of your compassion, to the empty bowels of my famine.

Merc. Were you not charged to return no more? I'll cut you into quarters, and hang you upon the shambles.

Sof. You'll get but little credit by me. Alas, Sir, I am but mere carrion! Brave Sofia, compassionate coward Sofia; and beat not thyself, in beating me.

Merc. Who gave you that privilege, sirrah, to assume my name? Have you not been sufficiently warned of it, and received part of punishment already?

Sof. May it please you, Sir, the name is big enough for both of us. I would have obeyed you, and quitted my title to it; but, wherever I come, the malicious world will call me Sofia, in spite of me. I am sensible there are two Amphitryons; and why may not there be two Sofias? Let those two cut one another's throats at their own pleasure; but you and I will be wiser, by my consent, and hold good intelligence together.

Merc. No, no; two Sofias would make but two fools.

Sof. Then let me be the fool, and be you the prudent person, and chuse for yourself some wiser name; or you shall be the elder brother, and I'll be content to be the younger, tho' I lose my inheritance.

Merc. I tell thee, I am the only son of our family.

Sof. Ah! then let me be your bastard brother, and the son of a whore—I hope that's but reasonable.

Merc. No, thou shalt not disgrace my father; for there are few bastards now-a-days worth owning.

Sof. Ah, poor Sofia! what will become of thee?

Merc. Yet again profanely using my proper name!

Sof. I did not mean myself—I was thinking of another Sofia, a poor fellow, that was once of my acquaintance,
                                      unfortu-

unfortunately banifhed out of doors, when dinner was juft coming upon the table.

Enter Phædra.

Phæd. Sofia, you and I muft——Blefs me! what have we here?—A couple of you! or do I fee double?

Sof. I would fain bring it about, that I might make one of them; but he's unreafonable, and will needs incorporate me, and fwallow me whole into himfelf. If he would be content to be but one and a half, 'twould never grieve me.

Merc. 'Tis a perverfe rafcal. I kick him, and cudgel him to no purpofe; for ftill he's obftinate to ftick to me; and I can never beat him out of my refemblance.

Phæd. Which of you two is Sofia? For t'other muft be the devil.

Sof. You had beft afk him, that has played the devil with my back and fides.

Merc You had beft afk him, who gave you the gold goblet.

Phæd. No, that's already given; but he fhall be my Sofia, that will give me fuch another.

Merc. I find you have been interloping, firrah.

Sof. No, indeed, Sir; I only promifed her a gold thimble; which was as much as comes to my proportion of being Sofia.

Phæd. This is no Sofia for my money. Beat him away, t'other Sofia; he grows infufferable.

Sof. [*Afide.*] Would I were valiant, that I might beat him away, and fucceed him at the dinner, for a pragmatical fon of a whore, as he is.

Merc. What's that you are muttering betwixt your teeth, of a fon of a whore, firrah?

Sof. I am fure I meant you no offence; for, if I am not Sofia, I am the fon of a whore, for ought I know; and, if you are Sofia you may be the fon of a whore, for ought you know.

Merc. Whatever I am, I will be Sofia as long as I pleafe; and whenever you vifit me, you fhall be fure of the civility of the cudgel.

Sof. If you will promife to beat me into the houfe, you may begin when you pleafe with me; but to be beaten

out

out of the houfe, at dinner-time, flefh and blood can never bear it.

[Mercury beats him about, and Sofia *is ftill making towards the door: but Mercury gets betwixt; and at length drives him off the ftage.*

Phæd. In the name of wonder, what are you that are Sofia, and are not Sofia ?

Merc. If thou wouldft know more of me, my perfon is freely at thy difpofing.

Phæd. Then I difpofe of it to you again; for 'tis fo ugly, 'tis not for my ufe.

Merc. I can be ugly or handfome, as I pleafe; go to bed old, and rife young. I have fo many fuits of perfons by me, I can fhift 'em when I will.

Phæd. You are a fool then, to put on your worft clothes when you come a wooing.

Merc. Go to: afk no more queftions. I am for thy turn; for I know thy heart, and fee all thou haft about thee. In thy right pocket—let me fee—three love-letters from Judge Gripus, written to the bottom, on three fides; full of fuftian paffion, and hearty nonfenfe: as alfo in the fame pocket, a letter of thine intended to him; confifting of nine lines and a half, fcrawl'd and falfe fpell'd, to fhew thou art a woman.

Phæd. Is the devil in you, to fee all this ? Now, for Heaven's fake, do not look in t'other pocket——

Merc. Nay, there's nothing there, but a bawdy lampoon, and ———

Phæd. [*Giving a great frifh.*] Look no farther, I befeech you———

Merc. And a filver fpoon——

Phæd. [*Shrieking.*] Ah !

Merc. Which you purloin'd laft night from Bromia.

Phæd. Keep my counfel, or I am undone for ever.

[*Holding up her hands to him.*

Merc. No: I'll mortify thee, now I have an handle to thy iniquity, if thou wilt not love me——

Phæd. Well, if you'll promife me to be fecret, I will love you : becaufe indeed I dare do no other.

Merc. 'Tis a good girl—I will be fecret; and further, I will be affifting to thee in thy filching: for thou and I were born under the fame planet.

Phæd.

Phæd. And we fhall come to the fame end too, I'm afraid.

Merc. No, no ; fince thou haft wit enough already to cozen a judge, thou need'ft never fear hanging.

Phæd. And will you make yourfelf a younger man, and be handfome too, and rich ? for you that know hearts, muft needs know, that I fhall never be conftant to fuch an ugly old Sofia.

Merc. As to my youth and beauty, thou fhalt know more of that another time. But, pr'ythee, why art thou fo covetous of riches ?

Phæd. Why ? becaufe riches will procure every thing elfe that I can wifh for.

Merc. But what if every thing elfe could be procur'd without riches : would not that do as well ?

Phæd. Why no ; there's a pleafure, methinks, in having the money before one lays it out.

Merc. And yet, till it is laid out, it is as ufelefs as fo much dirt.

Phæd. Aye—that may be—but when my heart dances to the chinking of money, it is not at leifure to think of that.

Merc. But fuppofe, that, without money, you could procure all that money could buy and more.

Phæd. Why, as well as I love money, I have no objection to any good thing that money won't buy : but pray, how is it to be had ?

Merc. To be had ? why, upon the eafieft terms in the world ; only by a motion of the finger, or a ftamp with the foot.

Phæd. Phoo, that's impoffible.

Merc. You fhall make the experiment.

Phæd. Shall I ? fo I will then, this minute. Muft I ftamp with my foot, or beckon with my finger ?

Merc. Firft try to find out what you wifh for, which I have known a difficult tafk for a woman.

Phæd. Let me fee——

Merc. Come, I'll help you—If you had been put into poffeffion of Gripus's wealth yefterday, what wou'd you have had to entertain you to-day ?

Phæd. Why, I wou'd have had——let me fee —— I wou'd have had, juft now, a band of the beft mufic in

4   Thebes,

Thebes, and a fong in the character of Plutus in praife
of money.

Merc. Well, now ftamp with your foot.

[Phædra *ftamps* ; *the muſic ſtrikes up* ; *ſhe ſtarts
and ſcreams out.*

Nay, nay, don't fpoil the mufic——there's a friend of
mine in the character of Plutus juft coming in.

Phæd. I am very much obliged to you and your
friend ; but, if you pleafe, I had rather keep a little farther out of his reach.

Merc. Pſhaw, pſhaw ! ſtay where you are ; my friends
hurt nobody without my leave.

SONG *by a perfon who enters in the character of* Plutus.

Away with the fables philofophers hold,
Of pleafure that honefty gains without gold :
To be rich is the bleffings of life to fecure ;
And the man muft be certainly wretched that's poor.

The virtue that claims all the gods for its friends,
On gold, mighty gold, for exiftence depends :
What wrongs, without gold, can a mortal redrefs ?
Or who, without gold, can get bleffings, or blefs ?

‘ The weak can you fuccour, the worthy reward,
‘ If money be wanting, the gift and the guard ?’
In gold there is ftrength which no foe can withftand ;
It conquers and triumphs, by fea and by land.

‘ In gold there are charms ; for the youth and the fair,
‘ Sigh one for an heirefs, and one for an heir.
‘ There's fenfe for each circle that liftens demure,
‘ Confents with a grin, and cries “ Yes to be fure !”
To be rich, if you truft your own ears and your eyes,
Is at once to be ftrong, to be fair, to be wife.

‘ *Phæd.* There's for you now—what have you to fay
‘ to that ?

‘ *Merc.* Why, Wit ſhall reply for me ; and, to mor-
‘ tify you the more, it ſhall be in the character of a wo-
‘ man.’

Phæd. [*To* Plutus, *who is going*] Stay then, Mr. Plutus, if you pleafe——let's hear what he'll fay, by way of reply.

Merc. That's but an ill-natur'd experiment; for Wit and Wealth have no kindnefs for one another: however, it fhall be as you pleafe for once.

[Mercury *waves his caduceus, a nymph enters, in the character of Wit.*

S O N G.

Plutus, vain is all your vaunting,
   Wit muft life with blifs fupply.
Gold, alas! fhould Wit be wanting,
   Would not find a joy to buy.

Wit alone creates the bleffing,
   Which, exchang'd for gold, you fhare:
Steril gold alone poffeffing,
   What has man but gloom and care?

Wit, of ev'ry art devifer,
   Every paffion can controul:
Can to pity move the mifer,
   Can with mirth dilate his foul.

Gold itfelf, on Wit depending,
   Thence derives its utmoft pow'r:
Folly all profufely fpending,
   Folly hoarding all is poor.

Phæd. To her, Mr. Plutus.

D U E T.

Plut. In vain wou'd your jargon our fenfes bewitch,
D'ye tell me that gold will not make a man rich?
Wit. It is Wit, Wit alone, that can keep it or ufe;
And it cannot enrich thofe that hide it or lofe.
Plut. Your quibbles I fcorn.
Wit. But you cannot reply.
Plut. I boldly affirm——
Wit. What I boldly deny.
Plut. I'll bet you ten millions.

                                      Wit.

Wit. No wagers I lay.

Plut. You dare not.

Wit. I scorn you.

Plut. I hate you.

Wit. Away——

Plut. I go—may great Jove in his mercy decree :
That we never may meet, since we ne'er can agree.

Wit. Go you to the foolish.

Plut. And you to the poor.

Wit. The poor I can bless, and their blessings secure.
[*Exeunt severally.*

' *Phæd.* Well, for all these fine promises of Wit, I
' have no great opinion of the happiness of poverty.

' *Merc.* If you will not yield to argument, let expe-
' riment convince you.

' [*Strikes the scene with his caduceus, and it changes to*
' *a rural prospect, with a dance of peasants to country*
' *music.*

' Well, what think you, Phædra——are these people
' happy ?

' *Phæd.* If they are happy, they owe their happiness
' as little to wit as to money, I believe.

' *Merc.* I beg your pardon—if it had not been for
' the arts that Wit has invented, they would have had
' neither pipe nor dance : and mere ease and content are
' but negative happiness at the best.

' *Phæd.* Well, I find 'tis in vain to dispute with you ;
' but I shall hold my opinion for all that. Adieu——If
' you make me happy according to my way of thinking,
' perhaps I may make you happy according to yours.
[*Exit.*

' *Merc.* Woman——mere woman !—however, I love
' thee but as mere woman, and only as mere woman
' thou art mine.

' Such bargain-loves as I with Phædra treat,

' Are all the leagues and friendships of the great.

' Our iron age is grown an age of gold :

' 'Tis who bids most—for all men wou'd be sold.'
[*Exit.*

END of the FOURTH ACT.

ACT

ACT V.

Enter Gripus *and* Phædra. Gripus *has the goblet in his hand.*

PHÆDRA.

YOU will not be so base to take it from me ?

Grip. 'Tis my proper chattel: and I'll seize my own in whatever hands I find it.

Phæd. You know I only shew'd it to you to provoke your generosity, that you might out-bid your rival with a better present.

Grip. My rival is a thief: and I'll indite you for a receiver of stolen goods.

Phæd. Thou hide-bound lover !

Grip. Thou very mercenary mistress !

Phæd. Thou most mercenary magistrate !

Grip. Thou seller of thyself !

Phæd. Thou seller of other people ! Thou weather-cock of government : that when the wind blows for the subject, point'st to privilege; and when it changes for the sovereign, veer'st to prerogative.

Grip. Will you compound, and take it as my present ?

Phæd. No: but I'll send thy rival to force it from thee.

Grip. When a thief is rival to his judge, the hangman will soon decide the difference. [*Exit* Phædra.

Enter Mercury, *with two swords.*

Merc. [*Bowing.*] Save your good lordship.

Grip. From an impertinent coxcomb——I am out of humour, and am in haste—Leave me.

Merc. 'Tis my duty to attend on your lordship, and to ease you of that indecent burthen.

Grip. Gold was never any burthen to one of my profession.

Merc. By your lordship's permission, Phædra has sent me to take it from you.

Grip. What, by violence ?

Merc. [*Still bowing.*] No ; but by your honour's permission, I am to restore it to her, and persuade your lordship to renounce your pretensions to her.

Grip.

Grip. Tell her flatly, I will neither do one, nor t'other.

Merc. O, my good lord, I dare pass my word for your free consent to both.——Will your honour be pleas'd to take your choice of one of these ?

Grip. Why these are swords : what have I to do with them ?

Merc. Only to take your choice of one of them—— which your lordship pleases ; and leave the other to your most obedient servant.

Grip. What, one of these ungodly weapons ? Take notice, I'll lay you by the heels, sirrah : this has the appearance of an unlawful bloody challenge.

Merc. You magistrates are pleased to call it so, my lord ; but with us sword-men, 'tis an honourable invitation to the cutting of one another's throats.

Grip. Be answer'd ; I have no throat to cut. The law shall decide our controversy.

Merc. By your permission, my lord, it must be dispatch'd this way.

Grip. I'll see thee hang'd before I give thee any such permission, to dispatch me into another world.

Merc. At the least, my lord, you have no occasion to complain of my want of respect to you : you will neither restore the goblet, nor renounce Phædra : I offer you the combat ; you refuse it ; all this is done in the forms of honour : it follows, that I am to affront, cudgel you, or kick you, at my own arbitrement ; and I suppose, you are too honourable not to approve of my proceeding.

Grip. Here's a new sort of process, that was never heard of in any of our courts.

Merc. This, my good lord, is law in short-hand ; without your long preambles, and tedious repetitions, that signify nothing but to squeeze the subject : therefore, with your lordship's favour, I begin.

[*Fillips him under the chin.*

Grip. What's this for ?

Merc. To give you an occasion of returning me a box o'th' ear ; that so, all things may proceed methodically.

Grip. I put in no answer, but suffer a non-suit.

Merc.

Merc. No, my lord ; for the cofts and charges are to be paid : will you pleafe to reftore the cup ?

Grip. I have told thee, no.

Merc. Then from your chin, I muft afcend to your lordfhip's ears.

Grip. Oh, oh, oh, oh !--Wilt thou never leave lugging me by the ears ?

Merc. Not till your lordfhip will be pleas'd to hear reafon.   [*Pulling again.*

Grip. Take the cup, and the devil give thee joy on't.

Merc. [*Still holding him.*] And your lordfhip will farther be gracioufly pleafed, to releafe all claims, titles, and actions whatfoever to Phædra : you muft give me leave to add one fmall *memento*, for that too.

[*Pulling him again.*

Grip. I renounce her, I releafe her.

Enter Phædra.

Merc. [*To her.*] Phædra, my lord has been pleafed to be very gracious, without pufhing matters to extremity.

Phæd. I over-heard it all. But give me livery and feifin of the goblet, in the firft place.

Merc. There's an act of oblivion fhou'd be pafs'd too.

Phæd. Let him begin to remember quarrels, when he dare ; now I have him under my girdle, I'll cap verfes with him to the end of the chapter.

Enter Amphitryon *and Guards.*

Am. [*To* Gripus.] At laft I have got poffeffion without your lordfhip's warrant. Phædra, tell Alcmena I am here.

Phæd. I'll carry no fuch lying meffage—You are not here, and you cannot be here ; for, to my knowledge, you are above with my lady in the chamber.

Am. All of a piece, and all witchcraft ! Anfwer me precifely ; doft thou not know me for Amphitryon ?

Phæd. Anfwer me firft : Did you give me a diamond, and a purfe of gold ?

Am. Thou know'ft I did not.

Phæd. Then by the fame token, I know you are not the true Amphitryon.

4   *Am.*

Am. I'll undo this enchantment with my fword, and kill the forcerer: come up, gentlemen, and follow me.

[*To the Guards.*

Phæd. I'll fave you the labour, and call him down to confront you, if you dare attend him.   [*Exit* Phædra.

Merc. [*Afide.*] Now the fpell is ended, and Jupiter can enchant no more; or elfe Amphitryon had not entered fo eafily.——[Gripus *is ftealing off.*] Whither now, Gripus? I have bufinefs for you. If you offer to ftir, you know what follows.

Enter Jupiter, *followed by* Tranio *and* Polidas.

Jup. Who dares to play the mafter in my houfe? What noife is this that calls me from above, Invades my foft recefs, And, like a tide, breaks in upon my love?

Am. O heav'ns! what's this I fee?

Tran. What a prodigy!

Pol. How! two Amphitryons!

Grip. I have beheld th' appearance of two funs, But ftill the falfe was dimmer than the true; Here, both fhine out alike.

Am. This is a fight, that, like the Gorgon's head, Chills all my blood, and ftiffens me to ftone. I need no more enquire into my fate; For what I fee refolves my doubts too plain.

Tran. Two drops of water cannot be more like.

Pol. They are two very fames.

' *Merc.* [*Afide.*] Our Jupiter is a great comedian, he ' counterfeits moft admirably.'

Am. Now I am gather'd back into myfelf; My heart beats high, and pufhes out the blood,

[*Drawing his fword.*

To give me juft revenge on this impoftor. If you are brave, affift me—[*To the Guards.*]—Not one ftirs!

What, are all brib'd to take th' enchanter's part! 'Tis true, the work is mine; and thus——

[*Going to rufh upon* Jupiter; *and is held by* Tranio *and* Polidas.

Pol. It muft not be.

Jup.

Jup. Give him his way : I dare the madman's worſt.
But ſtill take notice, that it looks not like
The true Amphitryon, to fly out at firſt
To brutal force : it ſhews he doubts his cauſe,
Who dares not truſt his reaſon to defend it.

  Am. [*Struggling.*] Thou baſe uſurper of my name
    and bed !
No leſs than thy heart's blood can waſh away
Th' affronts I have ſuſtain'd.

  Tran. We muſt not ſuffer
So ſtrange a duel, as Amphitryon
To fight againſt himſelf.

  Pol. Nor think we wrong you, when we hold your
    hands :
We know our duty to our general ;
We know the tyes of friendſhip to our friend ;
But who that friend, or who that gen'ral is,
Without more certain proofs betwixt you two,
Is hard to be diſtinguiſh'd by our reaſon,
Impoſſible by fight.

  Am. I know it ; and have ſatisfy'd myſelf,
I am the true Amphitryon.

  Jup. See again,
He ſhuns the certain proofs ; and dares not ſtand
Impartial judgment, and award of right.
But ſince Alcmena's honour is concern'd,
Whom, more than life and all the world, I love ;
This I propoſe, as equal to us both.
Tranio and Polidas, be you aſſiſtants ;
The guards be ready to ſecure th' impoſtor,
When once ſo prov'd, for public puniſhment ;
And, Gripus, be thou umpire of the cauſe.

  Am. I am content ; let him proceed to examination.

  Grip. [*Aſide to* Merc.] On whoſe ſide wou'd you pleaſe
that I ſhou'd give the ſentence ?

  Merc. [*Aſide to him.*] Follow thy conſcience for once :
but not to make a cuſtom of it neither ; ' nor to leave an
' evil precedent of uprightneſs to future judges—[*Aſide.*]
' 'Tis a good thing to have a magiſtrate under correction.
' Your old fornicating judge dares never give ſentence
' againſt him that knows his haunts.'

                Pol.

Polid. Your Lordſhip knows I was maſter of Amphitryon's ſhip; and I deſire to know of him, what paſſed in private betwixt us two at his landing, when he was juſt ready to engage the enemy?

Grip. Let the true Amphitryon anſwer firſt——

Jup. and Amp. together.—My Lord, I told him——

Grip. Peace both of you!—'Tis a plain caſe, they are both true; for they both ſpeak together: but for more certainty, let the falſe Amphitryon ſpeak firſt.

Merc. Now they are both ſilent——

Grip. Then 'tis as plain on t'other ſide, that they are falſe Amphitryons.

Merc. Which Amphitryon ſhall ſpeak firſt?

Grip. Let the choleric Amphitryon ſpeak: and let the peaceable hold his peace.

Amp. [*To* Polid.] You may remember that I whiſpered you, not to part from the ſtern, one ſingle moment.

Polid. You did ſo.

Grip. No more words then: I proceed to ſentence.

Jup. 'Twas I that whiſpered him; and he may remember I gave him this reaſon for it, that if our men were beaten, I might ſecure my own retreat.

Polid. You did ſo.

Grip. Now again he's as true as t'other.

Tran. You know I was pay-maſter: what directions did you give me the night before the battle?

Grip. To which of the You's art thou ſpeaking?

Am. I ordered you to take particular care of the great bag.

Grip. Why this is demonſtration.

Jup. The bag that I recommended to you, was of tiger's ſkin; and marked Beta.

Grip. In ſadneſs, I think, they are both jugglers: here's nothing, and here's nothing; and then *hiccius doccius*, and they are both here again.

Tran. You, peaceable Amphitryon, what money was there in that bag?

Jup. The ſum, in groſs, amounted juſt to fifty Attic talents.

Tran. To a farthing.

Grip. Paugh! Obvious, obvious.

Am.

Am. Two thoufand pieces of gold were tied up in a handkerchief by themfelves.

Tran. I remember it.

Grip. Then 'tis dubious again.

Jup. But the reft was not all filver; for there were juft four thoufand brafs halfpence.

Grip. Being but brafs, the proof is inconfiderable : if they had been filver, it had gone on your fide.

Am. [*To* Jup.] Death and hell, you will not perfuade me, that I did not kill Pterelas ?

Jup. Nor you me, that I did not enjoy Alcmena ?

Am. That laft was poifon to me——   [*Afide.*
Yet there's one proof thou canft not counterfeit :
In killing Pterelas, I had a wound
Full in the brawny part of my right arm ;
Where ftill the fcar remains : Now blufh, impoftor ;
For this thou canft not fhow.

[*Bares his arm, and fhews the fcar, which they all look on.*
Omnes. This is the true Amphitryon.

Jup. May your lordfhip pleafe——

Grip. No, firrah, it does not pleafe me : hold your tongue, I charge you, for the cafe is manifeft.

Jup. By your favour then, this fhall fpeak for me.
                              [*Bares his arm, and fhews it.*

Tran. 'Tis juft in the fame mufcle.

Polid. Of the fame length and breadth; and the fcar of the fame bluifh colour.

Grip. [*To* Jup.] Did not I charge you not to fpeak ?
'Twas plain enough before; and now you have puzzled it again.

Am. Good gods, how can this be !

Grip. For certain there was but one Pterelas ; and he muft have been in the plot againft himfelf too : for he was killed firft by one of them ; and then rofe again out of refpect to t'other Amphitryon, to be killed twice over.

                    Enter Alcmena, Phædra, *and* Bromia.

Alc. [*Turning to* Phædra *and* Bromia.] No more of
                this ; it founds impoffible
That two fhould be fo like, no difference found.

Phæd. You'll find it true.

Alc. Then where's Alcmena's honour and her fame ?
Farewel my needlefs fear, it cannot be :

                                                  This

This is a cafe too nice for vulgar fight—
But let me come, my heart will guide my eyes
To point, and tremble to its proper choice.

     [*Seeing* Amphitryon, *goes to him.*

There neither was, nor is, but one Amphitryon;
And I am only his —— [*Goes to take him by the hand.*

 Am. [*Pufhing her away from him.*] Away, adultrefs!

 Jup. My gentle love, my treafure and my joy,
Follow no more that falfe and foolifh fire,
That wou'd miflead thy fame to fure deftruction!
Look on thy better hufband, and thy friend,
Who will not leave thee liable to fcorn,
But vindicate thy honour from that wretch,
Who wou'd by bafe afperfions blot thy virtue.

 Alc. [*Going to him, who embraces her.*] I was indeed
  miftaken! thou art he!

Thy words, thy thoughts, thy foul is all Amphitryon.
Th' impoftor has thy features, not thy mind;
The face might have deceiv'd me in my choice,
Thy kindnefs is a guide that cannot err.

 Am. What! in my prefence to prefer the villain?
Oh, execrable cheat! I break the truce;
And will no more attend your vain decifions.
To this—and to the gods I'll truft my caufe.

    [*Is rufhing upon* Jupiter, *and is held again.*

 Jup. Poor man! how I contemn thofe idle threats!
Were I difpos'd, thou might'ft as fafely meet
The thunder launch'd from the red arm of Jove.
But in the face of Thebes fhe fhall be clear'd;
And what I am, and what thou art, be known.
Attend, and I will bring convincing proofs.

 Am. Thou wouldft elude my juftice, and efcape:
But I will follow thee, through earth, and feas;
Nor hell fhall hide thee from my juft revenge.

 Jup. I'll fpare thy pains: it fhall be quickly feen,
Betwixt us two, who feeks, and who avoids.——
Come in, my friends—and thou who feem'ftAmphitryon;
That all who are in doubt, may know the true.

 [Jupiter *re-enters the houfe; with him* Amphitryon,
  Alcmena, Polidas, Tranio, *and Guards.*

 Merc. Thou, Gripus, and you, Bromia, ftay with
  Phædra;

     [*To* Grip. *and* Brom. *who are following.*
              Let

Let their affairs alone, and mind we ours.
Amphitryon's rival fhall appear a god :
But know before-hand, I am Mercury ;
Who want not heav'n, while Phædra is on earth.

Brom. But, an't pleafe your Lordfhip, is my fellow
fervant, Phædra, to be exalted into the heav'ns, and made
a ftar ?

Phæd. When that comes to pafs, if you look up
a-nights, I fhall remember old kindnefs, and vouchfafe
to twinkle on you.

Enter Sofia, *peeping about him* ; *and feeing* Mercury, *is
ftarting back.*

Sof. Here he is again ; and there's no paffing by him
into the houfe, unlefs I were a fprite, to glide in through
the key-hole.——I am to be a vagabond, I find.

Merc. Sofia, come back.

Sof. No, I thank you—you may whiftle me long
enough ; a beaten dog has always the wit to avoid his
mafter.

Merc. I permit thee to be Sofia again.

Sof. 'Tis an unfortunate name, and I abandon it: he
that has an itch to be beaten, let him take it up for Sofia ;
—what have I faid now ! I mean for me; for I neither
am nor will be Sofia.

Merc. But thou mayft be fo in fafety : for I have acknowledged myfelf to be God Mercury.

Sof. I am your moft humble fervant, good Mr. Mercury. But how fhall I be fure that you will never affume
my fhape again ?

Merc. Becaufe I am weary of wearing fo villainous an
outfide.

Sof. Well, well ; as villainous as it is, here's old Bromia will be contented with it.

Brom. Yes, now I am fure that I may chaftife you
fafely.

Sof. Ay, but you had beft take heed you attempt it ;
for as Mercury has turned himfelf into me, fo I may
take the toy into my head, to turn myfelf into Mercury,
that I may fwinge you off, condignly.

Merc. In the mean time, be all my witneffes, that I
take Phædra for my wife of the left-hand ; that is, in
the nature of a lawful concubine.

Phæd.

Phæd. You fhall pardon me for believing you, for all you are a god : for you have a terrible ill name below ; and I'm afraid you'll get a footman, inftead of a prieft, to marry us.

Merc. But here's Gripus fhall draw up articles betwixt us.

Phæd. But he's terribly ufed to falfe conveyancing— Well, be it fo ; for my counfel fhall overlook them before I fign. Come on, Gripus ; that I may have him under black and white. [*Here* Grip. *gets ready pen, ink, and paper.*

Merc. With all my heart.

Phæd. [*To* Grip.] Begin, begin : Heads of articles to be made, &c. betwixt Mercury, god of thieves—

Merc. And Phædra, queen of gypfies——*Imprimis,* I promife to buy and fettle upon her an eftate, containing nine thoufand acres of land, in any part of Bœotia, to her own liking.

Phæd. Provided always, that no part of the faid nine thoufand acres fhall be upon, or adjoining to mount Parnaffus : for I will not be fobbed off with a poetical eftate.

Merc. Memorandum, that fhe be always conftant to me ; and admit of no other lover.

Phæd. Memorandum, unlefs it be a lover that offers more ; and that the conftancy fhall not exceed the fettlement.

' *Merc. Item,* that fhe fhall keep no male fervants in her houfe.

' *Brom.* Here's no provifion made for children yet.

' *Phæd.* Well remembered, Bromia ; I bargain that
' my eldeft fon fhall be a hero, and my eldeft daughter a
' king's miftrefs.

' *Merc.* That is to fay, a blockhead, and a harlot,
' Phædra.

' *Phæd.* That's true ; but who dares call them fo?
' Then for the younger children :—but now I think
' on't, we'll have no more, but mafter and mifs ; for the
' reft would be but chargeable, and a burden to the
' nation.

' *Merc.* Yes, yes ; the fecond fhall be a falfe prophet :
' he fhall have wit enough to fet up a new religion ;
' and too much wit to die a martyr for it.'

Phæd. Oh, what had I forgot ? there's pin-money,
and

and alimony, and feparate maintenance, and a thoufand things more to be confidered; that are all to be tacked to this act of fettlement.

Sof. I am a fool, I muft confefs—but yet I can fee as far into a mill-ftone as the beft of you. I have obferved, that you women-wits are commonly fo quick upon the fcent, that you often over-run it: now I would afk of Madam Phædra, that in cafe Mr. Heaven there, fhould be pleafed to break thefe articles, in what court of judicature fhe intends to fue him ?

Phæd. The fool has hit upon't:—Gods, and great men, are never to be fued ; for they can always plead privilege of peerage; and therefore for once, Monfieur, I'll take your word ; for as long as you love me, you'll be fure to keep it : and in the mean time I fhall be gaining experience how to manage fome rich cully; for no woman ever made her fortune by a wit.

[*It thunders* ; *and the company within doors*, Amphitryon, Alcmena, Polidas, *and* Tranio, *all come running out, and join with the reft, who were on the Theatre before.*

Am. Sure 'tis fome god ! He vanifh'd from our fight, And told us we fhould fee him foon return.

Alc. I know not what to hope, nor what to fear.
A fimple error, is a real crime ;
And unconfenting innocence is loft.

[*A fecond peal of thunder. After which,* Jupiter *appears in a machine.*

Jup. Look up, Amphitryon, and behold above
Th' impoftor god, the rival of thy love :
In thy own fhape fee Jupiter appear,
And let that fight fecure thy jealous fear.
Difgrace, and infamy, are turn'd to boaft ;
No fame, in Jove's concurrence, can be loft :
What he enjoys, he fanctifies from vice ;
And by partaking ftamps into a price.

' *Merc.* [*Afide.*] Amphitryon and Alcmena both ftand
' mute, and know not how to take it.'

Sof. [*Afide.*] Our fovereign lord Jupiter is a fly companion ; he knows how to gild a bitter pill.

Jup. From this aufpicious night fhall rife an heir,
Great like his fire, and like his mother fair :

Wrongs

Wrongs to redrefs, and tyrants to diffeize ;
Born for a world that wants a Hercules.
Monfters, and monfter-men he fhall engage,
And toil and ftruggle through an impious age.
Peace to his labours fhall at length fucceed ;
And murm'ring men, unwilling to be freed,
Shall be compell'd to happinefs, by need.

[Jupiter *is carried back to Heaven.*

Omnes. We all congratulate Amphitryon.

Sof. Ah, Bromia, Bromia, if thou hadft been as handfome and as young as Phædra ! I fay no more,—but
fomebody might have made his fortunes, as well as his
mafter, and never the worfe man neither.

But—down, ambition ! let me not complain—
Enough that I am Sofia once again !
Though not a cuckold, yet content I'll be ;
The great man's happinefs is not for me.
But of myfelf fhall I be robb'd no more ?
Your voice, " ye learned Thebans," I implore—
Give me your fuffrage, I'll be Sofia ftill ;
Let bully Merc'ry there, do what he will.

End of the Fifth Act.

EPILOGUE.

Spoken by PHÆDRA.

I'M thinking (and it almoſt makes me mad)
  How ſweet a time thoſe heathen ladies had.
Idolatry was ev'n their gods own trade ;
They worſhipp'd the fine creatures they had made.
Cupid was chief of all the deities ;
And love was all the faſhion in the ſkies.
When the ſweet nymph held up the lily hand,
Jove was her humble ſervant, at command.
The treaſury of heav'n was ne'er ſo bare,
But ſtill there was a penſion for the fair :
In all his reign, adultery was no ſin ;
For Jove the good example did begin.
Mark, too, when he uſurp'd the huſband's name,
How civilly he ſav'd the lady's fame.
The ſecret joys of love he wiſely hid ;
But you, Sirs, boaſt of more than e'er you did.
You teize your cuckolds, to their face torment them ;
But Jove gave his new honours, to content them :
And, in the kind remembrance of the fair,
On each exalted ſon beſtow'd a ſtar.
For thoſe good deeds, as by the date appears,
His godſhip flouriſh'd full two thouſand years.
At laſt, when he and all his prieſts grew old,
The ladies grew in their devotion cold ;
And that falſe worſhip would no longer hold.
Severity of life did next begin ;
(And always does, when we no more can ſin)
That doctrine too, ſo hard, in practice lies ;
Then the next age may ſee another riſe ;
Then pagan gods may once again ſucceed,
And Jove, or Mars, be ready, at our need,
To get young godlings, and ſo mend our breed.

Publish'd for Bell's British Theatre, May 5th 1777.　　Roberts del.

Mr DODD in the Character of TINSEL.
Have compassion on my Youth, & consider
I am but a Coxcomb.

BELL'S EDITION.

THE
D R U M M E R:
OR, THE
HAUNTED HOUSE.
A C O M E D Y,

As written by JOSEPH ADDISON, Esq.

DISTINGUISHING ALSO THE
VARIATIONS of the THEATRE,

AS PERFORMED AT THE

𝔗heatre-𝔯oyal in 𝔇rury-𝔏ane.

Regulated from the Prompt-Book.

By PERMISSION of the MANAGERS,

By Mr. H O P K I N S, Prompter.

———*Falsis terroribus implet*
Ut magnus.———

HOR.

L O N D O N:
Printed for JOHN BELL, near *Exeter-Exchange,* in the *Strand.*

MDCCLXXVII.

P R E F A C E.

HAVING recommended this play to the town, and delivered the copy of it to the bookseller, I think myself obliged to give some account of it.

It had been some years in the hands of the author, and falling under my perusal, I thought so well of it, that I persuaded him to make some additions and alterations to it, and let it appear upon the stage. I own I was very highly pleased with it, and liked it the better, for the want of those studied similes and repartees, which we, who have writ before him, have thrown into our plays, to indulge and gain upon a false taste that has prevailed for many years in the British theatre. I believe the author would have condescended to fall into this way a little more than he has, had he, before the writing of it, been often present at theatrical representations. I was confirmed in my thoughts of the play, by the opinion of better judges, to whom it was communicated, who observed, that the scenes were drawn after Moliere's manner, and that an easy and natural vein of humour ran through the whole.

I do not question but the reader will discover this, and see many beauties that escaped the audience; the touches being too delicate for every taste in a popular assembly. My brother sharers were of opinion, at the first reading of it, that it was like a picture in which the strokes were not strong enough to appear at a distance. As it is not in the common way of writing, the approbation was at first doubtful, but has risen every time it has been acted, and has given an opportunity, in several of its parts, for as just and good action as ever I saw on the stage.

The

The reader will confider that I fpeak here, not as the author, but as the patentee ; which is, perhaps, the reafon why I am not diffufe in the praifes of the play, left I fhould feem like a man who cries up his own wares, only to draw in cuftomers.

RICHARD STEELE.

PROLOGUE.

IN this grave age, when comedies are few,
  We crave your patronage for one that's new;
Tho' 'twere poor stuff, yet bid the author fair,
And let the scarceness recommend the ware.
Long have your ears been fill'd with tragic parts,
Blood and blank-verse have harden'd all your hearts;
If e'er you smile, 'tis at some party strokes,
Round-heads and wooden-shoes are standing jokes;
The same conceit gives claps and hisses birth,
You're grown such politicians in your mirth!
For once we try (though 'tis, I own, unsafe)
To please you all, and make both parties laugh.
Our author, anxious for his fame to-night,
And bashful in his first attempt to write,
Lies cautiously obscure and unreveal'd,
Like ancient actors in a mask conceal'd.
Censure, when no man knows who writes the play,
Were much good malice merely thrown away.
The mighty criticks will not blast, for shame,
A raw young thing, who dares not tell his name:
Good-natur'd judges will th' unknown defend,
And fear to blame, lest they should hurt a friend;
Each wit may praise it for his own dear sake,
And hint he writ it, if the thing should take:
But if you're rough, and use him like a dog,
Depend upon it —— he'll remain incog.
If you should hiss, he swears he'll hiss as high,
And, like a culprit, raise the hue and cry.
If cruel men are still averse to spare
These scenes, they fly for refuge to the fair.
Tho' with a ghost our comedy be heighten'd,
Ladies, upon my word, you shan't be frighten'd:
Oh, 'tis a ghost that scorns to be uncivil,
A well-spread, lusty, jointure-hunting devil:
An am'rous ghost, that's faithful, fond, and true,
Made up of flesh and blood — as much as you.
Then, ev'ry evening, come in flocks, undaunted;
We never think this house is too much haunted.

DRA-

DRAMATIS PERSONÆ.

M E N.

	Drury-Lane.	*Covent-Garden.*
Sir George Truman,	Mr. Aickin.	Mr. Smith.
Tinfel,	Mr. Dodd.	Mr. Woodward.
Fantome, the drummer,	Mr. Packer.	Mr. R. Smith.
Vellum, Sir George Truman's fteward,	Mr. Parfons.	Mr. Shuter.
Butler,	Mr. Baddeley.	Mr. Dunftall.
Coachman,	Mr. Moody.	Mr. Cufhing.
Gardener,	Mr. Baker.	Mr. Morris.

W O M E N.

Lady Truman,	Mrs. Hopkins.	Mrs. Ward.
Abigail,	Mifs Pope.	Mrs. Green.

THE

THE

DRUMMER.

*** *The lines marked with inverted commas, ' thus,' are omitted in the*
representation.

ACT I.

SCENE, *A great Hall.*

Enter the Butler, Coachman, *and* Gardener.

BUTLER.

THERE came another coach to town laſt night,
that brought a gentleman to enquire about this
ſtrange noiſe we hear in the houſe. This ſpirit will
bring a power of cuſtom to the George——if ſo be he
continues his pranks, I deſign to ſell a pot of ale, and ſet
up the ſign of the drum.

Coach. I'll give Madam warning, that's flat—I've always lived in ſober families. I'll not diſparage myſelf to
be a ſervant in a houſe that is haunted.

Gard. I'll e'en marry Nell, and rent a bit of ground
of my own, if both of you leave Madam ; not but that
Madam's a very good woman—if Mrs. Abigail did not
ſpoil her——Come, here's her health.

But. 'Tis a very hard thing to be a butler in a houſe
that is diſturbed. He made ſuch a racket in the cellar,
laſt night, that I'm afraid he'll four all the beer in my
barrels.

Coach. Why then, John, we ought to take it off as faſt
as we can——Here's to you——He rattled ſo loud under
the tiles, laſt night, that I verily thought the houſe
would have fallen over our heads. I durſt not go up into the cock-loft this morning, if I had not got one of the
maids to go along with me.

Gard. I thought I heard him in one of my bed-poſts.

I marvel

I marvel, John, how he gets into the houfe, when all the gates are fhut.

But. Why, look ye, Peter, your fpirit will creep you into an augre-hole————he'll whifk ye through a key-hole, without fo much as juftling againft one of the wards.

Coach. Poor Madam is mainly frighted, that's certain ; and verily believes it is my mafter, that was killed in the laft campaign.

But. Out of all manner of queftion, Robin, 'tis Sir George. Mrs. Abigail is of opinion, it can be none but his honour. He always loved the wars ; and, you know, was mightily pleafed, from a child, with the mufic of a drum.

Gard. I wonder his body was never found after the battle.

But. Found ! Why, ye fool, is not his body here about the houfe ? Doft thou think he can beat his drum without hands and arms ?

Coach. 'Tis mafter, as fure as I ftand here alive ; and I verily believe I faw him laft night in the town-clofe.

Gard. Ay ! How did he appear ?

Coach. Like a white horfe.

But. Phoo, Robin ! I tell ye, he has never appeared yet, but in the fhape of the found of a drum.

Coach. This makes one almoft afraid of one's own fha-dow. As I was walking from the ftable, t'other night, without my lanthorn, I fell acrofs a beam, that lay in my way ; and faith, my heart was in my mouth. I thought I had ftumbled over a fpirit.

But. Thou might'ft as well have ftumbled over a ftraw. Why, a fpirit is fuch a little thing, that I have heard a man, who was a great fcholar, fay, that he'll dance ye a Lancafhire hornpipe upon the point of a needle. As I fat in the pantry, laft night, counting my fpoons, the candle, methought, burnt blue, and the fpay'd bitch looked as if fhe faw fomething.

Coach. Ay, poor cur, fhe's almoft frightened out of her wits

Gard. Ay, I warrant ye, fhe hears him, many a time and often, when we don't.

But. My Lady muft have him laid, that's certain, whatever it coft her.

Gard.

Gard. I fancy, when one goes to market, one might hear of fomebody that can make a fpell.

Coach. Why, may not the parfon of our parifh lay him ?

But. No, no, no ; our parfon cannot lay him.

Coach. Why not he, as well as another man ?

But. Why, ye fool, he is not qualified. He has not taken the oaths.

Gard. Why, d'ye think, John, that the fpirit would take the law of him ? Faith, I could tell you one way to drive him off.

Coach. How's that ?

Gard. I'll tell you immediately.—[*Drinks.*]—I fancy Mrs. Abigail might fcold him out of the houfe.

Coach. Ay, fhe has a tongue that would drown his drum, if any thing could.

But. Pugh, this is all froth ; you underftand nothing of the matter. The next time it makes a noife, I tell you what ought to be done——I would have the fteward fpeak Latin to it.

Coach. Ay, that would do, if the fteward had but courage.

Gard. There you have it. He's a fearful man. If I had as much learning as he, and I met the ghoft, I'd tell him his own. But, alack ! what can one of us poor men do with a fpirit, that can neither write nor read ?

But. Thou art always cracking and boafting, Peter ; thou doft not know what mifchief it might do thee, if fuch a filly dog as thee fhould offer to fpeak to it. For ought I know, he might flea thee alive, and make parchment of thy fkin, to cover his drum with.

Gard. A fiddleftick ! tell not me——I fear nothing, not I ; I never did harm in my life ; I never committed murder.

But. I verily believe thee. Keep thy temper, Peter ; after fupper we'll drink each of us a double mug, and then let come what will.

Gard. Why, that's well faid, John—An honeft man, that is not quite fober, has nothing to fear——Here's to ye——Why, now if he fhould come this minute, here would I ftand——Ha ! what noife is that ?

But. and Coach. Ha ! where ?

Gard.

Gard. The devil! the devil! Oh, no; 'tis Mrs. Abigail.

But. Ay, faith! 'tis she; 'tis Mrs. Abigail! A good mistake; 'tis Mrs. Abigail.

Enter Abigail.

Ab. Here are your drunken sots for you! Is this a time to be guzzling, when gentry are come to the house! Why don't you lay your cloth? How come you out of the stables? Why are you not at work in your garden?

Gard. Why, yonder's the fine Londoner and Madam fetching a walk together; and methought they looked as if they should say they had rather have my room than my company.

But. And so forsooth being all three met together, we are doing our endeavours to drink this same drummer out of our heads.

Gard. For you must know, Mrs. Abigail, we are all of opinion that one can't be a match for him, unless one be as drunk as a drum.

Coach. I am resolved to give Madam warning to hire herself another coachman; for I came to serve my master, d'ye see, while he was alive: but do suppose that he has no further occasion for a coach, now he walks.

But. Truly, Mrs. Abigail, I must needs say, that this same spirit is a very odd sort of a body, after all, to fright Madam, and his old servants, at this rate.

Gard. And truly, Mrs. Abigail, I must needs say, I served my master contentedly, while he was living; but I will serve no man living (that is, no man that is not living) without double wages.

Ab. Ay, 'tis such cowards as you that go about with idle stories, to disgrace the house, and bring so many strangers about it: you first frighten yourselves, and then your neighbours.

Gard. Frightened! I scorn your words: frightened quoth-a!

Ab. What, you sot, are you grown pot-valiant?

Gard. Frightened with a drum! that's a good one! It will do us no harm, I'll answer for it: it will bring no blood-shed along with it, take my word. It sounds as like a train-band drum as ever I heard in my life.

But. Pr'ythee, Peter, don't be so presumptuous.

Ab.

Ab. Well, thefe drunken rogues take it as I could wifh.   *[Afide.*

Gard. I fcorn to be frightened, now I am in for't ; if old Dub-a-dub fhould come into the room, I would take him ——

But. Pr'ythee, hold thy tongue.

Gard. I would take him ——

    [*The drum beats: the Gardener endeavours to get off, and falls.*

But. and Coach. Speak to it, Mrs. Abigail.

Gard. Spare my life, and take all I have.

Coach. Make off, make off, good butler; and let us go hide ourfelves in the cellar.   [*They all run off.*

Ab. [*Alone.*] So, now the coaft is clear, I may venture to call out my drummer—But firft let me fhut the door, left we be furprifed. Mr. Fantome, Mr. Fantome ! [*He beats.*] Nay, nay, pray come out : the enemy's fled—I muft fpeak with you immediately—— Don't ftay to beat a parley.

    [*The back fcene opens, and difcovers* Fantome *with a drum.*

Fan. Dear Mrs. Nabby, I have overheard all that has been faid, and find thou haft managed this thing fo well, that I could take thee in my arms and kifs thee——If my drum did not ftand in my way.

Ab. Well, o' my confcience, you are the merrieft ghoft ! and the very picture of Sir George Truman.

Fan. There you flatter me, Mrs. Abigail : Sir George had that frefhnefs in his looks, that we men of the town can not come up to.

Ab. Oh, death may have altered you, you know—— Befides you muft confider, you loft a great deal of blood in the battle.

Fan. Ay, that's right ; let me look never fo pale, this cut crofs my forehead will keep me in countenance.

Ab. 'Tis juft fuch a one as my mafter received from a curfed French trooper, as my lady's letter informed her.

Fan. It happens luckily that this fuit of cloaths of Sir George's fits me fo well————I think I can't fail hitting the air of a man with whom I was fo long acquainted.

Ab.

Ab. You are the very man——I vow I almoſt ſtart when I look upon you.

Fan. But what good will this do me, if I muſt remain inviſible?

Ab. Pray what good did your being viſible do you? The fair Mr. Fantome thought no woman could with-ſtand him—But when you were ſeen by my Lady in your proper perſon, after ſhe had taken a full ſurvey of you, and heard all the pretty things you could ſay, ſhe very civilly diſmiſſed you for the ſake of this empty noiſy creature, Tinſel. She fancies you have been gone from hence this fortnight.

Fan. Why really I love thy Lady ſo well, that though I had no hopes of gaining her for myſelf, I could not bear to ſee her given to another, eſpecially ſuch a wretch as Tinſel.

Ab. Well, tell me truly, Mr. Fantome, have not you a great opinion of my fidelity to my dear Lady, that I would not ſuffer her to be deluded in this manner for leſs than a thouſand pound?

Fan. Thou art always reminding me of my promiſe—Thou ſhalt have it, if thou canſt bring our projeƈt to bear: doſt not know, that ſtories of ghoſts and appari-tions generally end in a pot of money.

Ab. Why truly now, Mr. Fantome, I ſhould think myſelf a very bad woman, if I had done what I do for a farthing leſs.

Fan. Dear Abigail, how I admire thy virtue!

Ab. No, no, Mr. Fantome, I defy the worſt of my enemies to ſay I love miſchief for miſchief's ſake.

Fan. But is thy Lady perſuaded that I'm the ghoſt of her deceaſed huſband?

Ab. I endeavour to make her believe ſo; and tell her every time your drum rattles, that her huſband is chiding her for entertaining this new lover.

Fan. Pr'ythee make uſe of all thy art: for I'm tired to death with ſtrolling round this wide old houſe, like a rat behind the wainſcot.

Ab. Did not I tell you 'twas the pureſt place in the world for you to play your tricks in? There's none of the family that knows every hole and corner in it, beſides myſelf.

Fan.

Fan. Ah, Mrs. Abigail! you have had your intrigues—

Ab. For you muft know when I was a romping young girl, I was a mighty lover of Hide and Seek.

Fan. I believe by this time, I am as well acquainted with the houfe as yourfelf.

Ab. You are very much miftaken, Mr. Fantome : but no matter for that; here is to be your ftation to-night. This place is unknown to any one living befides myfelf, fince the death of the joiner, who, you muft underftand, being a lover of mine, contrived the wainfcot to move to and fro, in the manner that you find it. I defigned it for a wardrobe for my lady's caft clothes. Oh, the ftomachers, ftays, petticoats, commodes, laced fhoes, and good things, that I have had in it !——Pray, take care you don't break the cherry brandy bottle that ftands up in the corner.

Fan. Well, Mrs. Abigail, I hire your clofet of you but for this one night—A thoufand pounds, you know, is a very good rent.

Ab. Well, get you gone : you have fuch a way with you, there's no denying you any thing.

Fan. I am thinking how Tinfel will ftare, when he fees me come out of the wall ; for I am refolved to make my appearance to-night.

Ab. Get you in, get you in, my Lady's at the door.

Fan. Pray take care fhe does not keep me up fo late as fhe did laft night, or depend upon it I'll beat the tattoo.

Ab. I'm undone, I'm undone——[*As he is going in.*] Mr. Fantome, Mr. Fantome, have you put the thoufand pound bond into my brother's hand ?

Fan. Thou fhalt have it ; I tell thee thou fhalt have it.
[Fantome *goes in.*

Ab. No more words——Vanifh, vanifh.

Enter Lady.

Ab. [*Opening the door.*] Oh, dear Madam, was it you that made fuch a knocking? My heart does fo beat—I vow you have frighted me to death——I thought verily it had been the drummer.

Lady T. I have been fhowing the garden to Mr. Tinfel : he's moft infufferably witty upon us about this ftory of the drum.

Ab.

Ab. Indeed, Madam, he's a very loose man : I'm afraid 'tis he that hinders my poor master from resting in his grave.

Lady T. Well, an infidel is such a novelty in the country, that I am resolved to divert myself a day or two at least with the oddness of his conversation.

Ab. Ah, Madam ! the drum began to beat in the house as soon as ever this creature was admitted to visit you. All the while Mr. Fantome made his addresses to you, there was not a mouse stirring in the family more than used to be——

Lady T. This baggage has some design upon me, more than I can yet discover. [*Aside.*]——Mr. Fantome was always thy favourite.

Ab. Ay, and should have been yours too, by my consent ! Mr. Fantome was not such a slight fantastic thing as this is——Mr. Fantome was the best built man one should see in a summer's day ! Mr. Fantome was a man of honour, and loved you. Poor soul, how has he sighed, when he has talked to me of my hard-hearted Lady—Well, I had as lief as a thousand pound you would marry Mr. Fantome.

Lady T. To tell thee truly, I loved him well enough till I found he loved me so much. But Mr. Tinsel makes his court to me with so much neglect and indifference, and with such an agreeable sauciness——Not that I say I'll marry him.

Ab. Marry him, quoth-a ! No, if you should, you'll be awakened sooner than married couples generally are —You'll quickly have a drum at your window.

Lady T. I'll hide my contempt of Tinsel for once, if it be but to see what this wench drives at. [*Aside.*

Ab. Why, suppose your husband, after this fair warning he has given you, should sound you an alarm at midnight ; then open your curtains with a face as pale as my apron, and cry out with a hollow voice, what dost thou do in bed with this spindle-shank'd fellow ?

Lady T. Why wilt thou needs have it to be my husband ? He never had any reason to be offended at me. I always loved him while he was living ; and should prefer him to any man, where he so still. Mr. Tinsel is indeed

very

very idle in his talk; but I fancy, Abigail, a difcreet woman might reform him.

Ab. That's a likely matter indeed! Did you ever hear of a woman who had power over a man when fhe was his wife, that had none while fhe was his miftrefs? Oh, there's nothing in the world improves a man in his complaifance, like marriage!

Lady T. He is, indeed, at prefent, too familiar in his converfation.

Ab. Familiar! Madam; in troth, he's downright rude.

Lady T. But that, you know, Abigail, fhews he has no diffimulation in him——Then he is apt to jeft a little too much upon grave fubjects.

Ab. Grave fubjects! he jefts upon the church.

' *Lady T.* But that, you know, Abigail, may be only
' to fhew his wit——Then it muft be owned he's ex-
' tremely talkative.

' *Ab.* Talkative, d'ye call it! he's downright imperti-
' nent.

' *Lady T.* But that, you know, Abigail, is a fign he
' has been ufed to good company——Then indeed he is
' very pofitive.

' *Ab.* Pofitive! why, he contradicts you in every
' thing you fay.

' *Lady T.* But then, you know, Abigail, he has been
' educated at the inns of court.

' *Ab.* A bleffed education indeed! It has made him
' forget his catechifm!'

Lady T. You talk as if you hated him.

Ab. You talk as if you loved him.

Lady T. Hold your tongue; here he comes.

Enter Tinfel.

Tin. My dear widow!

Ab. My dear widow! marry, come up!   [*Afide.*

Lady T. Let him alone, Abigail; fo long as he does not call me my dear wife, there's no harm done.

Tin. I have been moft ridiculoufly diverted fince I left you—Your fervants have made a convert of my booby: his head is fo filled with this foolifh ftory of a drummer, that I expect the rogue will be afraid hereafter to go upon a meffage by moon-light.

Lady T. Ay, Mr. Tinfel, what a lofs of billet-doux would that be to many a fine lady!

B 2

Ab.

Ab. Then you ſtill believe this to be a fooliſh ſtory ?
I thought my lady had told you, that ſhe had heard it
herſelf.

Tin. Ha, ha, ha !

Ab. Why, you would not perſuade us out of our ſenſes ?

Tin. Ha, ha, ha !

Ab. There's manners for you, Madam.   [*Aſide.*

Lady T. Admirably rally'd ! that laugh is unanſwer-
ble ! Now I'll be hanged if you could forbear being
witty upon me, if I ſhould tell you I heard it no longer
ago than laſt night !

Tin. Fancy !

Lady T. But what if I ſhould tell you my maid was
with me !

Tin. Vapours ! Vapours ! Pray, my dear widow, will
you anſwer me one queſtion ?——Had you ever this
noiſe of a drum in your head, all the while your huſband was living ?

' *Lady T.* And pray, Mr. Tinſel, will you let me aſk
' you another queſtion ? Do you think we can hear in
' the country, as well as you do in town ?'

Tin. Believe me, Madam, I could preſcribe you a
cure for theſe imaginations.

Ab. Don't tell my lady of imaginations, Sir, I have
heard it myſelf.

Tin. Hark thee, child—art thou not an old maid ?

Ab. Sir, if I am, it is my own fault.

Tin. Whims ! Freaks ! Megrims ! indeed Mrs. Abigail.

Ab. Marry, Sir, by your talk one would believe you
thought every thing that was good is a megrim.

' *Lady T.* Why truly I don't very well underſtand what
' you meant by your doctrine to me in the garden juſt
' now, that every thing we ſaw was made by chance.

' *Ab.* A very pretty ſubject indeed for a lover to divert
' his miſtreſs with.

' *Lady T.* But, I ſuppoſe, that was only a taſte of the
' converſation you would entertain me with after mar-
' riage.

' *Tin.* Oh, I ſhall then have time to read you ſuch lec-
' tures of motions, atoms, and nature—that you ſhall learn
' to think as freely as the beſt of us, and be convinced in
' leſs than a month, that all about us is chance-work.

' *Lady T.* You are a very complaiſant perſon indeed ;
                                            ' and

' and so you would make your court to me, by perfuading
' me that I was made by chance !

' *Tin.* Ha, ha, ha ! well faid, my dear ! why, faith,
' thou wert a very lucky hit, that's certain !

' *Lady T.* Pray, Mr. Tinfel, where did you learn this
' odd way of talking ?

' *Tin.* Ah, widow, 'tis your country innocence makes
' you think it an odd way of talking.'

Lady T. Though you give no credit to ftories of appa-
ritions, I hope you believe there are fuch things as fpirits.'

Tin. Simplicity !

Ab. I fancy you don't believe women have fouls, d'ye
Sir ?

Tin. Foolifh enough !

' *Lady T.* I vow, Mr. Tinfel, I'm afraid malicious
' people will fay I'm in love with an atheift.

' *Tin.* Oh, my dear, that's an old-fafhioned word——
' I'm a free-thinker, child !

' *Ab.* I'm fure you are a free-fpeaker !

' *Lady T.* Really, Mr. Tinfel, confidering that you are
' fo fine a gentleman, I'm amazed where you got all this
' learning ! I wonder it has not fpoiled your breeding.

' *Tin.* To tell you the truth, I have not time to look
' into thefe dry matters myfelf, but I am convinced by
' four or five learned men, whom I fometimes overhear
' at a coffee-houfe I frequent, that our forefathers were
' a pack of affes, that the world has been in an error for
' fome thoufands of years, and that all the people upon
' earth, excepting thofe two or three worthy gentlemen,
' are impofed upon, cheated, bubbled, abufed, bam-
' boozled——

' *Ab.* Madam, how can you hear fuch a profligate ?
' he talks like the London prodigal.

' *Lady T.* Why really, I'm thinking, if there be no
' fuch things as fpirits, a woman has no occafion for mar-
' rying——She need not be afraid to lie by herfelf.

' *Tin.* Ah, my dear ! are hufbands good for nothing
' but to frighten away fpirits ? Doft thou think I could
' not inftruct thee in feveral other comforts of matrimony.

' *Lady T.* Ah, but you are a man of fo much know-
' ledge, that you would always be laughing at my igno-
' rance——You learned men are fo apt to defpife one.

' *Tin.*

' *Tin.* No, child! I'd teach thee my principles, thou
' fhouldft be as wife as I am—in a week's time.

' *Lady T.* Do you think your principles would make
' a woman the better wife?

' *Tin.* Pr'ythee, widow, don't be queer.

' *Lady T.* I love a gay temper, but I would not have
' you rally things that are ferious.

' *Tin.* Well enough, faith! where's the jeft of rallying
' any thing elfe?

' *Ab.* Ah, Madam, did you ever hear Mr. Fantome
' talk at this rate?   [*Afide.*'

Tin. But where's this ghoft! this fon of a whore of a
drummer? I'd fain hear him, methinks.

Ab. Pray, Madam, don't fuffer him to give the ghoft
fuch ill language, efpecially when you have reafon to believe it is my mafter.

Tin. That's well enough, faith, Nab; doft think thy
mafter is fo unreafonable, as to continue his claim to his
relict after his bones are laid? Pray, widow, remember
the words of your contract, you have fulfilled them to a
tittle——Did not you marry Sir George to the tune of
'*till death us do part?*

Lady T. I muft not hear Sir George's memory treated
in fo flight a manner—' This fellow muft have been at
' fome pains to make himfelf fuch a finifhed coxcomb.
                            [*Afide.*'

Tin. Give me but poffeffion of your perfon, and I'll
whirl you up to town for a winter, and cure you at once.
' Oh, I have known many a country lady come to Lon-
' don with frightful ftories of the hall-houfe being haunt-
' ed, of fairies, fpirits, and witches; that by the time
' fhe had feen a comedy, played at an affembly, and
' ambled in a ball or two, has been fo little afraid of bug-
' bears, that fhe has ventured home in a chair at all hours
' of the night.

' *Ab.* Hum —— fauce-box.   [*Afide.*

' *Tin.* 'Tis the folitude of the country that creates
' thefe whimfies; there was never fuch a thing as a ghoft
' heard of at London, except in the play-houfe'—Oh,
we'd pafs all our time in London. 'Tis the fcene of pleafure and diverfions, where there's fomething to amufe you
every hour of the day. Life's not life in the country.

Lady T. Well then, you have an opportunity of fhowing

ing the fincerity of that love to me which you profefs.
You may give a proof that you have an affection to my
perfon, not my jointure.

Tin. Your jointure! How can you think me fuch a
dog! But, child, won't your jointure be the fame thing
in London, as in the country?

Lady T. No, you're deceived! You muft know it is
fettled on me by marriage articles, on condition that I live
in this old manfion-houfe, and keep it up in repair.

Tin. How!

Ab. That's well put, Madam.

Tin. Why faith I have been looking upon this houfe,
and think it is the prettieft habitation I ever faw in my
life.

Lady T. Ay, but then this cruel drum!

Tin. Something fo venerable in it!

Lady T. Ay, but the drum!

Tin. For my part, I like this Gothic way of building
better than any of your new orders——it would be a
thoufand pities it fhould fall to ruin.

Lady T. Ay, but the drum!

Tin. How pleafantly we two could pafs our time in
this delicious fituation. Our lives would be a continued
dream of happinefs. Come, faith, widow, let's go upon
the leads, and take a view of the country.

Lady T. Ay, but the drum! the drum!

Tin. My dear, take my word for't 'tis all fancy: befides, fhould he drum in thy very bed-chamber, I fhould
only hug thee the clofer.

Clafp'd in the folds of love, I'd meet my doom,
And act my joys though thunder fhook the room.

END of the FIRST ACT.

ACT II.

SCENE *opens and difcovers* Vellum *in his Office, and a
Letter in his Hand.*

VELLUM.

THIS letter aftonifheth; may I believe my own
eyes—or rather my fpectacles——To Humphrey
Vellum, Efq. fteward to the Lady Truman.

"VEL-

" Vellum,

I doubt not but you will be glad to hear your master is alive and designs to be with you in half an hour. The report of my being slain in the Netherlands, has, I find, produced some disorders in my family. I am now at the George-inn. If an old man with a grey beard, in a black cloak, enquires after you, give him admittance. He passes for a conjurer, but is really

Your faithful friend,
G. TRUMAN.

P. S. Let this be a secret, and you shall find your account in it."

This amazeth me! and yet the reasons why I should believe he is still living are manifold—First, because this has often been the case of other military adventurers.

Secondly, because this news of his death was first publish'd in Dyer's Letter.

Thirdly, because this letter can be written by none but himself—I know his hand and manner of spelling.

Fourthly———

Enter Butler.

But. Sir, here's a strange old gentleman that asks for you ; he says he's a conjurer, but he looks very suspicious ; I wish he ben't a Jesuit.

Vel. Admit him immediately.

But. I wish he ben't a Jesuit; but he says he's nothing but a conjurer.

Vel. He says right——He is no more than a conjurer. Bring him in and withdraw.   [*Exit* Butler.

And fourthly, as I was saying, because———

Enter Butler with Sir George.

But. Sir, here is the conjurer---What a devilish long beard he has! I warrant it has been growing these hundred years.   [*Aside. Exit.*

Sir G. Dear Vellum, you have receiv'd my letter : but before we proceed, lock the door.

Vel. It is his voice.   [*Shuts the door.*

Sir G. In the next place help me off with this cumbersome cloak.

Vel. It is his shape.

Sir G. So ; now lay my beard upon the table.

Vel.

Vel. [*After having looked on* Sir Geo. *thro' his spectacles.*]
It is his face, every lineament!

Sir G. Well, now I have put off the conjurer and the old man, I can talk to thee more at my ease.

Vel. Believe me, my good master, I am as much rejoiced to see you alive, as I was upon the day you were born. Your name was in all the news-papers in the list of those that were slain.

Sir G. We have not time to be particular. I shall only tell thee, in general, that I was taken prisoner in the battle, and was under close confinement several months. Upon my release, I was resolved to surprise my wife with the news of my being alive. I know, Vellum, you are a person of so much penetration, that I need not use any further arguments to convince you that I am so.

Vel. I am—and, moreover, I question not but your good lady will likewise be convinced of it. Her ho—nour is a discerning lady.

Sir G. I am only afraid she should be convinced of it to her sorrow. Is she not pleased with her imaginary widowhood? Tell me truly, was she afflicted at the report of my death?

Vel. Sorely.

Sir G. How long did her grief last?

Vel. Longer than I have known any widow's——at least three days.

Sir G. Three days, sayst thou? Three whole days! I'm afraid thou flatterest me—Oh, woman, woman!

Vel. Grief is twofold——

Sir G. This blockhead is as methodical as ever—but I know he is honest. [*Aside.*

Vel. There is a real grief, and there is a methodical grief: she was drowned in tears till such time as the taylor had made her widow's weeds——Indeed, they became her.

Sir G. Became her! and was that her comfort? Truly, a most seasonable consolation.

Vel. I must needs say she paid a due regard to your memory, and could not forbear weeping when she saw company.

Sir G. That was kind, indeed! I find she grieved with
a great

a great deal of good breeding.   But how comes this gang
of lovers about her ?

Vel. Her jointure is confiderable.

Sir G. How this fool torments me !   [*Afide.*

Vel. Her perfon is amiable.

Sir G. Death !   [*Afide.*

Vel. But her character is unblemifhed.   She has been
as virtuous in your abfence as a Penelope——

Sir G. And has had as many fuitors.

Vel. Several have made their overtures.

Sir G. Several !

Vel. But fhe has rejected all.

Sir G. There thou reviveft me.   But what means this
Tinfel ? Are his vifits acceptable ?

Vel. He is young.

Sir G. Does fhe liften to him ?

Vel. He is gay.

Sir G. Sure fhe could never entertain a thought of
marrying fuch a coxcomb !

Vel. He is not ill made.

Sir G. Are the vows and proteftations that paffed between us come to this ? I can't bear the thought of it !
Is Tinfel the man defigned for my worthy fucceffor ?

Vel. You do not confider that you have been dead thefe
fourteen months——

Sir G. Was there ever fuch a dog ?   [*Afide.*

Vel. And I have often heard her fay, that fhe muft never expect to find a fecond Sir George Truman—meaning
your ho—nour.

Sir G. I think fhe loved me ; but I muft fearch into
this ftory of the drummer, before I difcover myfelf to
her.   I have put on this habit of a conjurer, in order to
introduce myfelf.   It muft be your bufinefs to recommend
me as a moft profound perfon, that, by my great knowledge in the curious arts, can filence the drummer, and
difpoffefs the houfe.

Vel. I am going to lay my accounts before my Lady ;
and I will endeavour to prevail upon her ho—nour to admit the trial of your art.

Sir G. I have fcarce heard of any of thefe ftories, that
did not arife from a love-intrigue.   Amours raife as many
ghofts as murders.

Vel.

Vel. Mrs. Abigail endeavours to perfuade us, that 'tis your ho—nour who troubles the houfe.

Sir G. That convinces me 'tis a cheat ; for I think, Vellum, I may be pretty well affured it is not me.

Vel. I am apt to think fo, truly. Ha, ha, ha !

Sir G. Abigail had always an afcendant over her lady ; and if there is a trick in this matter, depend upon it, fhe is at the bottom of it. I'll be hanged if this ghoft be not one of Abigail's familiars.

Vel. Mrs. Abigail has of late been very myfterious.

Sir G. I fancy, Vellum, thou couldft worm it out of her. I know formerly there was an amour between you.

Vel. Mrs. Abigail hath her allurements ; and fhe knows I have pick'd up a competency in your ho—nour's fervice.

Sir G. If thou haft, all I afk of thee, in return, is, that thou wouldft immediately renew thy addreffes to her. Coax her up. Thou haft fuch a filver tongue, Vellum, as 'twill be impoffible for her to withftand. Befides, fhe is fo very a woman, that fhe'll like thee the beter for giving her the pleafure of telling a fecret. In fhort, wheedle her out of it, and I fhall act by the advice which thou giveft her.

Vel. Mrs. Abigail was never deaf to me, when I talked upon that fubject. I will take an opportunity of addref-fing myfelf to her in the moft pathetic manner.

Sir G. In the mean time, lock me up in your office, and bring me word what fuccefs you have——Well, fure I am the firft that ever was employed to lay himfelf.

Vel. You act, indeed, a threefold part in this houfe ; you are a ghoft, a conjurer, and my ho—noured mafter, Sir George Truman ; he, he, he ! You will pardon me for being jocular.

Sir G. Oh, Mr. Vellum, with all my heart ! You know I love you men of wit and humour. Be as merry as thou pleafeft, fo thou doft thy bufinefs. [*Mimicking him.*] You will remember, Vellum, your commiffion is twofold, firft, to gain admiffion for me to your lady, and fecondly, to get the fecret out of Abigail.

Vel. It fufficeth. [*The Scene fhuts.*

Enter Lady Truman.

Lady T. Women who have been happy in a firft mar-riage, are the moft apt to venture upon a fecond. But, for my part, I had a hufband fo every way fuited to my incli-nations,

nations, that I muſt entirely forget him, before I can like another man. I have now been a widow but fourteen months, and have had twice as many lovers, all of them profeſſed admirers of my perſon, but paſſionately in love with my jointure. I think it is a revenge I owe my ſex, to make an example of this worthleſs tribe of fellows, ' who ' grow impudent, dreſs themſelves fine, and fancy we are ' obliged to provide for them. But of all my captives, Mr. ' Tinſel is the moſt extraordinary in his kind. I hope the ' diverſion I give myſelf with him is unblameable. I'm ' ſure 'tis neceſſary to turn my thoughts off from the me- ' mory of that dear man, who has been the greateſt hap- ' pineſs and affliction of my life. My heart would be a ' prey to melancholy, if I did not find theſe innocent ' methods of relieving it.' But here comes Abigail ; I muſt teize the baggage ; for I find ſhe has taken it into her head, that I'm entirely at her diſpoſal.

Enter Abigail.

Ab. Madam, Madam, yonder's Mr. Tinſel has as good as taken poſſeſſion of your houſe. Marry, he ſays, he muſt have Sir George's apartment enlarged ; for, truly, ſays he, I hate to be ſtraitened. Nay, he was ſo impudent as to ſhew me the chamber where he intends to con- ſummate, as he calls it.

Lady T. Well, he's a wild fellow.

Ab. Indeed, he's a very ſad man, Madam.

Lady T. He's young, Abigail ; 'tis a thouſand pities he ſhould be loſt ; I ſhould be mighty glad to reform him.

Ab. Reform him ! marry, hang him !

Lady T. Has he not a great deal of life ?

Ab. Ay, enough to make your heart ake.

Lady T. I dare ſay thou think'ſt him a very agreeable fellow.

Ab. He thinks himſelf ſo, I'll anſwer for him.

Lady T. He's very good-natured.

Ab. He ought to be ſo ; for he's very ſilly.

Lady T. Doſt thou think he loves me ?

Ab. Mr. Fantome did, I'm ſure.

Lady T. With what raptures he talk'd !

Ab. Yes ; but 'twas in praiſe of your jointure-houſe.

Lady T. He has kept bad company.

3   *Ab.*

Ab. They muſt be very bad, indeed, if they were worſe than himſelf.

Lady T. I have a ſtrong fancy a good woman might reform him.

Ab. It would be a fine experiment, if it ſhould not ſucceed.

Lady T. Well, Abigail, we'll talk of that another time. Here comes the ſteward. I have no further occaſion for you at preſent.   [*Exit* Ab.

Enter Vellum.

Vel. Madam, is your ho-nour at leiſure to look into the accounts of the laſt week? They riſe very high. Houſe-keeping is chargeable in a houſe that is haunted.

Lady T. How comes that to paſs? I hope the drum neither eats nor drinks. But read your account, Vellum.

Vel. [*Putting on and off his ſpectacles in this ſcene.*] A hogſhead and a half of ale—It is not for the ghoſt's drinking; but your ho--nour's ſervants ſay, they muſt have ſomething to keep up their courage againſt this ſtrange noiſe. They tell me, they expect a double quantity of malt in their ſmall beer, ſo long as the houſe continues in this condition.

Lady T. At this rate, they'll take care to be frightened all the year round, I'll anſwer for them. But go on.

Vel. *Item*, Two ſheep, and a—Where is the ox?—Oh, here I have him – and an ox—Your ho-nour muſt always have a piece of cold beef in the houſe, for the entertainment of ſo many ſtrangers, who come from all parts, to hear this drum. *Item*, Bread, ten peck loaves—They cannot eat beef without bread. *Item*, Three barrels of table-beer—They muſt have drink with their meat.

Lady T. Sure no woman in England has a ſteward that makes ſuch ingenious comments on his works!   [*Aſide.*

Vel. *Item*, To Mr. Tinſel's ſervants five bottles of port wine—It was by your ho-nour's order. *Item*, Three bottles of ſack, for the uſe of Mrs. Abigail.

Lady T. I ſuppoſe that was by your own order.

Vel. We have been long friends; we are your ho-nour's ancient ſervants. Sack is an innocent cordial, and gives her ſpirit to chide the ſervants, when they are tardy in their buſineſs; he, he, he! Pardon me, for being jocular.

Lady T. Well, I ſee you'll come together at laſt.

Vel. Item, A dozen pound of watch-lights, for the use of the servants.

Lady T. For the use of the servants! What, are the rogues afraid of sleeping in the dark! What an unfortunate woman am I! This is such a particular distress, it puts me to my wits end. Vellum, what would you advise me to do?

Vel. Madam, your ho-nour has two points to consider. *Imprimis*, To retrench these extravagant expences, which bring so many strangers upon you—Secondly, To clear the house of this invisible drummer.

Lady T. This learned division leaves me just as wise as I was. But how must we bring these two points to bear?

Vel. I beseech your ho-nour to give me the hearing.

Lady T. I do. But, pr'ythee, take pity on me, and be not tedious.

Vel. I will be concise. There is a certain person arrived this morning, an aged man, of a venerable aspect, and of a long, hoary beard, that reacheth down to his girdle. The common people call him a wizard, a white-witch, a conjurer, a cunning-man, a necromancer, a————

Lady T. No matter for his titles. But what of all this?

Vel. Give me the hearing, good my Lady. He pretends to great skill in the occult sciences, and is come hither upon the rumour of this drum. If one may believe him, he knows the secret of laying ghosts, or of quieting houses that are haunted.

Lady T. Pho! these are idle stories, to amuse the country people: this can do us no good.

Vel. It can do us no harm, my Lady.

Lady T. I dare say, thou dost not believe there is any thing in it thyself.

Vel. I cannot say I do; there is no danger, however, in the experiment. Let him try his skill; if it should succeed, we are rid of the drum; if it should not, we may tell the world that it has, and by that means, at least, get out of this expensive way of living; so that it must turn to your advantage, one way or another.

Lady T. I think you argue very rightly. But where is the man? I would fain see him. He must be a curiosity.

Vel. I have already discoursed him, and he is to be with

3   me,

me, in my office, half an hour hence. He afks nothing for his pains, till he has done his work—No cure, no money.

Lady T. That circumftance, I muft confefs, would make one believe there is more in his art than one would imagine. Pray, Vellum, go and fetch him hither immediately.

Vel. I am gone. He fhall be forth-coming forthwith.
[*Exeunt.*

Enter Butler, Coachman, *and* Gardener.

But. Rare news, my lads ! rare news !

Gard. What's the matter ? Haft thou got any more vails for us ?

But. No, 'tis better than that.

Coach. Is there another ftranger come to the houfe ?

But. Ay, fuch a ftranger, as will make all our lives eafy.

Gard. What, is he a lord ?

But. A lord ! No, nothing like it—He's a conjurer.

Coach. A conjurer ! What, is he come a wooing to my Lady ?

But. No, no, you fool, he's come a purpofe to lay the fpirit.

Coach. Ay, marry, that's good news indeed. But where is he ?

But. He is locked up with the fteward in his office. They are laying their heads together very clofe. I fancy they are cafting a figure.

Gard. Pr'ythee, John, what fort of a creature is a conjurer ?

But. Why, he's made much as other men are, if it was not for his long grey beard.

Coach. Look ye, Peter, it ftands with reafon that a conjurer fhould have a long grey beard ; for, did ye ever know a witch that was not an old woman ?

Gard. Why, I remember a conjurer, once, at a fair, that, to my thinking, was a very fmock-faced man, and yet he fpewed out fifty yards of green ferret. I fancy, John, if thou'dft get him into the pantry, and give him a cup of ale, he'd fhew us a few tricks. Doft think we could not perfuade him to fwallow one of thy cafe-knives, for his diverfion ? He'll certainly bring it up again.

But. Peter, thou art fuch a wife-acre !—Thou doft not know the difference between a conjurer and a juggler.

This

This man muft be a very great mafter of his trade. His beard is at leaft half a yard long ; he's dreffed in a ftrange dark cloak, as black as a coal. Your conjurer always goes in mourning.

Gard. Is he a gentleman ? Had he a fword by his fide ?

But. No, no, he's too grave a man for that ; a conjurer is as grave as a judge. But he had a long white wand in his hand.

Coach. You may be fure there's a good deal of virtue in that wand—I fancy 'tis made out of witch-elm.

Gard. I warrant you, if the ghoft appears, he'll whifk ye that wand before his eyes, and ftrike you the drumftick out of his hand.

But. No, the wand, look ye, is to make a circle, and if he once gets the ghoft in a circle, then he has him ; let him get out again, if he can. A circle, you muft know, is a conjurer's trap.

Coach. But what will he do with him, when he has him there ?

But. Why, then he'll overpower him with his learning.

Gard. If he can once compafs him, and get him in Lob's-pound, he'll make nothing of him, but fpeak a few hard words to him, and, perhaps, bind him over to his good behaviour, for a thoufand years.

Coach. Ay, ay, he'll fend him packing to his grave again, with a flea in his ear, I warrant him.

But. No, no, I would advife Madam to fpare no coft. If the conjurer be but well paid, he'll take pains upon the ghoft, and lay him, look ye, in the Red Sea——and then he's laid for ever.

Coach. Ay, marry, that would fpoil his drum for him.

Gard. Why, John, there muft be a power of fpirits in that fame Red Sea——I warrant ye, they are as plenty as fifh.

Coach. Well, I wifh, after all, that he may not be too hard for the conjurer. I'm afraid he'll find a tough bit of work on't.

Gard. I wifh the fpirit may not carry a corner of the houfe off with him.

But. As for that, Peter, you may be fure that the fteward has made his bargain with the cunning-man beforehand, that he fhall ftand to all cofts and damages——

But,

But, hark! yonder's Mrs. Abigail; we fhall have her with us immediately, if we do not get off.

Gard. Ay, lads, if we could get Mrs. Abigail well laid too, we fhould lead merry lives.

For, to a man, like me, that's ftout and bold,
A ghoft is not fo dreadful as a fcold.   [*Exeunt.*

END of the SECOND ACT.

ACT III.

SCENE *opens, and difcovers* Sir George *in* Vellum's *Office.*

SIR GEORGE.

I Wonder I don't hear of Vellum yet. But I know his wifdom will do nothing rafhly. The fellow has been fo ufed to form in bufinefs, that it has infected his whole converfation. But I muft not find fault with that punctual and exact behaviour which has been of fo much ufe to me; my eftate is the better for it.

Enter Vellum.

Well, Vellum, I'm impatient to hear your fuccefs.

Vel. Firft, let me lock the door.

Sir G. Will your lady admit me?

Vel. If this lock is not mended foon, it will be quite fpoiled.

Sir G. Pr'ythee, let the lock alone at prefent, and anfwer me.

Vel. Delays in bufinefs are dangerous—I muft fend for the fmith next week; and, in the mean time, will take a minute of it.

Sir G. But what fays your lady?

Vel. This pen is naught, and wants mending——My Lady, did you fay?

Sir G. Does fhe admit me?

Vel. I have gained admiffion for you as a conjurer.

Sir G. That's enough—I'll gain admiffion for myfelf, as a hufband. Does fhe believe there's any thing in my art?

Vel. It is hard to know what a woman believes.

Sir G. Did fhe afk no queftions about me?

Vel. Sundry——She defires to talk with you herfelf, before you enter upon your bufinefs.

Sir G. But when?

Vel.

Vel. Immediately——this inftant.

Sir G. Pugh ! what haft thou been doing all this while ? Why didft not tell me fo ? Give me my cloak— Have you yet met with Abigail ?

Vel. I have not yet had an opportunity of talking with her ; but we have interchanged fome languifhing glances.

Sir G. Let thee alone for that, Vellum. I have formerly feen thee ogle her through thy fpectacles. Well, this is a moft venerable cloak. After the bufinefs of this day is over, I'll make thee a prefent of it. 'Twill become thee mightily.

Vel. He, he, he ! Would you make a conjurer of your fteward ?

Sir G. Pr'ythee, don't be jocular ; I'm in hafte. Help me on with my beard.

Vel. And what will your ho—nour do with your caft beard ?

Sir G. Why, faith, thy gravity wants only fuch a beard to it. If thou would'ft wear it with the cloak, thou would'ft make a moft complete heathen philofopher. But, where's my wand ?

Vel. A fine taper ftick—It is well chofen. I will keep this till you are fheriff of the county. It is not my cuftom to let any thing be loft.

Sir G. Come, Vellum, lead the way. You muft introduce me to your Lady. Thou art the fitteft fellow in the world to be mafter of the ceremonies to a conjurer.

[*Exeunt.*

Enter Abigail, *croffing the ftage.* Tinfel *following.*

Tin. Nabby, Nabby, whither fo faft, child ?

Ab. Keep your hands to yourfelf. I'm going to call the fteward to my Lady.

Tin. What, Goodman Twofold ? I met him walking with a ftrange old fellow, yonder. I fuppofe he belongs to the family too. He looks very antique. He muft be fome of the furniture of this old manfion-houfe.

Ab. What does the man mean ? Don't think to palm me, as you do my Lady.

Tin. Pr'ythee, Nabby, tell me one thing—What's the reafon thou art my enemy ?

Ab. Marry, becaufe I'm a friend to my Lady.

Tin. Doft thou fee any thing about me thou doft not like ?

like? Come hither, huffy. Give me a kifs. Don't be ill-natured.

Ab. Sir, I know how to be civil. [*Kiffes her.*] This rogue will carry off my Lady, if I don't take care. [*Afide.*

Tin. Thy lips are as foft as velvet, Abigail. I muft get thee a hufband.

Ab. Ay, now you don't fpeak idly, I can talk to you.

Tin. I have one in my eye for thee. Doft thou love a young lufty fon of a whore?

Ab. Lud, how you talk!

Tin. This is a thundering dog.

Ab. What is he?

Tin. A private gentleman.

Ab. Ay! Where does he live?

Tin. In the Horfe-guards—But he has one fault I muft tell thee of; if thou canft bear with that, he's a man for thy purpofe.

Ab. Pray, Mr. Tinfel, what may that be?

Tin. He's but five-and-twenty years old.

Ab. 'Tis no matter for his age, if he has been well educated.

Tin. No man better, child; he'll tie a wig, tofs a die, make a pafs, and fwear with fuch a grace, as would make thy heart leap to hear him.

Ab. Half thefe accomplifhments will do, provided he has an eftate——Pray, what has he?

Tin. Not a farthing.

Ab. Pox on him! what do I give him the hearing for?
[*Afide.*

Tin. But as for that, I would make it up to him.

Ab. How?

Tin. Why, look ye, child, as foon as I have married thy Lady, I defign to difcard this old prig of a fteward, and to put this honeft gentleman, I am fpeaking of, into his place.

Ab. [*Afide.*] This fellow's a fool——I'll have no more to fay to him——Hark! my Lady's a coming.

Tin. Depend upon it, Nab, I'll remember my promife.

Ab. Ay, and fo will I too, to your coft.   [*Afide.*
[*Exit* Abigail.
Tin.

Tin. My dear is purely fitted up with a maid But I shall rid the houfe of her.

Enter Lady Truman.

Lady T. Oh, Mr. Tinfel, I am glad to meet you here! I am going to give you an entertainment that won't be difagreeable to a man of wit and pleafure of the town——There may be fomething diverting in a converfation between a conjurer, and this conceited afs. [*Afide.*

Tin. She loves me to diftraction, I fee that. [*Afide.*]—Pr'ythee, Widow, explain thyfelf.

Lady T. You muft know, here is a ftrange fort of a man come to town, who undertakes to free the houfe from this difturbance. The fteward believes him a conjurer.

Tin. Ay, thy fteward is a deep one.

Lady T. He's to be here immediately. It is, indeed, an odd figure of a man.

Tin. Oh, I warrant you, he has ftudied the black art! Ha, ha, ha! Is he not an Oxford fcholar?——Widow, thy houfe is the moft extraordinarily inhabited of any widow's this day in Chriftendom. I think thy four chief domeftics are, a withered Abigail, a fuperannuated fteward, a ghoft, and a conjurer.

Lady T. [*Mimicking* Tinfel.] And you would have it inhabited by a fifth, who is a more extraordinary perfon than any of all thefe four.

Tin. 'Tis a fure fign a woman loves you, when fhe imitates your manner. [*Afide.*] Thou'rt very fmart, my dear. But fee, fmoke the doctor!

Enter Vellum *and* Sir George, *in his conjurer's habit.*

Vel. I will introduce this profound perfon to your ladyfhip, and then leave him with you——Sir, this is her ho-nour.

Sir G. I know it well. [*Exit* Vellum.

[*Afide, walking in a mufing pofture.*] That dear woman! The fight of her unmans me. I could weep for tendernefs, did not I, at the fame time, feel an indignation rife in me to fee that wretch with her. And yet, I cannot but fmile to fee her in the company of her firft and fecond hufband at the fame time.

Lady T. Mr. Tinfel, do you fpeak to him; you are ufed to the company of men of learning.

Tin. Old gentleman, thou doft not look like an inhabitant

bitant of this world; I suppose thou art lately come down from the stars. Pray, what news is stirring in the Zodiack?

Sir G. News that ought to make the heart of a coward tremble. Mars is now entering into the first house, and will shortly appear in all his domal dignities——

Tin. Mars! Pr'ythee, father Grey-beard, explain thyself.

Sir G. The entrance of Mars into his house, portends the entrance of a master into this family——and that soon.

Tin. D'ye hear that, widow? The stars have cut me out for thy husband. This house is to have a master, and that soon——Hark thee, old Gadbury? Is not Mars very like a young fellow called Tom Tinsel?

Sir G. Not so much as Venus is like this lady.

Tin. A word in your ear, doctor; these two planets will be in conjunction by and by; I can tell you that.

Sir G. [*Aside, walking disturbed.*] Curse on this impertinent fop! I shall scarce forbear discovering myself—— Madam, I am told that your house is visited with strange noises.

Lady T. And I am told that you can quiet them. I must confess I had a curiosity to see the person I had heard so much of; and, indeed, your aspect shews that you have had much experience in the world. You must be a very aged man.

Sir G. My aspect deceives you: what do you think is my real age?

Tin. I should guess thee within three years of Methusalah. Pr'ythee tell me, wast not thou born before the flood?

Lady T. Truly I should guess you to be in your second or third century, ' I warrant you, you have great grand-' children with beards a foot long.'

Sir G. Ha, ha, ha! If there be truth in man, I was but five and thirty last August. Oh, the study of the occult sciences makes a man's beard grow faster than you would imagine.

Lady T. What an escape you have had, Mr. Tinsel, that you were not bred a scholar!

Tin. And fo I fancy, Doctor, thou thinkeft me an illiterate fellow, becaufe I have a fmooth chin ?

Sir G. Hark ye, Sir, a word in your ear. You are a
coxcomb, by all the rules of phyfiognomy : but let that
be a fecret between you and me.   [*Afide to* Tinfel.

Lady T. Pray, Mr. Tinfel, what is it the doctor whifpers ?

Tin. Only a compliment, child, upon two or three of
my features. It does not become me to repeat it.

Lady T. Pray, Doctor, examine this gentleman's face,
and tell me his fortune.

Sir G. If I may believe the lines of his face, he likes
it better than I do, or—than you do, fair Lady.

Tin. Widow, I hope now thou'rt convinced he's a cheat.

Lady T. For my part, I believe he's a witch——Go
on, Doctor.

Sir G. He will be croffed in love ; and that foon.

Tin. Pr'ythee, Doctor, tell us the truth. Doft not
thou live in Moor-fields ?

Sir G. Take my word for it, thou fhalt never live in
my Lady Truman's manfion-houfe.

Tin. Pray, old gentleman, haft thou never been
plucked by the beard when thou wert faucy ?

Lady T. Nay, Mr. Tinfel, you are angry ! do you
think I would marry a man that dares not have his fortune told ?

Sir G. Let him be angry——I matter not——He is
but fhort-lived. He will foon die of——

Tin. Come, come, fpeak out, old Hocus, he, he, he !
This fellow makes me burft with laughing.
                                   [*Forces a laugh.*

Sir G. He will foon die of a fright——or of the——
let me fee your nofe——Ay——'tis fo !

Tin. You fon of a whore ! I'll run ye thro' the body.
I never yet made the fun fhine thro' a conjurer——

Lady T. Oh, fy, Mr. Tinfel ! you will not kill an old
man ?

Tin. An old man ! The dog fays he's but five and thirty.

Lady T. Oh, fy ; Mr. Tinfel, I did not think you
could have been fo paffionate, I hate a paffionate man.
Put up your fword, or I muft never fee you again.

Tin. Ha, ha, ha ! I was but in jeft, my dear. I had a
                                              mind

mind to have made an experiment upon the Doctor's body. I would but have drilled a little eyelet hole in it, and have seen whether he had art enough to close it up again.

Sir G. Courage is but ill shown before a lady. But know, if ever I meet thee again, thou shalt find this arm can wield other weapons besides this wand.

Tin. Ha, ha, ha!

Lady T. Well, learned Sir, you are to give a proof of your art, not of your courage. Or if you will show your courage, let it be at nine o'clock——for that is the time the noise is generally heard.

Tin. And look ye, old gentleman, if thou dost not do thy business well, I can tell thee by the little skill I have, that thou wilt be tossed in a blanket before ten. We'll do our endeavour to send thee back to the stars again.

Sir G. I'll go and prepare myself for the ceremonies— And, Lady, as you expect they should succeed to your wishes, treat that fellow with the contempt he deserves.

[*Exit Sir* George.

Tin. The saucieft dog I ever talked with in my whole life!

Lady T. Methinks he's a diverting fellow; one may see he's no fool.

Tin. No fool! Ay, but thou dost not take him for a conjurer.

Lady T. Truly I don't know what to take him for; I am resolved to employ him however. When a sickness is desperate, we often try remedies that we have no great faith in.

Enter Abigail.

Ab. Madam, the tea is ready in the parlour as you ordered.

Lady T. Come, Mr. Tinsel, we may there talk of the subject more at leisure. [*Exeunt Lady* T. *and* Tinsel.

Abigail sola.

Sure never any lady had such servants as mine has! Well, if I get this thousand pounds, I hope to have some of my own. Let me see, I'll have a pretty tight girl— just such as I was ten years ago (I'm afraid I may say twenty) she shall dress me and flatter me—for I will be flattered, that's pos! My Lady's cast suits will serve her

after

after I have given them the wearing. Befides, when I am worth a thoufand pound, I fhall certainly carry off the fteward—Madam Vellum—— how prettily that will found ! Here, bring out Madam Vellum's chaife – Nay, I do not know but it may be a chariot—It will break the attorney's wife's heart——for I fhall take place of every body in the parifh but my Lady. If I have a fon, he fhall be called Fantome. But fee, Mr. Vellum, as I could wifh. I know his humour, and will do my utmoft to gain his heart.

Enter Vellum, *with a pint of fack.*

Vel. Mrs. Abigail, don't I break in upon you unfeafonably !

Ab. Oh, no, Mr. Vellum, your vifits are always feafonable !

Vel. I have brought with me a tafte of frefh canary, which I think is delicious.

Ab. Pray fet it down——I have a dram-glafs juft by —— [*Brings in a rummer.*] I'll pledge you ; my Lady's good health.

Vel. And your own with it——fweet Mrs. Abigail.

Ab. Pray, good Mr. Vellum, buy me a little parcel of this fack, and put it under the article of tea—I would not have my name appear to it.

Vel. Mrs Abigail, your name feldom appears in my bills——and yet——if you will allow me a merry expreffion——You have been always in my books, Mrs. Abigail. Ha, ha, ha !

Ab. Ha, ha, ha ! Mr. Vellum, you are fuch dry jefting man !

Vel. Why, truly Mrs. Abigail, I have been looking over my papers——and I find you have been a long time my debtor.

Ab. Your debtor ! For what, Mr. Vellum !

Vel. For my heart, Mrs. Abigail—And our accounts will not be balanced between us till I have yours in exchange for it. Ha, ha, ha.

Ab. Ha, ha, ha ! Your are the moft gallant dun, Mr. Vellum.

Vel. But I am not ufed to be paid by words only, Mrs. Abigail ; when will you be out of my debt ?

Ab.

Ab. Oh, Mr. Vellum, you make one blush——My humble fervice to you.

Vel. I muſt anſwer you, Mrs. Abigail, in the country phraſe.———Your love is ſufficient. Ha, ha, ha!

Ab. Ha, ha, ha! Well, I muſt own I love a merry man!

Vel. Let me ſee how long is it, Mrs. Abigail, ſince I firſt broke my mind to you——' It was, I think, *unde-* ' *cimo Gulielmi?'*———We have converſed together theſe fifteen years——and yet, Mrs. Abigail, I muſt drink to our better acquaintance. He, he, he——Mrs. Abigail, you know I am naturally jocoſe.

Ab. Ah! you men love to make ſport with us ſilly creatures.

Vel. Mrs. Abigail, I have a trifle about me, which I would willingly make you a preſent of. It is indeed but a little toy.

Ab. You are always exceedingly obliging.

Vel. It is but a little toy——ſcarce worth your ac-ceptance.

Ab. Pray don't keep me in ſuſpence; what is it, Mr. Vellum?

Vel. A ſilver thimble.

Ab. I always ſaid Mr. Vellum was a generous lover.

Vel. But I muſt put it on myſelf, Mrs. Abigail—— You have the prettieſt tip of a finger—I muſt take the freedom to ſalute it.

' *Ab.* Oh, fy! you make me aſhamed, Mr. Vellum;
' how can you do ſo? I proteſt I am in ſuch a con-
' fuſion—— [*A feigned ſtruggle.*

' *Vel.* This finger is not the finger of idleneſs; it bears
' the honourable ſcars of the needle'—But why are you ſo cruel as not to pare your nails?

Ab. Oh, I vow you preſs it ſo hard! pray give me my finger again.

Vel. This middle finger, Mrs. Abigail, has a pretty neighbour—A wedding ring would become it mightily ——He, he, he.

Ab. You're ſo full of your jokes. Ay, but where muſt I find one for't.

Vel. I deſign this thimble only as the forerunner of it, they will ſet off each other, and are——indeed a
D two.

twofold emblem. The firſt will put you in mind of being a good houſewife, and the other of being a good
wife. Ha, ha, ha !

Ab. Yes, yes, I ſee you laugh at me.

Vel. Indeed I am ſerious.

Ab. I thought you had quite forſaken me—I am ſure
you cannot forget the many repeated vows and promiſes
you formerly made me.

Vel. I ſhould as ſoon forget the multiplication table.

Ab. I have always taken your part before my Lady.

Vel. You have ſo, and I have *itemed* it in my memory.

Ab. For I have always looked upon your intereſt as
my own.

Vel. It is nothing but your cruelty can hinder them
from being ſo.

Ab. I muſt ſtrike while the iron's hot. [*Aſide.*]——
Well, Mr. Vellum, there is no refuſing you, you have
ſuch a bewitching tongue !

Vel. How ? Speak that again !

Ab. Why then, in plain Engliſh, I love you.

Vel. I am overjoy'd !

Ab. I muſt own my paſſion for you.

Vel. I'm tranſported !   [*Catching her in his arms.*

Ab. Dear charming man !

Vel. Thou ſum total of all my happineſs ! I ſhall grow
extravagant ! I can't forbear !—to drink thy virtuous inclinations in a bumper of ſack. Your Lady muſt make
haſte, my duck, or we ſhall provide a young ſteward to
the eſtate, before ſhe has an heir to it——pr'ythee, my
dear, does ſhe intend to marry Mr. Tinſel.

Ab. Marry him ! my love. No, no! we muſt take
care of that ! there would be no ſtaying in the houſe for
us if ſhe did. That young rake-hell would ſend all the
old ſervants a grazing. You and I ſhould be diſcarded
before the honey-moon was at an end.

Vel. Pr'ythee, ſweet one, does not this drum put the
thoughts of marriage out of her head ?

Ab. This drum, my dear, if it be well managed, will
be no leſs than a thouſand pounds in our way.

Vel. Ay, ſay'ſt thou ſo, my turtle ?

Ab. Since we are now as good as man and wife——
I mean, almoſt as good as man and wife——I ought to
conceal nothing from you.

Vel.

Vel. Certainly, my dove, not from thy yoke-fellow, thy help mate, thy own flesh and blood!

Ab. Hush! I hear Mr. Tinsel's laugh; my Lady and he are a coming this way; if you will take a turn without, I'll tell you the whole contrivance.

Vel. Give me your hand, chicken.

Ab. Here take it, you have my heart already.

Vel. We shall have much issue.   [*Exeunt.*

END of the THIRD ACT.

ACT   IV.

Enter Vellum *and* Butler.

VELLUM.

JOHN, I have certain orders to give you—and therefore be attentive.

But. Attentive! Ay, let me alone for that——I suppose he means being sober.   [*Aside.*

Vel. You know I have always recommended to you a method in your business; I would have your knives and forks, your spoons and napkins, your plate and glasses laid in a method.

But. Ah, master Vellum! you are such a sweet-spoken man, it does one's heart good to receive your orders.

Vel. Method, John, makes business easy; it banishes all perplexity and confusion out of families.

But. How he talks! I could hear him all day.

Vel. And now, John, let me know whether your table-linen, your side-board, your cellar, and every thing else within your province, are properly and methodically disposed for an entertainment this evening.

But. Master Vellum, they shall be ready at a quarter of an hour's warning. But pray, Sir, is this entertainment to be made for the conjurer?

Vel. It is, John, for the conjurer, and yet it is not for the conjurer.

But. Why, look you, Master Vellum, if it is for the conjurer, the cook-maid should have orders to get him some dishes to his palate. Perhaps he may like a little brimstone in his sauce.

Vel. This conjurer, John, is a complicated creature, an amphibious animal, a perſon of a twofold nature—— But he eats and drinks like other men.

But. Marry, maſter Vellum, he ſhould eat and drink as much as two other men, by the account you give of him.

Vel. Thy conceit is not amiſs, he is indeed a double man ; ha, ha, ha !

But. Ha ! I underſtand you ; he's one of your hermaphrodites, as they call them.

Vel. He is married, and he is not married ——He hath a beard, and he hath no beard. He is old, and he is young.

But. How charmingly he talks ! I fancy, maſter Vellum, you could make a riddle. The ſame man old and young ! How do you make that out, maſter Vellum ?

Vel. Thou haſt heard of a ſnake caſting his ſkin, and recovering his youth. Such is this ſage perſon.

But. Nay, 'tis no wonder a conjurer ſhould be like a ſerpent.

Vel. When he has thrown aſide the old conjurer's ſlough that hangs about him, he'll come out as fine a young gentleman as ever was ſeen in this houſe.

But. Does he intend to ſup in his ſlough ?

Vel. That time will ſhow.

But. Well, I have not a head for theſe things. Indeed, Mr. Vellum, I have not underſtood one word you have ſaid this half hour.

Vel. I did not intend thou ſhouldſt——But to our buſineſs—Let there be a table ſpread in the great hall. Let your pots and glaſſes be waſhed, and in a readineſs. Bid the cook provide a plentiful ſupper, and ſee that all the ſervants be in their beſt liveries.

But. Ay, now I underſtand every word you ſay. But I would rather hear you talk a little in that t'other way.

Vel. I ſhall explain to thee what I have ſaid by and by —Bid Suſan lay two pillows upon your lady's bed.

But. Two pillows ! Madam won't ſleep upon them both ! She is not a double woman too ?

Vel. She will ſleep upon neither. But hark, Mrs. Abigail, I think I hear her chiding the cook-maid.

But. Then I'll away, or it will be my turn next: ſhe, I am ſure, ſpeaks plain Engliſh, one may eaſily underſtand every word ſhe ſays.   [*Exit* Butler.

Vellum

Vellum *folus.*

Servants are good for nothing, unlefs they have an opinion of the perfon's underftanding who has the direction of them.——But fee, Mrs. Abigail! fhe has a bewitching countenance; I wifh I may not be tempted to marry her in good earneft.

Enter Abigail.

Ab. Ha! Mr. Vellum.

Vel. What brings my fweet one hither?

Ab. I am coming to fpeak to my friend behind the wainfcot. It is fit, child, he fhould have an account of this conjurer, that he may not be furprized.

Vel. That would be as much as thy thoufand pounds is worth.

Ab. I'll fpeak low——Walls have ears.

                                [Pointing at the wainfcot.

Vel. But hark you, duckling! be fure you do not tell him that I am let into the fecret.

Ab. That's a good one indeed! as if I fhould ever tell what paffes between you and me.

Vel. No, no, my child, that muft not be! he, he, he! that muft not be; he, he, he!

Ab. You will always be waggifh.

Vel. Adieu, and let me hear the refult of your conference.

Ab. How can you leave one fo foon? I fhall think it an age 'till I fee you again.

Vel. Adieu, my pretty one.

Ab. Adieu, fweet Mr. Vellum.

Vel. My pretty one————   *[As he is going off.*

Ab. Dear Mr. Vellum.

Vel. My pretty one!   *[Exit* Vellum.

Ab. [*Sola.*] I have him—If I can but get this thoufand pounds.

    [Fant. gives three raps upon his drum behind the wainfcot.

Ab. Ha. Three raps upon the drum! the fignal Mr. Fantome and I agreed upon, when he had a mind to fpeak with me.   *[Fantome raps again.*

Ab. Very well, I hear you: come, fox, come out of your hole.

SCENE *opens, and* Fantome *comes out.*

Ab. You may leave your drum in the wardrobe, 'till you have occafion for it.

Fan. Well, Mrs. Abigail, I want to hear what's doing in the world.

Ab. You are a very inquifitive fpirit. But I muft tell you, if you do not take care of yourfelf, you will be laid this evening.

Fan. I have overheard fomething of that matter. But let me alone for the doctor—I'll engage to give a good account of him. I am more in pain about Tinfel. When a lady's in the cafe, I'm more afraid of one fop than twenty conjurers.

Ab. To tell you truly, he preffes his attacks with fo much impudence, that he has made more progrefs with my Lady in two days, than you did in two months.

Fan. I fhall attack her in another manner, if thou canft but procure me another interview. There's nothing makes a lover fo keen, as being kept up in the dark.

Ab. Pray, no more of your diftant bows, your refpectful compliments—Really, Mr. Fantome, you're only fit to make love acrofs a tea-table.

Fan. My dear girl, I can't forbear hugging thee for thy good advice.

Ab. Ay, now I have fome hopes of you; but why don't you do fo to my Lady ?

Fan. Child, I always thought your Lady loved to be treated with refpect.

Ab. Believe me, Mr. Fantome, there is not fo great a difference between woman and woman, as you imagine. You fee Tinfel has nothing but his faucinefs to recommend him.

Fan. Tinfel is too great a coxcomb to be capable of love—And let me tell thee, Abigail, a man, who is fincere in his paffion, makes but a very aukward profeffion of it——But I'll mend my manners.

Ab. Ay, or you'll never gain a widow——Come, I muft tutor you a little; fuppofe me to be my Lady, and let me fee how you'll behave yourfelf.

Fan. I'm afraid, child, we han't time for fuch a piece of mummery.

Ab.

Ab. Oh, it will be quickly over, if you play your part well.

Fan. Why then, dear Mrs. Ab——I mean, my Lady Truman.

Ab. Ay, but you han't faluted me.

Fan. That's right; faith, I forgot that circumftance. [*Kiffes her.*] Nectar and Ambrofia!

Ab. That's very well——

Fan. How long muft I be condemned to languifh! when fhall my fufferings have an end! My life, my happinefs, my all is wound up in you——

Ab. Well! why don't you fqueeze my hand.

Fan. What, thus?

Ab. Thus? Ay—Now throw your arm about my middle: hug me clofer.——You are not afraid of hurting me! Now pour forth a volley of rapture and nonfenfe till you are out of breath.

Fan. Tranfport and ecftacy! where am I!—my life, my blifs!——I rage, I burn, I bleed, I die.

Ab. Go on, go on.

Fan. Flames and darts——Bear me to the gloomy fhade, rocks, and grottos————Flowers, zephyrs, and purling ftreams.

Ab. Oh, Mr. Fantome, you have a tongue would undo a veftal! You were born for the ruin of our fex.

Fan. This will do then, Abigail?

Ab. Ay, this is talking like a lover, though I only reprefent my Lady, I take pleafure in hearing you. Well, o'my confcience, when a man of fenfe has a little dafh of the coxcomb in him, no woman can refift him. Go on at this rate, and the thoufand pounds is as good as in my pocket.

Fan. I fhall think it an age till I have an opportunity of putting this leffon in practice.

Ab. You may do it foon, if you make good ufe of your time. Mr. Tinfel will be here with my Lady at eight, and at nine the conjurer is to take you in hand.

Fan. Let me alone with both of them.

Ab. Well! forewarn'd, forearm'd. Get into your box, and I'll endeavour to difpofe every thing in your favour.   [*Fantome goes in. Exit* Abigail.

Enter

Enter Vellum.

Vel. Mrs. Abigail is withdrawn.——I was in hopes to have heard what paſſed between her and her inviſible correſpondent.

Enter Tinſel.

Tin. Vellum ! Vellum !

Vel. [*Aſide.*] Vellum ! We are, methinks, very fami- liar ; I am not uſed to be called ſo by any but their ho—nours——What would you, Mr. Tinſel ?

Tin. Let me beg a favour of thee, old gentleman.

Vel. What is that, good Sir ?

Tin. Pr'ythee run and fetch me the rent-roll of thy Lady's eſtate.

Vel. The rent-roll !

Tin. The rent-roll ! Ay, the rent-roll ! Doſt not un- derſtand what that means ?

Vel. Why, have you thoughts of purchaſing of it ?

Tin. Thou haſt hit it, old boy ; that is my very in- tention.

Vel. The purchaſe will be conſiderable.

Tin. And for that reaſon I have bid thy Lady very high——She is to have no leſs for it than this entire perſon of mine.

Vel. Is your whole eſtate perſonal, Mr. Tinſel—he, he, he !

Tin. Why, your queer old dog, you don't pretend to jeſt, d'ye ? Look ye, Vellum, if you think of being con- tinued my ſteward, you muſt learn to walk with your toes out.

Vel. [*Aſide.*] An inſolent companion !

Tin. Thou'rt confounded rich, I ſee, by that dang- ling of thy arms.

Vel. [*Aſide.*] An ungracious bird !

Tin. Thou ſhalt lend me a couple of thouſand pounds.

Vel. [*Aſide.*] A very profligate !

Tin. Look ye, Vellum, I intend to be kind to you— I'll borrow ſome money of you.

Vel. I cannot but ſmile to conſider the diſappointment this young fellow will meet with ; I will make myſelf merry with him. [*Aſide.*] And ſo, Mr. Tinſel, you pro- miſe you will be a very kind maſter to me.

[*Stifling a laugh.*
Tin.

Tin. What will you give for a life in the houſe you live in ?

Vel. What do you think of five hundred pounds ?— Ha, ha, ha !

Tin. That's too little.

Vel. And yet it is more than I ſhall give you—And I will offer you two reaſons for it.

Tin. Pr'ythee, what are they ?

Vel. Firſt, becauſe the tenement is not in your diſpoſal ; and, ſecondly, becauſe it never will be in your diſpoſal, and ſo fare you well, good Mr. Tinſel. Ha, ha, ha ! You will pardon me for being jocular.

[*Exit* Vellum.

Tin. This rogue is as ſaucy as the conjurer : I'll be hanged if they are not a-kin.

Enter Lady.

Lady T. Mr. Tinſel ! what, all alone ? You free-thinkers are great admirers of ſolitude.

Tin. No, faith, I have been talking with thy ſteward ; a very groteſque figure of a fellow, ' the very picture of ' one of our benchers.' How can you bear his converſation ?

Lady T. I keep him for my ſteward, and not my companion. He's a ſober man.

Tin. Yes, yes, he looks like a put, a queer old dog, as ever I ſaw in my life : we muſt turn him off, widow. He cheats thee confoundedly, I ſee that.

Lady T. Indeed you're miſtaken ; he has always had the reputation of being a very honeſt man.

Tin. What ! I ſuppoſe he goes to church.

Lady T. Goes to church ! ſo do you too, I hope.

Tin. I would for once, widow, to make ſure of you.

Lady T. Ah, Mr. Tinſel ! a huſband who would not continue to go thither, would quickly forget the promiſes he made there.

Tin. Faith, very innocent, and very ridiculous ! Well then, I warrant thee, widow, thou wouldſt not for the world marry a ſabbath-breaker !

Lady T. Truly they generally come to a bad end. I remember the conjurer told you, you were ſhort-liv'd.

Tin. The conjurer ! Ha, ha, ha !

Lady T. Indeed, you're very witty ?

' *Tin.*

' *Tin.* Indeed you're very handfome.' [*Kiſſes her hand.*

' *Lady T.* I wiſh the fool does not love me.' [*Aſide.*

Tin. Thou art the idol I adore : here muſt I pay my devotion——Pr'ythee, widow, haſt thou any timber upon thy eſtate.

Lady T. The moſt impudent fellow I ever met with.

[*Aſide.*

Tin. I take notice thou haſt a great deal of old plate here in the houſe, widow.

Lady T. Mr. Tinſel, you are a very obſerving man.

Tin. Thy large ſilver ciſtern would make a very good coach : and half a dozen ſalvers that I ſaw on the ſideboard, might be turned into ſix as pretty horſes as any that appear in the ring.

Lady T. You have a very good fancy, Mr. Tinſel.— What pretty transformations you could make in my houſe——But I'll ſee where 'twill end. [*Aſide.*

Tin. Then I obſerve, child, you have two or three ſervices of gilt plate ; we'd eat always in china, my dear.

Lady T. I perceive you are an excellent manager--How quickly you have taken an inventory of my goods !

Tin. Now, hark ye, widow, to ſhew you the love that I have for you——

Lady T. Very well ; let me hear.

Tin. You have an old-faſhioned gold caudle cup, with a figure of a ſaint upon the lid on't.

Lady T. I have : what then ?

Tin. Why, look ye, I'd ſell the caudle-cup with the old ſaint for as much money as they'd fetch, which I would convert into a diamond buckle, and make you a preſent of it.

Lady T. Oh, you are generous to an extravagance. But, pray, Mr. Tinſel, don't diſpoſe of my goods before you are ſure of my perſon. I find you have taken a great affection to my moveables.

Tin. My dear, I love every thing that belongs to you.

Lady T. I ſee you do, Sir ; you need not make any proteſtations upon that ſubject.

Tin. Pho, pho, my dear, we are growing ſerious ; and let me tell you that's the very next ſtep to being dull. ' Come, that pretty face was never made to look grave ' with.'

Lady

Lady T. Believe me, Sir, whatever you think, marriage is a serious subject.

Tin. For that very reason, my dear, let us run over it as fast as we can.

' *Lady T.* I should be very much in haste for a husband, if I married within fourteen months after Sir George's decease.

' *Tin.* Pray, my dear, let me ask you a question: dost not thou think that Sir George is as dead at present to all intents and purposes, as he will be a twelve-month hence?

' *Lady T.* Yes; but decency, Mr. Tinsel.——

' *Tin.* Or dost thou think thou'lt be more a widow then, than thou art now?

' *Lady T.* The world would say I never loved my first husband.

' *Tin.* Ah, my dear, they would say you loved your second; and they would own I deserved it, for I shall love thee most inordinately.

' *Lady T.* But what would people think?

' *Tin.* Think! why they would think thee the mirror of widowhood——That a woman should live fourteen whole months after the decease of her spouse, without having engaged herself. Why, about town, we know many a woman of quality's second husband, several years before the death of the first.

' *Lady T.* Ay, I know you wits have your common-place jests upon us poor widows.'

Tin. I'll tell you a story, widow: I know a certain lady, who, considering the craziness of her husband, had, in case of mortality, engaged herself to two young fellows of my acquaintance. They grew such desperate rivals for her, while her husband was alive, that one of them pinked the other in a duel. But the good lady was no sooner a widow, but what did my dowager do? Why, faith, being a woman of honour, she married a third, to whom, it seems, she had given her first promise.

Lady T. And this is a true story upon your own knowledge?

Tin. Every tittle, as I hope to be married, or never believe Tom Tinsel.

Lady T. Pray, Mr. Tinfel, do you call this talking like a wit, or like a rake?

' *Tin.* Innocent enough. He, he, he! Why, where's
' the difference, my dear.

' *Lady T.* Yes, Mr. Tinfel, the only man I ever loved
' in my life, had a great deal of the one, and nothing of
' the other in him.'

Tin. Nay, now you grow vapourifh; thou'lt begin to fancy thou heareft the drum by and by.

Lady T. If you had been here laft night about this time, you would not have been fo merry.

Tin. About this time, fay'ft thou! Come, faith, for humour's fake, we'll fit down and liften.

Lady T. I will, if you'll promife to be ferious.

Tin. Serious! never fear me, child; ha, ha, ha! Doft not hear him?

Lady T. You break your word already. ' Pray, Mr.
' Tinfel, do you laugh to fhew your wit, or your teeth?
' *Tin.* Why both, my dear———I'm glad, however,
' that fhe has taken notice of my teeth. [*Afide.*] But
' you look ferious, child; I fancy thou heareft the drum,
' doft not?

' *Lady T.* Don't talk fo rafhly.'

Tin. Why, my dear, you could not look more frighted if you had Lucifer's drum-major in your houfe.

' *Lady T.* Mr. Tinfel, I muft defire to fee you no
' more in it, if you do not leave this idle way of talking.

' *Tin.* Child, I thought I had told you what is my
' opinion of fpirits, as we were drinking a difh of tea
' but juft now———There is no fuch thing, I give
' thee my word.

' *Lady T.* Oh, My Tinfel, your authority muft be of
' great weight to thofe that know you.

' *Tin.* For my part, child, I have made myfelf eafy in
' thofe points.

' *Lady T.* Sure nothing was ever like this fellow's va-
' nity, but his ignorance. [*Afide.*

' *Tin.*' I'll tell thee what now, widow———I would engage, by the help of a white fheet, and a penny-worth of link, in a dark night, to frighten you a whole country village out of their fenfes, and the vicar into the bargain. [*Drum beats.*] Hark, hark!
what

what noife is that ? Heaven defend us ! this is more than fancy.

Lady T. It beats more terrible than ever.

Tin. 'Tis very dreadful ! What a dog have I been, to fpeak againft my confcience only to fhew my parts !

Lady. It comes nearer and nearer. I wifh you have not angered it by your foolifh difcourfe.

Tin. Indeed, Madam, I did not fpeak from my heart. I hope it will do me no hurt, for a little harmlefs raillery.

Lady T. Harmlefs, d'ye call it ? It beats hard by us, as if it would break through the wall.

Tin. What a devil had I to do with a white fheet ?

[*Scene opens, and difcovers* Fantome.

Mercy on us, it appears !

Lady T. Oh, 'tis he ! 'tis he himfelf ! 'tis Sir George ! 'tis my hufband ! [*She faints.*

Tin. Now would I give ten thoufand pounds that I were in town. [Fantome *advances to him, drumming.*] I beg ten thoufand pardons : I'll never talk at this rate any more. [Fantome *ftill advances, drumming.*] By my foul, Sir George, I was not in earneft. [*Falls on his knees.*] Have compaffion on my youth, and confider I am but a coxcomb. [Fantome *points to the door.*] But fee, he waves me off——Ay, with all my heart—— What a devil had I to do with a white fheet ?

{*He fteals off the ftage, mending his pace as the drum beats.*

Fan. The fcoundrel is gone, and has left his miftrefs behind him ; I'm miftaken if he makes love in this houfe any more. I have now only the conjurer to deal with. I don't queftion but I fhall make his reverence fcamper as faft as the lover ; and then the day's my own. But the fervants are coming ; I muft get into my cupboard.

[*He goes in.*

Enter Abigail *and Servants.*

Ab. Oh, my poor Lady ! This wicked drum has frighted Mr. Tinfel out of his wits, and my Lady into a fwoon. Let me bend her a little forward. She revives. Here, carry her into the frefh air, and fhe'll recover. [*They carry her off.*] This is a little barbarous to my Lady ; but 'tis all for her good : and I know her fo well, that fhe would not be angry with me, if fhe knew what I was to

E get

get by it. And if any of her friends fhould blame me for it hereafter,

I'll clap my hand upon my purfe, and tell 'em,
'Twas for a thoufand pounds, and Mr. Vellum. *Exit.*

END of the FOURTH ACT.

ACT V.

Enter Sir George *in his conjurer's habit*; *the* Butler *marching before him, with two large candles*; *and the two Servants coming after him, one bringing a little table, and another a chair.*

BUTLER.

AN'T pleafe your worfhip, Mr. Conjurer, the ftew-ard has given all of us orders to do whatfoever you fhall bid us, and to pay you the fame refpect as if you were our mafter.

Sir G. Thou fay'ft well.

Gard. An't pleafe your conjurerfhip's worfhip, fhall I fet the table down here?

Sir G. Here, Peter.

Gard. Peter!—He knows my name by his learning.
[*Afide.*

Coach. I have brought you, reverend Sir, the largeft elbow-chair in the houfe; 'tis that the fteward fits in, when he holds a court.

Sir G. Place it there.

But. Sir, will you pleafe to want any thing elfe?

Sir G. Paper, and a pen and ink.

But. Sir, I believe we have paper that is fit for your purpofe; my Lady's mourning paper, that is blacked at the edges. Would you choofe to write with a crow-quill?

Sir G. There is none better.

But. Coachman, go fetch the paper and ftandifh out of the little parlour.

Coach. [*To* Gard.] Peter, pr'ythee, do thou go along with me—I'm afraid——You know I went with you, laft night, into the garden, when the cook-maid wanted a handful of parfley.

But. Why, you don't think I'll ftay with the conjurer by myfelf?

Gard. Come, we'll all three go and fetch the pen and ink together.   *[Exeunt Servants.*

Sir G. There's nothing, I see, makes such strong alliances as fear. These fellows are all entered into a confederacy against the ghost. There must be abundance of business done in the family, at this rate. But here comes the triple-alliance. Who could have thought these three rogues could have found each of them an employment in fetching a pen and ink?

Enter Gardiner *with a sheet of paper,* Coachman *with a standish, and* Butler *with a pen.*

Gard. Sir, there is your paper.

Coach. Sir, there is your standish.

But. Sir, there is your crow-quill pen——I'm glad I have got rid on't.   *[Aside.*

Gard. [*Aside.*] He forgets that he's to make a circle—Doctor, shall I help you to a bit of chalk?

Sir G. It is no matter.

But. Look ye, Sir, I show'd you the spot where he's heard oftenest. If your worship can but ferret him out of that old wall in the next room——

Sir G. We shall try.

Gard. That's right, John. His worship must let fly all his learning at that old wall.

But. Sir, if I was worthy to advise you, I would have a bottle of good October by me. Shall I set a cup of old stingo at your elbow?

Sir G. I thank thee——we shall do without it.

Gard. John, he seems a very good-natured man, for a conjurer.

But. I'll take this opportunity of enquiring after a bit of plate I have lost. I fancy, whilst he is in my Lady's pay, one may hedge in a question or two into the bargain. Sir, Sir, may I beg a word in your ear.

Sir G. What wouldst thou?

But. Sir, I know I need not tell you, that I lost one of my silver spoons last week.

Sir G. Marked with a swan's neck——

But. My Lady's crest! He knows every thing. [*Aside.* How would your worship advise me to recover it again?

Sir G. Hum——

But. What must I do to come at it?

Sir G. Drink nothing but small-beer for a fortnight—
But. Small-beer! rot-gut!

Sir G. If thou drink'st a single drop of ale before fifteen days are expired——it is as much——as thy spoon ——is worth.

But. I shall never recover it that way—I'll e'en buy a new one. [*Aside.*

Coach. D'ye mind how they whisper?

Gard. I'll be hanged if he be not asking him something about Nell——

Coach. I'll take this opportunity of putting a question to him, about poor Dobbin. I fancy he could give me better counsel than the farrier.

But. [*To* Gard.] A prodigious man! he knows every thing. Now is the time to find out thy pick-ax.

Gard. I have nothing to give him. Does not he expect to have his hand cross'd with silver?

Coach. [*To* Sir G.] Sir, may a man venture to ask you a question?

Sir G. Ask it.

Coach. I have a poor horse, in the stable, that's bewitch'd——

Sir G. A bay gelding.

Coach. How could he know that? [*Aside.*

Sir G. Bought at Banbury.

Coach. Whew!—So it was, o'my conscience. [*Whistles.*

Sir G. Six years, old last Lammas.

Coach. To a day. [*Aside.*] Now, Sir, I would know whether the poor beast is bewitch'd by Goody Crouch, or Goody Fly?

Sir G. Neither.

Coach. Then it must be Goody Gurton; for she is the next oldest woman in the parish.

Gard. Hast thou done, Robin?

Coach. [*To* Gard.] He can tell thee any thing.

Gard. [*To* Sir G.] Sir I would beg to take you a little further out of hearing——

Sir G. Speak.

Gard. The butler and I, Mr. Doctor, were both of us in love, at the same time, with a certain person.

Sir G. A woman.

Gard. How could he know that? [*Aside.*

Sir

Sir G. Go on.

Gard. This woman has lately had two children at a birth.

Sir G. Twins.

Gard. Prodigious ! Where could he hear that ? [*Afide.*

Sir G. Proceed.

Gard. Now, becaufe I ufed to meet her fometimes in the garden, fhe has laid them both——

Sir G. To thee.

Gard. What a power of learning he muft have ! he knows every thing. [*Afide.*

Sir G. Haft thou done ?

Gard. I would defire to know, whether I am really father to them both ?

Sir G. Stand before me ; let me furvey thee round.

[*Lays his wand upon his head, and makes him turn about.*

Coach. Look yonder, John, the filly dog is turning about under the conjurer's wand. If he has been faucy to him, we fhall fee him puffed off in a whirlwind immediately.

Sir G. Twins, doft thou fay ? [*Still turning him.*

Gard. Ay, are they both mine, d'ye think ?

Sir G. Own but one of them.

Gard. Ay, but Mrs. Abigail will have me take care of them both—fhe's always for the butler——If my poor mafter, Sir George, had been alive, he would have made him go halves with me.

Sir G. What, was Sir George a kind mafter.

Gard. Was he ! Ay, my fellow-fervants will bear me witnefs.

Sir G. Did ye love Sir George ?

But. Every body loved him——

Coach. There was not a dry eye in the parifh, at the news of his death——

Gard. He was the beft neighbour——

But. The kindeft hufband——

Coach. The trueft friend to the poor——

But. My Lady took on mightily ; we all thought it would have been the death of her——

Sir G. I proteft thefe fellows melt me——I think the time long, till I am their mafter again, that I may be kind to them. [*Afide.*

Enter

Enter Vellum.

Vel. Have you provided the doctor every thing he has
occafion for ?——If fo——you may depart.

                [*Exeunt Servants.*

  Sir G. I can, as yet, fee no hurt in my wife's behaviour ; but ftill have fome certain pangs and doubts, that
are natural to the heart of a fond man. ' I muft take the
' advantage of my difguife, to be thoroughly fatisfied.
' It would neither be for her happinefs nor mine, to
' make myfelf known to her, till I am fo.' [*Afide.*] Dear
Vellum, I am impatient to hear fome news of my wife.
How does fhe, after her fright ?

  Vel. It is a faying fomewhere in my Lord Coke, that a
widow———

  Sir G. I afk of my wife, and thou talk'ft to me of my
Lord Coke——Pr'ythee, tell me how fhe does ; for I am
in pain for her.

  Vel. She is pretty well recovered. Mrs. Abigail has
put her in good heart ; and I have given her great hopes
from your fkill.

  Sir G. That, I think, cannot fail, fince thou haft got
this fecret out of Abigail. But I could not have thought
my friend Fantome would have ferved me thus.

  Vel. You will ftill fancy you are a living man.

  Sir G. That he fhould endeavour to enfnare my wife——

  : *Vel.* You have no right in her after your demife.
Death extinguifhes all property—*Quoad hanc*—It is a
maxim in the law.

  Sir G. A pox on your learning ! Well, but what is become of Tinfel ?

  Vel. He rufhed out of the houfe, called for his horfe,
clapped fpurs to his fides, and was out of fight in lefs
time than I can tell ten.

  Sir G. This is whimfical enough. My wife will have
a quick fucceffion of lovers in one day. Fantome has
driven out Tinfel, and I fhall drive out Fantome.

  Vel. Even as one wedge driveth out another—He, he,
he ! You muft pardon me for being jocular.

  Sir G. Was there ever fuch a provoking blockhead ?
But he means me well—' Well, I muft have fatisfaction
' of this traitor, Fantome ; and cannot take a more pro-
' per one, than by turning him out of my houfe, in a

                            manner

' manner that fhall throw fhame upon him, and make him
' ridiculous as long as he lives.'—You muſt remember,
Vellum, you have abundance of bufinefs upon your
hands ; and I have but juſt time to tell it you over. All
I require of you is difpatch ; therefore, hear me.

Vel. There is nothing more requiſite in bufinefs than
difpatch——

Sir G. Then hear me.

Vel. It is, indeed, the life of bufinefs——

Sir G. Hear me then, I fay.

Vel. And, as one hath rightly obferved, the benefit that
attends it is fourfold. Firſt——

Sir G. There is no bearing this. Thou art going to
defcribe difpatch, when thou fhould'ſt be practifing it.

Vel. But your ho—nour will not give me the hearing——

Sir G. Thou wilt not give me the hearing. [*Angrily.*
Vel. I am ſtill.

Sir G. In the firſt place, you are to lay my wig, hat,
and fword ready for me in the clofet, and one of my
fcarlet coats. You know how Abigail has defcribed the
ghoſt to you.

Vel. It ſhall be done.

Sir G. Then you muſt remember, whilſt I am laying
this ghoſt, you are to prepare my wife for the reception of
her real hufband. Tell her the whole ſtory, and do it
with all the art you are maſter of, that the furprife may
not be too great for her.

Vel. It ſhall be done. But fince her ho-nour has feen
this apparition, ſhe defires to fee you once more, before
you encounter it.

Sir G. I ſhall expect her impatiently ; for now I can
talk to her without being interrupted by that impertinent
rogue, Tinfel. I hope thou haſt not told Abigail any
thing of the fecret.

Vel. Mrs. Abigail is a woman ; there are many reafons
why ſhe ſhould not be acquainted with it : I ſhall only
mention fix——

Sir G. Huſh, here ſhe comes ! Oh, my heart !

Enter Lady Truman *and* Abigail.

Sir G. [*Afide, while* Vellum *talks in dumb ſhew to Lady* Trum.] Oh, that lov'd woman ! How I long to take
                                                        her

her in my arms ! If I find I am still dear to her memory, it will be a return to life indeed. But I must take care of indulging this tenderness, and put on a behaviour more suitable to my present character.

[*Walks at a distance in a pensive posture, waving his wand.*

Lady T. [*To* Vellum.] This is surprising indeed ! So all the servants tell me ; they say he knows every thing that has happened in the family.

Ab. [*Aside.*] A parcel of credulous fools ; they first tell him their secrets, and then wonder how he comes to know them.

[*Exit* Vellum, *exchanging fond looks with* Abigail.

Lady T. Learned Sir, may I have some conversation with you, before you begin your ceremonies ?

Sir G. Speak—But hold—First, let me feel your pulse.

Lady T. What can you learn from that ?

Sir G. I have already learned a secret from it, that will astonish you.

Lady T. Pray, what is it ?

Sir G. You will have a husband within this half hour.

Ab. [*Aside.*] I am glad to hear that—He must mean Mr. Fantome. I begin to think there's a good deal of truth in his art.

Lady T. Alas ! I fear you mean I shall see Sir George's apparition a second time.

Sir G. Have courage ; you shall see the apparition no more. The husband I mention, shall be as much alive as I am.

Ab. Mr. Fantome, to be sure. [*Aside.*]

Lady T. Impossible ; I loved my first too well.

Sir G. You could not love the first better than you will love the second.

' *Ab.* [*Aside.*] I'll be hanged if my dear steward has
' not instructed him. He means Mr. Fantome, to be sure.
' The thousand pound is our own.'

Lady T. Alas, you did not know Sir George !

Sir G. As well as I do myself—I saw him with you in the red damask room, when he first made love to you ; your mother left you together, under pretence of receiving a visit from Mrs. Hawthorn, on her return from London.

Lady

Lady T. This is aftonifhing!

Sir G. You were a great admirer of a fingle life for the firft half hour; your refufals then grew ftill fainter and fainter. With what ecftacy did Sir George kifs your hand, when you told him you fhould always follow the advice of your mamma!

Lady T. Every circumftance, to a tittle!

Sir G. Then, Lady, the wedding-night! I faw you in your white fattin night-gown. You would not come out of your dreffing-room, till Sir George took you out by force. He drew you gently by the hand——You ftruggled——but he was too ftrong for you——You blufhed; he——

Lady T. Oh, ftop there! go no further—He knows every thing. [*Afide.*

Ab. Truly, Mr. Conjurer, I believe you have been a wag in your youth.

Sir G. Mrs. Abigail, you know what your good word coft Sir George; a purfe of broad pieces, Mrs. Abigail——

Ab. The devil's in him. [*Afide.*] Pray, Sir, fince you have told fo far, you fhould tell my Lady, that I refufed to take them.

Sir G. 'Tis true, child, he was forced to thruft them in—to your bofom.

Ab. This rogue will mention the thoufand pounds, if I don't take care. [*Afide.*] Pray, Sir, though you are a conjurer, methinks you need not be a blab.

Lady T. Sir, fince I have now no reafon to doubt of your art, I muft befeech you to treat this apparition gently, It has the refemblance of my deceafed hufband. If there be any undifcovered fecret, any thing that troubles his reft, learn it of him.

Sir G. I muft, to that end, be fincerely informed by you, whether your heart be engaged to another. Have not you received the addreffes of many lovers, fince his death?

Lady T. I have been obliged to receive more vifits than have been agreeable.

Sir G. Was not Tinfel welcome?—I'm afraid to hear an anfwer to my own queftion. [*Afide.*

Lady T. He was well recommended.

Sir G. Racks! [*Afide.*
Lady T.

Lady T. Of a good family.

Sir G. Tortures !   [*Afide.*

Lady T. Heir to a confiderable eftate.

Sir G. Death ! [*Afide.*] And you ftill love him ?——
I'm diftracted !   [*Afide.*

Lady T. No, I defpife him. I found he had a defign
upon my fortune ; was bafe, profligate, cowardly, and
every thing that could be expected from a man of the
vileft principles.

Sir G. I'm recovered.   [*Afide.*

Ab. Oh, Madam, had you feen how like a fcoundrel he
looked, when he left your ladyfhip in a fwoon ! Where
have you left my Lady ? fays I. In an elbow-chair child,
fays he. And where are you going ? fays I. To town,
child, fays he ? for, to tell thee truly, child, fays he, I
don't care for living under the fame roof with the devil,
fays he.

Sir G. Well, Lady, I fee nothing in all this, that may
hinder Sir George's fpirit from being at reft.

Lady T. If he knows any thing of what paffes in my
heart he cannot but be fatisfied of that fondnefs which I
bear to his memory. My forrow for him is always frefh
when I think of him. He was the kindeft, trueft, tendereft——Tears will not let me go on——

Sir G. This quite overpowers me—I fhall difcover myfelf before my time. [*Afide.*] Madam, you may now retire, and leave me to myfelf.

Lady T. Succefs attend you.

Ab. I wifh Mr. Fantome gets well off from this old
Don——I know he'll be with him immediately.

      [*Exeunt* Lady Truman *and* Abigail.

Sir G. My heart is now at eafe ; fhe is the fame dear
woman I left her. Now for my revenge upon Fantome.
I fhall cut the ceremonies fhort—A few words will do his
bufinefs—Now, let me feat myfelf in form—A good eafy
chair for a conjurer, this—Now for a few mathematical
fcratches—A good lucky fcrawl, that—Faith, I think it
looks very aftrological—Thefe two or three magical pot-
hooks about it, make it a complete conjurer's fcheme.
[*Drum beats.*] Ha, ha, ha, Sir! are you there? Enter
drummer—Now muft I pore upon my paper.

           Enter

Enter Fantome, *beating his drum.*

Pr'ythee don't make a noife, I'm bufy. [Fantome *beats.*] A pretty march! pr'ythee beat that over again. [*He beats and advances.*] [*Rifing.*] Ha! you're very perfect in the ftep of a ghoft. You ftalk it majefti-cally. [Fantome *advances.*] How the rogue ftares, he acts it to admiration; I'll be hanged, if he has not been practifing this half hour in Mrs. Abigail's wardrobe. [Fantome *ftarts, gives a rap with his drum.*] Pr'ythee don't play the fool. [Fantome *beats.*] Nay, nay, enough of this, good Mr. Fantome.

Fan. [*Afide.*] Death! I am difcovered. This jade, Abigail, has betrayed me.

Sir G. Mr. Fantome, upon the word of an aftrologer, your thoufand pound bribe will never gain my Lady Truman.

Fan. 'Tis plain, fhe has told him all.   [*Afide.*

Sir G. Let me advife you to make off as faft as you can, or I plainly perceive by my art, Mr. Ghoft will have his bones broke.

Fan. [*To Sir G.*] Look ye, old gentleman, I perceive you have learned this fecret from Mrs. Abigail.

Sir G. I have learned it from my art.

Fan. Thy art! pr'ythee no more of that. Look ye, I know you are a cheat as much as I am. And if thou'lt keep my counfel, I'll give thee ten broad pieces.

Sir G. I am not mercenary! Young man, I fcorn thy gold.

Fan. I'll make them up twenty.——

Sir G. Avaunt! and that quickly, or I'll raife fuch an apparition as fhall——

Fan. An apparition, old gentleman! you miftake your man, I'm not to be frighted with bugbears!——

Sir G. Let me retire but for a few moments, and I will give thee fuch a proof of my art——

Fan. Why, if thou haft any *hocus-pocus* tricks to play, why can'ft thou not do them here?

Sir G. The raifing of a fpirit, requires certain fecret myfteries to be performed, and words to be muttered in private————

Fan. Well, if I fee through your trick, will you pro-mife to be my friend?

Sir G. I will——attend and tremble.   [*Exit.*

Fan. [*Alone.*] A very folemn old afs! But I fmoke him, ——he has a mind to raife his price upon me. I could not think this flut would have ufed me thus.—I begin to grow horribly tired of my drum. I wifh I was well rid of it. However, I have got this by it, that it has driven off Tinfel for good and all; I fhan't have the mortification to fee my miftrefs carried off by fuch a rival. Well, whatever happens, I muft ftop this old fellow's mouth; I muft not be fparing in hufh-money. But here he comes.

Enter Sir George *in his own habit.*

Ha! what's that! Sir George Truman! This can be no counterfeit. His drefs! his fhape! his face! the very wound of which he died! Nay, then 'tis time to de-camp!   [*Runs off.*

Sir G. Ha, ha, ha! Fare you well, good Sir George— The enemy has left me mafter of the field: here are the marks of my victory. This drum will I hang up in my great hall as the trophy of the day.

Enter Abigail.

Sir George *ftands with his hand before his face in a mufing pofture.*

Ab. Yonder he is. O'my confcience, he has driven off the conjurer. Mr. Fantome, Mr. Fantome! I give you joy, I give you joy. What do you think of your thoufand pounds now, why does not the man fpeak?

[*Pulls him by the fleeve.*

Sir G. Ha!   [*Taking his hand from his face.*

Ab. Oh, 'tis my mafter!   [*Shrieks.*

[*Running away he catches her.*

Sir G. Good Mrs. Abigail, not fo faft.

Ab. Are you alive, Sir? He has given my fhoulder fuch a curfed tweak! they muft be real fingers, I feel them I'm fure.

Sir G. What doft thou think?

Ab. Think, Sir! think! Troth, I don't know what to think. Pray, Sir, how——

Sir G. No queftions, good Abigail; thy curiofity fhall be fatisfied in due time. Where's your Lady?

Ab. Oh, I'm fo frighted!——and fo glad ——

Sir

Sir G. Where's your Lady ? I afk you——

Ab. Marry, I don't know where I am myfelf—I can't forbear weeping for joy————

Sir G. Your Lady ! I fay your Lady ! I muft bring you to yourfelf with one pinch more——

Ab. Oh, fhe has been talking a good while with the fteward.

Sir G. Then he has opened the whole ftory to her. I'm glad he has prepared her. Oh, here fhe comes.

Enter Lady Truman *followed by* Vellum.

Lady T. Where is he ? let me fly into his arms ! my life ! my foul ! my hufband !

Sir G. Oh, let me catch thee to my heart, deareft of women.

Lady T. Are you then ftill alive, and are you here ! I can fcarce believe my fenfes ! Now am I happy indeed !

Sir G. My heart is too full to anfwer thee.

' *Lady T.* How could you be fo cruel to defer giving
' me that joy which you knew I muft receive from your
' prefence ? You have robbed my life of fome hours of
' happinefs that ought to have been in it.

' *Sir G.* It was to make our happinefs the more fincere
' and unmixed : there will be now no doubts to difh it.
' What has been the afflicion of our lives, has given a
' variety to them, and will hereafter fupply us with a
' thoufand materials to talk of.

' *Lady T.* I am now fatisfied that it is not in the power
' of abfence to leffen your love towards me.

' *Sir G.* And I am fatisfied that it is not in the power
' of death to deftroy that love which makes me the hap-
' pieft of men.'

Lady T. Was ever woman fo bleffed ! to find again the darling of her foul, when fhe thought him loft for ever ! to enter into a kind of fecond marriage with the only man whom fhe was ever capable of loving !

Sir G. May it be as happy as our firft, I defire no more ! Believe me, my dear, I want words to exprefs thofe tranfports of joy and tendernefs which are every moment rifing in my heart whilft I fpeak to thee.

Enter Servants.

But. Juft as the fteward told us, lads !——Look you there, if he ben't with my Lady already ?

F

Gard.

Gard. He, he, he! what a joyful night will this be for Madam.

Coach. As I was coming in at the gate, a ftrange gentleman, whifked by me; but he took to his heels, and made away to the George. If I did not fee mafter before me, I fhould have fworn it had been his honour!

Gard. Haft thou given orders for the bells to be fet a ringing?

Coach. Never trouble thy head about that, 'tis done.

Sir G. [*To Lady* T.] My dear, I long as much to tell you my whole ftory, as you do to hear it. In the mean while I am to look upon this as my wedding-day. I'll have nothing but the voice of mirth and feafting in my houfe. My poor neighbours and my fervants fhall rejoice with me. My hall fhall be free to every one, and let my cellars be thrown open.

But. Ah, blefs your honour, may you never die again!

Coach. The fame good man that ever he was!

Gard. Whurra!

Sir G. Vellum, thou haft done me much fervice to-day. I know thou loveft Abigail; but fhe's difappointed in a fortune. I'll make it up to both of you. I'll give thee a thoufand pounds with her. It is not fit there fhould be one fad heart in my houfe to-night.

' *Lady T.* What you do for Abigail, I know is meant
' as a compliment to me. This is a new inftance of your
' love.'

Ab. Mr. Vellum, you are a well-fpoken man: pray do you thank my mafter and my lady.

Sir G. Vellum, I hope you are not difpleafed with the gift I make you.

Vel. The gift is twofold. I receive from you
    A virtuous partner, and a portion too;
    For which in humble wife, I thank the donors:
    And fo we bid good-night to both your ho—hours.

END of the FIFTH ACT.

EPI-

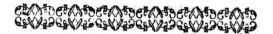

EPILOGUE.

Spoken by Lady TRUMAN.

TO-night, the poet's advocate I stand;
 And he deserves the favour at my hand,
Who in my equipage their cause debating,
Has plac'd two lovers, and a third in waiting:
If both the first should from their duty swerve,
There's one behind the wainscot in reserve.
In his next play, if I would take this trouble,
He promis'd me to make the number double:
In troth 'twas spoke like an obliging creature,
For though 'tis simple, yet it shews good-nature.
My help thus ask'd, I could not choose but grant it,
And really I thought the play would want it,
Void as it is of all the usual arts
To warm your fancies, and to steal your hearts:
No court-intrigue, nor city cuckoldom,
No song, no dance, no music——but a drum——
No smutty thought in doubtful phrase exprest,
And, gentlemen, if so, pray where's the jest?
When we would raise your mirth, your hardly know
Whether, in strictness, you should laugh or no;
But turn upon the ladies in the pit,
And if they redden, you are sure 'tis wit.
Protect him then, ye fair ones; for the fair
Of all conditions are his equal care.
He draws a widow, who, of blameless carriage,
True to her jointure, hates a second marriage;
And, to improve a virtuous wife's delights,
Out of one man, contrives two wedding nights;
Nay, to oblige the sex in ev'ry state,
A nymph of five and forty finds her mate.
Too long has marriage, in this tasteless age,
With ill-bred raillery supply'd the stage:

No little fcribbler is of wit fo bare,
But has his fling at the poor wedded pair.
Our author deals not in conceits fo ftale:
For fhould th' examples of his play prevail,
No man need blufh, though true to marriage-vows,
Nor be a jeft, though he fhould love his fpoufe.
Thus has he done you Britifh conforts right,
Whofe hufbands, fhould they pry like mine to-night,
Would never find you in your conduct flipping,
Though they turn'd conjurers to take you tripping.

L. Roberts del.

Publish'd for Bells British Theatre May 2d 1777.

Mrs YATES *in the Character of* BERINTHIA.

O Heavens! I would not be in the dark with you
for all the World.

BELL'S EDITION.

THE
R E L A P S E:

O R,

VIRTUE IN DANGER.

A COMEDY,

As written by Sir JOHN VANBRUGH.

DISTINGUISHING ALSO THE

VARIATIONS OF THE THEATRE,

AS PERFORMED AT THE

Theatre-Royal in Covent-Garden.

Regulated from the Prompt-Book.

By PERMISSION of the MANAGERS,

By Mr. WILD, Prompter.

LONDON:

Printed for JOHN BELL, near *Exeter-Exchange*, in the *Strand.*

MDCCLXXVII.

THE

P R E F A C E.

TO go about to excuse half the defects this abortive brat is come into the world with, would be to provoke the town with a long useless preface, when it is, I doubt, sufficiently soured already by a tedious play.

I do therefore (with the humility of a repenting sinner) confess, it wants every thing—but length ; and in that, I hope, the severest critic will be pleased to acknowledge I have not been wanting. But my modesty will sure atone for every thing, when the world shall know it is so great, I am even to this day insensible of those two shining graces in the play, (which some part of the town is pleased to compliment me with) blasphemy and bawdy.

For my part, I cannot find them out : if there were any obscene expressions upon the stage, here they are in the print ; for I have dealt fairly, I have not sunk a syllable, that could (though by racking of mysteries) be ranged under that head ; and yet I believe with a steddy faith, there is not one woman of a real reputation in town, but when she has read it impartially over in her closet, will find it so innocent, she will think it no affront to her prayer-book, to lay it upon the same shelf. So to them (with all manner of deference) I entirely refer my cause ; and I am confident they will justify me against those pretenders to good-manners, who at the same time, have so little respect for the ladies, they would extract a bawdy jest from an ejaculation, to put them out of countenance. But I expect to have these well-bred persons always my enemies, since I am sure I shall never write any thing lewd enough to make them my friends.

As for the saints (your thorough-paced ones, I mean, with skrewed faces and wry mouths) I despair of them ; for they are friends to nobody : they love nothing but

A 2   their

their altars and themselves; they have too much zeal to
have any charity; they make debauchees in piety, as
sinners do in wine; and are as quarrelsome in their religion, as other people are in their drink: so I hope nobody will mind what they say. But if any man (with
flat plod shoes, a little band, greasy hair, and a dirty
face, who is wiser than I, at the expence of being forty
years older) happens to be offended at a story of a cock
and a bull, and a priest and a bull-dog, I beg his pardon with all my heart; which, I hope, I shall obtain,
by eating my words, and making this public recanta-
tion. I do therefore, for his satisfaction, acknowledge I
lied, when I said, they never quit their hold; for in
that little time I have lived in the world, I thank God I
have seen them forced to it more than once; but next
time I will speak with more caution and truth, and only
say, they have very good teeth.

If I have offended any honest gentleman of the town,
whose friendship or good word is worth the having, I
am very sorry for it; I hope they will correct me as gently as they can, when they consider I have had no other
design, in running a very great risk, than to divert (if
possible) some part of their spleen, in spite of their wives
and their taxes.

One word more about the bawdy, and I have done.
I own the first night this thing was acted, some indecencies had like to have happened; but it was not my
fault.

The fine gentleman of the play, drinking his mistress's health in Nants brandy, from six in the morning
to the time he waddled on upon the stage in the evening,
had toasted himself up to such a pitch of vigour, I confess I once gave Amanda for gone, and am since (with all
due respect to Mrs. Rogers) very sorry she escaped; for
I am confident a certain lady (let no one take it to herself that is handsome) who highly blames the play, for
the barrenness of the conclusion, would then have allowed it a very natural close.

PROLOGUE.

LADIES, this play in too much in haste was writ,
  To be o'ercharg'd with either plot or wit ;
'Twas got, conceiv'd, and born in six weeks space,
And wit, you know, 's as slow in growth——as grace.
Sure it can ne'er be ripen'd to your taste ;
I doubt 'twill prove our author bred too fast :
For mark them well, who with the muses marry,
They rarely do conceive, but they miscarry.
'Tis the hard fate of those who are big with rhime,
Still to be brought to bed before their time.
Of our late poets nature few has made ;
The greatest part——are only so by trade.
Still want of something brings the scribbling fit ;
For want of money some of 'em have writ,
And others do't, you see——for want of wit.
Honour, they fancy, summons 'em to write,
So out they lug in resty nature's spight,
As some of your spruce beaux do——when you fight.
Yet let the ebb of wit be ne'er so low,
Some glimpse of it a man may hope to show,
Upon a theme so ample——as a beau.
So, howsoe'er true courage may decay,
Perhaps there's not one smock-face here to-day,
But's bold as Cæsar, to attack a play.
Nay, what's yet more, with an undaunted face,
To do the thing with more heroic grace,
'Tis six to four y' attack the strongest place.
You are such Hotspurs in this kind of venture,
Where there's no breach, just there you needs must enter.
But be advis'd——
E'en give the hero and the critique o'er,
For nature sent you on another score ;
She form'd her beau, for nothing but her whore.

DRA-

DRAMATIS PERSONÆ.

M E N.

Covent-Garden.

Sir *Novelty Fashion*, newly created Lord *Foppington*, ———	Mr. Woodward.
Young *Fashion*, his brother —	Mr. Dyer.
Lovelefs, hufband to *Amanda*, —	Mr. Smith.
Worthy, a gentleman of the town,	Mr. Hull.
Sir *Tunbelly Clumfey*, a country gentleman, ——— ———	Mr. Dunftall.
Sir *John Friendly*, his neighbour,	Mr. Davis.
Coupler, a matchmaker, —	Mr. Quick.
Bull, chaplain to Sir *Tunbelly*,	Mr. Saunders.
Syringe, a furgeon, ———	Mr. Shuter.
Lory, fervant to young *Fashion*,	Mr. Cufhing.
La Varole, ——— —.	Mr. Holtom.
Page, ——— ———	Mr. Harris.
Hofier, ——— ·———	Mr. Thompfon.
Shoe-maker ——— ———	Mr. Hamilton.
Taylor, ——— —	Mr. Fox.

W O M E N.

Amanda, wife to *Lovelefs*, ———	Mrs. Vincent.
Berinthia, her coufin, a young widow, ——— ———	Mrs. Bellamy.
Mifs *Hoyden*, a great fortune, daughter to Sir *Tunbelly*, ———	Mrs. Mattocks.
Nurfe, her governante, ———	Mrs. Pitt.
Sempftrefs, ——— ——	Mrs. White.
Amanda's woman, — —	Mrs. Evans.

THE

THE

R E L A P S E.

*_** *The lines marked with inverted commas, 'thus,' are omitted in the reprefentation.*

A C T I.

Enter Lovelefs *reading.*

' HOW true is that philofophy which fays
' Our heaven is feated in our minds !
' Through all the roving pleafures of my youth,
' (Where nights and days feem all confum'd in joy,)
' I never knew one moment's peace like this.'
Here—in this little foft retreat,
The raging flame of wild deftructive luft
Reduc'd to a warm pleafing fire of lawful love,
My life glides on, and all is well within.

Enter Amanda.

How does the happy caufe of my content, my dear
You find me mufing on my happy ftate,   [Amanda ?
And full of grateful thoughts to Heaven, and you.

Aman. Thofe grateful offerings Heaven can't receive
With more delight than I do :
Would I could fhare with it as well
The difpenfations of its blifs ;
That I might fearch its choiceft favours out,
And fhower them on your head for ever.

Lov. The largeft boons that Heaven thinks fit to grant,
To things it has decreed fhall crawl on earth,
Are in the gift of women form'd like you.
' Perhaps, when time fhall be no more,
' When the afpiring foul fhall take its flight,
' And drop this pond'rous lump of clay behind it,

' It may have appetites we know not of,
' And pleasures as refin'd as its desires——
' But till that day of knowledge shall instruct me,
The utmost blessing that my thought can reach,
[*Taking her in his arms.*] Is folded in my arms, and rooted
        in my heart.

   Aman. There let it grow for ever.

   Lov. Well said, Amanda—let it be for ever—
Wou'd Heaven grant that—

   Aman. 'Twere all the heaven I'd ask.
But ' we are clad in black mortality,
' And the dark curtain of eternal night,
' At last must drop between us.

   ' *Lov.* It must: that mournful separation we must see.
' A bitter pill it is to all; but doubles its ungrateful taste,
' When lovers are to swallow it.

   ' *Aman.* Perhaps that pain may only be my lot,
' You possibly may be exempted from it ;
' Men find out softer ways to quench their fires.'

   Lov. Can you then doubt my constancy, Amanda ?
You'll find 'tis built upon a steddy basis—
The rock of reason now supports my love ;
On which it stands so fix'd,
The rudest hurricane of wild desire
Wou'd like the breath of a soft slumbering babe,
Pass by, and never shake it.

   Aman. Yet still 'tis safer to avoid the storm ;
The strongest vessels, if they put to sea,
May possibly be lost.
Wou'd I cou'd keep you here in this calm port for ever.
Forgive the weakness of a woman,
I am uneasy at your going to stay so long in town ;
I know its false insinuating pleasures;
I know the force of its delusions ;
I know the strength of its attacks ;
I know the weak defence of nature ;
I know you are a man—and I—a wife.

   Love. You know then all that needs to give you rest,
For wife's the strongest claim that you can urge.
When you would plead your title to my heart,
On this you may depend ; therefore be calm,
' Banish your fears, for they are traitors to your peace;

                                     ' Be-

‘ Beware of them, they are infinuating bufy things,
‘ That goffip to and fro, and do a world of mifchief
‘ Where they come: but you fhall foon be miftrefs of ’em
‘ I’ll aid you with fuch arms for their deftruction,   [all.
‘ They never fhall erect their heads again.’
You know the bufinefs is indifpenfible, that obliges
Me to go to London, and you have no reafon, that I
Know of, to believe that I’m glad of the occafion :
‘ For my honeft confcience is my witnefs,
‘ I have found a due fucceffion of fuch charms
‘ In my retirement here with you,
‘ I have never thrown one roving thought that way,’
But fince, againft my will, I’m dragg’d once more
To that uneafy theatre of noife,
I am refolv’d to make fuch ufe on’t,
As fhall convince you ’tis an old caft miftrefs,
Who has been fo lavifh of her favours,
She’s now grown bankrupt of her charms,
And has not one allurement left to move me.
    Aman. Her bow, I do believe, is grown fo weak,
Her arrows, at this diftance, cannot hurt you,
But in approaching ’em you give ’em ftrength :
The dart that has not far to fly,
Will put the beft of armour to a dangerous trial.
    Lov. That trial paft, you are at eafe for ever ;
‘ When you have feen the helmet prov’d,
‘ You’ll appprehend no more for him that wears it :’
Therefore to put a lafting period to your fears,
I am refolv’d, this once, to launch into temptation ;
‘ I’ll give you an effay of all my virtues ;’
My former boon companions of the bottle
Shall fairly try what charms are left in wine :
They fhall hem me in,
Sing praifes to their God, and drink his glory ;
Turn wild enthufiafts for his fake,
And beafts to do him honour :
While I, a ftubborn atheift,
Sullenly look on,
Without one reverend glafs to his divinity.
That for my temperance :
Then for my conftancy——
    Aman. Ay, there take heed.

Love. Indeed the danger's fmall.

Aman. And yet my fears are great.

Love. Why are you fo timorous?

Aman. Becaufe you are fo bold.

Love. My courage fhould difperfe your apprehenfions.

Aman. My apprehenfions fhould alarm your courage.

Lov. Fy, fy, Amanda, it is not kind thus to diftruft me.

Aman. And yet my fears are founded on my love.

Love. Your love then is not founded as it ought;
For if you can believe 'tis poffible
I fhou'd again relapfe to my paft follies,
I muft appear to you a thing
Of fuch an undigefted compofition,
That but to think of me with inclination,
Wou'd be a weaknefs in your tafte,
Your virtue fcarce cou'd anfwer.

Aman. 'Twou'd be a weaknefs in my tongue
My prudence cou'd not anfwer,
If I fhou'd prefs you farther with my fears;
I'll therefore trouble you no longer with 'em.

Lov. Nor fhall they trouble you much longer,
A little time fhall fhew you they were groundlefs;
This winter fhall be the fiery trial of my virtues.
Which, when it once has paft,
You'll be convinc'd 'twas of no falfe allay,
There all your cares will end——

Aman. Pray heaven they may. [*Exeunt hand in hand.*

SCENE, *Whitehall.*

Enter Young Fafhion *and* Lory.

Y. Fafh. Come, pay the waterman, and take the port-mantle.

Lory. Faith, Sir, I gave the waterman the portmantle, to pay himfelf.

Y. Fafh. Why fure there's fomething left in't.

Lory. But a folitary old waiftcoat, upon my honour, Sir.

Y. Fafh. Why, what's become of the blue coat, firrah?

Lory. Sir, 'twas eaten at Gravefend; the reckoning came to thirty fhillings, and your privy-purfe was worth but two half-crowns.

Y. Fafh. 'Tis very well.

' *Enter*

' *Enter* Waterman.

' *Wat.* Pray, mafter, will you pleafe to difpatch me?

' *Y. Fafh.* Ay, here a――――Canft thou change me a
' guinea?

' *Lory.* [*Afide.*] Good.

' *Wat.* Change a guinea, mafter! Ha, ha, your ho-
' nour's pleafed to compliment.

' *Y. Fafh.* 'Egad I don't know how I fhall pay thee
' then, for I have nothing but gold about me.

' *Lory.* [*Afide.*]――――Hum, hum.

' *Y. Fafh.* What doft thou expect, friend?

' *Wat.* Why, mafter, fo far againft wind and tide, is
' richly worth half a piece.

' *Y. Fafh.* Why, faith, I think thou art a good con-
' fcionable fellow. 'Egad, I begin to have fo good an
' opinion of thy honeft, I care not if I leave my port-
' mantle with thee, till I fend thee thy money.

' *Wat.* Ha! God blefs your honour; I fhould be as
' willing to truft you, mafter, but that you are, as a
' man may fay, a ftranger to me, and thefe are nimble
' times; there are a great many fharpers ftirring. [*Taking
' up the portmantle.*] Well, mafter, when your worfhip
' fends the money, your portmantle fhall be forth-coming.
' My name's Tugg, my wife keeps a brandy-fhop in Drab-
' Ally, at Wapping,

' *Y. Fafh.* Very well; I'll fend for't to-morrow.

' [*Exit* Waterman.'

Lory. So—Now, Sir, I hope you'll own yourfelf a
happy man, you have outlived all your cares.

Y. Fafh. How fo, Sir?

Lory. Why you have nothing left to take care of.

Y. Fafh. Yes, firrah, I have myfelf and you to take
care of ftill.

Lory. Sir, if you could but prevail with fome body
elfe to do that for you, I fancy we might both fare the
better for't.

Y. Fafh. Why, if thou canft tell me where to apply
myfelf, I have at prefent fo little money, and fo much
humility about me, I don't know but I may follow a
fool's advice.

Lory. Why then, Sir, your fool advifes you to lay afide
all animofity, and apply to Sir Novelty your elder brother.

Y. Fafh.

Y. Faſh. Damn my elder brother.

Lory. With all my heart; but get him to redeem your annuity however.

Y. Faſh. My annuity! 'Sdeath, he's ſuch a dog, he would not give his powder puff to redeem my ſoul.

Lory. Look you, Sir, you muſt wheedle him, or you muſt ſtarve.

Y. Faſh. Look you, Sir, I will neither wheedle him, nor ſtarve.

Lory. Why, what will you do then?

Y. Faſh. I'll go into the army.

Lory. You can't take the oaths; you are a Jacobite.

Y. Faſh. Thou may'ſt as well ſay I can't take orders, becauſe I'm an atheiſt.

' *Lory.* Sir, I aſk your pardon; I find I did not know
' the ſtrength of your conſcience, ſo well as I did the
' weakneſs of your purſe.

' *Y. Faſh.* Methinks, Sir, a perſon of your experience
' ſhould have known, that the ſtrength of the conſcience
' proceeds from the weakneſs of the purſe.'

Lory. Sir, I am very glad to find you have a conſcience able to take care of us, let it proceed from what it will;
' but I deſire you'll pleaſe to conſider, that the army
' alone will be but a ſcanty maintenance for a perſon of
' your generoſity (at leaſt as rents now are paid);' I ſhall fee you ſtand in damnable need of ſome auxiliary guineas for your *menu plaiſirs*; I will therefore turn fool once more for your ſervice, and adviſe you to go directly to your brother.

Y. Faſh. Art thou then ſo impregnable a blockhead, to believe he'll help me with a farthing.

Lory. Not if you treat him, *de haut en bas*, as you uſe to do.

Y. Faſh. Why, how wouldſt have me treat him?

Lory. Like a trout, tickle him.

Y. Faſh. I can't flatter——

Lory. Can you ſtarve?

Y. Faſh. Yes——

Lory. I can't: good-by-t'ye, Sir.   [*Going.*

Y. Faſh. Stay, thou wilt diſtract me. What wouldſt thou have me to ſay to him?

Lory. Say nothing to him; apply yourſelf to his favourites;

vourites; fpeak to his periwig, his cravat, his feather, his fnuff-box, and when you are well with them——defire him to lend you a thoufand pounds. I'll engage you profper.

T. Fafh. 'Sdeath and furies! Why was that coxcomb thruft into the world before me? Oh, Fortune—Fortune—Thou art a bitch, by gad—— [*Exeunt.*

SCENE, *a Dreffing-room.*

Enter Lord Foppington *in his night-gown.*

Lord Fop. Page——

Enter Page.

Page. Sir.

Lord Fop. Sir! Pray, Sir, do me the favour to teach your tongue the title the king has thought fit to honour me with.

Page. I afk your Lordfhip's pardon, my Lord.

Lord F. Oh, you can pronounce the word, then. I thought it would have choaked you ——D'ye hear?

Page. My Lord.

Lord Fop. Call *La Varole*, I would drefs—[*Exit* Page.] Well, 'tis an unfpeakable pleafure to be a man of quality——Strike me dumb ——My Lord ——Your Lordfhip——My Lord Foppington——*Ah! c'eft quelque chofe de beau, que le diable m'emporte*——Why, the ladies were ready to pewk at me, whilft I had nothing but Sir Novelty to recommend me to them——Sure, whilft I was but a knight, I was a very naufeous fellow——Well, 'tis ten thoufand pawnd well given——flap my vitals—

Enter La Varole.

La Var. Me Lord, de fhoemaker, de taylor, de hofier, de fempftrefs, de peruquier, be all ready, if your Lordfhip pleafe to drefs.

Lord Fop. 'Tis well, admit 'em.

La Var. Hey, meilieurs, entrez.

Enter Taylor, &c.

Lord Fop. So, gentleman, I hope you have all taken pains to fhew yourfelves matters in your profeffions.

Tay. I think I may prefume to fay, Sir——

La Var. My Lord—You clown you.

Tay. Why, is he made a Lord?——My Lord, I afk your Lordfhip's pardon; my Lord, I hope, my Lord,

B　　　　　　　　　　your

your lordſhip will pleaſe to own, I have brought your lordſhip as accompliſhed a ſuit of cloaths, as ever peer of England trod the ſtage in, my Lord. Will your lordſhip pleaſe to try them now?

Lord Fop. Ay; but let my people diſpoſe the glaſſes ſo, that I may ſee myſelf before and behind; for I love to ſee myſelf all raund——

[*Whilſt he puts on his cloaths, enter* Young Faſhion *and* Lory.

Y. Faſh. Hey-day! what the devil have we here? Sure my gentleman's grown a favourite at court, he has got ſo many people at his levee.

Lor. Sir, theſe people come in order to make him a favourite at court; they are to eſtabliſh him with the ladies.

Y. Faſh. Good God! to what an ebb of taſte are women fallen, that it ſhould be in the power of a laced coat to recommend a gallant to them——

Lor. Sir, taylors and periwig-makers are now become the bawds of the nation; 'tis they debauch all the women.

Y. Faſh. Thou ſay'ſt true; for there's that fop now, has not, by nature, wherewithal to move a cook-maid; and by that time theſe fellows have done with him, 'egad, he ſhall melt down a counteſs——But, now for my reception: I engage it ſhall be as cold a one, as a courtier's to his friend, who comes to put him in mind of his promiſe.

Lord Fop [*To his Taylor.*] Death, and eternal tartures! Sir, I ſay the packet's too high, by a foot.

Tay. My Lord, if it had been an inch lower, it would not have held your lordſhip's pocket-handkerchief.

Lord Fop. Rat my packet-handkerchief! Have not I a page to carry it? You may make him a packet up to his chin a purpoſe for it; but I will not have mine come ſo near my face.

Tay. 'Tis not for me to diſpute your lordſhip's fancy.

Y. Faſh. [*To* Lory.] His lordſhip, Lory! Did you obſerve that?

Lory. Yes, Sir, I always thought 'twould end there. Now, I hope, you'll have a little more reſpect for him.

Y. Faſh. Reſpect! Damn him, for a coxcomb; now has he ruined his eſtate to buy a title, that he may be a
fool

fool of the firſt rate. But let's accoſt him——[*To* Lord
Fop.] Brother, I'm your humble ſervant.

Lord Fop. Oh, lard, Tam ! I did not expeĉt you in
England   Brother, I'm glad to ſee you——[*Turning to
his Taylor.*] Look you, Sir, I ſhall never be reconciled to
this nauſeous packet; therefore, pray, get me another
ſuit, with all manner of expedition ; for this is my eternal averſion. Mrs. Callicoe, are not you of my mind ?

Semp. Oh, direĉtly, my Lord ! it can never be too low.

Lord Fop. You are paſitively in the right on't ; for
the packet becomes no part of the body but the knee.

Semp. I hope your lordſhip is pleaſed with your
ſteinkirk.

Lord Fop. In love with it, ſtap my vita's. Bring your
bill ; you ſhall be paid to-morrow——

Semp. I humbly thank your honour.   [*Exit Semp.*

Lord Fop. Hark thee, ſhoemaker ; theſe ſhoes an't
ugly ; but they don't fit me.

Shoe. My Lord, methinks, they fit you very well.

Lord Fop. They hurt me juſt below the inſtep.

Shoe. [*Feeling his foot.*] My Lord, they don't hurt
you there.

Lord Fop. I tell thee, they pinch me execrably.

Shoe. My Lord, if they pinch you, I'll be bound to be
hang'd, that's all.

Lord Fop. Why, wilt thou undertake to perſuade me I
cannot feel ?

Shoe. Your lordſhip may pleaſe to feel what you think
fit ; but that ſhoe does not hurt you——I think I underſtand my trade——

Lord Fop. Now, by all that's great and powerful, thou
art an incomprehenſible coxcomb; but thou makeſt good
ſhoes ; and ſo I'll bear with thee.

Shoe. My Lord, I have worked for half the people of
quality in town, theſe twenty years ; and 'tis very hard
I ſhould not know when a ſhoe hurts, and when it don't.

Lord Fop. Well, pr'ythee, begone about thy buſineſs.
[*Exit Shoe.*
[*To the Hoſier.*] Mr. Mendlegs, a word with you ; the
calves of the ſtockings are thickened a little too much.
They make my legs look like a chairman's.

Mend. My Lord, methinks, they look mighty well.

Lord Fop. Ay, but you are not fo good a judge of thofe things as I am ; I have ftudied them all my life : therefore, pray, let the next be the thicknefs of a crawn-piece lefs—[*Afide.*] If the town takes notice my legs are fallen away, 'twill be attributed to the violence of fome new intrigue——[*To the Periwig-maker.*] Come, Mr. Foretop, let me fee what you have done, and then the fatigue of the morning will be over.

' *Fore.* My Lord, I have done what I defy any prince
' in Europe to out-do ; I have made you a perriwig fo
' long, and fo full of hair, it will ferve you for a hat and
' cloak in all weathers.

' *Lord Fop.* Then thou haft made me thy friend to
' eternity. Come, comb it out.'

Y. Fafh. Well, Lory, what doft think on't ? A very friendly reception for a brother, after three years abfence!

Lor. Why, Sir, 'tis your own fault; we feldom care for thofe that don't love what we love. If you would creep into his heart, you muft enter into his pleafures— Here you have ftood ever fince you came in, and have not commended any one thing that belongs to him.

Y. Fafh. Nor never fhall, while they belong to a coxcomb.

Lor. Then, Sir, you muft be content to pick a hungry bone.

Y. Fafh. No, Sir, I'll crack it, and get to the marrow, before I have done.

' *Lord Fop.* Gad's curfe ! Mr. Foretop, you don't in-
' tend to put this upon me for a full periwig ?

' *Fore.* Not a full one, my Lord ! I don't know what
' your lordfhip may pleafe to call a full one ; but I have
' crammed twenty ounces of hair into it.

' *Lord Fop.* What it may be by weight, Sir, I fhall
' not difpute ; but by tale, there are not nine hairs on
' a fide.

' *Fore.* Oh, Lord! Oh, Lord ! Oh, Lord ! Why, as
' Gad fhall judge me, your honour's fide-face is reduced
' to the tip of your nofe.

' *Lord Fop.* My fide-face may be in an eclipfe, for
' ought

‘ ought I know; but I'm fure my full-face is like the
‘ full-moon.

‘ *Fore.* Heaven blefs my eye-fight! [*Rubbing his eyes.*]
‘ Sure I look through the wrong end of the perfpective!
‘ for, by my faith, an't pleafe your honour, the broadeft
‘ place I fee in your face, does not feem to me to be two
‘ inches diameter.

‘ *Lord Fop.* If it did, it would be juft two inches too
‘ broad; for a periwig to a man, fhould be like a mafk to
‘ a woman, nothing fhould be feen but his eyes.

‘ *Fore.* My Lord, I have done. If you pleafe to have
‘ more hair in your wig, I'll put it in.

‘ *Lord Fop.* Pafitively, yes.

‘ *Fore.* Shall I take it back now, my Lord?

‘ *Lord Fop.* No, I'll wear it to-day; tho' it fhew fuch
‘ a manftrous pair of cheeks, ftap my vitals, I fhall be
‘ taken for a trumpeter.   [*Exit* Fore.

‘ *T. Fafh.*’ Now your people of bufinefs are gone,
brother, I hope I may obtain a quarter of an hour's audience of you.

Lord Fop. Faith, Tam, I muft beg you'll excufe me at
this time; for I muft away to the houfe of lards immediately: my Lady Teafor's cafe is to come on to-day,
and I would not be abfent for the falvation of mankind.
Hey, page! is the coach at the door?

Page. Yes, my Lord.

Lord Fop. You'll excufe me, brother.   [*Going.*

T. Fafh. Shall you be back at dinner?

Lord Fop. As Gad fhall judge me, I can't tell; for 'tis
paffible I may dine with fome of aur haufe at Lacket's.

T. Fafh. Shall I meet you there? For I muft needs
talk with you.

Lord Fop. That, I'm afraid, mayn't be fo praper; far
the lards I commonly eat with, are a people of a nice
converfation; and you know, Tam, your education has
been a little at large: but if you'll ftay here, you'll find a
family dinner. Hey, fellow! What is there for dinner?
There's beef. I fuppofe my brother will eat beef. Dear
Tam, I'm glad to fee thee in England, ftap my vitals.

[*Exit, with his equipage.*

T. Fafh. Hell and furies! is this to be borne?

Lor. Faith, Sir, I could have almoſt given him a knock o'the pate myſelf.

Y. Faſh. 'Tis enough—I will now ſhew you the ex-ceſs of my paſſion, by being very calm. Come Lory, lay your loggerhead to mine, and, in cool blood, let us con-trive his deſtruction.

Lor. Here comes a head, Sir, would contrive it better than us both, if he would but join in the confederacy.

Enter Coupler.

Y. Faſh. By this light, old Coupler alive ſtill! Why, how now, match-maker; art thou here ſtill, to plague the world with matrimony? You old bawd, how have you the impudence to be hobbling out of your grave, twenty years after you are rotten?

Coup. When you begin to rot, ſirrah, you'll go off like a pippin; one winter will ſend you to the devil. 'What ' miſchief brings you home again? Ha! You young laſ-' civious rogue you: let me put my hand into your bo-' ſom, ſirrah.

' *Y. Faſh.* Stand off, old Sodom.

' *Coup.* Nay, pr'ythee, now, don't be ſo coy.

' *Y. Faſh.* Keep your hands to yourſelf, you old dog ' you, or I'll wring your noſe off.

' *Coup.* Haſt thou then been a year in Italy, and ' brought home a fool at laſt? By my conſcience, the ' young fellows of this age profit no more by their going ' abroad, than they do by their going to church. Sirrah, ' ſirrah, if you are not hanged before you come to my ' years, you'll know a cock from a hen.' But come, I'm ſtill a friend to thy perſon, tho' I have a contempt of thy underſtanding: and therefore I would willingly know thy condition, that I may ſee whether thou ſtandeſt in need of my aſſiſtance; for widows ſwarm, my boy; the town's infeſted with them.

Y. Faſh. I ſtand in need of any body's aſſiſtance, that will help me to cut my elder brother's throat, without the riſque of being hanged for him.

Coup. 'Egad, ſirrah, I could help thee to do him almoſt as good a turn, without the danger of being burnt in the hand for it.

Y. Faſh. Say'ſt thou ſo, old Satan? Shew me but that, and my ſoul is thine.

' *Coup.*

' *Coup.* Pox o' thy foul! give me thy warm body,
' firrah ; I fhall have a fubftantial title to it, when I tell
' thee my project.

' *Y. Fafh.* Out with it then, dear dad, and take pof-
' feffion as foon as thou wilt.

' *Coup.* Sayeft thou fo, my Hepheftion ? Why, then,
' thus lies the fcene—But hold—who's that ? If we are
' heard, we are undone.

' *Y. Fafh.* What, have you forgot Lory ?

' *Coup.* Who, trufty Lory, is it thee ?

' *Lory.* At your fervice, Sir.

' *Coup.* Give me thy hand, old boy. 'Egad, I did not
' know thee again ; but I remember thy honefty, tho' I
' did not thy face ; I think thou hadft like to have been
' hanged once or twice for thy mafter.

' *Lor.* Sir, I was very near once having that honour.

' *Coup.* Well, live and hope ; don't be difcouraged ; eat
' with him, and drink with him, and do what he bids thee,
' and it may be thy reward at laft, as well as another's.'
[*To* Y. Fafh.] Well, Sir, you muft know, I have done
you the kindnefs to make up a match for your brother.

Y. Fafh. I am very much beholden to you.

Coup. You may be, firrah, before the wedding-day
yet ; the lady is a great heirefs, fifteen hundred pounds
a year, and a great bag of money ; the match is concluded, the writings are drawn, and the pipkin's to be
crack'd in a fortnight—Now, you muft know, ftripling,
(with refpect to your mother) your brother's the fon of
a whore.

Y. Fafh. Good.

Coup. He has given me a bond of a thoufand pounds,
for helping him to this fortune, and has promifed me as
much more, in ready money, upon the day of marriage ;
which, I underftand by a friend, he ne'er defigns to pay
me. If, therefore, you will be a generous young dog,
and fecure me five thoufand pounds, I'll be a covetous
old rogue, and help you to the lady.

Y. Fafh. 'Egad, if thou canft bring this about, I'll have
thy ftatue caft in brafs. But don't you doat, you old pan-
dar you, when you talk at this rate ?

Coup. That your youthful parts fhall judge of. This
plump partridge, that I tell you of, lives in the country,
fifty

fifty miles off, with her honoured parents, in a lonely old houſe, which nobody comes near; ſhe never goes abroad, nor ſees company at home. To prevent all miſfortunes, ſhe has her breeding within doors; the parſon of the pariſh teaches her to play on the baſs-viol, the clerk to ſing, her nurſe to dreſs, and her father to dance. In ſhort, nobody can give you admittance there but I; nor can I do it any other way, than by making you paſs for your brother.

Y. Faſh. And how the devil wilt thou do that?

Coup. Without the devil's aid, I warrant thee. Thy brother's face not one of the family ever ſaw; the whole buſineſs has been managed by me, and all the letters go thro' my hands. The laſt that was writ to Sir Tunbelly Clumſey (for that's the old gentleman's name) was to tell him, his lordſhip would be down in a fortnight, to conſummate. Now, you ſhall go away immediately, pretend you writ that letter only to have the romantic pleaſure of ſurprizing your miſtreſs; fall deſperately in love, as ſoon as you ſee her; make that your plea for marrying her immediately; and when the fatigue of the wedding-night's over, you ſhall ſend me a ſwinging purſe of gold, you dog you.

Y. Faſh. 'Egad, old dad, I'll put my hand in thy boſom now.

' *Coup.* Ah, you young, hot, luſty thief, let me muzzle
' you. [*Kiſſing.*] Sirrah, let me muzzle you.

' *Y. Faſh.* Ffha! the old letcher——'   [*Aſide.*

Coup. Well, I'll warrant thou haſt not a farthing of money in thy pocket now; no, one may ſee it in thy face——

Y. Faſh. Not a ſouſe, by Jupiter.

Coup. Muſt I advance, then?—Well ſirrah, be at my lodgings in half an hour, and we'll ſee what may be done. We'll ſign and ſeal, and eat a pullet; and when I have given thee ſome farther inſtructions, thou ſhalt hoiſt ſail, and begone——[*Kiſſing.*]——T'other buſs; and ſo, adieu.

Y. Faſh. Um——Pſha!

Coup. Ah, you young warm dog you! what a delicious night will the bride have on't!   [*Exit* Coup.

Y. Fash. So, Lory, Providence, thou feeſt, at laſt, takes care of men of merit. We are in a fair way to be great people.

Lor. Ay, Sir, if the devil don't ſtep between the cup and the lip, as he uſes to do.

Y. Fash. Why, faith, he has played me many a damn'd trick, to ſpoil my fortune ; and, 'egad, I'm almoſt afraid he's at work about it again now : but if I ſhould tell thee how, thou'dſt wonder at me.

Lor. Indeed, Sir, I ſhould not.

Y. Fash. How doſt know ?

Lor. Becauſe, Sir, I have wondered at you ſo often, I can wonder at you no more.

Y. Fash. No ! What wouldſt thou ſay, if a qualm of conſcience ſhould ſpoil my deſign ?

Lor. I would eat my words, and wonder more than ever.

Y. Fash. Why, faith, Lory, tho' I am a young rake-hell, and have played many a roguiſh trick, this is ſo full-grown a cheat, I find I muſt take pains to come up to it. I have ſcruples——

Lor. They are ſtrong ſymptoms of death ; if you find they increaſe, pray, Sir, make your will.

Y. Fash. No, my conſcience ſhan't ſtarve me neither. But thus far I'll hearken to it ; before I execute this pro-ject, I'll try my brother to the bottom ; I'll ſpeak to him with the temper of a philoſopher ; my reaſons (tho' they preſs him home) ſhall yet be cloathed with ſo much mo-deſty, not one of all the truths they urge, ſhall be ſo na-ked to offend his ſight. If he has yet ſo much humanity about him, as to aſſiſt me, (tho' with a moderate aid) I'll drop my project at his feet, and ſhew him how I can do for him, much more than what I aſk he'd do for me. This one concluſive trial of him I reſolve to make——

Succeed or no, ſtill victory's my lot;
If I ſubdue his heart, 'tis well ; if not,
I ſhall ſubdue my conſcience to my plot.

[Exeunt.

END of the FIRST **A**CT.

ACT

ACT II.

Enter Lovelefs *and* Amanda.

LOVELESS.

HOW do you like thefe lodgings, my dear? For my part, I am fo well pleafed with them, I fhall hardly remove whilft we ftay in town, if you are fatisfied.

Am. I am fatisfied with every thing that pleafes you; elfe I had not come to town at all. ·

Lov. Oh, a little of the noife and buftle of the world fweetens the pleafures of retreat! We fhall find the charms of retirement doubled, when we return to it.

Am. That pleafing profpeft will be my chiefeft entertainment, whilft, much againft my will, I am obliged to ftand furrounded with thefe empty pleafures, which 'tis fo much the fafhion to be fond of.

Lov. I own moft of them are, indeed, but empty; nay, fo empty, that one would wonder by what magic power they aft, when they induce us to be vicious for their fakes; yet fome there are we may fpeak kindlier of; there are delights, of which a private life is deftitute, which may divert an honeft man, and be a harmlefs entertainment to a virtuous woman. The converfation of the town is one; and, truly, (with fome fmall allowances) the plays, I think, may be efteemed another.

Am. The plays, I muft confefs, have fome fmall charms; and would have more, would they reftrain that loofe, obfcene encouragement to vice, which fhocks, if not the virtue of fome women, at leaft, the modefty of all.

Lov. But, till that reformation can be made, I would not leave the wholefome corn, for fome intruding tares, that grow among it. Doubtlefs, the moral of a well-wrought fcene is of prevailing force—Laft night there happened one that moved me ftrangely.

Am. Pray, what was that?

Lov. Why, 'twas about—but 'tis not worth repeating.

Am. Yes, pray, let me know it.

Lov. No, I think 'tis as well let alone.

Am. Nay, now you make me have a mind to know.

Lov. 'Twas a foolifh thing. You'd, perhaps, grow
jealous,

jealous, fhould I tell it you, tho' without a caufe, Heaven knows.

Am. I fhall begin to think I have caufe, if you perfift in making it a fecret.

Lov. I'll then convince you you have none, by making it no longer fo. Know, then, I happened, in the play, to find my very character, only with the addition of a re-lapfe; which ftruck me fo, I put a fudden ftop to a moft harmlefs entertainment, which, till then, diverted me be-tween the acts: 'twas to admire the workmanfhip of na-ture, in the face of a young lady, that fat at fome diftance from me; fhe was fo exquifitely handfome——

Am. So exquifitely handfome !

Lov. Why do you repeat my words, my dear ?

Am. Becaufe you feemed to fpeak them with fuch pleafure, I thought I might oblige you with their echo.

Lov. Then you are alarm'd, Amanda ?

Am. It is my duty to be fo, when you are in danger.

Lov. You are too quick in apprehending for me. All will be well, when you have heard me out. I do confefs I gazed upon her; nay, eagerly I gazed upon her.

Am. Eagerly, that's with defire.

Lov. No, I defired her not. I viewed her with a world of admiration, but not one glance of love.

Am. Take heed of trufting to fuch nice diftinctions.

Lov. I did take heed; for, obferving in the play, that he who feemed to reprefent me there, was, by an accident like this, unwarily furprifed into a net, in which he lay a poor entangled flave, and brought a train of mifchiefs on his head, I fnatched my eyes away; they pleaded hard for leave to look again; but I grew abfolute, and they obeyed.

Am. Were they the only things that were inquifitive ? Had I been in your place, my tongue, I fancy, had been curious too. I fhould have afked her name, and where fhe lived (yet ftill without defign :)——Who was fhe, pray ?

Lov. Indeed, I cannot tell.

Am. You will not tell.

Lov. By all that's facred, then, I did not afk.

Am. Nor do you know what company was with her ?

Lov. I do not.

Am.

Am. Then I am calm again.

Lov. Why, were you difturb'd ?

Am. Had I then no caufe ?

Lov. None, certainly.

Am. I thought I had.

Lov. But you thought wrong, Amanda : for, turn the cafe, and let it be your ftory ; fhould you come home, and tell me you had feen a handfome man, fhould I grow jealous, becaufe you had eyes ?

Am. But fhould I tell you he were exquifitely fo ; that I had gazed on him with admiration ; that I had looked with eager eyes upon him ; fhould you not think 'twere poffible I might go one ftep further, and enquire his name ?

Lov. [*Afide.*] She has reafon on her fide ; I have talk'd too much ; but I muft turn it off another way. [*To* Am.] Will you then make no difference, Amanda, between the language of our fex and yours ? There is a modefty reftrains your tongues, which makes you fpeak by halves, when you commend ; but roving flattery gives a loofe to ours, which makes us ftill fpeak double what we think. You fhould not, therefore, in fo ftrict a fenfe, take what I faid to her advantage.

Am. ' Thofe flights of flattery, Sir, are to our faces ' only. When women once are out of hearing, you are ' as modeft in your commendations as we are. But I ' fhan't put you to the trouble of farther excufes.' If you pleafe, this bufinefs fhall reft here. Only give me leave to wifh, both for your peace and mine, that you may never meet this miracle of beauty more.

Lov. I am content.

Enter Servant.

Serv. Madam, there is a young lady at the door, in a chair, defires to know whether your ladyfhip fees company. I think her name is Berinthia.

Am. Oh, dear ! 'tis a relation I have not feen thefe five years. Pray her to walk in. [*Exit Servant.*] [*To* Lov.] Here's another beauty for you. She was young when I faw her laft ; but I hear fhe's grown extremely handfome.

Lov. Don't be jealous, now ; for I fhall gaze upon her too.

Enter

Enter Berinthia.

Ha! By heavens, the very woman! [*Aside.*

Ber. [*Saluting* Amanda.] Dear Amanda, I did not expect to meet with you in town.

Am. Sweet coufin, I'm overjoyed to fee you. [*To* Lov.]
Mr. Lovelefs, here's a relation and a friend of mine, I
defire you'll be better acquainted with.

Lov. [*Saluting* Ber.] If my wife never defires a harder
thing, Madam, her requeft will be eafily granted.

Ber. [*To* Amanda.] I think, Madam, I ought to wifh
you joy.

Am. Joy! Upon what?

Ber. Upon your marriage. You were a widow when
I faw you laft.

Lov. You ought, rather, Madam, to wifh me joy upon
that, fince I am the only gainer.

Ber. If fhe has got fo good a hufband as the world re-
ports, fhe has gained enough to expect the compliment
of her friends upon it.

Lov. If the world is fo favourable to me, to allow I
deferve that title, I hope 'tis fo juft to my wife, to own I
derive it from her.

Ber. Sir, 'tis fo juft to you both, to own you are, and
deferve to be, the happieft pair that live in it.

Lov. I'm afraid we fhall lofe that character, Madam,
whenever you happen to change your condition.

Enter Servant.

Ser. Sir, my Lord Foppington prefents his humble fervice to you, and defires to know how you do. He but
juft now heard you were in town. He's at the next door;
and, if it be not inconvenient, he'll come and wait upon
you.

Lov. Lord Foppington!—I know him not.

Ber. Not his dignity, perhaps, but you do his perfon.
'Tis Sir Novelty; he has bought a barony, in order to
marry a great fortune. His patent has not been paffed
above eight-and-forty hours, and he has already fent
how do-ye's to all the town, to make them acquainted
with his title.

Lov. Give my fervice to his lordfhip, and let him
know I am proud of the honour he intends me. [*Ex. Ser.*
Sure this addition of quality muft have fo improved this

C coxcomb,

coxcomb, he can't but be very good company for a quarter of an hour.

Am. Now it moves my pity more than my mirth, to fee a man whom nature has made no fool, be fo very induftrious to pafs for an afs.

Lov. No, there you are wrong, Amanda; you fhould never beftow your pity upon thofe who take pains for your contempt; pity thofe whom nature abufes, but never thofe who abufe nature.

' *Ber.* Befides, the town would be robbed of one of its ' chiefeft diverfions, if it fhould become a crime to laugh ' at a fool.

' *Am.* I could never yet perceive the town inclined to ' part with any of its diverfions, for the fake of their being ' crimes; but I have feen it very fond of fome, I think, ' had little elfe to recommend them.

' *Ber.* I doubt, Amanda, you are grown its enemy, ' you fpeak with fo much warmth againft it.

' *Am.* I muft confefs, I am not much its friend.

' *Ber.* Then give me leave to make you mine, by not ' engaging in its quarrel.

' *Am.* You have many ftronger claims than that, Berinthia, whenever you think fit to plead your title.

' *Lov.* You have done well to engage a fecond, my ' dear; for here comes one will be apt to call you to an ' account for your country principles.'

Enter Lord Foppington.

Lord Fop. [*To* Lov.] Sir, I am your moft humble fervant.

Lov. I wifh you joy, my Lord.

Lord Fop. Oh, Lard, Sir!———Madam, your Ladyfhip's welcome to tawn.

Am. I wifh your Lordfhip joy.

Lord Fop. Oh, heavens, Madam!———

Lov. My Lord, this young lady is a relation of my wife's.

Lord Fop. [*Saluting her.*] The beatifulleft race of people upon earth, rat me. Dear Lovelefs, I am overjoyed to fee you have brought your family to tawn again: I am, ftap my vitals.———[*Afide.*] For I defign to lie with your wife———[*To* Am.] Far Gad's fake, Madam, haw has your

2

your Ladyſhip been able to ſubſiſt thus long, under the fatigue of a country life ?

Aman. My life has been very far from that, my Lord, it has been a very quiet one.

Lord Fop. Why that's the fatigue I ſpeak of, Madam : for 'tis impoſſible to be quiet, without thinking : now thinking is to me the greateſt fatigue in the world.

Am. Does not your Lordſhip love reading then ?

Lord Fop. Oh, paſſionately, Madam———But I never think of what I read.

Ber. Why, can your Lordſhip read without thinking ?

Lord Fop. Oh, lard———Can your Ladyſhip pray without devotion———Madam ?

Am. Well, I muſt own I think books the beſt entertainment in the world.

Lord Fop. I am ſo much of your Ladyſhip's mind, Madam, that I have a private gallery, where I walk ſometimes, is furniſhed with nothing but books and looking-glaſſes. Madam, I have gilded them, and ranged them ſo prettily, before gad, it is the moſt entertaining thing in the world to walk and look upon them.

Am. Nay, I love a neat library too ; but 'tis, I think, the inſide of a book ſhould recommend it moſt to us.

Lord Fop. That, I muſt confeſs, I am not altogether ſo fond of : far to my mind the inſide of a book, is to entertain one's ſelf with the forced product of another man's brain. Now, I think, a man of quality and breeding, may be much diverted with the natural ſprauts of his own. But to ſay the truth, Madam, let a man love reading never ſo well, when once he comes to know this tawn, he finds ſo many better ways of paſſing away the four and twenty hours, that 'twere ten thouſand pities he ſhould conſume his time in that. Far example, Madam, my life ; my life, Madam, is a perpetual ſtream of pleaſure, that glides through with ſuch a variety of entertainments, I believe the wiſeſt of our anceſtors never had the leaſt conception of any of them. I riſe, Madam, about ten o'clock. I don't riſe ſooner, becouſe 'tis the worſt thing in the world for the complection ; nat that I pretend to be a beau ; but a man muſt endeavour to look wholeſome, leſt he makes ſo nauſeous a figure in the ſide-box, the ladies ſhould be compelled to turn their eyes upon the

play.

play. So at ten o'clock, I say, I rise. Naw, if I find it a good day, I resolve to take a turn in the park, and see the fine women ; so huddle on my clothes, and get dressed by one. If it be nasty weather, I take a turn in the chocolate house ; where, as you walk, Madam, you have the prettiest prospect in the world : you have looking glasses all around you————But I'm afraid I tire the company.

Ber. Not at all ; pray go on.

Lord Fop. Why then, ladies, from thence I go to dinner at Lacket's, and there you are so nicely and delicately served, that, stap my vitals, they can compose you a dish, no bigger than a saucer, shall come to fifty shillings ; between eating my dinner, and washing my mouth, ladies, I spend my time, till I go to the play ; where, till nine o'clock, I entertain myself with looking upon the company ; and usually dispose of one hour more in leading them aut. So there's twelve of the four and twenty pretty well over. The other twelve, Madam, are disposed of in two articles : in the first four I toast myself drunk, and in t'other eight I sleep myself sober again. Thus, ladies, you see my life is an eternal raund O of delights.

Love. 'Tis a heavenly one, indeed.

Am. But, my Lord, you beaus spend a great deal of your time in intrigues. You have given us no account of them yet.

Lord Fop. [*Aside.*] Soh, she would enquire into my amours————That's jealousy————She begins to be in love with me. [*To* Aman.] Why, Madam——as to time for my intrigues, I usually make detachments of it from my other pleasures, according to exigency. Far your Ladyship may please to take notice, that those who intrigue with women of quality, have rarely occasion for above half an hour at a time : people of that rank being under those decornms, they can seldom give you a larger view, than will just serve to shoot them flying. So that the course of my other pleasures is not very much interrupted by my amours.

Love. But your Lordship now is become a pillar of the state ; you must attend the weighty affairs of the nation.

Lord Fop. Sir——as to weighty affairs——I leave
them

them to weighty heads. I never intend mine ſhall be a burden to my body.

Love. Oh, but you'll find the houſe will expect your attendance.

Lord Fop. Sir, you'll find the houſe will compound for my appearance.

Love. But your friends will take it ill if you don't attend their particular cauſes.

Lord Fop. Not, Sir, if I come time enough to give them my particular vote.

Ber. But pray, my Lord, how do you difpofe of your ſelf on Sundays? for that, methinks, ſhould hand wretchedly on your hands.

Lord Fop. Why faith, Madam ——— Sunday——— is a vile day, I muſt confeſs; I intend to move for leave to bring in a bill, that players may work upon it, as well as the hackney coaches. Though this I muſt ſay for the government, it leaves us the churches to entertain us ——— But then again, they begin ſo abominably early, a man muſt rife by candle-light to get dreſſed by the pſalm.

Ber. Pray, which church does your Lordſhip moſt oblige with your preſence?

Lord Fop. Oh, St. James's, Madam——— There's much the beſt company.

Am. Is there good preaching too?

Lord Fop. Why faith, Madam ——— I can't tell. A man muſt have very little to do there, that can give an account of the ſermon.

Ber. You can give us an account of the ladies, at leaſt.

Lord Fop. Or I deferve to be excommunicated—There is my Lady Tattle, my Lady Prate, my Lady Titter, my Lady Leer, my Lady Giggle, and my Lady Grin: theſe fit in the front of the boxes, and all church-time are the prettieſt company in the world, ſtap my vitals. [*To* Aman.] May'not we hope for the honour to ſee you Ladyſhip added to our ſociety, Madam?

Am. Alas, my Lord, I am the worſt company in the world at church: I'm apt to mind the prayers, or the ſermon, or———

Lord Fop. One is indeed ſtrangely apt at church to mind what one ſhould not do. But I hope, Madam, at

C 3   one

one time or other, I fhall have the honour to lead your Ladyfhip to your coach there. [*Afide.*] Methinks fhe feems ftrangely pleafed with every thing I fay to her—'Tis a vaft pleafure to receive encouragement from a woman before her hufband's face—I have a good mind to purfue my conqueft, and fpeak the thing plainly to her at once—'Egad I'll do't, and that in fo cavalier a manner, fhe fhall be furprifed at it——Ladies, I'll take my leave: I'm afraid I begin to grow troublefome with the length of my vifit.

Aman. Your Lordfhip is too entertaining to grow troublefome any where.

Lord Fop. [*Afide.*] That now was as much as if fhe had faid—— Pray lie with me. I'll let her fee I'm quick of apprehenfion. [*To* Aman.] Oh, lard, Madam, I had like to have forgot a fecret, I muft needs tell your Ladyfhip. [*To* Love.] Ned, you muft not be fo jealous now as to liften.

Love. Not I, my Lord; I'm too fafhionable a hufband to pry into the fecrets of my wife.

Lord Fop. [*To* Aman. *fqueezing her hand*] I am in love with you to defperation, ftrike me fpeechlefs.

Am. [*Giving him a box o'the car.*] Then thus I return your paffion——An impudent fool!

Lord Fop. Gad's curfe, Madam, I'm a peer of the realm.

Love. Hey! what the devil do you affront my wife, Sir? Nay, then—[*They draw and fight. The women run fhrieking for help.*

Am. Ah! What has my folly done? 'Help! Murder! help! Part them, for heaven's fake.'

Lord Fop. [*Falling back, and leaning upon his fword.*] Ah——quite through the body——Stap my vitals.

Enter Servants.

Love. [*Running to him.*] I hope I han't killed the fool however—Bear him up! Where's your wound?

Lord Fop. Juft through the guts.

Love. Call a furgeon there: unbutton him quickly.

Lord Fop. Ay, pray make hafte.

Love. This mifchief you may thank yourfelf for.

Lord Fop. I may fo—Love's the devil indeed, Ned.

Enter

Enter Syringe *and Servant.*

Serv. Here's Mr. Syringe, Sir, was juſt going by the door.

Lord Fop. He's the welcomeſt man alive.

Syr. Stand by, ſtand by, ſtand by. Pray, gentlemen, ſtand by. Lord have mercy upon us! Did you never fee a man run through the body before? Pray ſtand by.

Lord Fop. Ah, Mr. Syringe——I'm a dead man.

Syr. A dead man, and I by——I ſhould laugh to fee that, 'egad.

Love. Pr'ythee, don't ſtand prating, but look upon his wound.

Syr. Why, what if I won't look upon his wound this hour, Sir?

Love. Why then he'll bleed to death, Sir.

Syr. Why then I'll fetch him to life again, Sir.

Love. 'Slife, he's run through the guts, I tell thee.

Syr. Would he were run through the heart, I ſhould get the more credit by his cure. Now I hope you are ſatisfied?——Come, now let me come at him; now let me come at him. [*Viewing his wound.*] Oons, what a gaſh is here!—Why, Sir, a man may drive a coach and fix horſes into your body.

Lord Fop. Ho——

Syr. Why, what the devil have you run the gentleman through with a ſcythe?—[*Aſide.*] A little prick between the ſkin and the ribs, that's all.

Love. Let me fee his wound.

Syr. Then you ſhall dreſs it, Sir; for if any body looks upon it, I won't.

Love. Why, thou art the verieſt coxcomb I ever ſaw.

Syr. Sir, I am not maſter of my trade for nothing.

Lord Fop. Surgeon!

Syr. Well, Sir.

Lord Fop. Is there any hopes?

Syr. Hopes!——I can't tell——What are you willing to give for your cure?

Lord Fop. Five hundred paunds with pleaſure.

Syr. Why then perhaps there may be hopes. But we muſt avoid further delay. Here, help the gentleman into a chair, and carry him to my houſe preſently, that's the propereſt place, [*Aſide.*] to bubble him out of his money.

ney. Come, a chair, a chair quickly——There, in with him.   [_They put him into a chair._

Lord Fop. Dear Lovelefs——Adieu. If I die——I forgive thee; and if I live——I hope thou wilt do as much by me. I am very forry you and I fhould quarrel; but I hope here's an end on't, for if you are fatisfied——I am.

Love. I fhall hardly think it worth my profecuting any further, fo you may be at reft, Sir.

Lord Fop. Thou art a generous fellow, ftrike me dumb. [_Afide._] But thou haft an impertinent wife, ftap my vitals.

Syr. So, carry him off, carry him off, we fhall have him prate himfelf into a fever by and by; carry him off.   [_Exit_ Servant _with Lord_ Foppington.

_Am._ Now on my knees, my dear, let me afk your pardon for my indifcretion, my own I never fhall obtain.

Love. Oh, there's no harm done: you ferved him well.

_Am._ He did indeed deferve it. But I tremble to think how dear my indifcreet refentment might have coft you.

Love. Oh, no matter, never trouble yourfelf about that.

‘ _Ber._ For heaven's fake, what was't he did to you?

‘ _Am._ Oh, nothing; he only fqueezed me kindly by
‘ the hand, and frankly offered me a coxcomb's heart.
‘ I know I was to blame to refent it as I did, fince no-
‘ thing but a quarrel could enfue. But the fool fo fur-
‘ prized me with his infolence, I was not miftrefs of my
‘ fingers.

‘ _Ber._ Now I dare fwear he thinks you had them at
‘ great command, they obeyed you fo readily.’

Enter Worthy.

Wor. Save you, fave you, good people; I'm glad to find you all alive; I met a wounded peer carrying off: for heaven's fake what was the matter?

Love. Oh, a trifle! he would have lain with my wife before my face, fo fhe obliged him with a box of the ear, and I run him through the body: that was all.

Wor. Bagatelle on all fides. But, pray, Madam, how long has this noble lord been an humble fervant of yours?

_Am._ This is the firft I have heard on't. So, I fuppofe, 'tis his quality, more than his love, has brought him into this

this adventure. He thinks his title an authentic paſſ-
port to every woman's heart, below the degree of a
peereſs.

Wor. He's coxcomb enough to think any thing. But
I would not have you brought into trouble for him : I
hope there's no danger of his life?

Love. None at all : he's fallen into the hands of a
roguiſh ſurgeon, who, I perceive, deſigns to frighten a
little money out of him. But I ſaw his wound, 'tis nothing ; he may go to the play to-night, if he pleaſes.

Wor. I'm glad you have corrected him without farther
miſchief. And now, Sir, if theſe ladies have no farther
ſervice for you, you'll oblige me if you can go to the
place I ſpoke to you of t'other day.

Lov. With all my heart. [*Aſide.*] Tho' I could wiſh,
methinks, to ſtay and gaze a little longer on that creature. Good gods ! how beautiful ſhe is—But what have
I to do with beauty ? I have already had my portion,
and muſt not covet more. Come, Sir, when you pleaſe.
[*To* Wor.

Wor. Ladies, your ſervant.

Am. Mr. Loveleſs, pray one word with you before
you go.

Lov. '[*To* Wor.] I'll overtake you, Sir.' What would
my dear ? [*Exit* Worthy.

Am. Only a woman's fooliſh queſtion. How do you
like my couſin here ?

Lov. Jealous already, Amanda ?

Am. Not at all ; I aſk you for another reaſon.

Lov. [*Aſide.*] Whate'er her reaſon be, I muſt not
tell her true. [*To* Aman.] Why, I confeſs ſhe's handſome.
But you muſt not think I ſlight your kinſwoman, if I
own to you, of all the women who may claim that character, ſhe is the laſt would triumph in my heart.

Am. I'm ſatisfied.

Lov. Now tell me why you aſk'd ?

Am. At night I will. Adieu.

Lov. I'm yours. [*Kiſſing her.*] [*Exit* Lov.

Am. [*Aſide.*] I'm glad to find he does not like her ;
for I have a great mind to perſuade her to come and live
with me. [*To* Ber.] Now, dear Berinthia, let me enquire
a little into your affairs : for I do aſſure you, I am
enough

enough your friend, to intereſt myſelf in every thing
that concerns you.

Ber. You formerly have given me ſuch proofs on't, I
ſhould be very much to blame to doubt it; I am ſorry
I have no ſecrets to truſt you with, that I might convince you how entire a confidence I durſt repoſe in
you.

Am. Why is it poſſible, that one ſo young and beautiful as you, ſhou'd live and have no ſecrets?

Ber. What ſecrets do you mean?

Am. Lovers.

Ber. O twenty; but not one ſecret one amongſt 'em.
Lovers in this age have too much honour to do any thing
under-hand; they do all above-board.

Am. That now, methinks, would make me hate a
‘ man.

‘ *Ber.* But the women of the town are of another
‘ mind: for by this means a lady may (with the expence
‘ of a few coquet glances) lead twenty fools about in a
‘ ſtring, for two or three years together. Whereas, if
‘ ſhe ſhould allow 'em greater favours, and oblige them to
‘ ſecrecy, ſhe would not keep one of 'em a fortnight.

‘ *Am.* There's ſomething indeed in that to ſatisfy the
‘ vanity of a woman; but I can't comprehend how the
‘ men find their account in it.

‘ *Ber.* Their entertainment, I muſt confeſs, is a rid-
‘ dle to me: for there's very few of them ever get far-
‘ ther than a bow and an ogle. I have half a ſcore for
‘ my ſhare, who follow me all over the town; and at
‘ the play, the Park, and the church, do (with their eyes)
‘ ſay the violent'ſt things to me—But I never hear any
‘ more of 'em.

‘ *Am.* What can be the reaſon of that?

‘ *Ber.* One reaſon is, they don't know how to go far-
‘ ther. They have had ſo little practice, they don't un-
‘ derſtand the trade. But beſides their ignorance, you
‘ muſt know, there is not one of my half ſcore lovers, but
‘ what follows half a ſcore miſtreſſes. Now their af-
‘ fections being divided amongſt ſo many, are not ſtrong
‘ enough for any one, to make 'em purſue her to the
‘ purpoſe. Like a young puppy in a warren, they have a
‘ ſlirt at all, and catch none.

‘ *Am.*

' *Am.* Yet they feem to have a torrent of love to dif-
' pofe of.

' *Ber.* They have fo : but 'tis like the river of a mo-
' dern philofopher (whofe works, tho' a woman, I have
' read) it fets out with a violent ftream, fplits in a thou-
' fand branches, and is all loft in the fands.

' *Am.* But do you think this river of love runs all its
' courfe without doing any mifchief ? Do you think it
' overflows nothing ?

' *Ber.* O yes; 'tis true, it never breaks into any body's
' ground that has the leaft fence about it ; but overflows
' all the commons that lie in its way. And this is the
' utmoft achievement of thofe dreadful champions in
' the field of love—the beau.'

Am. But pr'ythee, Berinthia, inftruct me a little farther ; for I am fo great a novice, I'm almoft afhamed
on't. My hufband's leaving me whilft I was young and
fond, threw me into that depth of difcontent, that ever
fince I have led fo private and reclufe a life, my ignorance is fcarce conceivable. I therefore fain wou'd be
inftructed : not (Heaven knows) that what you call intrigues have any charms for me : the practic part of all
unlawful love is———

Ber. O 'tis abominable : but for the fpeculative; that
we muft all confefs, is entertaining. The converfation
of all the virtuous women in the town turns upon that
and new clothes.

Am. Pray be fo juft then to me, to believe, 'tis with a
world of innocency I would enquire, whether you think
thofe women we call women of reputation, do really
'fcape all other men, as they do thofe fhadows of 'em,
the beaus.

Ber. O no, Amanda : there a fort of men make dreadful work amongft 'em : men that may be called, the beaus
antipathy ; for they agree in nothing but walking upon
two legs. Thefe have brains : the beau has none.
Thefe are in love with their miftrefs : the beau with
himfelf. They take care of her reputation : he's induftrious to deftroy it. They are decent : he's a fop.
They are men : he's an afs.

Am. If this be their character, I fancy we had here
e'en now a pattern of 'em both.

Ber.

Ber. His Lordſhip and Mr. Worthy.

Am. The ſame.

Ber. As for the Lord he's eminently ſo : and for the other, I can aſſure you, there's not a man in town who has a better intereſt with the women, that are worth having an intereſt with. But 'tis all private : ' he's like a ' back-ſtair miniſter at court, who, whilſt the reputed ' favourites are ſauntering in the bed-chamber, is ruling ' the roaſt in the cloſet.

Am. ' He anſwers then the opinion I had ever of ' him. Heaven's ! what a difference there is between a ' man like him, and that vain nauſeous fop, Sir Novelty. ' [*Taking her hand.*]' I muſt acquaint you with a ſecret, couſin ; 'tis not that fool alone has talk'd to me of love, Worthy has been tampering too : 'tis true, he has done it in vain : not all his charms or art have power to ſhake me. My love, my duty, and my virtue, are ſuch faithful guards, I need not fear my heart ſhould e'er betray me. But what I wonder at is this : I find I did not ſtart at his propoſal, as when it came from one whom I contemn'd. ' I thefore mention this attempt, that I ' may learn from you whence it proceeds ; that vice, ' which cannot change its nature, ſhould ſo far change at ' leaſt its ſhape, as that the ſelf-ſame crime propoſed from ' one ſhall ſeem a monſter gaping at your ruin, when ' from another it ſhall look ſo kind, as tho' it were your ' friend, and never meant to harm you.' Whence think you, can this difference proceed ? For 'tis not love, Heaven knows.

Ber. O no ; I wou'd not for the world believe it were. But poſſibly, ſhould there a dreadful ſentence paſs upon you, to undergo the rage of both their paſſions ; the pain you apprehend from one might ſeem ſo trivial to the other, the danger would not quite ſo much alarm you.

Am. Fy, fy, Berinthia, you would indeed alarm me, could you incline me to a thought, that all the merit of mankind combined, could ſhake that tender love I bear my huſband : no, he ſits triumphant in my heart, and nothing can dethrone him.

' *Ber.* But ſhould he abdicate again, do you think ' you ſhould preſerve the throne ten tedious winters ' more, in hopes of his return ?

' Am.

' *Am.* Indeed I think he fhould. Tho' I confefs, after
' thofe obligations he has to me, fhould he abandon me
' once more, my heart would grow extremely urgent
' with me to root him thence, and caft him out for
' ever.'

Ber. Were I that thing they call a flighted wife, fome
body fhould run the rifque of being that thing they call—
a hufband.

Am. O fy, Berinthia, no revenge fhould ever be taken
againft a hufband: but to wrong his bed is a vengeance,
which of all vengeance——

Ber. Is the fweeteft, ha, ha, ha! Don't I talk madly?
Am. Madly indeed.

Ber. Yet I'm very innocent.

Am. That I dare fwear you are. I know how to make
allowances for your humour: You were always very entertaining company; but I find fince marriage and widowhood have fhewn you the world a little, you are very
much improved.

Ber. [*Afide.*] Alack-a-day, there has gone more than
that to improve me, if fhe knew all.

Am. For Heaven's fake, Berinthia, tell me what way
I fhall take to perfuade you to come and live with me?

Ber. Why, one way in the world there is——and
but one.

Am. Pray which is that?

Ber. It is to affure me—I fhall be very welcome.

Am. If that be all, you fhall e'en lie here to-night.

Ber. To-night?

Am. Yes, to-night.

Ber. Why, the people where I lodge will think me
mad.

Am. Let 'em think what they pleafe.

Ber. Say you fo, Amanda? Why then they fhall think
what they pleafe: for I'm a young widow, and I care not
what any body thinks. Ah, Amanda! it's a delicious
thing to be a young widow.

Am. You'll hardly make me think fo.

Ber. Phu, becaufe you are in love with your hufband:
but that is not every woman's cafe.

Am. I hope 'twas yours at leaft.

D

Ber.

Ber. Mine, fay ye ? Now I have a great mind to tell you a lie, but I fhould do it fo aukwardly, you'd find me out.

Am. Then e'en fpeak the truth.

Ber. Shall I?—Then, after all, I did love him, Amanda—as a nun does penance.

Am. Why did not you refufe to marry him then ?

Ber. Becaufe my mother would have whipped me.

Am. How did you live together ?

Ber. Like man and wife – afunder. He lov'd the country, I the town ; he hawks and hounds, I coaches and equipage ; he eating and drinking, I carding and playing ; he the found of a horn, I the fqueak of a fiddle ; we were dull company at table, worfe a-bed : Whenever we met, we gave one another the fpleen ; and never agreed but once, which was about lying alone.

Am. But tell me one thing truly and fincerely.

' *Ber.* What's that ?'

Am. Notwithftanding all thefe jars, did not his death at laft, extremely trouble you ?

Ber. O yes : ' not that my prefent pangs were fo very ' violent, but the after-pains were intolerable.' I was forced to wear a beaftly widow's band a twelvemonth for't.

Am. Women, I find, have different inclinations.

Ber. Women, I find, keep different company. When your hufband ran away from you, if you had fallen into fome of my acquaintance, 'twou'd have fav'd you many a tear. But you go and live with a grandmother, a bifhop, and an old nurfe, which was enough to make any woman break her heart for her hufband. Pray, Amanda, if ever you are a widow again, keep yourfelf fo, as I do.

Am. Why, do you then refolve you'll never marry ?

Ber. O no ; I refolve I will.

Am. How fo ?

Ber. That I never may.

Am. You banter me.

Ber. Indeed I don't. But I confider I'm a woman, and form my refolutions accordingly.

Am. Well, my opinion is, form what refolution you will, matrimony will be the end on't.

Ber.

Ber. Faith it won't.

Am. How do you know?

Ber. I'm fure on't.

Am. Why, do you think 'tis impoffible for you to fall in love?

Ber. No.

Am. Nay, but to grow fo paffionately fond, that nothing but the man you love can give you reft.

Ber. Well, what then?

Am. Why, then you'll marry him.

Ber. How do you know that?

Am. Why, what can you do elfe?

Ber. Nothing—but fit and cry.

Am. Pfha!

Ber. Ah, poor Amanda, you have led a country life: but if you'll confult the widows of this town they'll tell you, you fhould never take a leafe of a houfe you can hire for a quarter's warning. [*Exeunt.*

END of the SECOND ACT.

ACT III.

Enter Lord Foppington *and Servant.*

LORD FOPPINGTON.

HEY, fellow, let the coach come to the door.

Serv. Will your lordfhip venture fo foon to expofe yourfelf to the weather?

Lord Fop. Sir, I will venture as foon as I can, to expofe myfelf to the ladies: ' tho' give me my cloak how-' ever; for in that fide-bax, what between the air that ' comes in at the door on one fide, and the intolerable ' warmth of the mafks on t'other, a man gets fo many ' heats and colds, 'twou'd deftroy the canftitution of a ' harfe.

Serv. ' [*Putting on his cloke.*]' I wifh your lordfhip would pleafe to keep houfe a little longer; I'm afraid your honour does not well confider your wound.

Lord Fop. My wound!——I would not be in eclipfe another day, tho' I had as many wounds in my guts as I have had in my heart.

Enter

Enter Young Fashion.

Y. Fash. Brother, your servant. How do you find yourself to-day ?

Lord Fop. So well, that I have arder'd my coach to the door. So there's no great danger of death this baut, Tam.

Y. Fash. I'm very glad of it.

Lord Fop. [*Aside.*] That I believe's a lie. Pr'ythee, Tam, tell me one thing ; did not your heart cut a caper up to your mauth, when you heard I was run thro' the bady ?

Y. Fash. Why do you think it should ?

Lord Fop. Becaufe I remember mine did fo, when I heard my father was fhat thro' the head.

Y. Fash. It then did very ill.

Lord Fop. Pr'ythee, why fo ?

Y. Fash. Becaufe he us'd you very well.

Lord Fop. Well !—naw ftrike me dumb, he ftarv'd me. He has let me want a thaufand women for want of a thaufand paund.

Y. Fash. Then he hindered you from making a great many ill bargains ; for I think no woman is worth money that will take money.

Lord Fop. If I were a younger brother, I fhould think fo too.

Y. Fash. Why, is it poffible you can value a woman that's to be bought ?

Lord Fop. Pr'ythee, why not as well as a pad-nag ?

Y. Fash. Becaufe a woman has a heart to difpofe of ; a horfe has none.

Lord Fop. Look you, Tam, of all things that belang to a woman, I have an averfion to her heart ; far when once a woman has given you her heart——you can never get rid of the reft of her bady.

Y. Fash. This is ftrange doctrine : but pray in your amours how is it with you own heart ?

Lord Fop. Why, my heart in my amours —— is like—my heart aut of my amours ; *à la glace.* My bady, Tam, is a watch ; and my heart is the pendulum to it ; whilft the finger runs raund to every hour in the circle, that ftill beats the fame time.

Y. Fash. Then you are feldom much in love ?

Lord

Lord Fop. Never, ſtap my vitals.

Y. Faſh. Why then did you make all this buſtle about Amanda ?

Lord Fop. Becauſe ſhe was a woman of an inſolent virtue, and I thought myſelf piqu'd in honour to debauch her.

Y. Faſh. Very well. [*Aſide.*] Here's a rare fellow for you, to have the ſpending of five thouſand pounds a-year. But now for my buſineſs with him. [*To Lord* Fop.] Brother, tho' I know to talk of buſineſs (eſpecially of money) is a theme not quite ſo entertaining to you as that of the ladies, my neceſſities are ſuch, I hope you'll have patience to hear me.

Lord Fop. The greatneſs of your neceſſities, Tam, is the worſt argument in the warld for your being patiently heard. I do believe you are going to make a very good ſpeech, but, ſtrike me dumb, it has the worſt beginning of any ſpeech I have heard this twelvemonth.

Y. Faſh. I'm very ſorry you think ſo.

Lord Fop. I do believe thou art. But come, let's know thy affair quickly ; for 'tis a new play, and I ſhall be ſo rumpled and ſqueezed with preſſing thro' the crawd, to get to my ſervant, the women will think I have lain all night in my clothes.

Y. Faſh. Why then (that I may not be the author of ſo great a misfortune) my caſe in a word is this. The neceſſary expences of my travels have ſo much exceeded the wretched income of my annuity, that I have been forced to mortgage it for five hundred pounds, which is ſpent ; ſo that unleſs you are ſo kind to aſſiſt me in redeeming it, I know no remedy but to take a purſe.

Lord Fop. Why faith, Tam—to give you my ſenſe of the thing, I do think taking a purſe the beſt remedy in the warld ; for if you ſucceed, you are relieved that way ; if you are taken—you are relieved t'other.

Y. Faſh. I'm glad to ſee you are in ſo pleaſant a humour, I hope I ſhall find the effects on't.

Lord Fop. Why, do you then really think it a reaſonable thing I ſhou'd give you five hundred paunds ?

Y. Faſh. I do not aſk it as a due, brother, I am willing to receive it as a favour.

Lord

Lord Fop. Thau art willing to receive it in any haw, ftrike me fpeechlefs. But thefe are damned times to give money in: taxes are fo great, repairs fo exorbitant, tenants fuch rogues, and periwigs fo dear, that the devil take me, I am reduced to that extremity in my cafh, I have been farc'd to retrench in that one article of fweet pawder, till I have braught it dawn to five guineas a manth. Now judge, Tam, whether I can fpare you five hundred paunds?

Y. Fafh. If you can't, I muft ftarve, that's all. [*Afide.*] Damn him.

Lord Fop. All I can fay is, you fhould have been a better hufband.

Y. Fafh. 'Oons, if you can't live upon five thoufand a-year, how do you think I fhould do't upon two hundred?

Lord Fop. Don't be in a paffion, Tam; far paffion is the moft unbecoming thing in the warld---to the face. Look you, I don't love to fay any thing to you to make you melancholy; but upon this occafion I muft take leave to put you in mind, that a running horfe does require more attendance than a coach-horfe. Nature has made fome difference 'twixt you and I.

Y. Fafh. Yes, fhe has made you older. [*Afide.*] Pox take her.

Lord Fop. That is nat all, Tam.

Y. Fafh. Why what is there elfe?

Lord Fop. [*Looking firft upon himfelf, then upon his brother.*]——Afk the ladies.

Y. Fafh. Why, thou effence bottle! thou mufk-cat! doft thou then think thou haft any advantage over me, but what fortune has given thee?

Lord Fop. I do——flap my vitals.

Y. Fafh. Now, by all that's great and powerful, thou art the prince of coxcombs.

Lord Fop. Sir——I am praud of being at the head of fo prevailing a party.

Y. Fafh. Will nothing then provoke thee?——Draw, coward.

Lord Fop. Look you, Tam, you know I have always taken you for a mighty dull fellow, and here is one of the foolifheft plats broke out, that I have feen a long time,

time. Your paverty makes your life fo burthenfome to
you, you would provoke me to a quarrel, in hopes either
to flip thro' my lungs into my eftate, or to get yourfelf
run thro' the guts, to put an end to your pain. But I
will difappoint you in both your defigns; far with the
temper of a philafapher, and the difcretion of a ftatefman
——I will go to the play with my fword in my fcabbard.
                                            [*Exit.*

Y. Fafh. So! Farewel, fnuff-box. And now, confcience, I defy thee; Lory !
                    Enter Lory.

Lory. Sir.

Y. Fafh. Here's rare news, Lory; his lordfhip has given me a pill has purged off all my fcruples.

Lory. Then my heart's at eafe again : for I have been
in a lamentable fright, Sir, ever fince your confcience had
the impudence to intrude into your company.

Y. Fafh. Be at peace, it will come there no more :
my brother has given it a wring by the nofe, and I have
kicked it down ftairs. So run away to the inn; get the
horfes ready quickly, and bring them to old Coupler's,
without a moment's delay.

Lory. Then, Sir, you are going ftraight about the fortune.

Y. Fafh. I am : away ; fly, Lory.

Lory. The happieft day I ever faw. I'm upon the
wing already.   [*Exeunt feveral ways.*

SCENE, *a Garden.*

Enter Lovelefs *and a Servant.*

Lov. Is my wife within ?

Serv. No, Sir, fhe has been gone out this half hour.

Lov. 'Tis well ; leave me.

‘ Sure, Fate has yet fome bufinefs to be done,
‘ Before Amanda's heart and mine muft reft ;
‘ Elfe, why amongft thofe legions of her fex,
‘ Which throng the world,
‘ Should fhe pick out for her companion
‘ The only one on earth
‘ Whom Nature has endowed for her undoing ?
‘ Undoing was't, I faid——Who fhall undo her ?
‘ Is not her empire fix'd ? Am I not hers ?

                                            ‘ Did

‘ Did she not rescue me, a groveling slave,
‘ When chain’d and bound by that black tyrant Vice,
‘ I labour’d in its vilest drudgery ?
‘ Did she not ransom me, and set me free ?
‘ Nay more :
‘ When by my follies sunk
‘ To a poor tatter’d despicable beggar,
‘ Did she not lift me up to envy’d fortune,
‘ Give me herself, and all that she possest,
‘ Without a thought of more return,
‘ Than what a poor repenting heart might make her ?
‘ Han’t she done this ? And if she has,
‘ Am I not strongly bound to love her for it ?
‘ To love her—Why, do I not love her then ?
‘ By earth and Heaven I do.
‘ Nay, I have demonstration that I do :
‘ For I would sacrifice my life to serve her.
‘ Yet hold—if laying down my life
‘ Be demonstration of my love,
‘ What is’t I feel in favour of Berinthia ?
‘ For should she be in danger, methinks, I could incline
‘ To risk it for her service too ; and yet I do not love
‘ How then subsists my proof ?———   [her.
‘ ———O, I have found it out.
‘ What I would do for one, is demonstration of my love ;
‘ and if I’d do as much for t’other, it there is demonstra-
‘ tion of my friendship——— Ay——— it must be so.
‘ I find I’m very much her friend.—Yet let me ask my-
‘ self one puzzling question more :   Whence springs
‘ this mighty friendship all at once ?   For our acquain-
‘ tance is of a later date.   Now friendship’s said to be a
‘ plant of tedious growth, its root composed of tender
‘ fibres, nice in their taste, cautious in spreading, check-
‘ ed with the least corruption in the soil, long ere it
‘ take, and longer still ere it appear to do so : whilst
‘ mine is in a moment shot so high, and fixed so fast, it
‘ seems beyond the power of storms to shake it.   I doubt
‘ it thrives too fast.   [*Musing.*’

Enter Berinthia.

—Ah, she here !—Nay, then take heed, my heart, for
there are dangers towards.

                                        Ber.

Ber. What makes you look fo thoughtful, Sir? I hope you are not ill.

Lov. I was debating, Madam, whether I was fo or not ; and that was it which made me look fo thoughtful.

Ber. Is it then fo hard a matter to decide ? I thought all people had been acquainted with their own bodies, tho' few people know their own minds.

Lov. What if the diftemper I fufpect be in the mind ?

Ber. Why then I'll undertake to prefcribe you a cure.

Lov. Alas ! you undertake you know not what.

Ber. So far at leaft then allow me to be a phyfician.

Lov. Nay, I'll allow you fo yet farther : for I have reafon to believe, fhould I put myfelf into your hands, you would increafe my diftemper.

Ber. Perhaps I might have reafons from the college not to be too quick in your cure ; for 'tis poffible, I might find ways to give you often eafe, Sir.

Lov. Were I but fure of that, I'd quickly lay my cafe before you.

Ber. Whether you are fure of it or no, what rifk do you run in trying ?

Lov. O, a very great one.

Ber. How?

Lov. You might betray my diftemper to my wife.

Ber. And fo lofe all my practice.

Lov. Will you then keep my fecret ?

Ber. I will, if it don't burft me.

Lov. Swear.

Ber. I do.

Lov. By what ?

Ber. By woman.

Lov. That's fwearing by my deity. Do it by your own, or I fhan't believe you.

Ber. By man then.

Lov. I'm fatisfied. Now hear my fymptoms, and give me your advice. The firft were thefe :

When 'twas my chance to fee you at the play,

A random glance you threw, at firft alarm'd me,

I could not turn my eyes from whence the danger came :

I gazed upon you, till you fhot again,

And then my fears came on me ;

My

My heart began to pant, my limbs to tremble,
My blood grew thin, my pulfe beat quick,
My eyes grew hot and dim, and all the frame of nature
Shook with apprehenfion.
'Tis true, fome fmall recruits of refolution
My manhood brought to my affiftance,
And by their help I made a ftand awhile,
But found at laft your arrows flew fo thick,
They could not fail to pierce me ;
So left the field,
And fled for fhelter to Amanda's arms.
What think you of thefe fymptoms, pray ?

Ber. Feverifh every one of 'em.
But what relief pray did your wife afford you ?

Lov. Why ' inftantly fhe let me blood which,' for
the prefent much affuaged my flame. But when I faw
you, out it burft again, and raged with greater fury than
before. Nay, fince you now appear, 'tis fo increafed,
that in a moment, if you do not help me, I fhall, whilft
you look on, confume to afhes.

[*Taking hold of her hand.*

Ber. [*Breaking from him.*] O lard, let me go ; 'tis the
plague, and we fhall all be infected.

Lov. [*Catching her in his arms, and kiffing her.*] Then
we'll die together, my charming angel.

Ber. O ged——the devil's in you. Lord, let me go,
here's fomebody coming.

Enter Servant.

Serv. Sir, my lady ' is come home, and ' defires to
fpeak with you ; fhe's in her chamber.

Lov. Tell her, I'm coming. [*Exit Serv.*
But before I go, one glafs of nectar more to drink her
health.

Ber. Stand off, or I fhall hate you, by Heavens.

Lov. [*Kiffing her.*] In matters of love, a woman's
oath is no more to be minded than a man's.

Ber. Um——

Enter Worthy.

Wor. Ha ! what's here ? my ' old' miftrefs, and fo
clofe, i'faith ! I would not fpoil her fport for the uni-
verfe. [*He retires.*

Ber.

Ber. O ged————Now do I pray to Heaven, [*Exit*
Lovelefs, *running.*] with all my heart and foul, that the
devil in hell may take me, if ever—I was better pleafed
in my life—This man has bewitched me, that's certain.
[*Sighing.*] ' Well, I am condemn'd, but thanks to Hea-
' ven, I feel myfelf each moment more and more pre-
' pared for my execution. Nay, to that degree, I don't
' perceive I have the leaft fear of dying. No, I find,
' let the executioner be but a man, and there's nothing
' will fuffer with more refolution than a woman. Well,
' I never had but one intrigue yet ; but, I confefs, I
' long to have another. Pray Heaven it end as the firft
' did tho', that we may both grow weary at a time ; for
' 'tis a melancholy thing for lovers to outlive one ano-
' ther.'

Enter Worthy.

Wor. [*Afide.*] This difcovery's a lucky one, I hope to
make a happy ufe on't. That gentlewoman there is no
fool ; fo I fhall be able to make her underftand her intereft. [*To* Ber.] Your fervant, Madam ; I need not afk
you how you do, you have got fo good a colour.

Ber. No better than I ufed to have, I fuppofe.

Wor. A little more blood in your cheeks.

Ber. The weather's hot.

Wor. If it were not, a woman may have a colour.

Ber. What do you mean by that ?

Wor. Nothing.

Ber. Why do you fmile then ?

Wor. Becaufe the weather's hot.

Ber. You'll never leave roguing, I fee that.

Wor. [*Putting his finger to his nofe.*] You'll never leave
————I fee that.

Ber. Well, I can't imagine what you drive at. Pray
tell me what you mean ?

Wor. Do you tell me, it's the fame thing ?

Ber. I can't.

Wor. Guefs !

Ber. I fhall guefs wrong.

Wor. Indeed you won't.

Ber. Pfha ! either tell, or let it alone.

Wor. Nay, rather than let it alone, I will tell. But
firft I muft put you in mind, that after what has paft
'twixt

'twixt you and I, very few things ought to be secrets between us.

Ber. Why, what secrets do we hide? I know of none.

Wor. Yes, there are two; one I have hid from you, and t'other you would hide from me. You are fond of Lovelefs, which I have difcovered; and I am fond of his wife——

Ber. Which I have difcovered.

Wor. Very well, now I confefs your difcovery to be true: what do you fay to mine?

Ber. Why, I confefs——I would fwear 'twere falfe, if I thought you were fool enough to believe me.

' *Wor.* Now am I almoft in love with you again. Nay,
' I don't know but I might be quite fo, had I made one
' fhort campaign with Amanda. Therefore, if you find
' 'twould tickle your vanity, to bring me down once more
' to your lure, e'en help me quickly to difpatch her bufi-
' nefs, that I may have nothing elfe to do, but to apply
' myfelf to yours.

' *Ber.* Do you then think, Sir, I am old enough to be
a bawd?'

Wor. ' No,' but I think you are wife enough to——

Ber. To do what?

Wor. To hoodwink Amanda with a gallant, that fhe mayn't fee who is her hufband's miftrefs.

Ber. [*Afide.*] He has reafon: the hint's a good one.

Wor. Well, Madam, what think you on't?

Ber. I think you are fo much a deeper politician in thefe affairs than I am, that I ought to have a very great regard to your advice.

Wor. Then give me leave to put you in mind, that the moft eafy, fafe, and pleafant fituation for your own a-mour, is the houfe in which you now are; provided you keep Amanda from any fort of fufpicion. That the way to do that, is to engage her in an intrigue of her own, making yourfelf her confident. And the way to bring her to intrigue, is to make her jealous of her hufband in a wrong place; which the more you foment, the lefs you'll be fufpected. This is my fcheme, in fhort; which if you follow, as you fhould do, (my dear Berinthia) we may all four pafs the winter very pleafantly.

' *Ber.*

3

' *Ber.* Well, I could be glad to have no body's fins to
' anfwer for but my own. But where there is a neceffity—

' *Wor.* Right, as you fay, where there is a neceffity, a
' Chriftian is bound to help his neighbour.' So, good
Berinthia, lofe no time, but let us begin the dance as faft
as we can.

Ber. Not till the fiddles are in tune, pray Sir. ' Your
' lady's ftrings will be very apt to fly, I can tell you that,
' if they are wound up too haftily. But if you'll have pa-
' tience to fkrew them to a pitch by degrees, I don't doubt
' but fhe may endure to be played upon.

' *Wor.* Ay, and will make admirable mufic too, or
' I'm miftaken ;' but have you had no private clofet difcourfe with her yet about males and females, and fo forth,
which may give you hopes in her conftitution! for I
know her morals are the devil againft us.

Ber. I have had fo much difcourfe with her, that I believe were fhe once cured of her fondnefs to her hufband,
the fortrefs of her virtue would not be fo impregnable as
fhe fancies.

Wor. What! fhe runs, I'll warrant you, into that common miftake of fond wives, who conclude themfelves virtuous, becaufe they can refufe a man they don't like,
when they have got one they do.

Ber. True, and therefore I think 'tis a prefumptuous
thing in a woman to affume the name of virtuous, till fhe
has heartily hated her hufband, and been foundly in love
with fomebody elfe; whom, if fhe has withftood—then
—much good may it do her.

Wor. Well, fo much for her virtue. Now, one word
of her inclinations, and every one to their poft. What
opinion do you find fhe has of me ?

Ber. What you could wifh ; fhe thinks you handfome
and difcreet.

Wor. Good, that's thinking half feas over. One tide
more brings us into port.

Ber. Perhaps it may, though ftill remember, there's a
difficult bar to pafs.

Wor. I know there is, but I don't queftion I fhall get
well over it, by the help of fuch a pilot.

Ber. You may depend upon your pilot, fhe'il do the
E   beft

beſt ſhe can; ſo weigh anchor and be gone as ſoon as you pleaſe.

Wor. I'm under ſail already. Adieu.   [*Exit* Wor.

Ber. [*Alone.*] *Bon Voyage.* So, here's fine work. What a buſineſs have I undertaken? I'm a very pretty gentlewoman truly; but there was no avoiding it: he'd have ruined me, if I had refuſed him. ' Beſides, faith, I be-
' gin to fancy there may be as much pleaſure in carrying
' on another body's intrigue, as one's own. This at leaſt
' is certain; it exerciſes almoſt all the entertaining facul-
' ties of a woman: for there's employment for hypocriſy,
' invention, deceit, flattery, miſchief, and lying.'

    Enter Amanda, *her Woman following her.*

Wom. If you pleaſe, Madam, only to ſay, whether you'll have me buy them or not.

Am. Yes; no; go fiddle; I care not what you do. Pr'ythee leave me.

   ' *Wom.* I have done.'   [*Exit Woman.*

Ber. What in the name of Jove's the matter with you?

Am. The matter, Berinthia! I'm almoſt mad, I'm plagued to death.

Ber. Who is it that plagues you?

Am. Who do you think ſhould plague a wife, but her huſband?

Ber. Oh, ho, is it come to that? We ſhall have you wiſh yourſelf a widow by and by.

Am. Would I were any thing but what I am; a baſe ungrateful man, after what I have done for him, to uſe me thus!

Ber. What, he has been ogling now, I'll warrant you?

Am. Yes, he has been ogling.

Ber. And ſo you are jealous? Is that all?

Am. That all! Is jealouſy then nothing?

Ber. It ſhould be nothing, if I were in your caſe.

Am. Why, what would you do?

Ber. I'd cure myſelf.

Am. How?

Ber. ' Let blood in the fond vein:' care as little for my huſband, as he did for me.

Am. That would not ſtop his courſe.

Ber. Nor nothing elſe, when the wind's in the warm corner. Look you, Amanda, you may build caſtles in the air, ' and fume, and fret, and grow thin and lean,
                               ' and

' and pale and ugly, if you pleafe.' But I tell you, no man worth having is true to his wife, or can be true to his wife, or ever was, or ever will be fo.

Am. Do you then really think he's falfe to me? for I did not fufpect him.

Ber. Think fo! I know he's fo.

Am. Is it poffible? Pray tell me what you know?

Ber. Don't prefs me then to name names; for that I have fworn I won't do.

Am. Well, I won't; but let me know all you can without perjury.

' *Ber.* I'll let you know enough to prevent any wife wo-
' man's dying of the pip; and, I hope, you'll pluck up
' your fpirits, and fhew, upon occafion, you can be as
' good a wife as the beft of them.

' *Am.* Well, what a woman can do I'll endeavour.

' *Ber.* Oh, a woman can do a great deal, if once fhe
' fets her mind to it. Therefore, pray don't ftand trifling
' any longer, and teazing yourfelf with this and that, and
' your love and your virtue, and I know not what; but
' refolve to hold up your head, get a tiptoe, and look over
' them all; for, to my certain knowledge, your hufband
' is a pickeering elfewhere.

' *Am.* You are fure on't?'

Ber. Pofitively; he fell in love at the play.

Am. Right, the very fame; do you know the ugly thing?

Ber. Yes, I know her well enough; but fhe's no fuch ugly thing neither.

Am. Is fhe very handfome?

Ber. Truly I think fo.

Am. Hey ho!

Ber. What do you figh for now?

Am. Oh, my heart!

' *Ber.* [*Afide.*] Only the pangs of nature! fhe's in la-
' bour of her love; heaven fend her a quick delivery,
' I'm fure fhe has a good midwife.

' *Am.*' I'm very ill, I muft go to my chamber. Dear Berinthia, don't leave me a moment.

Ber. No, don't fear. [*Afide.*] I'll fee you fafe brought to bed, I'll warrant you.

[*Exit* Amanda *leaning upon* Berinthia.

SCENE, *a Country-House*.

Enter Young Fashion *and* Lory.

Young Fash. So, here's our inheritance, Lory, if we can but get into possession. But, methinks, the seat of our family looks like Noah's ark, as if the chief part on't were designed for the fowls of the air, and the beasts of the field.

Lory. Pray, Sir, don't let your head run upon the orders of building here; get but the heiress, let the devil take the house.

Young Fash. Get but the house, let the devil take the heiress, I say; at least if she be as old Coupler describes her. But come, we have no time to squander. Knock at the door. [Lory *knocks two or three times.*] What the devil, have they got no ears in this house? Knock harder.

Lory. 'Egad, Sir, this will prove some inchanted castle; we shall have the giant come out by and by with his club, and beat our brains out. [*Knocks again.*

Young Fash. Hush; they come.

From within.] Who is there?

Lory. Open the door and see: is that your country breeding?

Within.] Ay, but two words to a bargain: Tummis, is the blunderbuss primed?

Young Fash. 'Oons, give them good words, Lory; we shall be shot here a fortune-catching.

Lory. 'Egad, Sir, I think y'are in the right on't. Ho, Mr. What d'ye-call-um.—[*Servant appears at the window with a blunderbuss.*]

Serv. Weal naw, what's yare business.

Young Fash. Nothing, Sir, but to wait upon Sir Tunbelly, with your leave.

Ser. To weat upon Sir Tunbelly? Why, you'll find that's just as Sir Tunbelly pleases.

Young Fash. But will you do me the favour, Sir, to know whether Sir Tunbelly pleases or not?

Ser. Why, look you, do you see, with good words much may be done. Ralph, go thy waes, and ask Sir Tunbelly, if he pleases to be waited upon. And, do'st hear? Caull to nurse, that she may lock up Miss Hoyden before the geat's open.

Young Fash. D'ye hear that, Lory?

' *Lory.*

' *Lory.* Ay, Sir, I'm afraid we fhall find a difficult job
' on't. Pray heaven, that old rogue, Coupler, han't fent
' us to fetch milk out of the gunroom.

' *Young Fafh.* I'll warrant thee all will go well: fee,
' the door opens.'

Enter Sir Tunbelly, *with his fervants armed with guns,*
clubs, pitchforks, fcythes, &*c.*

' *Lory.* [*Running behind his mafter.*] Oh, lord, Oh,
' lord, Oh, lord, we are both dead men.

' *Young Fafh.* Take heed, fool; thy fear will ruin us.

' *Lory.* My fear, Sir; 'fdeath, Sir, I fear nothing.
' [*Afide.*] Would I were well up to the chin in a horfe-
' pond.'

Sir Tun. Who is it here has any bufinefs with me?

Young Fafh. Sir, 'tis I, if your name be Sir Tunbelly
Clumfey.

Sir Tun. Sir, my name is Sir Tunbelly Clumfey, whether you have any bufinefs with me or not. So you fee
I am not afhamed of my name—nor my face—neither.

Young Fafh. Sir, you have no caufe, that I know of.

Sir Tun. Sir, if you have no caufe neither, I defire to
know who you are; for till I know your name, I fhall
not afk you to come into my houfe, and when I know your
name—'tis fix to four I don't afk you neither.

Young Fafh. [*Giving him a letter.*] Sir, I hope you'll
find this letter an authentic paffport.

Sir Tun. Cod's my life, I afk your Lordfhip's pardon
ten thoufand times. [*To his fervants.*] Here, run in doors
quickly: get a Scotch-coal fire in the great parlour; fet
all the Turkey-work-chairs in their places; get the great
brafs candlefticks out, and be fure ftick the fockets full of
laurel: run. [*Turning to* Young Fafhion.] My Lord, I
afk your Lordfhip's pardon. [*To other Servants.*] And do
you hear, run away to nurfe, bid her let Mifs Hoyden
loofe again; and if it was not fhifting day, let her put on
a clean tucker, quick. [*Exeunt Servants confufedly.*] [*To*
Young Fafhion.] I hope your honour will excufe the diforder of my family, we are not ufed to receive men of
your Lordfhip's great quality every day. Pray where are
your coaches and fervants, my Lord?

Young Fafh. Sir, that I might give you and your fair
daughter a proof how impatient I am to be nearer a-kin

to you, I left my equipage to follow me, and came away post with only one servant.

Sir Tun. Your Lordship does me too much honour. It was exposing your person to too much fatigue and danger, I protest it was; but my daughter shall endeavour to make you what amends she can; and though I say it, that should not say it—Hoyden has charms.

Young Fash. Sir, I am not a stranger to them, though I am to her. Common fame has done her justice.

Sir Tun. My Lord, I am common fame's very grateful humble servant. My Lord——my girl's young: Hoyden is young, my Lord; but this I must say for her, what she wants in art, she has by nature; what she wants in experience, she has in breeding; and what's wanting in her age, is made good in her constitution. So pray, my Lord, walk in; pray, my Lord, walk in.

Young Fash. Sir, I wait upon you. [*Exeunt.*

Enter Miss Hoyden.

Miss Hoy. Sure never no body was used as I am. I know well enough what other girls do, for all they think to make a fool of me: it's well I have a husband a coming, or I-cod, I'd marry the baker, I would so. No body can knock at the gate, but presently I must be locked up; and here's the young greyhound bitch can run loose about the house all the day long, she can; 'tis very well. [*Nurse without, opening the door.*] Miss Hoyden, Miss, Miss, Miss; Miss Hoyden.

Enter Nurse.

Miss. Well, what do you make such a noise for, ha! What do you din a body's ears for? Can't one be at quiet for you.

Nurse. What do I din your ears for? Here's one come will din you ears for you.

Miss. What care I who comes; I care not a fig, who comes, nor who goes, as long as I must be locked up like the ale-cellar.

Nurse. That, Miss, is for fear you should be drank before you are ripe.

Miss. Oh, don't you trouble your head about that: I'm as ripe as you, though not so mellow.

Nurse. Very well; now I have a good mind to lock you up again, and not let you see my Lord to-night.

Miss.

Mifs. My Lord! Why, is my hufband come?

Nurfe. Yes, marry is he, and a goodly perfon too.

Mifs. [*Hugging Nurfe.*] Oh, my dear Nurfe, forgive me this once, and I'll never mifufe you again; no, if I do, you fhall give me three thumps on the back, and a great pinch by the cheek.

Nurfe. Ah, the poor thing! fee how it melts; it's as full of good-nature, as an egg's full of meat.

Mifs. But, my dear nurfe, don't lie now; is he come by your troth?

Nurfe. Yes, by my truly, is he.

Mifs. Oh, lord! I'll go and put on my laced fmock, though I'm whipped till the blood run down my heels for't.   [*Exit running.*

' *Nurfe.* Eh——the Lord fuccour thee, how thou art
' delighted?   [*Exit after her.*

' *Enter Sir* Tunbelly, *and* Young Fafhion. *A fervant with wine.*

' *Sir Tun.* My Lord, I'm proud of the honour to fee
' your Lordfhip within my doors: and I humbly crave
' leave to bid you welcome in a cup of fack wine.

' *Young Fafh.* Sir, to your daughter's health. [*Drinks.*

' *Sir Tun.* Ah, poor girl! fhe'll be fcared out of her
' wits on her wedding night; for, honeftly fpeaking, fhe
' does not know a man from a woman, but by his beard,
' and his breeches.

' *Young Fafh.* Sir, I don't doubt fhe has had a virtuous
' education, which, with the reft of her merit, makes me
' long to fee her mine. I wifh you would difpenfe with
' the canonical hour, and let it be this very night.

' *Sir Tun.* Oh, not fo foon neither; that's fhooting my
' girl before you bid her ftand. No, give her fair warn-
' ing, we'll fign and feal to-night, if you pleafe; and
' this day feven-night——let the jade look to her quar-
' ters.

' *Young Fafh.* This day feven-night——Why, what do
' you take me for a ghoft, Sir? 'Slife, Sir, I'm made of
' flefh and blood, and bones and finews, and can no more
' live a week without your daughter——than I can live a
' month with her.   [*Afide.*

' *Sir Tun.* Oh, I'll warrant you, my hero; young men
' are hot, I know, but they don't boil over at that rate,
                          ' neither;

' neither; befides, my wench's wedding gown is not
' come home yet.

' *Young Fafh.* Oh, no matter, Sir, I'll take her in her
' fhift. [*Afide.*] A pox of this old fellow, he'll delay the
' bufinefs till my damned ftar finds me out, and difcovers
' me. [*To Sir* Tun.] Pray, Sir, let it be done without ce-
' remony, 'twill fave money.

' *Sir Tun.* Money——Save money when Hoyden's to
' be married? Udfwoons, I'll give my wench a wedding-
' dinner, though I go to grafs with the king of Affyria
' for't, and fuch a dinner it fhall be, as is not to be
' cooked in the poaehing of an egg. Therefore, my
' noble Lord, have a little patience, we'll go and look
' over our deeds and fettlements immediately; and as for
' your bride, though you may be fharp-fet before fhe's
' quite ready, I'll engage for my girl, fhe ftays your fto-
' mach at laft.'   [*Exeunt.*

END of the THIRD ACT.

ACT IV.

Enter Mifs Hoyden *and* Nurfe.

NURSE.

WELL, Mifs, how do you like your hufband that is
to be?

Mifs. Oh, Lord, nurfe, I'm fo overjoyed, I can fcarce
contain myfelf.

Nurfe. Oh, but you muft have a care of being too
fond; for men now a-days hate a woman that loves them.

Mifs. Love him! Why do you think I love him,
nurfe? I-cod, I would not care if he were hanged, fo I
were but once married to him——No——that which
pleafes me, is to think what work I'll make when I get
to London; for when I am a wife and a lady both,
Nurfe, I-cod I'll flant it with the beft of them.

Nurfe. Look, look, if his honour be not a coming to
you; now if I were fure you would behave yourfelf hand-
fomely, and not difgrace me that have brought you up,
I'd leave you alone together.

Mifs. That's my beft nurfe, do as you would be done
by;

by; truſt us together this once, and if I don't ſhew my
breeding from the head to the foot of me, may I be twice
married, and die a maid.

Nurſe. Well, this once I'll venture you; but if you
diſparage me———

Miſs. Never fear, I'll ſhew him my parts, I'll warrant
him. [*Exit* Nurſe.] Theſe old women are ſo wiſe when
they get a poor girl into their clutches; but ere it be
long, I ſhall know what's what, as well as the beſt of
them.

Enter Young Faſhion.

Young Faſh. Your ſervant, Madam, I'm glad to find you
alone; for I have ſomething of importance to ſpeak to
you about.

Miſs. Sir, (my Lord, I meant) you may ſpeak to me,
about what you pleaſe, I ſhall give you a civil anſwer.

Young Faſh. You give me ſo obliging a one, it encou-
rages me to tell you in few words, what I think both for
your intereſt and mine. Your father, I ſuppoſe you
know, has reſolved to make me happy in being your huſband, and I hope I may depend upon your conſent, to
perform what he deſires.

Miſs. Sir, I never diſobey my father in any thing but
eating of green gooſeberries.

Young Faſh. So good a daughter muſt needs be an admirable wife; I am therefore impatient till you are mine,
and hope you will ſo far conſider the violence of my
love, that you won't have the cruelty to defer my happineſs, ſo long as your father deſigns it.

Miſs. Pray, my Lord, how long is that?

Young Faſh. Madam, a thouſand year—a whole week.

Miſs. A week——why I ſhall be an old woman by that
time.

Young Faſh. And I an old man, which you'll find a
greater misfortune than t'other.

Miſs. Why I thought it was to be to-morrow morning, as ſoon as I was up; I'm ſure nurſe told me ſo.

Young Faſh. And it ſhall be to-morrow morning ſtill,
if you'll conſent.

Miſs. If I conſent! Why, I thought I was to obey
you as my huſband.

Y. Faſh.

Y. Fash. That's when we are married; till then,
to obey you.

Miss. Why then, if we are to take it by turns, it's the
same thing. I'll obey you now, and when we are married, you shall obey me.

Y. Fash. With all my heart. But I doubt we must
get nurse on our side, or we shall hardly prevail with the
chaplain.

Miss. No more we shan't, indeed; for he loves her
better than he loves his pulpit, and would always be a
preaching to her by his good will.

Y. Fash. Why, then, my dear little bedfellow, if
you'll call her hither, we'll try to persuade her presently.

Miss. Oh, lord! I can tell you a way to persuade her
to any thing.

Y. Fash. How's that?

Miss. Why, tell her she's a wholesome, comely woman,
and give her half a crown.

Y. Fash. Nay, if that will do, she shall have half a
score of them.

Miss. Oh, Gemini! for half that she'd marry you herself. I'll run and call her. [*Exit Miss.*

Y. Fash. So, matters go swimmingly; this is a rare
girl, i'faith. I shall have a fine time of it with her at
London. ' I'm much mistaken, if she don't prove a
' March hare all the year round. What a scampering
' chace will she make on't, when she finds the whole ken-
' nel of beaus at her tail! Hey to the park and the play,
' and the church, and the devil! She'll shew them sport,
' I'll warrant them.' But, no matter; she brings an
estate will afford me a separate maintenance.

Enter Miss *and* Nurse.

How do you do, good Mistress Nurse? I desired your
young lady would give me leave to see you, that I might
thank you for your extraordinary care and conduct in her
education. Pray, accept of this small acknowledgment
for it at present; and depend upon my farther kindness,
when I shall be that happy thing, her husband.

Nurse. [*Aside.*] Gold, by mackins! Your honour's
goodness is too great. Alas! all I can boast of is, I gave
her pure good milk, and so your honour would have said,
an you had seen how the poor thing suck'd it—Eh, God's
blessing

blessing on the sweet face on't; how it used to hang at at this poor teat, and suck, and squeeze, and kick, and sprawl, it would, till the belly on't was so full, it would drop off like a leech.

Miss. [*To* Nurse, *taking her angrily aside.*] Pray, one word with you; pr'ythee, Nurse, don't stand ripping up old stories, to make one ashamed before one's love. Do you think such a fine proper gentleman as he is, cares for a fiddlecome tale of a draggle-tail'd girl? If you have a mind to make him have a good opinion of a woman, don't tell him what one did then, tell him what one can do now. [*To* Y. Fash.] I hope your honour will excuse my mismanners to whisper before you; it was only to give some orders about the family.

Y. Fash. Oh, every thing, Madam, is to give way to business! besides, good housewifery is a very commendable quality in a young lady.

Miss. Pray, Sir, are young ladies good housewives at London town? Do they darn their own linen?

Y. Fash. Oh, no! they study how to spend money, not to save it.

Miss. I'cod, I don't know but that may be better sport than t'other, ha, Nurse!

Y. Fash. Well, you shall have your choice, when you come there.

Miss. Shall I?——Then, by my troth, I'll get there as fast as I can—[*To* Nurse.] His honour desires you'll be so kind as to let us be married to-morrow.

Nurse. To-morrow, my dear Madam!

Y. Fash. Yes, to-morrow, sweet Nurse, privately.
' Young folks, you know, are impatient, and Sir Tun-
' belly would make us stay a week for a wedding-dinner.
' Now, all things being signed and sealed, and agreed, I
' fancy there could be no great harm in practising a
' scene or two of matrimony in private, if it were only
' to give us the better assurance, when we come to play
' it in public.'

Nurse. Nay, I must confess, stolen pleasures are sweet. But if you should be married now, what will you do when Sir Tunbelly calls for you to be wedded?

Miss. Why, then we will be married again.

Nurse. What, twice, my child?

Miſs. I'cod, I don't care how often I'm married, not **I.**

' *Y. Faſh.* Pray, Nurſe, don't you be againſt your young lady's good ; for, by this means, ſhe'll have the pleaſure of two wedding-days.

' *Miſs.* [*To* Nurſe, *ſoftly.*] And of two wedding-nights, ' too, Nurſe.'

Nurſe. Well, I'm ſuch a tender-hearted fool, I find I can refuſe you nothing ; ſo you ſhall e'en follow your own inventions.

Miſs. Shall I ? [*Aſide*] Oh, Lord, I could leap over the moon !

Y. Faſh. Dear Nurſe, this goodneſs of yours ſhan't go unrewarded ; but now you muſt employ your power with Mr. Bull, the chaplain, that he may do his friendly office too ; and then we ſhall be all happy. Do you think you can prevail with him ?

Nurſe. Prevail with him !——or he ſhall never prevail with me, I can tell him that.

Miſs. My Lord, ſhe has had him upon the hip this ſeven year.

Y. Faſh. I'm glad to hear it : however, to ſtrengthen your intereſt with him, you may let him know, I have ſeveral fat livings in my gift, and that the firſt that falls ſhall be in your diſpoſal.

Nurſe. Nay then, I'll make him marry more folks than one, I'll promiſe him.

Miſs. Faith, do, Nurſe, make him marry you, too. I'm ſure he'll do it for a fat living ; for he loves eating more than he loves his bible ; and I have often heard him ſay, **a** fat living was the beſt meat in the world.

Nurſe. Ay, and I'll make him commend the ſauce, too, or I'll bring his gown to a caſſock, I will ſo.

Y. Faſh. Well, Nurſe, whilſt you go and ſettle matters with him, your lady and I will go and take a walk in the garden.

Nurſe. I'll do your honour's buſineſs in the catching up of a garter. [*Exit* Nurſe.

Y. Faſh. [*Giving her his hand.*] Come, Madam, dare you venture yourſelf alone with me ?

Miſs. Oh, dear, yes, Sir ! I don't think you'll do any thing to me I need be afraid on.

[*Exeunt.*
[*Enter*

Enter Amanda *and* Berinthia.

'A   S O N G.

' I ſmile at love, and all its arts,
   ' The charming Cynthia cry'd ;
' Take heed, for love has piercing darts,
   ' A wounded ſwain reply'd.
' Once free and bleſs'd, as you are now,
   ' I trifled with his charms,
' I pointed at his little bow,
   ' And ſported with his arms :
' Till urg'd too far, revenge, he cries,
   ' A fatal ſhaft he drew ;
' It took its paſſage thro' your eyes,
   ' And to my heart it flew.

' To tear it thence I try'd in vain ;
   ' To ſtrive, I quickly found,
' Was only to encreaſe the pain,
   ' And to enlarge the wound.
' Ah, much too well, I fear, you know
   ' What pain I'm to endure ;
' Since what your eyes alone could do,
   ' Your heart alone can cure !
' And that (grant, Heaven, I may miſtake)
   ' I doubt, is doom'd to bear
' A burden for another's ſake,
   ' Who ill rewards its care.'

Am. Well, now, Berinthia, I'm at leiſure to hear what
'twas you had to ſay to me.

Ber. What I had to ſay, was only to echo the ſighs and
groans of a dying lover.

Am. Phoo ! will you never learn to talk in earneſt of
any thing ?

Ber. Why, this ſhall be in earneſt, if you pleaſe ; for
my part, I only tell you matter of fact ; you may take it
wh ch way you like beſt : ' but if you'll follow the women
' of the town, you'll take it both ways : for when a man
' offers himſelf to one of them, firſt ſhe takes him in jeſt,
' and then ſhe takes him in earneſt,'

F   *Am.*

Am. ' I'm sure there's so much jest and earnest in what ' you say to me,' I scarce know how to take it. But I think you have bewitched me ; for I don't find it possible to be angry with you, say what you will.

Ber. I'm very glad to hear it ; for I have no mind to quarrel with you, for some reasons that I'll not brag of. But quarrel or not, smile or frown, I must tell you what I have suffered upon your account.

Am. Upon my account !

Ber. Yes, upon yours—I have been forced to sit still, and hear you commended for two hours together, without one compliment to myself. Now, don't you think a woman has a blessed time of that ?

Am. ' Alas, I should have been unconcerned at it ! I ' never knew where the pleasure lay of being praised by ' the men.' But, pray, who was this that commended me so ?

Ber. One you have a mortal aversion to ; Mr. Worthy. ' He used you like a text ; he took you all to pieces ; but ' spoke so learnedly upon every point, one might see the ' spirit of the church was in him. If you are a woman, ' you'd have been in an extasy to have heard how feeling- ' ly he handled your hair, your eyes, your nose, your ' mouth, your teeth, your tongue, your chin, your neck, ' and so forth. Thus he preached for an hour ; but ' when he came to use an application, he observed, that ' all these, without a gallant, were nothing—Now, con- ' sider of what has been said ; and Heaven give you grace ' to put it in practice.'

Am. Alas, Berinthia ! did I incline to a gallant, (which you know I do not) do you think a man so nice as he, could have the least concern for such a plain, unpolished thing as I am ? It is impossible !

Ber. Now have you a great mind to put me upon commending you.

Am. Indeed, that was not my design.

Ber. Nay, if it were, it's all one ; for I won't do't ; I'll leave that to your looking-glass. But, to shew you I have some good-nature left, I'll commend him ; and may be that may do as well.

Am. You have a great mind to persuade me I am in love with him.

Ber. I have a great mind to perfuade you, you don't know what you are in love with.

Am. I am fure I am not in love with him, nor never fhall be; fo let that pafs. But you were faying fomething you would commend him for.

Ber. Oh, you'd be glad to hear a good character of him, however.

Am. Pfha!

Ber. Pfha! ——— Well, 'tis a foolifh undertaking for women, in thefe kind of matters, to pretend to deceive one another——Have not I been bred a woman, as well as you?

Am. What then?

Ber. Why, then, I underftand my trade fo well, that, whenever I am told of a man I like, I cry, Pfha! But, that I may fpare you the pains of putting me a fecond time in mind to commend him, I'll proceed, and give you this account of him; that, tho' 'tis poffible he may have had women with as good faces as your ladyfhip's, (no difcredit to it neither) yet, you muft know, your cautious behaviour, with that referve in your humour, has given him his death's wound. He mortally hates a coquette. He fays, 'tis impoffible to love, where we cannot efteem; and that no woman can be efteemed by a man who has fenfe, if fhe makes herfelf cheap in the eye of a fool. ' That pride to a woman, is as neceffary as humility to a ' divine; and that far-fetch'd, and dear-bought, is meat ' for gentlemen, as well as for ladies.' In fhort, that every woman who has beauty, may fet a price upon herfelf; and that, by under-felling the market, they ruin the trade. This is his doctrine; how do you like it?

Am. So well, that, fince I never intend to have a gallant for myfelf, if I were to recommend one to a friend, he fhould be the man.

Enter **Worthy.**

Blefs me, he's here! Pray Heaven, he did not hear me!

Ber. If he did, it won't hurt your reputation; your thoughts are as fafe in his heart, as in your own.

Wor. I venture in at an unfeafonable time of night, ladies; I hope, if I am troublefome, you'll ufe the fame freedom in turning me out again.

Am.

Am. I believe it can't be late; for Mr. Lovelefs is not come home yet, and he ufually keeps good hours.

Wor. Madam; I'm afraid he'll tranfgrefs a little to-night; for he told me, about half an hour ago, he was going to fup with fome company, he doubted would keep him out till three or four o'clock in the morning; and defired I would let my fervant acquaint you with it, that you might not expect him. But my fellow's a blunder-head; fo, left he fhould make fome miftake, I thought it my duty to deliver the meffage myfelf.

Am. I'm very forry he fhould give you that trouble, Sir; but——

Ber. But fince he has, will you give me leave, Madam, to keep him to play at ombre with us ?

Am. Coufin, you know you command my houfe.

Wor. [*To* Ber.] And, Madam, you know you command me; tho' I'm a very wretched gamefter.

Ber. Oh, you play well enough to lofe your money, and that's all the ladies require; and fo, without any more ceremony, let's go into the next room, and call for the cards.

Am. With all my heart.   [*Ex.* Wor. *leading out* Am.

Ber. Well, how this bufinefs will end, Heaven knows ! but fhe feems to be in as fair a way——as a boy is to be a rogue, when he's put clerk to an attorney.   [*Exit.*

S C E N E, Berinthia's *Chamber.*

Enter Lovelefs *cautioufly in the dark.*

Lov. So, thus far all's well. I'm got into her bed-chamber, and I think nobody has perceived me fteal into the houfe: my wife don't expect me home till four o'clock; fo if Berinthia comes to bed by eleven, I fhall have a chace of five hours. Let me fee; where fhall I hide myfelf? Under her bed? No; we fhall have her maid fearching there for fomething or other: her clofet's a better place, and I have a mafter-key will open it : I'll e'en in there, ' and attack her juft when fhe comes to her ' prayers; that's the moft like to prove her critical mi- ' nute; for then the devil will be there to affift me.'

[*He opens the clofet, goes in, and fhuts the door after him. Enter* Berinthia, *with a candle in her hand.*

Ber. Well, fure I am the beft natured woman in the world.

world. I, that love cards so well, (there is but one thing
upon the earth that I love better) have pretended letters to
write to give my friends a *tête-à-tête*. However, I'm innocent; for picquet is the game I set them to: at her
own peril be it, if she ventures to play with him at any
other. But now, what shall I do with myself? I don't
know how in the world to pass my time. Would Loveless were here, to *badiner* a little—Well, he's a charming
fellow; I don't wonder his wife's so fond of him—What
if I should sit down and think of him till I fall fast asleep,
and dream of the Lord knows what? Oh, but then if I
should dream we were married, I should be frightened out
of my wits. [*Seeing a book.*] What's this book? I think I
had best go read. Oh, splenetique! it's a sermon. Well,
I'll go into my closet, and read the Plotting Sisters. [*She
opens the closet, sees* Loveless, *and shrieks out.*] Oh, Lord,
a ghost, a ghost, a ghost, a ghost!

Enter Loveless *running to her.*

Lov. Peace, my dear; it's no ghost; take it in your
arms; you'll find 'tis worth a hundred of them.

Ber. Run in again; here's somebody coming.

Enter Maid.

Maid. Oh, Lord, Madam! what's the matter?

Ber. Oh, heavens, I'm almost frighted out of my wits!
I thought, verily, I had seen a ghost; and 'twas nothing
but the white curtain, with a black hood pinned up against
it. You may begone again—I am the fearfullest fool—
[*Exit Maid.*

Re-enter Loveless.

Lov. Is the coast clear?

Ber. The coast clear! I suppose you are clear; you'd
never play such a trick as this else.

Lov. I am very well pleased with my trick thus far;
and shall be so till I have played it out, if it ben't your
fault. Where's my wife?

Ber. At cards.

Lov. With whom?

Ber. With Worthy.

Lov. Then we are safe enough.

Ber. You are so! Some husbands would be of another
mind, if he were at cards with their wives.

Lov. And they'd be in the right on't too. But I dare
trust

truft mine. Befides, I know he's in love in another place ; and he's not one of thofe who court half a dozen at a time.

Ber. Nay, the truth on't is, you'd pity him if you faw how uneafy he is, at being engaged with us; but 'twas my malice. I fancied he was to meet his miftrefs ſomewhere elfe ; fo did it to have the pleafure of feeing him fret.

Lov. What fays Amanda to my ſtaying abroad fo late ?

Ber. Why, fhe's as much out of humour as he ; I be-lieve they wifh one another at the devil.

Lov. Then I'm afraid they'll quarrel at play, and foon throw up the cards. [*Offering to pull her into the clofet.*] Therefore, my dear, charming angel, let us make good ufe of our time.

Ber. Heavens ! what do you mean ?

Lov. Pray, what do you think I mean ?

Ber. I don't know.

Lov. I'll fhew you.

Ber. You may as well tell me.

Lov. No, that would make you blufh worfe than t'other.

Ber. Why, do you intend to make me blufh ?

Lov. Faith, I can't tell that ; but if I do, it fhall be in the dark. [*Pulling her.*

Ber. Oh, heavens ! I would not be in the dark with you for all the world.

Lov. I'll try that. [*Puts out the candle.*

Ber. Oh, Lord ! are you mad ? What fhall I do for light ?

Lov. You'll do as well without it.

Ber. Why, one can't find a chair to fit down ?

Lov. Come into the clofet, Madam ; there's moon-fhine upon the couch.

Ber. Nay, never pull ; for I will not go.

Lov. Then you muft be carried. [*Carrying her.*

Ber. ' Help, help ! I'm ravifh'd, ruin'd, undone !' Oh, Lord, I fhall never be able to bear it ! [*Very foftly.*

[*Exeunt.*

SCENE, Sir Tunbelly's *Houfe.*

Enter Mifs Hoyden, Nurfe, Young Fafhion, *and* Bull.

Y. Faſh. This quick difpatch of yours, Mr. Bull, I take

ſo

fo kindly, it fhall give you claim to my favour as long as
I live, I do affure you.

Mifs. And to mine too, I promife you.

Bull. I moft humbly thank your honours ; and I hope,
‘ fince it has been my lot to join you in the holy bands
‘ of wedlock, you will fo well cultivate the foil which I
‘ have craved a bleffing on, that’ your children may fwarm
about you like bees about a honey-comb.

Mifs. I’cod, with all my heart ; the more the merrier,
I fay : ha, Nurfe.

Enter Lory, *taking his mafter haftily afide.*

Lor. One word with you, for Heaven’s fake.

Y. Fafh. What the devil’s the matter ?

Lor. Sir, your fortune’s ruined ; ‘ and I don’t think
‘ your life’s worth a quarter of an hour’s purchafe.’
Yonder’s your brother arrived, with two coaches and fix
horfes, twenty footmen and pages, a coat worth fourfcore
pounds, and a periwig down to his knees : fo judge what
will become of your lady’s heart.

Y. Fafh. Death and furies, ’tis impoffible !

Lor. Fiends and fpectres, Sir ! ’tis true.

Y. Fafh. Is he in the houfe yet ?

Lor. No, they are capitulating with him at the gate ;
the porter tells him, he’s come to run away with Mifs
Hoyden, and has cock’d the blunderbufs at him ; your
brother fwears, Gad damme, they are a parcel of clawns,
‘ and he had a good mind to break off the match ; but
‘ they have given the word for Sir Tunbelly ; fo, I doubt,
‘ all will come out, prefently.’ Pray, Sir, refolve what
you’ll do, this moment ; ‘ for, ’egad, they’ll maul you.’

Y. Fafh. Stay a little——[*To* Mifs.] My dear, here’s a
troublefome bufinefs, my man tells me of ; but don’t be
frightened ; we fhall be too hard for the rogue. Here’s
an impudent fellow at the gate, (not knowing I was come
hither *incognito)* has taken my name upon him, in hopes
to run away with you.

Mifs. Oh, the brazen-fac’d varlet ! It’s well we are
married, or may be we might never have been fo.

Y. Fafh. [*Afide.*] ’Egad, like enough—Pr’ythee, dear
Doctor, run to Sir Tunbelly, and ftop him from going to
the gate, before I fpeak with him.

Bull. I fly, my good Lord——   [*Exit* Bull.
                                                    Nurfe.

Nurſe. An't pleaſe your honour, my Lady and I had beſt lock ourſelves up till the danger be over.

Y. Faſh. Ay, by all means.

Miſs. Not ſo faſt; I won't be locked up any more; I'm married.

Y. Faſh. Yes, pray, my dear, do, till we have ſeized this raſcal.

Miſs. Nay, if you pray me, I'll do any thing.

[*Exeunt* Miſs *and* Nurſe.

Y. Faſh. Oh, here's Sir Tunbelly coming—[*To* Lory.] Hark you, Sirrah, things are better than you imagine; the wedding's over.

Lor. The devil it is, Sir.

Y. Faſh. Not a word, all's ſafe; but Sir Tunbelly don't know it, nor muſt not yet; ſo I am reſolved to brazen the buſineſs out, and have the pleaſure of turning the impoſtor upon his lordſhip, which I believe may eaſily be done.

Enter Sir Tunbelly, Chaplain, *and* Servants, *armed.*

Y. Faſh. Did you ever hear, Sir, of ſo impudent an undertaking?

Sir Tun. Never, by the maſs; but we'll tickle him, I warrant you.

Y. Faſh. They tell me, Sir, he has a great many people with him, diſguiſed like ſervants.

Sir Tun. Ay, ay, rogues enow; but I'll ſoon raiſe the poſſe upon him.

Y. Faſh. Sir, if you'll take my advice, we'll go a ſhorter way to work; I find, whoever this ſpark is, he knows nothing of my being privately here; ſo, if you pretend to receive him civilly, he'll enter without ſuſpicion; and as ſoon as he is within the gate, we'll whip up the drawbridge upon his back, let fly the blunderbuſs to diſperſe the crew, and ſo commit him to gaol.

Sir Tun. 'Egad, your lordſhip is an ingenious perſon, and a very great general; but ſhall we kill any of them, or not?

Y. Faſh. No, no, fire over their heads, only to fright them; I'll warrant the regiment ſcours, when the colonel's a priſoner.

Sir Tun. Then come along, my boys; and let your courage be great—for your danger is but ſmall. [*Exeunt.*

SCENE,

SCENE, *the Gate.*

Enter Lord Foppington *and Followers.*

Lord Fop. A pax of thefe bumkinly people ! will they open the gate, or do they defire I fhould grow at their moat-fide, like a willow ? [*To the Porter.*] Hey, fellow ! Pr'ythee, do me the favour, in as few words as thou canft find to exprefs thyfelf, to tell me whether thy mafter will admit me or not, that I may turn about my coach, and begone ?

Por. Here's my mafter himfelf now at hand ; he's of age, he'll give you his anfwer.

Enter Sir Tunbelly *and his Servants.*

Sir Tun. My moft noble Lord, I crave your pardon for making your honour wait fo long ; but my orders to my fervants have been to admit nobody without my know-ledge, for fear of fome attempt upon my daughter, the times being full of plots and roguery.

Lord Fop. Much caution, I muft confefs, is a fign of great wifdom. But, ftap my vitals, I have got a cold enough to deftroy a porter——He, hem——

Sir Tun. I am very forry for it, indeed, my Lord ; but if your lordfhip pleafe to walk in, we'll help you to fome brown fugar-candy. My Lord, I'll fhew you the way.

Lord Fop. Sir, I follow with pleafure.   [*Exeunt.*
[*As Lord* Foppington's *Servants go to follow him in, they clap the door againft* La Verole.

Servants. [*Within.*] Nay, hold you me there, Sir.

' *La Ver.* Jernie, qu'eft ce que veut dire ça ?'

Sir Tun. [*Within.*] Fire, porter.

' *La Ver.* Ah, je fuis mort'— [*The Servants all run off.*

' *Port.* Not one foldier left, by the mafs.'

SCENE *changes into a Hall.*

Enter Sir Tunbelly, *the* Chaplain *and* Servants, *with* Lord Foppington *difarmed.*

Sir Tun. Come, bring him along, bring him along.

Lord Fop. What the pax do you mean, gentlemen ? Is it fair-time, that you are all drunk before dinner ?

Sir Tun. Drunk, firrah ! Here's an impudent rogue for you. Drunk or fober, bully, I'm a juftice of the peace, and know how to deal with ftrollers.

Lord Fop. Strollers !

Sir Tun. Ay, ſtrollers. Come, give an account of your-ſelf. What's your name ? Where do you live ? Do you pay ſcot and lot ? Are you a Williamite, or a Jacobite ? Come——

Lord Fop. And why doſt thou aſk me ſo many imper-tinent queſtions ?

Sir Tun. Becauſe I'll make you anſwer them before I have done with you, you raſcal you.

Lord Fop. Before Gad, all the anſwer I can make thee to them is, that thou art a very extraordinary old fellow, ſtap my vitals.

Sir Tun. Nay, if you are for joking with deputy lieu-tenants, we know how to deal with you. Here, draw a warrant for him immediately.

Lord Fop. A warrant !——What the devil is it thou would be at, old gentleman ?

Sir Tun. I would be at you, ſirrah, (if my hands were not tied as a magiſtrate) and with theſe two double fiſts, beat your teeth down your throat, you dog you.

Lord Fop. And why wouldſt thou ſpoil my face at that rate ?

Sir Tun. For your deſign to rob me of my daughter, villain.

Lord Fop. Rab thee of thy daughter !—Now do I be-gin to believe I'm a-bed and aſleep, and that all this is but a dream—If it be, it will be an agreeable ſurpriſe enough, to waken by and by, and, inſtead of the imperti-nent company of a naſty country juſtice, find myſelf, per-haps, in the arms of a woman of quality—[*To* Sir Tun.] Pr'ythee, old father, wilt thou give me leave to aſk thee one queſtion ?

Sir Tun. I can't tell whether I will or not, till I know what it is.

Lord Fop. Why, then, it is, whether thou didſt not write to my Lord Foppington, to come down and marry thy daughter ?

Sir Tun. Yes, marry, did I ; and my Lord Foppington is come down, and ſhall marry my daughter before ſhe's a day older.

Lord Fop. Now give me thy hand, dear dad ; I thought we ſhould underſtand one another at laſt.

Sir Tun. This fellow's mad—Here, bind him hand and foot.   [*They bind him down.*

Lord Fop. Nay, pr'ythee, knight, leave fooling; thy jeft begins to grow dull.

Sir Tun. Bind him, I fay; he's mad——Bread and water, a dark room, and a whip, may bring him to his fenfes again.

Lord Fop. [*Afide.*] 'Egad, if I don't waken quickly, by all that I can fee, this is like to prove one of the moft impertinent dreams that ever I dreamt in my life.

    Enter Mifs *and* Nurfe.

Mifs. [*Going up to him.*] Is this he that would have run away with me? Fough, how he ftinks of fweets!—Pray, father, let him be dragged through the horfe-pond.

Lord Fop. [*Afide.*] This muft be my wife, by her natural inclination to her hufband.

Mifs. Pray, father, what do you intend to do with him? Hang him?

Sir Tun. That a leaft, child.

Nurfe. Ay, and it's e'en too good for him, too.

Lord Fop. [*Afide.*] *Madame la governante*, I prefume. Hitherto, this appears to me to be one of the moft extraordinary families that ever man of quality matched into.

Sir Tun. What's become of my Lord, daughter?

Mifs. He's juft coming, Sir.

Lord Fop. [*Afide.*] My Lord——What does he mean by that, now?

    Enter Young Fafhion *and* Lory.

[*Seeing him.*] Stap my vitals, Tam, now the dream's out.

Y. Fafh. Is this the fellow, Sir, that defigned to trick me of your daughter?

Sir Tun. This is he my Lord; how do you like him? Is not he a pretty fellow to get a fortune?

Y. Fafh. I find, by his drefs, he thought your daughter might be taken with a beau.

Mifs. Oh, Gemini! is this a beau? Let me fee him again—Ha! I find a beau is no fuch ugly thing neither.

Y. Fafh. 'Egad, fhe'll be in love with him prefently; I'll e'en have him fent away to gaol—[*To* Lord Fop.] Sir, tho' your underftanding fhews you a perfon of no extraordinary modefty, I fuppofe you han't confidence enough to expect much favour from me.

             Lord

3

Lord Fop. Strike me dumb, Tam, thou art a very impudent fellow.

Nurſe. Look, if the varlet has not the frontery to call his lordſhip plain Thomas.

' *Bull.* The buſineſs is, he would feign himſelf mad, ' to avoid going to gaol.

' *Lord Fop.* [*Aſide.*] That muſt be the chaplain, by ' his unfolding of myſteries.'

Sir Tun. Come, is the warrant writ?

Cler. Yes, Sir?

Sir Tun. Give me the pen, I'll ſign it—So, now, conſtable, away with him.

Lord Fop. Hold one moment, pray, gentlemen——My Lord Foppington, ſhall I beg one word with your Lordſhip?

Nurſe. Oh, ho! is it my Lord with him now? See how afflictions will humble folks.

Miſs. Pray, my Lord, don't let him whiſper too cloſe, leſt he bite your ear off.

Lord Fop. I am not altogether ſo hungry as your Ladyſhip is pleaſed to imagine—[*To* Y. Faſh.] Look you, Tam, I am ſenſible I have not been ſo kind to you as I ought; but I hope you'll forgive what's paſt, and accept of the five thauſand paunds I offer : thou may'ſt live in extreme ſplendor with it, ſtap my vitals.

Y. Faſh. It's a much eaſier matter to prevent a diſeaſe, than to cure it ; a quarter of that ſum would have ſecured your miſtreſs; twice as much won't redeem her.

[*Leaving him.*

Sir Tun. Well, what ſays he?

Y. Faſh. Only the raſcal offered me a bribe to let him go.

Sir Tun. Ay, he ſhall go, with a pox to him. Lead on, conſtable.

Lord Fop. One word more, and I have done.

Sir Tun. Before gad, thou art an impudent fellow, to trouble the court at this rate, after thou art condemned. But ſpeak, once for all.

Lord Fop. Why, then, once for all ; I have, at laſt, luckily called to mind, that there is a gentleman of this country, who, I believe, cannot live far from this place, if he were here, would ſatisfy you I am Navelty, Baron of of Foppington, with five thaufand paunds a year, and that fellow there, a rafcal, not worth a groat.

Sir Tun. Very well ; now who is this honeft gentleman you are fo well acquainted with?—— [*To* Y. Fafh.] Come, Sir, we fhall hamper him.

Lord Fop. 'Tis Sir John Friendly.

Sir Tun. So—he lives within half a mile, and came down into the country but laft night. This bold-faced fellow thought he had been at London ftill, and fo quoted him ; now we fhall difplay him in his colours ; I'll fend for Sir John immediately. Here, fellow, away prefently, and defire my neighbour he'll do me the favour to ftep over, upon an extraordinary occafion ; and, in the mean while, you had beft fecure this fharper in the gate-houfe.

Conft. An't pleafe your worfhip, he may chance to give us the flip thence. If I were worthy to advife, I think the dog-kennel's a furer place.

Sir Tun. With all my heart, any where.

Lord Fop. Nay, for Heaven's fake, Sir, do me the favour to put me in a clean room, that I mayn't daub my cloaths.

Sir Tun. Oh, when you have married my daughter, her eftate will afford you new ones. Away with him.

Lord Fop. A dirty country juftice is a barbarous magiftrate, ftap my vitals.

[*Exit Conftable with* **Lord** Foppington.

Y. Fafh. [*Afide.*] 'Egad, I muft prevent this knight's coming, or the houfe will foon grow too hot to hold me— [*To* Sir Tun.] Sir, I fancy 'tis not worth while to trouble Sir John upon this impertinent fellow's defire. I ll fend and call the meffenger back.

Sir Tun. Nay, with all my heart : for, to be fure, he thought he was far enough off, or the rogue would never have named him.

Enter Servant.

Serv. Sir, I met Sir John juft alighting at the gate ; he's come to wait upon you.

Sir Tun. Nay, then it happens as one could wifh.

Y. Fafh. [*Afide.*] The devil it does ! Lory, you fee how things are ; here will be a difcovery prefently, and we fhall have our brains beat out ; for my brother will be fure to fwear he don't know me : therefore, run into the ftable, take the two firft horfes you can light on, I'll flip out at the back-door, and we'll away immediately.

Lor. What, and leave your Lady, Sir ?

Y. Fafh. There's no danger in that, as long as I have taken poffeffion ; I fhall know how to treat with them well enough, if once I am out of their reach. Away ; I'll fteal after thee.

[*Exit* Lory ; *his mafter follows him out at one door, while* Sir *John enters at the other.*

Sir Tun. Sir John, you are the welcomeft man alive ; I had juft fent a meffenger to defire you'd ftep over, upon a very extraordinary occafion—We are all in arms here.

' *Sir John.* How fo ?

' *Sir Tun.* Why, you muft know, a finical fort of a taw-
' dry fellow here, (I don't know what the devil he is, not
' I) hearing, I fuppofe, that the match was concluded be-
' tweed my Lord Foppington and my girl, Hoyden, comes
' impudently to the gate, and, with a whole pack of rogues
' in liveries, would have paffed upon me for his Lordfhip.
' But what does I ? I comes up to him boldly, at the
' head of his guards, takes him by the throat, ftrikes up
' his heels, binds him hand and foot, difpatches a war-
' rant, and commits him prifoner to the dog-kennel.

' *Sir John.* So—But how do you know but this was
' my Lord ? For I was told he fet out from London the
' day before me, with a very fine retinue, and intended
' to come directly hither.

' *Sir Tun.* Why, now to fhew you how many lies people
' raife in that damn'd town, he came two nights ago, poft,
' with only one fervant, and is now in the houfe with
' me. But you don't know the cream of the jeft yet ;
' this fame rogue, (that lies yonder neck and heels among
' the hounds) thinking you were out of the country,
' quotes you for his acquaintance, and faid, if you were
' here, you'd juftify him to be Lord Foppington, and I
' know not what.'

Sir John. Your fervants told me the bufinefs ; and that the impofter quotes me for his acquaintance. Pray, let me fee him.

Sir Tun. Ay, that you fhall, prefently—Here, fetch the prifoner.   [*Exit Servant.*

' *Sir*

' *Sir Tun.* He was here juſt now ; ſee for him,' Doctor, tell my Lord, Sir John Friendly is here to wait upon
him.   [*Exit Chaplain.*

' *Sir John.* I hope, Sir Tunbelly, the young lady is
' not married yet.

' *Sir Tun.* No, things won't be ready this week ; but
' why do you ſay, you hope ſhe is not married ?

' *Sir John.* Some fooliſh fancies only ; perhaps I'm
' miſtaken.'

Re-enter Chaplain.

Bull Sir, his Lordſhip is juſt rid out to take the air.

Sir Tun. To take the air ! Is that his London breeding, to go to take the air, when gentlemen come to viſit
him.

' *Sir John.* 'Tis poſſible he might want it, he might
' not be well, ſome ſudden qualm perhaps.'

Enter Conſtable, &c. with Lord Foppington.

Lord Fop. Stap my vitals, I'll have ſatisfaction.

Sir John. [*Running to him.*] My dear Lord Foppington !

Lord Fop. Dear Friendly, thou art come in the critical minute, ſtrike me dumb.

Sir John. Why, I little thought to have found you in
fetters.

Lord Fop. Why truly the world muſt do me the juſtice to confeſs, I do uſe to appear a little more *degagé :*
but this old gentleman, not liking the freedom of my
air, has been pleaſed to ſkewer down my arms like a
rabbit.

Sir Tun. Is it then poſſible that this ſhould be the true
Lord Foppington at laſt ?

Lord Fop. Why, what do you ſee in his face to make
you doubt of it ? Sir, without preſuming to have any extraordinary opinion of my figure, give me leave to tell
you, if you had ſeen as many Lords as I have done, you
would not think it impoſſible a perſon of a worſe *taille*
than mine, might be a modern man of quality.

Sir Tun. Unbind him, ſlaves : my Lord, I'm ſtruck
dumb, I can only beg pardon by ſigns ; but if a ſacrifice will appeaſe you, you ſhall have it. Here, purſue
this Tartar, bring him back———Away, I ſay, a dog.
Oons———I'll cut off his ears and his tail, I'll draw out

76 **T H E R E L A P S E.**

all his teeth, pull his ſkin over his head——and——
what ſhall I do more?

Sir John. He does indeed deſerve to be made an example of.

Lord Fop. He does deſerve to be *chartré,* ſtap my vitals.

Sir Tun. May I then hope I have your honour's pardon?

Lord Fop. Sir, we courtiers do nothing without a
bribe; that fair young lady might do miracles.

Sir Tun. Hoyden, come hither, Hoyden.

Lord Fop. Hoyden is her name, Sir?

Sir Tun. Yes, my Lord.

Lord Fop. The prettieſt name for a ſong I ever heard.

Sir Tun. My Lord——here's my girl, ſhe's yours, ſhe
has a wholeſome body, and a virtuous mind: ſhe's a
woman complete, both in fleſh and in ſpirit; ſhe has a
bag of milled crowns, as ſcarce as they are, and fifteen
hundred a year ſtitched faſt to her tail: ſo go thy ways,
Hoyden.

Lord Fop. Sir, I do receive her like a gentleman.

Sir Tun. Then I'm a happy man, and if your Lordſhip will give me leave, I will, like a good Chriſtian at
Chriſtmas, be very drunk by way of thankſgiving. Come,
my noble peer, I believe dinner's ready; if your honour pleaſes to follow me, I'll lead you on to the attack
of a veniſon paſty.   [*Exit Sir* Tun.

Lord Fop. Sir, I wait upon you. Will your Ladyſhip
do me the favour of your little finger, Madam?

Miſs. My Lord, I'll follow you preſently. I have a
little buſineſs with my nurſe.

Lord Fop. Your Ladyſhip's moſt humble ſervant:
come, Sir John, the ladies have *des affaires.*

                    [*Exeunt Lord* Fop. *and Sir* John.

Miſs. So, nurſe, we are finely brought to bed: what
ſhall we do now?

Nurſe. Ah, dear Miſs, we are all undone. ' Mr. Bull,
' you were uſed to help a woman to a remedy.' [*Crying.*

' *Bull.* A lack a-day, but it's paſt my ſkill now, I can
' do nothing.

' *Nurſe.* Who would have thought that ever your in-
' vention ſhould have been drained ſo dry?'

Miſs. Well, I have often thought old folks fools, and
                                        now

now I'm sure they are so: I have found a way myself to secure us all.

Nurse. Dear lady, what's that?

Miss. Why, if you two will be sure to hold your tongues, and not say a word of what's past, I'll e'en marry this lord too.

Nurse. What! two husbands, my dear?

Miss. Why you had three, good nurse, you may hold your tongue.

Nurse. Ay, but not altogether, sweet child.

Miss. Psha! if you had, you'd ne'er a thought much on't.

' *Nurse.* Oh, but 'tis a sin——Sweeting.

' *Bull.* Nay, that's my business to speak to, nurse: I
' do confess, to take two husbands for the satisfaction of
' the flesh, is to commit the sin of exorbitancy; but to
' do it for the peace of the spirit, is no more than to be
' drunk by way of physic: besides, to prevent a parent's
' wrath, is to avoid the sin of disobedience; for when
' the parent's angry, the child is froward. So that upon
' the whole matter, I do think, though Miss should mar-
' ry again, she may be saved.

' *Miss.*' I-cod, and I will marry again then, and so
there is an end of the story.   [*Exeunt.*

*SCENE, Berinthia's *Apartment.*

Enter her Maid, passing the Stage, followed by Worthy.

Wor. Hem, Mrs. Abigail, is your mistress to be spoken with?

Ab. By you, Sir, I believe she may.

Wor. Why, 'tis by me I would have her spoken with.

Ab. I'll acquaint her, Sir.   [*Exit* Abigail.

Wor. [*Alone.*] One lift more I must persuade her to give
me, and then I'm mounted. ' Well, a young bawd, and
' a handsome one for my money, 'tis they do the execu-
' tion; I'll never go to an old one, but when I have oc-
' casion for a witch. Lewdness looks heavenly to a wo-
' man, when an angel appears in its cause; but when
' a hag is advocate, she thinks it comes from the devil.

---

* In the original, this is the second scene in the Fifth Act.

' An

'An old woman has fomething fo terrible in her looks,
'that whilft fhe is perfuading your miftrefs to forget fhe
'has a foul, fhe ftares hell and damnation full in her
'face.'

Enter Berinthia.

Ber. Well, Sir, what news bring you?

Wor. No news, Madam, there's a woman going to cuckold her hufband.

Ber. Amanda?

Wor. I hope fo.

Ber. Speed her well.

Wor. Ay, but there muft be a more than a 'God'-fpeed, or your charity won't be worth a farthing.

Ber. Why, han't I done enough already?

Wor. Not quite.

Ber. What's the matter?

Wor. The lady has a fcruple ftill, which you muft remove.

Ber. What's that?

Wor. Her virtue——fhe fays.

Ber. And do you believe her?

Wor. No, but I believe it's what fhe takes for her virtue; it's fome relics of lawful love! She is not yet fully fatisfied her hufband has got another miftrefs, which, unlefs I can convince her of, I have opened the trenches in vain; for the breach muft be wider, before I dare ftorm the town.

Ber. And fo I'm to be your engineer?

Wor. I'm fure you know beft how to manage the battery.

Ber. What think you of fpringing a mine? I have a thought juft now come into my head, how to blow her up at once.

Wor. That would be a thought indeed.

Ber. Faith, I'll do't, and thus the execution of it fhall be. We are all invited to my Lord Foppington's to-night to fupper; 'he's come to town with his bride, 'and gives a ball with an entertainment of mufic.' Now you muft know, my undoer here, Lovelefs, fays, he muft needs meet me about fome private bufinefs (I don't know what 'tis) before we go to the company. To which end, he has told his wife one lie, and I have told her another.

But

But to make her amends, I'll go immediately, and tell her a folemn truth.

Wor. What's that?

Ber. Why, I'll tell her, that to my certain knowledge her hufband has a rendezvous with his miftrefs this afternoon : and that, if fhe'll give me her word, fhe will be fatisfied with the difcovery, without making any violent inquiry after the woman, I'll direct her to a place where fhe fhall fee them meet——Now, friend, this, I fancy, may help you to a critical minute. For home fhe muft go again to drefs. You, with your good breeding, come to wait upon us to the ball, find her all alone, her fpirit enflamed againft her hufband for his treafon, and her flefh in a heat from fome contemplations upon the treachery, her blood on a fire, her confcience in ice ; a lover to draw, and the devil to drive ———Ah, poor Amanda !

Wor. [*Kneeling.*] Thou angel of light, let me fall down and adore thee !

Ber. Thou minifter of darknefs, get up again, for I hate to fee the devil at his devotions.

Wor. Well, my incomparable Berinthia———How fhall I requite you———

Ber. Oh, ne'er trouble yourfelf about that : virtue is its own reward. There's a pleafure in doing good, which fufficiently pays itfelf. Adieu.

Wor. Farewel, thou beft of women.

[*Exeunt feveral ways.*

Enter Amanda, *meeting* Berinthia.

Am. Who was that went from you ?

Ber. A friend of yours.

Am. What does he want ?

Ber. Something you might fpare him, and be ne'er the poorer.

Am. I can fpare him nothing but my friendfhip ; my love already's all difpofed of : though, I confefs, to one ungrateful to my bounty.

Ber. Why there's the myftery ! You have been fo bountiful, you have cloyed him. ' Fond wives do by ' their hufbands, as barren wives do by their lap-dogs ; ' cram them with fweetmeats till they fpoil their fto- ' machs.'

Am.

Am. Alas! Had you but feen how paffionately fond
he has been fince our laft reconciliation, you would have
thought it were impoffible he ever fhould have breathed
an hour without me.

Ber. Ay, but there you thought wrong again, Amanda; ' you fhould confider, that in matters of love men's
' eyes are always bigger than their bellies. They have
' violent appetites, 'tis true, but they have foon dined.'

Am. Well; there's nothing upon earth aftonifhes me
more than men's inconftancy.

Ber. Now there's nothing upon earth aftonifhes me
lefs, when I confider what they and we are compofed of:
for nature has made them children, and us babies. Now,
Amanda, how we ufed our babies, you may remember.
We were mad to have them, as foon as we faw them;
kiffed them to pieces, as foon as we got them; then
pulled off their clothes, faw them naked, and fo threw
them away.

Am. But do you think all men are of this temper?

Ber. All but one.

Am. Who's that?

Ber. Worthy.

Am. Why, he's weary of his wife too, you fee.

Ber. Ay, that's no proof.

Am. What can be a greater?

Ber. Being weary of his miftrefs.

Am. Don't you think 'twere poffible he might give
you that too?

Ber. Perhaps he might, if he were my gallant; not
if he were yours.

Am. Why do you think he fhould be more conftant
to me, than he would to you? I'm fure I'm not fo handfome.

Ber. Kiffing goes by favour: he likes you beft.

' *Am.* Suppofe he does; that's no demonftration he
' would be conftant to me.

' *Ber.* No, that I'll grant you: but there are other
' reafons to expect it; for you muft know after all,
' Amanda, the inconftancy we commonly fee in men of
' brains, does not fo much proceed from the uncertainty
' of their temper, as from the misfortunes of their love.
' A man fees, perhaps, an hundred women he likes well
                                            ' enough

'   enough for an intrigue, and away; but possibly, thro'
'   the whole course of his life, does not find above one,
'   who is exactly what he could wish her: now her, 'tis a
'   thousand to one, he never gets. Either she is not to be
'   had at all (though that seldom happens, you'll say) or
'   he wants those opportunities that are necessary to gain
'   her; either she likes somebody else much better than
'   him, or uses him like a dog, because he likes nobody
'   so well as her. Still something or other Fate claps in
'   the way between them and the woman they are capa-
'   ble of being fond of: and this makes them wander
'   about from mistress to mistress, like a pilgrim from
'   town to town, who every night must have a fresh lodg-
'   ing, and is in haste to be gone in the morning.'

Am. 'Tis possible there may be something in what you
say; but what do you infer from it, as to the man we
were talking of?

Ber. Why, I infer, that you being the woman in the
world, the most to his humour, 'tis not likely he would
quit you for one that is less.

Am. That is not to be depended upon, for you see Mr.
Loveless does so.

Ber. What does Mr. Loveless do?

Am. Why, he runs after something for variety, I'm
sure he does not like so well as he does me.

Ber. That's more than you know, Madam.

Am. No, Im sure on't: I am not very vain, Berinthia; and yet I'll lay my life, if I could look into his
heart, he thinks I deserve to be preferred to a thousand
of her.

Ber. Don't be too positive in that neither: a million
to one, but she has the same opinion of you. What
would you give to see her?

Am. Hang her, a dirty trull; though I really believe
she's so ugly, she'd cure me of my jealousy.

Ber. All the men of sense about town say she's handsome.

Am. They are as often out in those things as any
people.

Ber. Then I'll give you farther proof——all the women about town say, she's a fool: now I hope you are
convinced?

Am. Whate'er she be, I'm satisfied he does not like her
well

well enough to beftow any thing more than a little outward gallantry upon her.

Ber. Outward gallantry!—[*Afide.*] I can't bear this.
[*To Aman.*] Don't you think fhe's a woman to be fobbed
off fo. Come, I'm too much your friend, to fuffer you
fhould be thus grofsly impofed upon, by a man who does
not deferve the leaft part about you, unlefs he knew how
to fet a greater value upon it. Therefore, in one word,
to my certain knowledge, he is to meet her now, within
a quarter of an hour, ' fomewhere about that Babylon of
' wickednefs, Whitehall.' And if you'll give me your
word that you'll be content with feeing her without pulling her headclothes off, I'll ftep immediately to the perfon from whom I have my intelligence, and fend you
word whereabouts you may ftand to fee them meet. ' My
' friend and I'll watch them from another place, and
' dodge them to their private lodging: but don't you
' offer to follow them, left you do it aukwardly, and fpoil
' all. I'll come home to you again, as foon as I have
' earthed them, and give you an account in what corner
' of the houfe the fcene of their lewdnefs lies.'

Am. If you can do this, Berinthia, he's a villain.

Ber. I can't help that, men will be fo.

Am. Well! I'll follow your directions; for I fhall
never reft till I know the werft of this matter.

Ber. Pray, go immediately, and get yourfelf ready
then. Put on fome of your woman's clothes, a great
fcarf and a mafk, and you fhall prefently receive orders.
' [*Calls within.*] Here, who's there? get me a chair
' quickly.

' *Serv.* There are chairs at the door, Madam.

' *Ber.* 'Tis well, I'm coming.'

Am. But, pray, Berinthia, before you go, tell me how
I may know this filthy thing, if fhe fhould be fo forward
(as I fuppofe fhe will) to come to the rendezvous firft;
for, methinks, I would fain view her a little.

Ber. Why, fhe's about my heighth? and very well
fhaped.

Am. I thought fhe had been a little crooked.

Ber. Oh, no, fhe's as ftraight as I am. But we lofe
time; come away.

END of the FOURTH ACT.

ACT V.

SCENE, *London.*

Enter Coupler, Young Fashion, *and* Lory.

COUPLER.

' WELL, and so Sir John coming in——
' *Young F.* And so Sir John coming in, I thought
' it might be manners in me to go out, which I did, and
' getting on horseback as fast as I could, rid away as if
' the devil had been at the rear of me; what has hap-
' pened since, heaven knows.

' *Coup.* 'Egad, sirrah, I know as well as heaven.
' *Young F.* What do you know?
' *Coup.* That you are a cuckold.
' *Young F.* The devil I am! By who?
' *Coup.* By your brother.
' *Young F.* My brother! which way?
' *Coup.* The old way: he has lain with your wife.
' *Young F.* Hell and furies, what dost thou mean?
' *Coup.* I mean plainly, I speak no parable.
' *Young F.* Plainly thou dost not speak common
' sense, I cannot understand one word thou sayest.

' *Coup.* You will do soon, youngster. In short, you
' left your wife a widow, and she married again.

' *Young Fash.* It's a lie.

' *Coup.* ——I-cod, if I were a young fellow, I'd
' break your head, sirrah.

' *Young F.* Dear dad, don't be angry, for I am as mad
' as Tom of Bedlam.

' *Coup.* When I had fitted you with a wife, you should
' have kept her.

' *Young F.* But is it possible the young strumpet could
' play me such a trick?

' *Coup.* A young strumpet, Sir——can play twenty
' tricks.

' *Young F.* But, pr'ythee, instruct me a little farther;
' whence comes thy intelligence?

' *Coup.* From your brother, in this letter; there, you
' may read it.' *Now you have told me your story, I'll let
you into mine in this letter, read it.* [Young Fashion *reads.*

3   " Dear

" Dear Coupler,

" [*Pulling off his hat.*] I have only time to tell thee in three lines, or thereabouts, that here has been the devil: that rafcal, Tam, having ftole the letter thou hadft formerly writ for me to bring to Sir Tunbelly, formed a damnable defign upon my miftrefs, and was in a fair way of fuccefs when I arrived. But after having fuffered fome indignities (in which I have all daubed my embroidered coat) I put him to flight. I fent out a party of horfe after him, in hopes to have made him my prifoner, which, if I had done, I would have qualified him for the feraglio, ftap my vitals. The danger, I have thus narrowly efcaped, has made me fortify myfelf againft further attempts, by entering immediately into an affociation with the young lady, by which we engage to ftand by one another, as long as we both fhall live.   In fhort, the papers are fealed, and the contract is figned, fo the bufinefs of the lawyer is *achevé*; but I defer the divine part of the thing till I arrive at London, not being willing to confummate in any other bed but my own.

" *P. S.* 'Tis poffible I may be in the tawn as foon as this letter ; for I find the lady is fo violently in love with me, I have determined to make her happy with all the difpatch that is practicable, without difardering my coach horfes."

So here's rare work, i'faith !

Lory. 'Egad, Mifs Hoyden has laid about her bravely.

Coup. I think my country-girl has played her part, as well as if fhe had been born and bred in St. James's parifh.

Young F.——That rogue the chaplain.

Lory. And then that jade the nurfe, Sir.

Young F. And then that drunken fot, Lory, Sir; that could not keep himfelf fober to be a witnefs to the marriage.

Lory. Sir——with refpect ——I know very few drunken fots that do keep themfelves fober.

Young F. Hold your prating, firrah, or I'll break your head. Dear Coupler, what's to be done ?

Coup. Nothing's to be done till the bride and bridegroom come to town.

Young F. Bride and bridegroom; hell and furies! I can't bear you should call them so.

Coup. Why, what shall I call them, dog and cat?

Young F. Not for the world, that sounds more like man and wife than t'other.

Coup. Well, call them what you will, there's nothing to be done without them. But you have been an idle young rogue, or the girl would never have left thee.

[*Exeunt.*

Enter Amanda, *in a scarf, &c. as just returned,* ' *her wo-*
' *man following her.* *

' *Am.* Pr'ythee, what care I who has been here?

' *Wom.* Madam, 'twas my Lady Bridle, and my Lady
' Tiptoe.

' *Am.* My Lady Fiddle and my Lady Faddle. What
' dost stand troubling me with the visits of a parcel of
' impertinent women? When they are well seamed with
' the small pox, they won't be so fond of shewing their
' faces—There are more coquettes about this town——

' *Wom.* Madam, I suppose, they only came to return
' your Ladyship's visit, according to the custom of the
' world.

' *Am.* Would the world were on fire, and you in the
' middle on't. Begone; leave me.   [*Exit Woman.*'

Am. [*Alone.*] At last I am convinc'd. My eyes are
     testimonies of his falshood.
The base, ungrateful, perjur'd villain——
' Good Gods—What slippery stuff are men compos'd of?
' Sure the account of their creation's false,
' And 'twas the woman's rib that they were form'd of.'
But why am I thus angry?
This poor relapse shou'd only move my scorn.
' 'Tis true; the roving flights of his unfinish'd youth,
' Had strong excuses from the plea of nature:
' Reason had thrown the reins loose on his neck,
' And slipt him to unlimited desire.
' If therefore he went wrong, he had a claim
' To my forgiveness, and I did him right:
' But since the years of manhood rein him in,
                    H   ' And

* In the Original, this Scene precedes the Scene between *Miss*
and *Nurse.* See p. 94.

' And reafon, well digefted into thought,
' Has pointed out the courfe he ought to run ;
' If now he ftrays,
' 'Twou'd be as weak, and mean in me to pardon,
' As it has been in him t'offend. But hold !
' 'Tis an ill caufe indeed, where nothing's to be faid for't.
' My beauty poffibly is in the wain :
' Perhaps fixteen has greater charms for him :
' Yes, there's the fecret. But let him know,
' My quiver's not entirely empty'd yet ;
' I ftill have darts, and I can fhoot 'em too :
' They're not fo blunt, but they can enter ftill ;
' The want's not in my power, but in my will.
' Virtue's his friend ; or, thro' another's heart,
' I yet cou'd find the way to make his fmart.'

[*Going off*, *fhe meets* Worthy.

Ha ! he here ! Protect me, heaven, for this looks omi-
nous.

Wor. You feem difordered, Madam ; I hope there's
no misfortune happened to you ?

Am. None that will long diforder me, I hope.

Wor. Whate'er it be difturbs you, I would to Heaven
'twere in my power to bear the pain, till I were able to
remove the caufe.

Am. I hope ere long it will remove itfelf ; at leaft, I
have given it warning to be gone.

' *Wor.* Wou'd I durft afk, where 'tis the thorn tor-
' ments you ?

' Forgive me, if I grow inquifitive ;

' 'Tis only with defire to give you eafe.

' *Am.* Alas ! 'tis in a tender part. It can't be drawn
' without a world of pain : yet out it muft ; for it be-
' gins to fefter in my heart.'

Wor. If 'tis the fting of unrequited love, remove it
inftantly : I have a balm will quickly heal the wound.

Am. You'd find the undertaking difficult : the furgeon, who already has attempted it, has much tormented
me.

Wor. I'll aid him with a gentler hand——if you will
give me leave.

Am. How foft foe'er the hand may be, there ftill is
terror in the operation.

Wor.

Wor. Some few preparatives would make it eafy, could I perfuade you to apply 'em. Make home reflections, Madam, on your flighted love : weigh well the ftrength and beauty of your charms : rouze up that fpirit women ought to bear, ' and flight your god, if he neglects his ' angel.' With arms of ice receive h's cold embraces, and keep your fire for thofe who come in flames. Behold a burning lover at your feet, his fever raging in his veins. ' See how he trembles, how he pants ! See how ' he glows, how he confumes ! ' Extend the arms of mercy to his aid : his zeal may give him title to your pity, altho' his merit cannot claim your love.

Am. Of all my feeble fex, fure I muft be the weakeft, fhould I again prefume to think on love. [*Sighing.*] ――Alas ! my heart has been too roughly treated.

Wor. 'Twill find the greater blifs in fofter ufage.

Am. But where's that ufage to be found ?

Wor. 'Tis here, within this faithful breaft ; which, if you doubt, I'll rip it up before your eyes ; lay all its fecrets open to your view ; and then you'll fee 'twas found.

Am. With juft fuch honeft words as thefe, the worft of men deceiv'd me.

Wor. He therefore merits all revenge can do : his fault is fuch, the extent and ftretch of vengeance cannot reach it. O make me but your inftrument of juftice ; you'll find me execute it with fuch zeal, as fhall convince you I abhor the crime.

Am. The rigour of an executioner, has more the face of cruelty than juftice : and he who puts the cord about the wretch's neck, is feldom know to exceed him in his morals.

Wor. What proof then can I give you of my truth ?

Am. There is on earth but one.

Wor. And is that in my power ?

Am. It is ; and one that would fo thoroughly convince me, I fhould be apt to rate your heart fo high, I poffibly might purchafe't with a part of mine.

Wor. ' Then, Heav'n, thou art my friend, and ' I am bleft ; ' for if 'tis in my power, my will I'm fure will ' reach it.' No matter what the terms may be, when fuch a recompence is offered. O tell me quickly what

H 2   this

this proof muſt be ? What is it will convince you of my love ?

Am. I ſhall believe you love me as you ought, if from this moment, you forbear to aſk whatever is unfit for me to grant————You pauſe upon it, Sir————I doubt on ſuch hard terms, a woman's heart is ſcarcely worth the having.

Wor. A heart like yours, on any terms is worth it; 'twas not on that I pauſed : but I was thinking [*Drawing nearer to her.*] whether ſome things there may not be, which women cannot grant without a bluſh, and yet which men may take without offence. [*Taking her hand.*] Your hand I fancy may be of the number : O pardon me, if I commit a rape upon it, [*Kiſſing it eagerly.*] and thus devour it with my kiſſes.

Am. O heavens ! let me go.

Wor. Never, whilſt I have ſtrength to hold you here. [*Forcing her.*] My life, my ſoul, my goddeſs—' O for-
' give me !

' *Am.* O whither am I going? Help, Heaven, or I
' am loſt.

' *Wor.* Stand neuter, gods, this once I do invoke
' you.

' *Am.* Then, ſave me, Virtue, and the glory's thine.

' *Wor.* Nay, never ſtrive.

' *Am.* I will ; and conquer too. My forces ral'y
' bravely to my aid, [*Breaking from him.*] and thus I
' gain the day.

Wor. ' Then mine as bravely double their attack ;
' [*Seizing her again.*] and thus I wreſt it from you.'
Nay, ſtruggle not ; for all's in vain : or death or victo-
ry ; I am determined.

Am. And ſo am I. [*Ruſhing from him.*] Now keep your diſtance, or we part for ever.

Wor. [*Offering again.*] For Heaven's ſake——

Am. [*Going.*] Nay then, farewel.

Wor. [*Kneeling, and holding by her clothes.*] O ſtay, and ſee the magic force of love: behold this raging lion at your feet, ſtruck dead with fear, and tame as charms can make him. What muſt I do to be forgiven by you ?

Am. Repent, and never more offend.

' *Wor.*

' *Wor.* Repentance for paft crimes, is juft and eafy ;
' but fin no more's a tafk too hard for mortals.

' *Am.* Yet thofe who hope for Heaven, muft ufe their
' beft endeavours to perform it.

' *Wor.* Endeavours we may ufe, but flefh and blood
' are got in t'other fcale ; and they are pond'rous
' things.

Am. ' Whate'er they are, there is a weight in refolu-
' tion fufficient for their balance. The foul, I do con-
' fefs, is ufually fo carelefs of its charge, fo foft, and fo
' indulgent to defire, it leaves the reins in the wild hand
' of Nature, who, like a Phaeton, drives the fiery cha-
' riot, and fets the world on flame. Yet ftill the fove-
' reignty is in the mind, whene'er it pleafes to exert its
' force. Perhaps you may not think it worth your
' while, to take fuch mighty pains for my efteem ; but
' that I leave to you.

' You fee the price I fet upon my heart,
' Perhaps 'tis dear : but fpite of all you art,
' You'll find on cheaper terms, we ne'er fhall part.'

[*Exit.*

Wor. Sure there's divinity about her ; and fhe's dif-
penfed fome portion on't to me. For what but now was
the wild flame of love, or (to diffect that fpacious term)
the vile, the grofs defires of flefh and blood, is in a moment turned to adoration. ' The coarfer appetite of na-
' ture's gone, and 'tis methinks, the food of angels I re-
' quire : how long this influence may laft, Heaven
' knows ; but in this moment of my purity, I could on
' her own terms accept her heart. Yes, lovely woman,
' I can accept it. For now 'tis doubly worth my care.
' Your charms are much increafed, fince thus adorned.'
When truth's extorted from us, then we own the robe
of virtue is a graceful habit.

Could women but our fecret counfels fcan,
Could they but reach the deep referves of man,
They'd wear it on, that that of love might laft ;
For when they throw off one, we foon the other caft.
Their fympathy is fuch——
The fate of one, the other fcarce can fly,
They live together; and together die.   [*Exit.*

Enter

Enter Young Fashion, '*meeting* Lory.

' *Y. Fash.* Well, will the doctor come?

' *Lory.* Sir, I sent a porter to him as you ordered me.
' He found him with a pipe of tobacco and a great tan-
' kard of ale, which, he said, he would dispatch while I
' could tell three, and be here.

' *Y. Fash.* He does not suspect 'twas I that sent for
' him.

' *Lory.* Not a jot, Sir; he divines as little for himself,
' as he does for other folks.

' *Y. Fash.* Will he bring nurse with him?

' *Lory.* Yes.

' *Y. Fash.* That's well; where's Coupler?

' *Lory.* He's half way up the stairs taking breath; he
' must play his bellows a little, before he can get to the
' top.

Enter Coupler.

' *Y. Fash.* O, here he is. Well, old Phthisic, the
' doctor's coming.

' *Coup.* Would the pox had the doctor——I'm quite
' out of wind. [*To* Lory.] Set me a chair, sirrah. Ah——
' [*Sits down.*] [*To* Y. Fash.] Why the plague can't not
' thou lodge upon the ground-floor?

' *Y. Fash.* Because I love to lie as near Heaven as I
' can.

' *Coup.* Pr'ythee, let Heaven alone; ne'er affect tend-
' ing that way: thy center's downwards.

' *Y. Fash.* That's impossible. I have too much ill-
' luck in this world to be damned in the next.

' *Coup.* Thou art out in thy logic. Thy major is
' true, but thy minor is false; for thou art the luckiest
' fellow in the universe.

' *Y. Fash.* Make out that.

' *Coup.* I'll do't: last night the devil ran away with
' the parson of Fat Goose living.

' *Y. Fash.* If he had run away with the parish too,
' what's that to me?

' *Coup.* I'll tell thee what it's to thee. This living is
' worth five hundred pounds a-year, and the presentation
' of it is thine, if thou can't prove thyself a lawful hus-
' band to Miss Hoyden.

' *Y. Fash.*

' *Y. Fa/h.* Say'ft thou fo, my protector ! then 'Egad
' I fhall have a brace of evidences here prefently.

' *Coup.* The nurfe and the doctor ?

' *Y. Fa/h.* The fame : the devil himfelf won't have
' intereft enough to make them withftand it.

' *Coup.* That we fhall fee prefently.—Here they come.
Enter Nurfe *and* Chaplain ; ' *they ftart back, feeing Young*
Fafhion.

' *Nurfe.* Ah goodnefs, Roger, we are betrayed.

' *Y. Fa/h.* [*Laying hold on them.*] Nay, nay, ne'er
' flinch for the matter ; for I have you fafe. Come to
' your trials immediately ; I have no time to give you
' copies of your indictment. There fits your judge.—
' [*Both kneeling.*] Pray, Sir, have compaffion on us.

' *Nurfe.* I hope, Sir, my years will move your pity ;
' I am an aged woman.

' *Coup.* That is a moving argument indeed. [*To* Bull.]
' Are not you a rogue of fanctity ?

' *Bull.* Sir, with refpect to my function, I do wear a
' gown. I hope, Sir, my character will be confidered :
' I am Heaven's ambaffador.

' *Coup.* Did not you marry this vigorous young fellow
' to a plump young buxom wench ?

' *Nurfe.* [*To* Bull.] Don't confefs, Roger, unlefs you
' are hard put to it indeed.

' *Coup.* Come, out with't——Now is he chewing the
' cud of his roguery, and grinding a lie between his
' teeth.

' *Bull.* Sir——I cannot pofitively fay——I fay, Sir
' ——pofitively I cannot fay——

' *Coup.* Come, no equivocation, no Roman turns up-
' on us. Confider thou ftand'ft upon Proteftant ground,
' which will flip from under thee, like a Tyburn cart ;
' for in this country, we have always ten hangmen for
' one Jefuit.

' *Bull.* [*To* Y. Fafh.] Pray, Sir, then will you but per-
' mit me to fpeak one word in private with nurfe?

' *Y. Fa/h.* Thou art always for doing fomething in
' private with nurfe.

' *Coup.* But pray let his betters be ferv'd before him
' for once. I would do fomething in private with her
' myfelf. Lory, take care of this reverend gown-man
' in

‘ in the next room a little. Retire, prieſt. [*Exit* Lory
‘ *with* Bull.] Now, virgin, I muſt put the matter home
‘ to you a little: do you think it might not be poſſible to
‘ make you ſpeak truth?

‘ *Nurſe.* Alas! Sir, I don’t know what you mean by
‘ truth.

‘ *Coup.* Nay, ’tis poſſible thou mayeſt be a ſtranger
‘ to it.

‘ *Υ. Faſh.* Come, nurſe, you and I were better friends
‘ when we ſaw one another laſt; and I ſtill believe you
‘ you are a very good woman in the bottom. I did de-
‘ ceive you and your young lady, ’tis true, but I always
‘ deſigned to make a very good huſband to her, and to be
‘ a very good friend to you. And ’tis poſſible in the
‘ end, ſhe might have found herſelf happier, and you
‘ richer, than ever my brother will make you.

‘ *Nurſe.* Brother! Why is your worſhip then his
‘ Lordſhip’s brother?

‘ *Υ. Faſh.* I am; which you ſhould have known, if I
‘ durſt have ſtaid to have told you; but I was forced to
‘ take horſe a little in haſte, you know.

‘ *Nurſe.* You were indeed, Sir. Poor young man,
‘ how he was bound to ſcaure for’t. Now won’t your
‘ worſhip be angry, if I confeſs the truth to you? When
‘ found you were a cheat (with reſpect be it ſpoken) I
‘ verily believed Miſs had got ſome pitiful ſkip-Jack
‘ varlet or other to her huſband, or I had ne’er let her
‘ think of marrying again.

‘ *Coup.* But where was your conſcience all this while,
‘ woman? Did not that ſtare you in the face with huge
‘ ſaucer-eyes, and a great horn upon the forehead? Did
‘ not you think you ſhould be damned for ſuch a ſin?
‘ Ha!

‘ *Υ. Faſh.* Well ſaid, divinity; preſs that home upon
‘ her.

‘ *Nurſe.* Why, in good truly, Sir, I had ſome fearful
‘ thoughts on’t, and could never be brought to conſent,
‘ till Mr. Bull ſaid it was a peckadilla, and he’d ſecure
‘ my ſoul for a tythe-pig.

‘ *Υ. Faſh.* There was a rogue for you.

‘ *Coup.* And he ſhall thrive accordingly: he ſhall
‘ have a good living. Come, honeſt nurſe, I ſee you
‘ have

' have butter in your compound ; you can melt. Some
' compaffion you can have of this handfome young fel-
' low.

' *Nurfe.* I have indeed, Sir.

Y. Fafh. ' Why then I'll tell you what you fhall do
' for me.' You know what a warm living here is fallen ;
and that it muft be in the difpofal of him who has the
difpofal of Mifs. Now if you and the doctor will agree
to prove my marriage, I'll prefent him to it, upon condition he make you his bride.

Nurfe. Now the blefling of the Lord follow your
good worfhip ' both by night and by day.' Let him be
fetched in by the ears ; I'll foon bring his nofe to the
grindftone.

Coup. [*Afide.*] Well faid, old whit-leather.   Hey ;
bring in the prifoner there.

Enter Lory *with* Bull.

' *Coup.* Come, advance, holy man : here's your duck
' does not think fit to retire with you into the chancel at
' this time ; but fhe has a propofal to make to you in the
' face of the congregation.   Come, nurfe, fpeak for
' yourfelf ; you are of age.

' *Nurfe.* Roger, are not you a wicked man, Roger, to
' fet your ftrength againft a weak woman, and perfuade
' her it was no fin to conceal Mifs's nuptials ? My con-
' fcience flies in my face for it, thou prieft of Baal ; and
' I find, by woeful experience, thy abfolution is not worth
' an old caffock : therefore I am refolved to confefs the
' truth to the whole world, though I die a beggar for it.
' But his worfhip overflows with his mercy, and his boun-
' ty : he is not only pleafed to forgive us our fins, but
' defigns thou fha't fquat thee down in Fat-goofe living
' and which is more than all, has prevailed with me to
' become the wife of thy bofom.'

Young F. All this I intend for you, doctor : what you
are to do for me, I need not tell ye.

Bull. Your worfhip's goodnefs is unfpeakable : ' yet
' there is one thing feems a point of confcience ; and
' confcience is a tender babe.   If I fhould bind myfelf,
' for the fake of this living, to marry nurfe, and main-
' tain her afterwards, I doubt it might be looked on as a
' kind of fimony.'

Coup.

Coup. ' [*Rifing up.*] If it were facrilege, the living's
' worth it : therefore,' no more words, good doctor ; but
with the [*Giving Nurfe to him.*] Parifh——here——take
the parfonage-houfe. 'Tis true, 'tis a little out of repair ; fome dilapidations there are to be made good ; the
windows are broke, the wainfcot is warped, the cielings
are peeled, and the walls are cracked ; but a little glaz-
ing, painting, whitewafh, and plaifter, will make it laft
thy time.

Bull. Well, Sir, if it muft be fo, ' I fhan't contend :
' What Providence orders,' I fubmit ' to.'

Nurfe. And fo do I, with all humility.

Coup. Why, that now was fpoke like good people :
Come, ' my turtle-doves,' let us go help this poor pigeon
to his wandering mate again ; and after inftitution and
induction, you fhall go a cooing together.   [*Exeunt.*

Enter Mifs *and* Nurfe.

Mifs. But is it fure and certain, fay you, he's my
Lord's own brother ?

Nurfe. As fure, as he's your lawful hufband.

Mifs. I'cad, if I had known that in time, I don't know
but I might have kept him : for, between you and I,
nurfe, he'd have made a hufband worth two of this I
have. But which do you think you fhould fancy moft,
nurfe ?

Nurfe. Why, truly, in my poor fancy, Madam, your
firft hufband is the prettier gentleman.

Mifs. I don't like my Lord's fhapes, nurfe.

Nurfe. Why in good truly, as a body may fay, he is
but a flam.

Mifs. What do you think now he puts me in mind of ?
Don't you remember a long, loofe, fhambling fort of a
horfe my father called Wafhy ?

Nurfe. As like as two twin-brothers.

Mifs. I'cod, I have thought fo a hundred times ; faith
I'm tired of him.

Nurfe. Indeed, Madam, I think you had e'en as good
ftand to your firft bargain.

Mifs. O but, nurfe, we han't confidered the main
thing yet. If I leave my lord, I muft leave my lady
too : and when I rattle about in the ftreets in my coach,
they'll only fay, there goes Miftrefs——Miftrefs——

Miftrefs

Miftrefs what? What's this man's name, I have married, nurfe?

Nurfe. 'Squire Fafhion.

Mifs. 'Squire Fafhion is it?——Well, 'fquire, that's better than nothing. Do you think one could not get him made a knight, nurfe?

Nurfe. I don't know but one might, Madam, when the king's in a good humour.

Mifs. I'cod, that would do rarely. For then he'd be as good a man as my father, you know.

Nurfe. By'rlady, and that's as good as the beft of 'em.

Mifs. So 'tis, faith; for then I fhall be my lady, and your ladyfhip at every word, that's all I have to care for. Ha, nurfe, but hark you me, one thing more, and then I have done. I'm afraid, if I change my hufband again, I fhan't have fo much money to throw about, nurfe.

Nurfe. Oh, enough's as good as a feaft: ' befides, Ma-
' dam, one don't know, but as much may fall to your
' fhare with the younger brother, as with the elder.' For
tho' thefe lords have a power of wealth indeed; yet as I
have heard fay, they give it all to their fluts and their
trulls, who joggle it about in their coaches, with a mur-
rain to 'em, whilft poor Madam fits fighing and wifhing,
and knotting and crying, and has not a fpare half-crown,
to buy her a Practice of Piety.

Mifs. O, but for that, don't deceive yourfelf, nurfe, for this I muft [*Snapping her fingers.*] fay for my Lord, and a——for him; he's as free as an open houfe at Chriftmas. For this very morning he told me, I fhould have two hundred a-year to buy pins. Now, nurfe, if he gives me two hundred a-year to buy pins, what do you think he'll give me to buy fine petticoats?

Nurfe. Ah, my deareft, he deceives thee foully, and he's no better than a rogue for his pains. Thefe Lon-
doners have got a gibberidge with 'em, would confound a gipfey. That which they call pin-money, is to buy their wives every thing in the verfal world, down to their very fhoe ties. ' Nay, I have heard folks fay, that fome
' ladies, if they will have gallants, as they call 'em, are
' forced to find them out of their pin-money too.'

Mifs.

Mifs. Has he ſerved me ſo, ſay ye?——Then I'll be his wife no longer, that's fixt. Look, here he comes, with all the fine folks at's heels. I'cod, nurſe, theſe London ladies will laugh till they crack again, to ſee me ſlip my collar, and run away from my huſband. But, d'ye hear, pray take care of one thing: when the buſineſs comes to break out, be ſure you get between me and my father, for you know his tricks; he'll knock me down.

Nurſe. I'll mind him, ne'er fear, Madam.

Enter Lord Foppington, Loveleſs, Worthy, Amanda,
and Berinthia.

Lord Fop. Ladies and gentlemen, you are all welcome. [*To* Lov.] Loveleſs——that's my wife; pr'ythee do me the favour to ſalute her: and do'ſt hear, [*Aſide to him.*] if thau haſt a mind ta try thy fartune, to be revenged of me, I won't take it ill, ſtap my vitals.

Lov. You need not fear, Sir, I'm too fond of my own wife, to have the leaſt inclination for yours.

[*All ſalute Mifs.*

Lord Fop. [*Aſide.*] I'd give a thouſand paund he would make love to her, that he may ſee ſhe has ſenſe enough to prefer me to him, tho' his own wife has not. [*Viewing him.*] ' He's a very beaſtly fellow, in my opinion.'

Mifs. [*Aſide.*] What a power of fine men there are in this London. He that kiſſed me firſt, is a goodly gentleman, I promiſe you. Sure thoſe wives have a rare time on't, that live here always.

Enter Sir Tunbelly, *with Muſicians, Dancers, &c.*

Sir Tun. Come, come in, good people, come in; come, tune your fiddles, tune your fiddles. [*To the hautboys.*] Bag-pipes, make ready there. Come, ſtrike up.

[*Sings.*

> For this is Hoyden's wedding day;
> And therefore we keep holy-day,
> And come to be merry.

Ha! there's my wench, i'faith: touch and take, I'll warrant her; ſhe'll breed like a tame rabbit.

Mifs. [*Aſide.*] I'cod, I think my father's gotten drunk before ſupper.

Sir

4

Sir Tun. [*To* Lov. *and* Wor.] Gentlemen, you are welcome. [*Saluting* Aman. *and* Ber.] Ladies, by your leave. Ha——they bill like turtles: udsookers, they set my old blood a-fire; I shall cuckold somebody before morning.

Lord Fop. [*To Sir* Tun.] Sir, you being master of the entertainment; will you desire the company to sit?

Sir Tun. Oons, Sir——I'm the happiest man on this side the Ganges.

Lord Fop. [*Aside.*] This is a mighty unaccountable old fellow. [*To Sir* Tun.] I said, Sir, it would be convenient to ask the company to sit.

Sir Tun. Sit——' with all my heart: come, take your 'places, ladies, take your places, gentlemen:' come, 'sit down, sit down;' a pox of ceremony, 'take your 'places.'   [*They sit, and the Mask begins.*

' DIALOGUE *between* Cupid *and* Hymen.

' CUPID.   I.

' Thou bane to my empire, thou spring of contest,
' Thou source of all discord, thou period to rest;
' Instruct me what wretches in bondage can see,
' That the aim of their life is still pointed to thee.

' HYMEN.   II.

' Instruct me, thou little impertinent god,
' From whence all thy subjects have taken the mode
' To grow fond of a change, to whatever it be,
' And I'll tell thee why those would be bound, who are
          free.

' CHORUS.

' For change, we're for change, to whatever it be,
' We are neither contented with freedom, nor thee.
     ' Constancy's an empty sound,
     ' Heaven, and earth, and all go round,
     ' All the works of nature move,
     ' And the joys of life and love
         ' Are in variety.

I   ' CUPID.

' CUPID.   III.

' Were love the reward of a pains-taking life,
' Had a hufband the art to be fond of his wife,
' Were virtue fo plenty, a wife could afford,
' Thefe very hard times, to be true to her lord,
' Some fpecious account might be given of thofe,
' Who are ty'd by the tail, to be led by the nofe.

' IV.

  But fince 'tis the fate of a man and his wife,
' To confume all their days in contention and ftrife :
' Since whatever the bounty of Heaven may create her,
  He's morally fure he fhall heartily hate her.
' I think 'twere much wifer to ramble at large,
' And the vollies of love on the head to difcharge.
'

  ' HYMEN.   V.

' Some colour of reafon thy counfel might bear,
' Could a man have no more than his wife to his fhare :
' Or were I a monarch fo cruelly juft,
' To oblige a poor wife to be true to her truft ;
' But I have not pretended, for many years paft,
' By marrying of people, to make 'em grow chafte.

' VI.

' I therefore advife thee to let me go on,
' Thou'lt find I'm the ftrength and fupport of thy
          throne ;
' For hadft thou but eyes, thou wouldft quickly perceive
          it,
    ' How fmoothly the dart
    ' Slips into the heart
    ' Of a woman that's wed,
    ' Whilft the fhivering maid
' Stands trembling, and wifhing, but dare not receive it.

' CHORUS.

  ' For change, &c.

2

The mask ended, enter Young Fashion, Coupler, *and* Bull.

Sir Tun. So, ' very fine, very fine; i'faith, this is
' something like a wedding.' Now, if supper were but
ready, I'd say a short grace; and if I had such a bedfellow
as Hoyden to-night—I'd say as short prayers ——[*Seeing
Y.* Fash.] How now, what have we got here? A ghost!
Nay, it must be so; for his flesh and blood could never
have dared to appear before me—[*To him.*] Ah, rogue!

Lord Fop. Stap my vitals, I am again!

Sir Tun. My Lord, will you cut his throat, or shall I?

Lord Fop. Thou art the impudenteft fellow that nature
has yet spawned into the warld, strike me speechless.

Y. Fash. Why, you know my modesty would have
starved me; I sent it a begging to you, and you would
not give it a groat.

Lord Fop. And dost thau expect, by an excefs of affurance, to extart a maintenance fram me?

Y. Fash. [*Taking* Mifs *by the hand.*] I do intend to ex-
tort your mistress from you, and that I hope will prove
one.

Lord Fop. I ever thaught Newgate or Bedlam would
be his fartune, and naw his fate's decided. Pr'ythee,
Lovelefs, doft knaw of ever a mad doctar hard by?

Y. Fash. There's one at your elbow will cure you presently.—[*To* Bull.] Pr'ythee, doctor, take him in hand
quickly.

Lord Fop. Shall I beg the favour of you, Sir, to pull
your fingers out of my wife's hand?

Y. Fash. His wife? Look you there. Now I hope
you are all satisfied he's mad.

Lord Fop. Naw is it impaffible far me to penetrate what
fpecies of fally it is thou art driving at.

Sir Tun. Here, here, here, let me beat out his brains,
and that will decide all.

Lord Fop. No, pray, Sir, hold; we'll destray him prefently, according to law.

Y. Fash. [*To* Bull.] Nay, then, advance, Doctor——
Come, you are a man of confcience; answer boldly to
the queftions I shall afk. Did not you marry me to this
young lady, before ever that gentleman there saw her
face?

Bull. Since the truth muft out, I did.

Y. Fash.

Y. Fash. Nurfe, fweet nurfe, were not you a witnefs to it?

Nurfe. Since my confcience bids me fpeak——I was.

Y. Fash. [*To* Mifs.] Madam, am not I your lawful hufband?

Mifs. Truly, I can't tell; but you married me firft.

Y. Fash. Now, I hope you are all fatisfied.

Sir Tun. [*Offering to ftrike him, is held by* Lov. *and* Wor.] Oons and thunder, you lie!

Lord Fop. Pray, Sir, be calm—the battle is in difarder; but requires more canduct than courage to rally our forces. Pray, Dactar, one word with you. [*To* Bull. *afide.*] Look you, Sir, ' tho' I will nat prefume to calcu-
' late your notions of damnation, fram the defcription you
' give us of hell; yet, fince there is a paffibility you
' may have a pitchfark thruft in your backfide,' methinks it fhould not be worth your while to rifque your
faul in the next warld, for the fake of a beggarly yaunger
brather, who is nat able to make your bady happy in
this.

Bull. Alas, my Lord, I have no worldly ends! I fpeak the truth, Heaven knows——

' *Lord Fop.* Nay, pr'ythee, never engage Heaven in
' the matter; far, by all I can fee, 'tis like to prove a
' bufinefs far the devil.'

Y. Fash. Come, pray, Sir, all above-board; no cor-
rupting of evidences, if you pleafe: this young lady is
my lawful wife, and I'll juftify it in all the courts in England. So, your Lordfhip (who had always a paffion for
variety) may go feek a new miftrefs if you think fit.

Lord Fop. I am ftruck dumb with his impudence, and
cannot pafitively tell whether ever I fhall fpeak again,
or nat.

Sir Tun. Then let me come and examine the bufinefs
a little; I'll jerk the truth out of them prefently. Here,
give me my dog-whip.

Y. Fash. Look you, old gentleman, 'tis in vain to make
a noife; if you grow mutinous, I have fome friends within call, have fwords by their fides above four foot long;
therefore, be calm, hear the evidence patiently, and when
the jury have given their verdict, pafs fentence according

to law. Here's honeft Coupler fhall be foreman, and afk as many queftions as he pleafes.

Coup. All I have to afk is, whether the nurfe perfifts in her evidence? The parfon, I dare fwear, will never flinch from his.

Nurfe. [*To Sir* Tun. *kneeling.*] I hope in heaven your worfhip will pardon me: I have ferved you long and faithfully; but in this thing I was over-reached. Your worfhip, however, was deceived as well as I; and if the wedding-dinner had been ready, you had put Madam to bed with him with your own hands.

Sir Tun. But how durft you do this, without acquainting of me.

Nurfe. Alas! if your worfhip had feen how the poor thing begged, and prayed, and clung, and twined about me, like ivy to an old wall, you would fay, I, who had fuckled it, and fwaddled it, and nurfed it both wet and dry, muft have had a heart of adamant to refufe it.

Sir Tun. Very well.

Y. Fafh. Foreman, I expect your verdict.

Coup. Ladies and gentlemen, what's your opinions?

All. A clear cafe, a clear cafe.

Coup. Then, my young folks, I wifh you joy.

Sir Tun. [*To* Y. Fafh.] Come hither, ftripling—If it be true, then, that thou haft married my daughter, pr'ythee, tell me who thou art.

Y. Fafh. Sir, the beft of my condition is, I am your fon-in-law; and the worft of it is, I am brother to that noble Peer there.

Sir Tun. Art thou brother to that noble Peer?—Why then, that noble Peer, and thee, and thy wife, and the nurfe, and the prieft—may all go and be damn'd together.

[*Exit* Sir Tun.

Lord Fop. [*Afide.*] Naw, for my part, I think the wifeft thing a man can do, with an aking heart, is to put on a ferene countenance; for a philofaphical air is the moft becoming thing in the warld to the face of a perfon of quality. I will therefore bear my difgrace like a great man, and let the people fee I am above an affrant.—[*To* Y. Fafh.] Dear Tam, fince things are thus fallen aut, pr'ythee, give me leave to wifh thee jay; I do it *de bon cœur,*

cœur, ftrike me dumb. You have married a woman, beautiful in her perfon, charming in her airs, prudent in her canduct, canftant in her inclinations, and of a nice marality, fplit my windpipe.

Y. Fafh. Your Lordfhip may keep up your fpirits with your grimace, if you pleafe ; I fhall fupport mine with this lady, and two thoufand pounds a year.——[*Taking* Mifs.] Come Madam :

We once again, you fee, are man and wife ;
And now, perhaps, the bargain's ftruck for life :
If I miftake, and we fhould part again,
At leaft, you fee you may have choice of men :
Nay, fhould the war at length fuch havock make,
That lovers fhould grow fcarce, yet for your fake,
Kind Heaven always will preferve a beau——

Pointing to Lord Fop] You'll find his Lordfhip ready to come to.

Lord Fop. Her Ladyfhip fhall ftap my vitals if I do.

[*Exeunt,*

END of the FIFTH ACT.

EPILOGUE.

Spoken by LORD FOPPINGTON.

Gentlemen and Ladies,

THESE people have regal'd you here to-day
    (In my opinion) with a saucy play;
In which the author does presume to show,
That coxcomb, ab origine—was beau.
Truly, I think the thing of so much weight,
That if some sharp chastisement ben't his fate,
Gad's curse, it may, in time, destroy the state.
I hold no one its friend, I must confess,
Who would discountenance you men of dress.
Far, give me leave t'observe, good cloaths are things
Have ever been of great support to kings.
All treasons come from slovens; it is nat
Within the reach of gentle beaus to plat;
They have no gall, no spleen, no teeth, no stings;
Of all Gad's creatures the most harmless things.
Thro' all recard, no prince was ever slain
By one who had a feather in his brain.
They're men of too refin'd an education,
To squabble with a court—for a vile dirty nation.
I'm very pasitive you never saw
A th'ro' republican a finish'd beau.
Nor, truly, shall you very often see
A Jacobite much better dress'd than he.
In short, thro' all the courts that I have been in,
Your men of mischief—still are in foul linen.
Did ever yet one dance the Tyburn jig,
With a free air, or a well pawder'd wig?
Did ever highwayman yet bid you stand,
With a sweet bawdy snuff-box in his hand?
Or do you ever find they ask your purse,
As men of breeding do?——Ladies, Gad's curse,
This author is a dag, and 'tis not fit
You should allow him ev'n one grain of wit;
To which, that his pretence may ne'er be nam'd,
My humble motion is——he may be damn'd.

AUTHOR/TITLE INDEX

Note to the Reader

These indexes cover the entire Bell's series. Roman numerals refer to the set in which the individual play appears, as follows: (I) Bell's British Theatre, 1776-1781; (II) Farces, 1784; (III) Selected Plays, 1791-1802 (and 1797). Arabic numerals indicate the volume number within each of the series.

AUTHOR/TITLE INDEX

TITLE/AUTHOR INDEX